Get the eBook FREE!
(PDF, ePub, Kindle, and liveBook all included)

We believe that once you buy a book from us, you should be able to read it in any format we have available. To get electronic versions of this book at no additional cost to you, purchase and then register this book at the Manning website.

Go to https://www.manning.com/freebook and follow the instructions to complete your pBook registration.

That's it!
Thanks from Manning!

D1597517

Bootstrapping Microservices
with Docker, Kubernetes, and Terraform

Bootstrapping Microservices with Docker, Kubernetes, and Terraform

A PROJECT-BASED GUIDE

ASHLEY DAVIS

MANNING
SHELTER ISLAND

For online information and ordering of this and other Manning books, please visit
www.manning.com. The publisher offers discounts on this book when ordered in quantity.
For more information, please contact

Special Sales Department
Manning Publications Co.
20 Baldwin Road
PO Box 761
Shelter Island, NY 11964
Email: orders@manning.com

Manning Publications Co.
20 Baldwin Road
PO Box 761
Shelter Island, NY 11964

Development editor:	Helen Sturgius
Technical development editor:	Jeanne Boyarsky
Review editor:	Aleks Dragosavljević
Production editor:	Lori Weidert
Copy editor:	Frances Buran
Proofreader:	Jason Everett
Technical proofreader:	Alain Couniot
Typesetter:	Gordan Salinovic
Cover designer:	Marija Tudor

ISBN 9781617297212
Printed in the United States of America

brief contents

contents

preface

I first tried building applications with microservices around 2013. That was the year Docker was initially released, but back then, I hadn't heard about it. At that time, we built an application with each microservice running on a separate virtual machine. As you might expect, that was a really expensive way to run microservices.

Because of the high running costs, we then opted to create fewer rather than more microservices, pushing more and more functionality into the existing microservices to the point where we couldn't really call these microservices. It was still a distributed application of course, just not *micro-sized* in the way we had hoped.

I already knew at that stage that microservices were a powerful idea, if only they were cheaper. I put microservices back on the shelf, but made a note that I should look at those again later.

Over the years, I watched from the sideline as the tools and technology around microservices developed, powered by the rise (*and rise*) of open source coding. And I looked on as the cost of cloud computing continued to drop, spurred on by competition between vendors. Over time, it was clear that building and running a distributed application with micro-sized components was becoming more cost effective.

After what seemed like a lifetime, in early 2018, I officially returned to the world of microservices. I had two opportunities for which I believed microservices were the right fit. Both were startups. The first was a contract job to bootstrap a new microservices application for a promising young company. The second was building a microservices application for my own startup.

To be successful, I knew that I needed new tools. I needed an effective way to package microservices. I needed a computing platform on which I could deploy microservices. Crucially, I needed to be able to automate deployments.

By then, Docker had already gained a big foothold in our industry, so I knew it was a safe bet as a way to package microservices. I also liked the look of Kubernetes as a computing platform for microservices, but early on, I was extremely uncertain about it. Kubernetes, however, promised a future of freedom from the tyranny of cloud vendor lockin—that was very appealing.

At this point, I'd read quite a few books on microservices. These were all interesting, providing good value on a theoretical level. I do enjoy reading the theory, but these books lacked the practical examples that would have helped me smash through my own learning curve. Even as an experienced developer, I was struggling to know where to start! I knew from past experience that bad technical decisions made at the beginning of a project would haunt me to the end.

Learning Kubernetes was especially difficult. From the outside, it seemed incredibly difficult to penetrate. But I had a job to do, and I needed a way to deliver software. So I pushed on. The going was tough, and I almost gave up on Kubernetes a few times.

The situation changed when I discovered Terraform. This was the missing piece of the puzzle for me. It's what made Kubernetes understandable and usable to the point where I could do nothing else but commit to using it.

Terraform is the tool that allowed me to describe the structure of my application. Terraform could then live in my continuous delivery (CD) pipeline and automatically keep my application up to date! I began writing *infrastructure as code*, and it felt like I had moved to the big league.

I forced my way through the learning curve, bolstered by my long-time experience of evaluating technology and learning quickly on the job, with a splash of trial and error mixed in for good measure. My efforts delivered software that is performant, flexible, reliable, scalable, extensible, and still running to this day. Through this time, my desire to write this book sparked and grew to the point where I had to take action.

A new mission formed—I wanted to *make microservices more accessible*. I felt compelled to write this book; it's the book I wanted but didn't have. I knew I could help people, and the best way to do that was with a practical book, this book. A book that shows you, step by step, that microservices *don't* have to be difficult or complex; it all depends on your approach and the perspective you take. You now have in your hands the fruits of that labor. I learned the hard way so that you don't have to.

acknowledgments

In *Bootstrapping Microservices*, I share my years of hard-won experience with you. Such experience wouldn't be possible without being surrounded by people who supported and encouraged me.

There are many who helped me get to where I am today. I wouldn't be a developer without my parents, Garry and Jan, who bought me my first PC. My partner in life, Antonella, who has tirelessly supported me through two books now. My partner in business, Majella, who listens to all my rants about technology, and still pushes me forward. Thank you all!

Of course, thank you to Manning for the opportunity and especially to Helen Stergius, who once again edited my book. Hopefully, I made your job easier this time, now that I'm a more experienced author. Thanks as well to the entire team at Manning for their efforts.

A big thank you to the technical proof reader, Alain Couniot, and all the reviewers who have played such a huge part in taking this book to the next level: Angelo Simone Scotto, Anupam Sengupta, Barnaby Norman, Björn Neuhaus, Bonnie Malec, Chris Kolosiwsky, Chris Viner, Dan Sheikh, Dhruvesh Patel, Donald McLamb, Eric Platon, Ernesto Bossi Carranza, Giampiero Granatella, John Guthrie, Julien Pohie, Marcin Sęk, Michele Adduci, Miguel Montalvo, Rich Ward, Rinor Maloku, Ruben Vandeginste, and Weyert de Boer.

Of course, Jeanne Boyarsky, the technical editor, deserves a special thank you. She did a wonderful job "nitpicking" (as she put it), and the book is so much better for her involvement.

Finally, I'd like to thank the development community. Your feedback and encouragement made this book a joy to write. I wrote this book for you!

about this book

Building applications with microservices—building *distributed applications*—can be a complicated process and can be difficult to learn. If you are plunged into a modern complex application, it can be difficult to see the trees from the forest. There's so much more to consider than simply coding. And this is not an easy journey to take on your own.

To use microservices, you must understand how to build a distributed application. But by itself, that's not enough. You also have to learn the deep and complex tools that are necessary to develop, test, and deploy such an application. How do we assemble a robust toolkit for development? Where do we start?

Along the way are many more questions. How do we package and deploy a microservice? How do we configure our development environment for local testing? How do we get our microservices communicating with each other, and how do we manage the data? Most importantly, how do we deploy our microservices to production? Then, once in production, how do we manage, monitor, and fix problems with potentially hundreds of microservices?

This book, *Bootstrapping Microservices*, answers these questions and more! It's your guide to building an application with microservices using the latest tools. We'll start from nothing and go all the way to a working microservices application running in production.

You won't find much theory in this book. *Bootstrapping Microservices* is practical and project-based. Together, we'll work through numerous examples of microservices, eventually getting to production, and covering everything you need to know to be a confident microservices developer.

Each example in this book comes with working code that is available on GitHub. You can try it out for yourself and make your own experimental changes.

Who should read this book

This book is aimed at anyone who wants to learn more about the practical aspects of working with microservices; those who need a clear guide on how to assemble their toolkit and take their application all the way to production. This book doesn't teach coding, so basic coding skills are advisable.

> **NOTE** If you have some basic or entry-level experience with modern programming languages like C#, Java, Python, or JavaScript, you should be able to follow along with this book.

The code examples are as simple as they can be, but this book isn't about the code. It's more about teaching you how to assemble the toolkit you need for building a microservices application.

If you don't have coding experience, but you are a fast learner, you can learn basic JavaScript (through another book, tutorials, videos, and so forth) while you read *Bootstrapping Microservices*. Like I said, the code examples are as simple as these can be, so you stand a good chance of being able to read the code and get the gist of it without much coding experience. Our coding adventure starts in chapter 2, where you learn how to build a simple microservice using JavaScript and Node.js.

How this book is organized: A roadmap

In the 11 chapters of this book, we go from building a single microservice all the way to running multiple microservices in a production-ready Kubernetes cluster.

- Chapter 1 is an introduction to microservices and explains why we want to use these.
- Chapter 2 works through building a simple microservice using Node.js and JavaScript. We learn how to use live reload for a more streamlined development process.
- Chapter 3 introduces Docker for packaging and publishing our microservice to get it ready for deployment.
- Chapter 4 scales up to multiple microservices and introduces Docker Compose for simulating our microservices application on your development workstation during development. We then cover data management for microservices, including having a database and external file storage.
- Chapter 5 upgrades our development environment for *whole application* live reload. We then cover communications among microservices, including HTTP for direct messaging and RabbitMQ for indirect messaging.

- Chapter 6 introduces Terraform and Kubernetes. We use Terraform to create a private container register and a Kubernetes cluster on Microsoft Azure.
- Chapter 7 uses Terraform to deploy microservices to our Kubernetes cluster. We deploy a database, a RabbitMQ server, and finally, a microservice. We also look at how to create a continuous delivery (CD) pipeline that automates the deployment of our application to production.
- Chapter 8 shows how we can apply multiple levels of automated testing to microservices.
- Chapter 9 is an overview of the example application and a review of the skills you learned thus far in the context of deploying the example application for yourself.
- Chapter 10 explores the ways that we can build reliable and fault-tolerant microservices and then monitor those to maintain a healthy application.
- Chapter 11 wraps up by showing practical ways that your microservices application can be scaled to support your growing business and organized to manage your growing development team. It also touches on security, refactoring a monolith, and how to build with microservices on a budget.

About the code

This book contains many examples of source code both in numbered listings and in line with normal text. In both cases, source code is formatted in a `fixed-width font like this` to separate it from ordinary text.

In many cases, the original source code has been reformatted; we've added line breaks and reworked indentation to accommodate the available page space in the book. In rare cases, even this was not enough, and listings include line-continuation markers (➥). Additionally, comments in the source code have often been removed from the listings when the code is described in the text. Code annotations accompany many of the listings, highlighting important concepts.

The code for the examples in this book is available for download from the Manning website at https://www.manning.com/books/bootstrapping-microservices-with-docker-kubernetes-and-terraform and from GitHub at https://github.com/bootstrapping-microservices.

You can download a zip file to accompany each chapter (chapters 2–9), or you can use Git to clone the Git code repository for each chapter. Each example is designed to be as simple as possible, self-contained, and easy to run. As you progress through the book, you will run the code in different ways.

We start by running code for a single microservice directly under Node.js (chapter 2), then under Docker (chapter 3). We then run multiple microservices under Docker Compose (chapters 4 and 5).

Next, we run code under Terraform, first locally (chapter 6) and then within our continuous delivery pipeline (chapter 7). Also, in chapters 6 and 7, we'll run our microservices on a Kubernetes cluster in the cloud. In chapter 8, we come back to

Node.js to run automated tests under Jest and Cypress. And, finally, in chapter 9, we revise the skills learned thus far (from chapters 2–8). The example code for chapter 9 is a simple, yet complete, microservices application that you can get running for yourself both in development and production.

Throughout the code examples, I aim to follow standard conventions and best practices. I ask that you provide feedback and report any issues through GitHub.

liveBook discussion forum

Purchase of *Bootstrapping Microservices with Docker, Kubernetes, and Terraform* includes free access to a private web forum run by Manning Publications where you can make comments about the book, ask technical questions, and receive help from the author and from other users. To access the forum, go to https://livebook.manning.com/#!/book/bootstrapping-microservices-with-docker-kubernetes-and-terraform/discussion. You can also learn more about Manning's forums and the rules of conduct at https://livebook.manning.com/#!/discussion.

Manning's commitment to our readers is to provide a venue where a meaningful dialogue between individual readers and between readers and the author can take place. It is not a commitment to any specific amount of participation on the part of the author, whose contribution to the forum remains voluntary (and unpaid). We suggest you try asking the author some challenging questions lest his interest stray! The forum and the archives of previous discussions will be accessible from the publisher's website as long as the book is in print.

about the author

ASHLEY DAVIS is a software craftsman, entrepreneur, and author with over 20 years of experience in software development, from coding to managing teams, then to founding companies. He has worked for a range of companies, from the tiniest startups to the largest internationals. Along the way, he has contributed back to the community through his writing and open source coding.

Ashley is the CTO of Sortal, a product that automatically sorts digital assets through the magic of machine learning. He is the creator of Data-Forge Notebook, a notebook-style desktop application for exploratory coding and data visualization using JavaScript and TypeScript. Ashley is also a keen algorithmic trader, actively trading and developing quantitative trading software.

For updates on his book, his open source coding, and more, follow Ashley on Twitter @ashleydavis75, follow him on Facebook at *The Data Wrangler*, or visit his blog at http://www.the-data-wrangler.com.

For more on Ashley's background, see his personal web page (http://www.codecapers .com.au) or his Linkedin profile (https://www.linkedin.com/in/ashleydavis75).

about the cover illustration

The figure on the cover of *Bootstrapping Microservices with Docker, Kubernetes, and Terraform* is captioned "Catalan" or a man from Catalonia, in northeast Spain. The illustration is taken from a collection of dress costumes from various countries by Jacques Grasset de Saint-Sauveur (1757–1810), titled *Costumes civils actuels de tous les peoples connus*, published in France in 1788. Each illustration is finely drawn and colored by hand. The rich variety of Grasset de Saint-Sauveur's collection reminds us vividly of how culturally apart the world's towns and regions were just 200 years ago. Isolated from each other, people spoke different dialects and languages. In the streets or in the countryside, it was easy to identify where they lived and what their trade or station in life was just by their dress.

The way we dress has changed since then and the diversity by region, so rich at the time, has faded away. It is now hard to tell apart the inhabitants of different continents, let alone different towns, regions, or countries. Perhaps we have traded cultural diversity for a more varied personal life—certainly for a more varied and fast-paced technological life.

At a time when it is hard to tell one computer book from another, Manning celebrates the inventiveness and initiative of the computer business with book covers based on the rich diversity of regional life of two centuries ago, brought back to life by Grasset de Saint-Sauveur's pictures.

Why microservices?

This chapter covers

- The learning approach of this book
- The what and why of microservices
- The benefits and drawbacks of using microservices
- What's wrong with the monolith?
- The basics of microservices design
- A quick overview of the application we build

As software continues to become larger and more complicated, we need better ways of managing and mitigating its complexity. As it grows alongside our business, we need better ways of dividing it up so that multiple teams can participate in the construction effort.

As our demanding customer base grows, we must also be able to expand our software. At the same time, our applications should be fault-tolerant and able to scale quickly to meet peak demand. How do we then meet the demands of modern business while evolving and developing our application?

Microservices are an architectural pattern that plays a pivotal role in contemporary software development. A *distributed application* composed of microservices solves these problems and more, but typically it is more difficult, more complex, and more time-consuming to architect than a traditional *monolithic application*. If these terms are new—microservices, distributed application, and monolithic application—they will be explained soon.

Conventional wisdom says that microservices are too difficult. We are told to start "monolith-first" and later restructure to microservices when necessary to scale. But I argue that this attitude doesn't make the job of building an application any easier! Your application is always going to tend toward complexity and, eventually, you will need to scale it. When you do decide you need to change, you now have the extremely difficult job of safely converting your monolith to microservices when staff and customers already depend on it.

Now is also the perfect time to be building microservices. The confluence of various factors—accessible and cheap cloud infrastructure, ever improving tools, and increasing opportunities for automation—is driving an industry-wide movement toward smaller and smaller services, aka *microservices*. Applications become more complex over time, but microservices offer us better ways to manage such complexity. There is no better time than now to go "microservices-first."

In this book, I will show you that a microservices-first approach is no longer as daunting as it once was. I believe the balance is firmly tipping toward microservices. The remaining problem is that *learning* microservices is difficult. The learning curve is steep and holds back many developers in their quest to build microservices. Together, we will break the learning curve. We will say "Boo" to the monolith, and we'll build from the ground up a simple but complete video-streaming application using microservices.

1.1   *This book is practical*

Why are you reading this book? You are reading this because you want or need to build a microservices application, which is an important skill set for modern developers, but it's a difficult skill set to obtain, and you need some guidance. You may have read other books on microservices and been left wondering *where do I begin?* I understand your torment.

Microservices are tough to learn. Not only do you have to learn deep and complicated tools, you must also learn to build a distributed application. This requires new design patterns, protocols, and methods of communication. That's a lot to learn in anyone's book.

In this book, we cut through the seemingly impenetrable learning curve of building microservices applications. The learning curve you must endure can seem insurmountable when tackled by yourself, but, rather than that, we'll undergo this development adventure together. We'll start as simple as possible and, piece-by-piece, we'll build up to deploying our application to production.

This book is about busting through the learning curve and bootstrapping a working application that will last indefinitely, an application that we can continuously update and build on to satisfy the ongoing and changing needs of our customers and users.

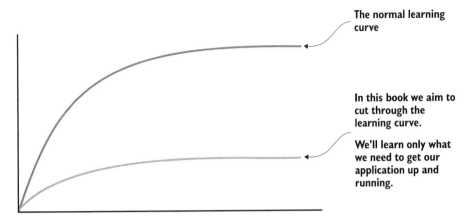

The normal learning curve

In this book we aim to cut through the learning curve.

We'll learn only what we need to get our application up and running.

Figure 1.1 Cutting through the learning curve. In this book, we'll learn only the bare minimum, just enough to bootstrap our application.

Figure 1.1 illustrates this idea of cutting through the learning curve. While our example application is small and simple, from the start, we will build-in pathways to scalability that will later allow it to be expanded out to a truly massive distributed application.

How is this book different from all the other books on microservices? Other books are notably theoretical. That's a good approach for an experienced developer or architect looking to broaden their knowledge, but acquiring practical skills that way is challenging and doesn't help you navigate the minefield of bootstrapping a new application. The technical choices you make at project inception can haunt you for a long time.

This book *is* different; this book *is not* theoretical. We will take a practical approach to learning. There is a small amount of theory interspersed throughout, and we will actually build a substantial microservices application. We will start from nothing and work through bringing our application into existence and getting it into production. We'll build and test the application on our development workstation (or personal computer), and ultimately, we'll deploy it to the cloud.

Together we'll get our microservices application off the ground without having to learn the deepest details of any of the tools or technologies. An example of this book's learning model is illustrated in figure 1.2.

This book is about building a microservices application, starting with nothing. Some people have already asked why I didn't write this book to show how to convert a monolith to a microservices application? This is something that many people would like to learn.

I wrote the book in this way because it's much easier to learn how to write an application from scratch than it is to learn how to refactor an existing application. I also believe these skills are useful because, in time, more and more applications will be written microservices-first.

In any case, refactoring an existing application is much more complicated than building a fresh application. It's a process with many complex variables and depends

Each of the technologies we'll learn is deep, complicated, and difficult to grasp (to varying degrees).

We'll keep things simple, and we'll only learn the thin crust of what's possible.

We will only use what's necessary to bootstrap our microservices application from scratch. That's what makes this book possible.

External references will help you find more information on each of these topics for when you need to go deeper.

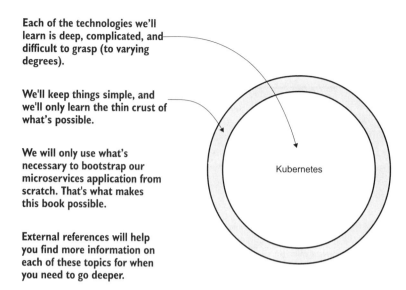

Kubernetes

Figure 1.2 The learning model for this book. We will skim the surface of these deep and complicated technologies to only use what is necessary to bootstrap our application.

heavily on the particulars of the legacy codebase. I make the presumption that it will be easier for you to figure out your own monolith conversion strategy once you know (indeed, once you have experienced) how to create a greenfield (new) microservices application.

I can assure you that when you can build an application microservices-first, you will be much better equipped to clearly see a route from your existing monolith to microservices. That journey from monolith to microservices will no doubt still be demanding, so stay tuned. In chapter 11, we will discuss more on this topic.

Throughout this book, you will learn concrete and practical techniques for getting a microservices application off the ground. Of course, there are many diverse ways to go about this and many different tools you can use. I am teaching you one single recipe and one set of tools (albeit a popular toolset). You will, no doubt, find many ways to improve on this recipe and enhance it for your own situation. Other experienced developers will, of course, already have their own recipes for doing this. What I'm trying to say is that this is my way, and it is just one of many ways that will work; however, I can attest that I have tried every technique in this book in production and found these to work well. So without further ado, let us commence our journey of learning and discovery.

1.2   What will I learn?

Throughout the book, we will progress from easy to more difficult. We'll start with the simplest task—creating a single microservice. Over 11 chapters, we'll build up to a more complex application and infrastructure, but we'll do it in incremental steps so that you never get lost. After reading this book and practicing the skills taught, you can expect to be able to

- Create individual microservices
- Package and publish microservices using Docker
- Develop a microservices application on your development workstation using Docker Compose
- Test your code, microservices, and application using Jest and Cypress
- Integrate third-party servers into your application (like MongoDB and RabbitMQ, as examples)
- Communicate between microservices using HTTP and RabbitMQ messages
- Store the data and files your microservices need to operate
- Create production infrastructure with Kubernetes using Terraform
- Deploy your microservices to production using Terraform
- Create a continuous delivery pipeline to automatically deploy your application as you update the code

1.3 *What do I need to know?*

You might be wondering, what you need to know going into this book. I have made an effort to write this book with as few assumptions as possible about what you already know. We are going on a journey that takes you from absolute basics all the way through to some rather complicated concepts. I think there's something here for everyone, no matter how much experience you might have already as a developer.

It's best coming into this book if you have some entry-level understanding of computer programming. I don't think you'll need much, so long as you can read code and get the gist of what it's doing. But don't worry; I'll explain as much as possible about anything important that is happening in the code.

If you have a background in programming, you'll have no problem following along with the examples in this book. If you are learning programming while reading this book, you could find it to be quite a bit more challenging, but not impossible, and you might have to put in some extra work.

This book uses Node.js for examples of microservices, but starting out, you don't need to know JavaScript or Node.js. You'll pick up enough along the way to follow along. This book also uses Microsoft Azure for examples of production deployment. Again, starting out, you don't need to know anything about Azure either.

Rest assured that this book isn't about Node.js or Azure; it's about building microservices applications using modern tooling like Docker, Kubernetes, and Terraform. Most of the skills you will take away from this book are transferable to other languages and other cloud providers. Because I had to pick a programming language and cloud vendor that I could use to demonstrate the techniques in this book, I chose Node.js and Azure. That's mostly what I use in production these days.

If Node.js and Azure aren't your thing, with some extra research and experimentation on your part, you'll be able to figure out how to replace Node.js and JavaScript with your favorite programming language and replace Azure with your preferred cloud vendor. In fact, the main reason I use Docker, Kubernetes, and Terraform in the first place is precisely because these tools offer freedom—freedom of choice for programming language and freedom from cloud vendor lock-in.

1.4 Managing complexity

A microservice application, like any application, will become more complex over time. But it doesn't need to start that way! This book takes the approach that we can begin from a simple starting point and that each iteration of development can also be just as simple. In addition, each microservice is small and simple. As you read this book, you'll find that it isn't as difficult as you might think to build applications with microservices (despite what some people say).

Microservices give us a way to manage complexity at a granular level, and it's the level we work at almost every day—the level of a single microservice. At that level, microservices are not complex. In fact, to earn the name *microservice*, they have to be small and simple. A single microservice is intended to be manageable by a single developer or a small team!

It is true, though, that through continued development and evolution, a complex system will emerge. There's no denying that a microservices application will become complex. But that doesn't happen immediately; it takes time. Along the way, we'll use microservices to manage the growing complexity of your application so that it doesn't become a burden.

A microservices application is a form of *complex adaptive system*, where complexity emerges naturally from the interactions of its constituent parts. Even though the system as a whole can become far too complex for any mere mortal to understand, each of its components remains small, manageable, and easy to understand. Don't worry though; the example application we build in this book isn't that complicated.

Development with this microservices attitude (with help from our tools and automation) allows us to build extremely large and scalable applications without being overwhelmed by the complexity. And, after reading this book, you'll be able to zoom in and look at any part of the most complex microservices application and find its components to be straightforward and understandable.

1.5 What is a microservice?

Before we can understand a microservices application, we must first understand what it means to be a microservice.

> **DEFINITION** A *microservice* is a tiny and independent software process that runs on its own deployment schedule and can be updated independently.

Let's break that definition down. A microservice is a small, independent software process that has its own separate deployment frequency. That is to say that it must be possible to update each microservice independently from other microservices.

A microservice can be owned and operated either by a single developer or a team of developers. A developer or team might also manage multiple other microservices. Each developer/team has the responsibility for the microservice(s) they own. In the modern world of programming, this often includes development, testing, deployment, and operations. We might find, however, that when we work for a small company or a startup (as I do), or when we are learning (as we are in this book), we must manage multiple microservices or, indeed, even an entire microservices application on our own.

An individual microservice might be exposed to the outside world so our customers can interact with it or it might be purely an internal service and not externally accessible. It typically has access to a database, file storage, or some other method of state persistence. Figure 1.3 illustrates these internal and external relationships.

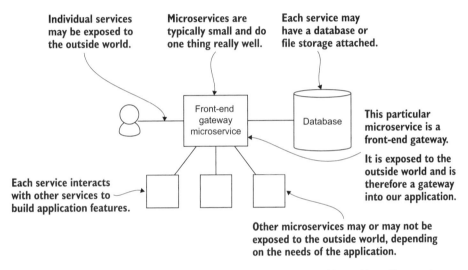

Figure 1.3   A single microservice can have connections to the outside world or other services, and it also can have a database and/or attached file storage.

By itself, a single microservice doesn't do much. A well-designed system, however, can be decomposed into such simple services. The services must collaborate with each other to provide the features and functionality of the greater application. This brings us to the topic of the microservices application.

1.6   *What is a microservices application?*

A microservices application is traditionally known as a *distributed application*, a system composed of tiny components that live in separate processes and communicate via the network. Each service or component resides on a logically distinct (virtual) computer and sometimes even on a physically separate computer.

DEFINITION   A *microservices application* is a distributed program composed of many tiny services that collaborate to achieve the features and functionality of the overall project.

Typically, a microservices application has one or more services that are externally exposed to allow users to interact with the system. Figure 1.4 shows two such services acting as gateways for web-based and mobile phone users. You can also see in figure 1.4 that many services are working together within the *cluster*. It is called a cluster because it is a group of computers that are represented to us (the developers) as a single cohesive slab of computing power to be directed as we will. Somewhere close by we also have a database server. In figure 1.4, it is shown to be outside the cluster, but it could just as easily be hosted inside the cluster. We'll talk more about this in chapter 4.

The cluster is hosted on a cluster orchestration platform, and we use Kubernetes for this purpose. *Orchestration* is the automated management of our services. This is what Kubernetes does for us—it helps us to deploy and manage our services.

The cluster itself, our database and other virtual infrastructure, are all hosted on our chosen cloud vendor. We will learn how to deploy this infrastructure on Microsoft Azure, but with some work on your own, you can change the examples in this book to deploy to Amazon Web Services (AWS) or Google Cloud Platform (GCP).

A microservices application can take many forms, is very flexible, and can be arranged to suit many situations. Any particular application might have a familiar overall structure, but the services it contains will do different jobs, depending on the needs of our customers and the domain of our business.

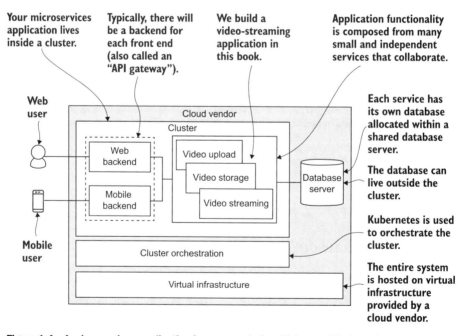

Figure 1.4   A microservices application is composed of multiple, small independent services running in a cluster.

1.7 What's wrong with the monolith?

What is a monolith and what is so wrong with it that we'd like to use microservices instead? Although distributed computing has been around for decades, applications were often built in the monolithic form. This is the way that the majority of software was developed before the cloud revolution and microservices. Figure 1.5 shows what the services in a simple video-streaming application might look like and compares the differences between a monolithic version of the application and a microservices version.

DEFINITION A *monolith* is an entire application that runs in a single process.

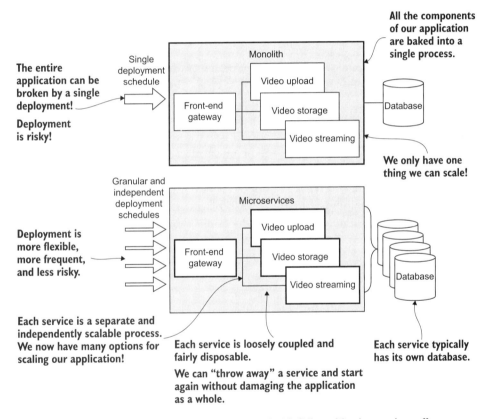

Figure 1.5   Monolith vs. microservices. You can see that building with microservices offers many advantages over the traditional monolithic application.

It is much easier to build a monolith than a microservices application. You need fewer technical and architectural skills. It's a great starting point when building a new application, say for an early-stage product, and you want to test the validity of the business model before you commit to the higher technical investment required by a microservices application.

A monolith is a great option for creating a throw-away prototype. It also might be all that you need for an application that has a small scope or an application that stabilizes quickly and does not need to evolve or grow over its lifetime. If your application will always be this small, it makes sense for it to be a monolith.

Deciding whether to go monolith-first or microservices-first is a balancing act that has traditionally been won by the monolith. However, in this book, I'll show you, given the improvements in modern tooling and with cheap and convenient cloud infrastructure, that it's important that you at least consider building microservices-first.

Most products generally need to grow and be evolved, and as your monolith grows bigger and has more useful features, it becomes more difficult to justify throwing away the throw-away prototype. So down the road, you could find yourself stuck with the monolith at a time when what you really need is the flexibility, security, and scalability of a microservices application.

Monoliths come with a host of potential problems. These start out small, and we always have the best of intentions of keeping the code clean and well organized. A good team of developers can keep a monolith elegant and well organized for many years. But as time passes, the vision can be lost or sometimes there wasn't a strong vision in the first place. All the code runs in the same process, so there are no barriers and nothing to stop us writing a huge mess of spaghetti code that will be near impossible to pick apart later.

Staff turnover also has a big effect. As developers leave the team they take crucial knowledge with them, and they are replaced by new developers who will have to develop their own mental model of the application, which could easily be at odds with the original vision. Time passes, code changes hands many times, and these negative forces conspire to devolve the codebase into what is called a *big ball of mud*. This name denotes the messy state of the application when there is no longer a discernible architecture.

Updating the code for a monolith is a risky affair. It's all or nothing. When you push a code change that breaks the monolith, the entire application ceases operation, your customers are left high and dry, and your company bleeds money. We might only want to change a single line of code, but still, we must deploy the entire monolith and risk breaking it. This risk stokes deployment fear. Fear slows the pace of development.

In addition, as the structure of the monolith degenerates, our risk of breaking it in unanticipated ways increases. Testing becomes harder and breeds yet more deployment fear. Have I convinced you that you should try microservices? Wait, there's more!

Due to the sheer size of an established monolith, testing is problematic, and because of its extremely low level of granularity, it is difficult to scale. Eventually, the monolith expands to consume the physical limits of the machine it runs on. As the aging monolith consumes more and more physical resources, it becomes more expensive to run. I have witnessed this! To be fair, this kind of eventuality might be a long way off for any monolith, but even after just a few years of growth, the monolith leads to a place that you would prefer not to be.

Despite the eventual difficulties with the monolith, it remains the simplest way to bootstrap a new application. Shouldn't we always start with a monolith and later restructure when we need to scale? My answer: *it depends*.

Many applications will always be small. There are plenty of small monoliths in the wild that do their job well and don't need to be scaled or evolved. Because these are not expanding, they do not suffer the problems of growth. If you believe your application will remain small and simple and doesn't need to evolve, you should definitely build it as a monolith.

There are many applications, however, that we can easily predict will benefit from a microservices-first approach. These are the kinds of applications we know will continually be evolved over many years. Other applications that can benefit are those that need to be flexible, scalable, or have security constraints from the start. Building these types of applications is much easier if you start with microservices because converting an existing monolith is difficult and risky.

By all means, if you need to validate your business idea first, do so by initially building a monolith. However, even in this case, I would argue that with the right tooling, prototyping with microservices isn't much more difficult than prototyping with a monolith. After all, what is a monolith if not a single large service?

You might even consider using the techniques in this book to bootstrap your monolith as a single service within a Kubernetes cluster. Now you have the best of both worlds! When the time comes to decompose to microservices, you are already in the best possible position to do so and, at your leisure, you can start chipping microservices off the monolith. And with the ease of automated deployment that modern tooling offers, it is easy to tear down and recreate your application or create replica environments for development and testing. If you want or need to create a monolith first, you can still benefit from the techniques and technologies presented in this book.

If you do start with a monolith, for your own sanity and as early as possible, either throw it away and replace it or incrementally restructure it into microservices. We'll talk more about breaking up existing monoliths in chapter 11.

1.8 *Why are microservices popular now?*

Why does it seem that right now microservices are exploding in popularity? Is this just a passing fad?

No, it is not a passing fad. Distributed computing has been around for a long time and has always had many advantages over monolithic applications. Traditionally though, it has been more complex and more costly to build applications in this way. Developers only reached for these more powerful application architectures for the most demanding problems: those where the value of the solution would outweigh the cost of the implementation.

In recent times, however, with the advent of cloud technology, virtualization, and the creation of automated tools for managing our virtual infrastructure, it has become much less expensive to build such distributed systems. As it became cheaper to replace monolithic applications with distributed applications, we naturally considered the ways this could improve the structure of our applications. In doing so, the components of our distributed systems have shrunk to the tiniest possible size so that now we call them *microservices.*

That's why microservices are popular now. Not only are they generally a worthwhile way to build complex modern applications, but they are also increasingly *cost-effective.* Distributed computing has become more accessible than ever before, so naturally more developers are using it. Right now, it appears to be nearing critical mass, and so it's reaching the mainstream.

But why are microservices so good? How do they improve the structure of our application? This question leads to the benefits of microservices.

1.9 *Benefits of microservices*

Building distributed applications brings many advantages. Each service can potentially have its own dedicated CPU, memory, and other resources. Typically though, we share physical infrastructure between many services and that's what makes microservices cost-effective. But we are also able to separate these out when necessary so that the services with the heaviest workloads can be allocated dedicated resources. We can say that each small service is independently scalable, and this gives us a fine-grained ability to tune the performance of our application. In this section, we look at these benefits:

- *Allows for fine-grained control*—Microservices allow us to build an application with fine-grained control over scalability
- *Minimizes deployment risk*—Microservices help us minimize deployment risk while maximizing the pace of development
- *Lets you choose your own tech stack*—Microservices allow us to choose the right stack for the task at hand so that we aren't constrained to a single tech stack

Having a distributed application offers us the potential for better reliability and reduced deployment risk. When we update a particular service we can do so without the risk of breaking the entire application. Of course, we might still risk breaking a part of the application, but that is better and easier to recover from than bringing down the entire application. When problems occur, it's easier to rollback just a small part of the system rather than the whole. Reduced deployment risk has the knock-on effect of promoting frequent deployments, and this is essential to agility and sustaining a fast pace of development.

These benefits are nothing new. After all, we have built distributed applications for a long time, but such systems have become cheaper to build and the tools have improved. It is easier than ever before to build applications this way and to reap the rewards. As costs decreased and deployment convenience increased, our services tended towards the micro-level, and this brought its own complement of benefits.

Smaller services are quicker to boot than larger services. This helps make our system easier to scale because we can quickly replicate any service that becomes overloaded.

Smaller services are also easier to test and troubleshoot. Even though testing an overall system can still be difficult, we can more easily prove that each individual part of it is working as expected.

Building applications with many small and independently upgradeable parts means we can have an application that is more amenable to being extended, evolved, and rearranged over its lifetime. The fact that we have enforced process boundaries between our components means that we will never be tempted to write spaghetti code. And, indeed, if we do write terrible code (we all have bad days, right?), the impact of bad code is controlled and isolated because every microservice (to earn the name) should be small enough that it can be thrown away and rewritten within a matter of weeks, if not days. In this sense, we are *designing our code for disposability*. We are designing it to be replaced over time. The ongoing and iterative replacement of our application is not only made possible, but it is actively encouraged, and this is what we need for our application architecture to survive the continuously evolving needs of the modern business.

Another benefit that really excites developers using microservices is that we are no longer constrained to a single technology stack for our application. Each service in our application can potentially contain any tech stack. For larger companies, this means that different teams can choose their own tech stack; they can choose it based on their experience or based on the stack that is best for the job at hand. Various tech stacks can co-exist within our cluster and work together using shared protocols and communication mechanisms.

Being able to change between tech stacks is important for the long-term health of the application. As the tech landscape evolves, as it always does, older tech stacks fall out of favor and must eventually be replaced by new ones. Microservices create a structure that can be progressively converted to newer tech stacks. As developers, we no longer need languish on out-of-date technologies.

Technology (tech) stack

Your technology stack is the combination of tools, software, and frameworks on which you build each microservice. You can think of it as the fundamental underlying elements needed by your application.

Some stacks have names. For example, MEAN (Mongo, Express, Angular, Node.js) or LAMP (Linux, Apache, MySQL, PHP). But your stack is just the combination of tools you use, and it doesn't need a name to be valid.

When building a monolith, we have to choose a single tech stack, and we have to stay with that stack for as long as the monolith remains in operation. The microservices architecture is appealing because it gives us the potential to use multiple tech stacks within one application. This allows us to change our tech stack over time as we evolve our application.

1.10 *Drawbacks of microservices*

This chapter would not be complete without addressing the two main problems that people have with microservices:

- Microservices are more difficult
- People often fear complexity

The first problem is the steep learning curve. Learning how to build microservices requires you to learn not just a complicated arrangement of technologies, but also the principles and techniques for building distributed applications. Although learning how to build microservices is difficult, this book will help you shortcut the learning curve.

> **NOTE** I can understand if you feel daunted by what's in front of you. But recently, huge progress has been made in the development of tooling for building distributed applications. Our tools are now more sophisticated, easier to use, and most importantly, more *automatable* than ever before.

These days, a single experienced developer is now capable of bootstrapping a microservices application on their own without the support of a team. I know this because I have done this multiple times for startups. Still, it surprises me how much can be achieved on one's own. We'll talk more about how startups, small teams, and solo developers can work with microservices quickly and effectively in chapter 11.

To be fair, the tools are *still* complicated. Ordinarily, it would take months or longer to conquer the learning curve on your own—mastering any of these tools takes significant time! But this book takes a different approach. Together we will only learn the bare minimum necessary to bootstrap our application and get it running in production. Together we will produce a simple but working microservices application. Along the way, we'll also learn the basics of structuring distributed applications.

As I mentioned, there are actually two problems facing microservices developers. The second is that building a microservices application, indeed any distributed application, is going to be more complicated than building the equivalent monolith. It is hard to argue with this. The first thing I would say is that yes, building a monolith is simpler in the beginning and in many cases it is the right decision. If your application is one of those that must later be converted or restructured to microservices however, then you should consider the eventual cost of unraveling your big ball of mud.

Don't be frightened by complexity; it happens whether you like it or not. Fortunately, microservices offer us tangible ways of managing complexity.

If you think this through, you might concede that building microservices, at least in certain situations, is actually less complicated than building a monolith. If this discussion hasn't convinced you, consider this: *any* significant application is going to become complex. If not at the start, it *will* grow more complex over time. You can't hide from complexity in modern software development, it *always* catches up with you, eventually. Instead, let's take control of this situation and meet the complexity head-on. What we want are better tools to help manage complexity. Microservices as an architectural pattern is one such tool.

Think of microservices as a way to bring the pain forward, to a place where it's more economical to deal with. What do we get in return for this pain? Microservices offer us tangible ways to manage complexity in our application. They provide hard boundaries that prevent us from writing spaghetti code. Microservices allow us to more easily rewire our application, scale it, and upgrade it over time. Microservices also force us to apply better design. We can't prevent complexity, but we can manage it, and modern tooling for distributed applications is already here to help us.

1.11 *Modern tooling for microservices*

This book is all about the tooling. Together, we will learn the basics of a number of different tools. To start with, we must be able to create a microservice. We'll use JavaScript and Node.js to do this, and the next chapter will teach you the basics of that.

We are using Node.js because that's my weapon of choice. However, as far as microservices are concerned, the technology stack within the service is not particularly important. We could just as easily build our microservices with Python, Ruby, Java, Go, or virtually any other language. We'll encounter numerous tools along our journey, but these are the most important ones:

- *Docker*—To package and deploy our services
- *Docker Compose*—To test our microservices application on our development workstation
- *Kubernetes*—To host our application in the cloud
- *Terraform*—To build our cloud infrastructure, our Kubernetes cluster, and deploy our application

The technological landscape is always changing and so are the tools. So why should we learn any particular toolset when the tools are constantly outdated and replaced? Well, it's because we will always need good tools to work effectively. And with better tools, we can do a better job, or maybe we just get to do the same job but more effectively. Either way, this helps us to be more productive.

I selected the tools for this book because these make the job of building microservices applications significantly easier and quicker. All technologies change in time, but I don't think these particular tools are going anywhere soon. They are popular, are currently the best we have, and all fill useful positions in one's toolkit.

Of course, these tools will eventually be replaced, but hopefully, in the meantime, we'll have extracted significant value from these and built many good applications. And when the tools do change, they will certainly be replaced by better tools that lift the bar of abstraction even higher, making our jobs easier and less frustrating.

Docker is the one tool out of all the tools that is more or less ubiquitous. It seems to have almost come from nowhere and has taken over our industry. Kubernetes on the other hand is not quite as ubiquitous as Docker, although it does have a strong future because it allows us to transcend the boundaries of cloud vendors. This is good news if you ever felt trapped with your particular cloud provider. We can run our Kubernetes-based application on pretty much any cloud platform, and we have freedom of movement when needed.

Terraform is a relative newcomer, but I think it's a game-changer. It's a declarative configuration language that allows us to script the creation of cloud resources and the deployment of our services. The important thing about Terraform is that it's one language that can work with potentially any cloud vendor. No matter which cloud vendor you choose, now or in the future, chances are that Terraform will support it, and you won't have to learn something new.

Think about this for a moment: *Terraform means we can easily code the creation of cloud infrastructure.* This is something! In the past, we would laboriously and physically piece together infrastructure, but now we are able to create it with code. This concept is called *infrastructure as code* and it is a key enabler for *continuous delivery*, something important to modern software development that we'll look at in chapter 7.

1.12 *Designing a microservices application*

This isn't a book about theory, but I do have to touch on some of the software design aspects before we get into the practical stuff. I promise this is just some foundational principles, and there are plenty of other books to help you get a better grounding in this space.

At the outset, I'd like to say that designing a microservices application isn't particularly different from designing any software. You can read any good book on software design and apply those same principles and techniques to microservices. There aren't many hard and fast rules that I follow, but I feel these few are especially important:

- Don't over design or try and future proof your architecture. Start with a simple design for your application.
- Apply continuous refactoring during development to keep it as simple as it can be.
- Let a good design emerge naturally.

I feel that the last rule is especially encouraged by microservices. You can't conclusively preplan a big microservices application. The architecture has to emerge during development and over the lifetime of the application.

I'm not saying that you shouldn't do any planning. You definitely should be planning at every stage of development. What I am saying is that you should be planning for your plan to change! You should be able to respond quickly to changing circumstances, and that's another thing that's well supported by microservices. Rules aside, let's briefly discuss three principles that seem particularly relevant to microservices:

- Single responsibility principle
- Loose coupling
- High cohesion

Generally, we'd like to have each microservice be as small and simple as possible. One individual service should cover only a single conceptual area of the business. That is to say that each service should have a single, well-defined area of responsibility. This is normally known as the *single responsibility principle*.

Microservices should be *loosely coupled* and have *high cohesion*. Loosely coupled means that the connections between services are minimal and that they don't share information unless necessary. When we reduce the connections and dependencies between microservices, we make it easier to upgrade individual services without having problems propagate through the application. Loose coupling helps us pull apart and rewire our application into new configurations. This makes our application more flexible and responsive to the changing needs of the business.

The code contained within a microservice should be highly cohesive. This means that all the code in a microservice *belongs together* and contributes to solve the problem that is the service's area of responsibility. If a microservice solves more than one problem or has a larger area of responsibility, then this is an indication that it is not highly cohesive.

A design paradigm that works well for microservices is called *domain driven design* (DDD). Using DDD is a great way to understand the domain of a business and to model the business as software. The technique comes from the book, *Domain Driven Design*, by Eric Evans (2003). I have used it multiple times myself and find that it maps well to designing distributed applications. Specifically, the concept of the *bounded context* fits well to the boundary of a microservice as illustrated in figure 1.6.

This figure shows how the boundaries of concepts in our video-streaming domain might fit into microservices. Concepts such as *User*, *Like*, and *Video* live within our microservices, and some concepts (like Video) create the relationships between microservices. For example, in figure 1.6, the idea of a video is almost the same (but

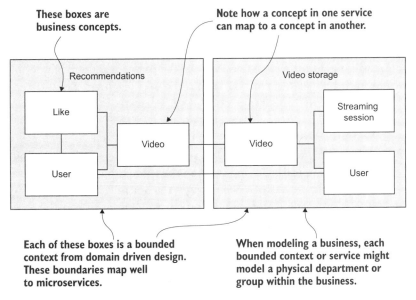

Figure 1.6 Bounded contexts from domain driven design (DDD) equate to the boundaries of microservices.

there can be differences) between the recommendations and the video-storage microservices.

There is a coding principle that seems like it might be under attack by microservices. Many developers live by the motto *don't repeat yourself* (DRY). But in the world of microservices, we are developing a higher tolerance for duplicated code than what was previously considered acceptable.

The hard process boundaries in a microservices application certainly make it more difficult to share code, and the practice of DDD seems to encourage duplicating concepts, if not replicating code. Also, when microservices are owned by separate teams, we then encounter all the usual barriers to sharing code that already exists between teams.

Be assured, there are good ways to share code between microservices, and we aren't simply going to throw out DRY. We'd still like to share code between microservices when it makes sense to do so.

1.13 *An example application*

By the end of this book, we'll have built a simple but complete microservices application. In this section, we'll develop an idea of what the final product looks like.

The example product we will build is a video-streaming application. Every good product deserves a name, so after much brainstorming and throwing around various ideas, I've landed on the name *FlixTube*, the future king of the video-streaming world. Gotta start somewhere right?

Why choose video streaming as the example? Simply because it's a fun example and is surprisingly easy to create (at least in a simple form). It's also a well-known use case for microservices, being the approach successfully taken to the extreme by Netflix. (Reports vary, but we know they run 100s if not 1,000s of microservices.)

We'll use the FlixTube example application to demonstrate the process of constructing a microservices application. It will only have a small number of microservices, but we will build-in the pathways we need for future scalability, including adding more virtual machines to the cluster, replicating services for scale and redundancy, and extracting services to separate code repositories so these can have separate deployment schedules and be managed by separate teams.

Our application will have a browser-based front end so our users can view a list of videos. From there they can select a video and it will begin playing. During development, we'll boot our application using Docker Compose, which we'll cover in chapters 4 and 5. We'll build and publish Docker images for our microservices in chapter 3. In chapters 6 and 7, we'll deploy our application to production. In chapter 8, we'll swing back to development for some automated testing.

Our application will contain services for video streaming, storage, and upload, plus a gateway for the customer-facing front end. We'll work up to deploying the full application in chapter 9, which figure 1.7 illustrates. In chapters 10 and 11, we'll look at all the ways this architecture can help us scale in the future as our application grows. Are you ready to start building with microservices?

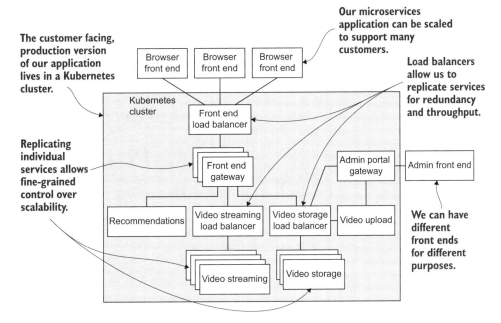

The customer facing, production version of our application lives in a Kubernetes cluster.

Our microservices application can be scaled to support many customers.

Load balancers allow us to replicate services for redundancy and throughput.

Replicating individual services allows fine-grained control over scalability.

We can have different front ends for different purposes.

Kubernetes cluster

Browser front end

Browser front end

Browser front end

Front end load balancer

Front end gateway

Admin portal gateway

Admin front end

Recommendations

Video streaming load balancer

Video storage load balancer

Video upload

Video streaming

Video storage

Figure 1.7   Our example application running in production on Kubernetes.

Summary

- We take a practical rather than a theoretical approach to learning how to build a microservices application.
- Microservices are small and independent processes that each do one thing well.
- A microservices application is composed of numerous small processes working together to create the application's features.
- A monolith is an application composed of a single massive service.
- Although building a microservices application is more complicated than building a monolith, it's not as difficult as you might think.
- Applications built from microservices are more flexible, scalable, reliable, and fault-tolerant than monolithic applications.
- The union of the modern tools like Docker, Kubernetes, and Terraform make building a microservices application much easier than previously possible.
- Domain driven design (DDD) is an effective way to design a microservices application.
- Bounded contexts from DDD map well to the boundaries of microservices.
- We previewed the example application that we'll build in this book.

Creating your first microservice

Our goal for this book is to assemble an application that consists of multiple microservices. But before we can build multiple microservices, we must first learn how to build a single microservice.

Because we have to start somewhere, in this chapter, we'll create our first microservice. It's a simple microservice, doing very little, but it illustrates the process so that you can understand it and repeat it. Indeed, it is the process we'll use to create multiple microservices through the course of the book.

This first microservice is a simple HTTP server that delivers streaming video to a user watching in a web browser. This is the first step on our road to building FlixTube, our video-streaming application. Video streaming might sound difficult, but the simple code we examine at this stage should not present much trouble.

In this book, our microservices are programmed with JavaScript and run on Node.js. It's important to note, though, that we could use any tech stack for our microservices. Building applications with microservices gives us a lot of freedom in the tech stack we use.

You don't have to use JavaScript to build microservices. You can just as easily build your microservices using Python, C#, Ruby, Java, Go, or whatever language is in vogue by the time you read this book. I had to make a choice, however, because this is a practical book, and we need to get down to the nitty-gritty of actual coding. But, keep in mind that you can just as easily use your own favorite programming language to build your microservices.

We are about to embark on a whirlwind tour of Node.js. Of course, we can't cover the full details, and as is the theme in this book, we are only going to skim the surface of what's possible. At the end of the chapter, you'll find references to other books on Node.js to drill down for a deeper knowledge.

If you already know Node.js, then you'll find much of this chapter to be familiar, and you might be tempted to skip it. But skim through it because there are some important notes on setting up your development environment, preparing for production deployment, and getting ready for fast iterative development that we'll rely on throughout the book.

Hold onto your hats! This book starts out simple, but in no time at all it turns into a pretty wild ride.

2.1 New tools

Because this book is all about the tools, in most chapters we'll start with the new tools you need to install to follow along with the examples in the chapter. Starting with our first microservice, table 2.1 shows the tools we need: Git, Node.js, and Visual Studio (VS) Code. We'll use Git to get the code. We'll use Node.js to run and test our first microservice, and we'll use VS Code to edit our code and work on our Node.js project.

Throughout the book, I'll tell you the version numbers for each tool used to develop the examples in this book. This gives you a version number that you can use to follow along with the examples.

Later versions of these tools should also work because good tools are usually backward compatible, but occasional major increments to versions can break old examples. If that happens, let me know by logging an issue in GitHub (see the next section).

Table 2.1 Tools introduced in chapter 2

Tool	Version	Purpose
Git	2.27.0	Version control is an essential part of day-to-day development, in this chapter, we use Git to get a copy of the chapter 2 code.
Node.js	12.18.1	We use Node.js to run our microservices.
Visual Studio (VS) Code	1.46.1	We use VS Code for editing our code and other assets.

Of course, you can use some other integrated development environment (IDE) or text editor for editing your code. I recommend VS Code because you can't go wrong with it!

2.2   Getting the code

Numerous working example projects accompany this book. The code for each project is available on GitHub. You can clone or download the code repositories there to follow along with the examples in the book. I strongly recommend that you run these examples as you work through the book. That's the best way for you to get practical experience and the most out of your learning.

Following standard conventions, these examples are easy to run and all have a similar setup. Once you understand the fundamentals (which we'll cover), you'll find it easy to run the examples. The examples become more complex as we progress, but still, I'll keep these as accessible as possible, explain how they work, and help you get them up and running.

To find the Bootstrapping Microservices organization on GitHub, point your web browser to https://github.com/bootstrapping-microservices. Here you will see a collection of code repositories organized by chapter, starting with the chapter-2 repository for this chapter.

Each chapter has its own code repository, for example, https://github.com/bootstrapping-microservices/chapter-2. Under each repository, you can find the code organized by the example project that is listed throughout that chapter. If you find any problems with the code, or you are having trouble getting it working, log an issue against the appropriate code repository on GitHub so that I can help you get it working.

2.3   Why Node.js?

In this book, we use Node.js to build our microservices. Why is that? One of the advantages of building microservices is that we can choose the tech stack that we like. I happen to like Node.js, but I also have other reasons for choosing it.

Building our microservices with Docker (which we look at in chapter 3) means we can actually compose applications from multiple tech stacks. That might sound like it just makes things more confusing, and it probably does, but it gives us the ability to mix and match technologies. We can use this to ensure we are using the most appropriate stack that each situation demands.

> **NOTE**   Node.js is well suited to building microservices. It's network oriented and high performance. We plan to build many services, so let's be kind to ourselves and choose a platform that makes our work easier.

Node.js is also popular and well known. That might not sound like much, but it's important because it means there's an ecosystem of people, tools, and resources around Node.js. Having a big community to fall back on when you need help is important. That makes it easier to find assistance while learning, and it's also good to have the support during ongoing software development.

Node.js is made for microservices. It's all there in the name. *Node* implies it's use for building nodes in distributed network-based applications. (JavaScript moved from the browser 11 years ago and has since established itself as an extremely competent server-side programming language.)

Node.js is made for creating small, high-performance and lightweight services, and it forgoes the baggage that comes with many other platforms. Building an HTTP server in Node.js is trivial. This makes it easy for us to bootstrap new microservices quickly. That's a good motivator because we are planning to create many small services. Node.js is also convenient for this book because it means that you don't need to spend a lot of time learning how to code a basic microservice and, as you'll soon see, that we can build a microservice with a small amount of code using Node.js.

Using JavaScript promotes full-stack coding. These days there aren't many places JavaScript doesn't go. We can use it in our application's backend to build microservices. We can use it in our web-based front end (that's where JavaScript was born of course). Not only that, but we can also use JavaScript for desktop development (Electron), mobile development (Ionic), embedded development (IoT devices), and as I showed in my previous book, *Data Wrangling with JavaScript*, we can use JavaScript when working with data, a domain normally dominated by Python. Using JavaScript as much as possible means we can go anywhere in our application without triggering a mental context switch.

The other big thing we get with Node.js is *npm*, the Node Package Manager, which is a command-line tool used to install Node.js code libraries. This isn't specifically related to building microservices, but it is extraordinarily useful to have a fantastic package manager and a vast amount of open-source packages at our fingertips. My superpower as a developer is that I have over 350,000 code libraries (when it was reported in 2017) within easy access. Whatever I need to do it is often just a quick npm search away!

NOTE Node.js is open source and you can find the code for it on GitHub at https://github.com/nodejs/node.

What is npm?

Npm is the Node Package Manager. It is a command-line application that talks to the npm repository online and allows you to manage third-party packages in your Node.js project. Installing a readily available package is a fast way to solve a problem you'd otherwise have to write more code to achieve! You can search for packages on the npm website at https://www.npmjs.com.

2.4   *Our philosophy of development*

Before we get into the coding, I want to brief you on my philosophy of development, which we'll use throughout this book. You will see this manifested time and again, so a quick explanation is in order. I'll sum up my philosophy of development with the following three points:

- Iterate
- Keep it working
- Move from simple to complex

Iteration is a key ingredient. I'm talking about personal iterations of coding and not the larger iterations in agile that are commonly known as sprints. We build the code for our application through a series of personal iterations. We'll add code, iteration by iteration, as shown in figure 2.1. Each iteration gives us feedback. Feedback allows us to discover when we are veering off track and to do immediate course corrections. Fast iteration allows us to align our work closely with our evolving goals.

> **NOTE**   Small, fast-paced increments of coding are essential for a productive software developer.

At each iteration, we do a small amount of coding. How small? It depends on what we are doing and how difficult it is. But the key is that it should be small enough so that we can easily understand and test the code we just wrote.

Each iteration must produce working and tested code. This is the most important factor. Have you ever typed in a whole page of code then struggled for hours to get it working? When we work in small and well-tested iterations of code, the sum total at the end of a day's coding is a large body of *working* code. You can see how this works in figure 2.1.

This notion of producing a large body of working code demonstrates my second point: *keep it working.* We will rarely get into trouble if we work in small, easily tested

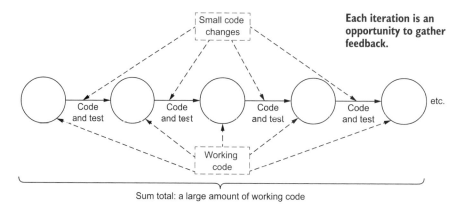

Figure 2.1   **A series of small code changes results in a large body of working code.**

increments. When typing large amounts of code, we face many difficulties getting that code to work. Most likely we'll have a large amount of broken (*non-working*) code. But even if the code does appear to work, it probably still harbors many "nasties" that are yet to be found.

> **NOTE** Each small iteration of coding should produce working and tested code. The sum total of a series of such iterations results in a large amount of rock-solid code.

When we get into trouble, we can easily wind our code back to the previous iteration to restore it to working order. Because each iteration of our code is small, we don't give up much progress when we need to revert back. Getting into trouble really isn't any trouble at all!

Of course, restoration of the previous iteration implies that you are staging or committing your code to Git or some other form of version control. That should go without saying. Even if you aren't using version control (you really should be), then it's up to you to find another way to preserve the results of your iterations.

The third and final point in my philosophy of coding is to *start simple*. We should start coding at the simplest possible starting point and iterate our application toward greater complexity. All applications grow complex over time; that's unavoidable in the long run. But we definitely shouldn't start with complexity. Don't try and lay down a complex system all at once in the "big bang" style. That probably won't work out well for you.

> **NOTE** Complexity is where applications *always* end up, but it doesn't mean that's where they have to start. Each code change should also be simple, avoiding too much complexity in any single iteration.

Start with the simplest possible code, then iteration by iteration, you can build it up to something more complex. This process is illustrated in figure 2.2. Don't be too eager to take on complexity. Keep it simple for as long as you can. As our application becomes more and more complex, we need to bring in tools, techniques, processes, and patterns to help us manage that complexity.

Building with microservices is one such tool for managing complexity. Again, any given microservice should be simple. It should be small. Making a small update to an existing microservice should be easy. And adding a new microservice to an existing application should be effortless. These statements are true, even when the application itself has become extremely complex.

As our code becomes more complex, it doesn't mean that our iterations need to be that way. We should strive to keep every modification to the code as simple as possible. Simple changes are easy to understand, simpler to test and to integrate into the application. All this increases the probability that the evolving system continues to behave as we had hoped it would.

TIP When solving problems in complex applications, don't be afraid to extract the problem from the application and reproduce it in a simpler environment. If you can isolate a problem with a smaller amount of code, that problem has less space in which to hide!

If we encounter problems in a complex application that we can't easily solve, we have a new option now. As indicated in figure 2.2, where the arrow goes from the end back to the beginning, at any time, we can extract our problematic code from the complex application and reproduce it in a simpler environment.

Thankfully, this is fairly easy to do when coding in JavaScript. We might load our code in a unit test where we can repeatedly run the code to troubleshoot and fix it. If that's not possible, we might extract the code to a separate Node.js project to isolate the problem and make it easier to solve. I often start up Data-Forge Notebook (an application that I built and have released to the public) to run isolated code and make it easier to solve problems.

But what can we do if the code isn't so easy to extract? In that situation, what I like to do is teardown the application around the problematic code. Pull code out of the application (as much as is possible) until you have isolated the problem as best you can.

Why would we do this? It's because when you have isolated a problem it has nowhere to hide. Finding problems is usually much more time-consuming than fixing them once they are found. So having faster ways to triangulate the location of problems in our code is one of the best ways for us to enhance our productivity. We'll talk more about the debugging process and isolating problems in chapter 10.

This is another thing to love about microservices. Our application is already compartmentalized, so it should be easy for us to tear out non-essential microservices. Having said that, eliminating code from your application in this way *is* an advanced technique and can easily result in a broken application!

I've covered my philosophy of development here because I think it can help you to be a better and more productive developer. The evolution of our software in small and well-tested increments is the main goal. We are taking our code on a journey of iterations from working state to working state. At no time should our code ever be fundamentally broken.

You'll see this philosophy in action in this chapter and throughout the book. Start simple. Start small. Iterate with small changes. Keep it working. Before you know it,

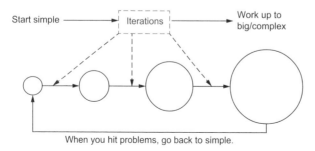

Figure 2.2 **Start simple and work up to complex through a series of small iterations**

we'll have built something big and complex! But that doesn't happen all at once. It happens through a series of small changes that, taken together, add up to something huge.

2.5 *Establishing our single-service development environment*

To create and work on a microservice, we need to set up our development environment. This provides a way for us to create and edit code and then run it to make sure it works. In this chapter, we'll build a single microservice and we'll run it using Node.js directly on our development workstation (or personal computer). We will edit our code using VS Code or some other IDE or text editor of your choice. Let's begin by setting up our environment.

Node.js itself is easy to install and run on any of the main operating systems, so you can choose Linux, Windows, or MacOS for the development of your microservice. (Your choices are summarized in table 2.2.)

Running a single service under Node.js directly is fairly easy, as you'll see in the coming sections of this chapter. But when it comes to developing and testing multiple microservices, which we'll cover in chapter 4, things become more complicated. That's when we'll need to enlist the help of Docker (from chapter 3 and on). For now, let's focus on running our microservice directly under Node.js in our chosen operating system.

Even after we start developing and testing multiple microservices, there will be times during development, testing, and troubleshooting that we'll want to pull a single microservice out of the application and run it so that we can focus on just that isolated part without having to worry about the application and all the baggage that it brings. Having a single-service development environment isn't just a convenient stepping stone in the early stages. It is useful to have on standby and ready to be called into action at any time during ongoing development.

Table 2.2 Options for running Node.js

Platform	Notes
Linux	Node.js was built for Linux, so it works pretty well there!
	For this book, I demonstrate most commands under Ubuntu Linux. If you also run Ubuntu or another variant of Linux, you are well placed to follow along with the examples in the book.
Windows	Node.js also works well under Windows. In fact, I do most of my day-to-day development, testing, and troubleshooting with Windows.
MacOS	Node.js also works well under MacOS.

> **NOTE** When working with just Node.js, you can use it on any platform, and there really isn't one that is better than any other!

Figure 2.3 gives you an indication of what our single-microservice development environment looks like. We will edit our code in VS Code or an alternative editor. Our

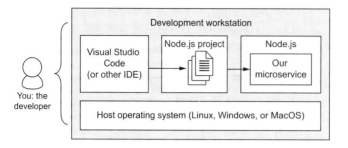

Figure 2.3   Our single-service development environment for chapter 2

microservice project is a Node.js project with JavaScript code. (I'll show you how to create this soon.) Executing our project under Node.js produces a running instance of our microservice. All of this is running on our development workstation on our host operating system of choice: Linux, Windows, or MacOS.

2.5.1   *Installing Git*

The example projects and code for this book are in GitHub under the Bootstrapping Microservices organization (see the links in section 2.2). Figure 2.4 shows how each code repository is structured. Each subdirectory (example-1, example-2, and so forth) are working projects that you can run yourself to follow along with the book (assuming you don't want to type in all the code yourself).

Each of these directories contains a complete working example.

You can run the code in each of these examples for yourself!

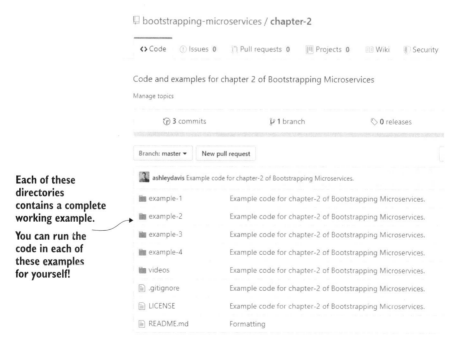

Figure 2.4   Each example project in the GitHub repository is a complete working project that you can run for yourself.

The simplest way to get the code is to *download* it as a zip file from GitHub. To do this, you should go to the code repository (e.g., the repository chapter-2 for chapter 2) and look for the Clone or Download button. Click it and then choose Download ZIP.

The best way to get the code, of course, is to use Git to *clone* the code repository. To do this, you first need to install Git. You might already have it installed, for instance, if you (like me) use it for everyday work. Or you might be running a variant of Linux that comes with Git pre-installed. On MacOS, you might have Xcode installed, which comes with Git.

How do we know if we have Git installed? To find out which version of Git you have (if any), open a terminal (on Windows open the Command Prompt, or even better install Windows Terminal from the Microsoft Store) and run the following command:

```
git --version
```

If Git is already installed, you'll see its version number, which is something like this:

```
git version 2.27.0
```

If you don't already have Git, installing it isn't difficult. See the Git website at https://git-scm.com and follow the instructions there to download and install on your platform.

> **New to using the command line?**
> Using the command line is one of the best and most productive ways to work as a software developer. Using UIs and visual editors is great for doing the most common everyday tasks, but for more complex or customized tasks, we need to be comfortable using the command line. If you are new to it, consider first doing a tutorial for using the command line for your operating system.

2.5.2   Cloning the code repo

With Git installed, you can now clone the code repository for each chapter of this book. For example, at this point, you should clone the repo for chapter 2 so you can follow along with this chapter:

git clone https://github.com/bootstrapping-microservices/chapter-2.git

This command gets a copy of the code repository from GitHub and places it on your local hard drive (in the current working directory) under a directory named chapter-2. I won't explain how to clone a repository again in future chapters. But at the start of each new chapter, I'll show you where to get the code for that chapter, then you can use Git to get your own copy. Feel free to return here at any time for a reminder of how to use Git.

2.5.3   *Getting Visual Studio (VS) Code*

I use Visual Studio (VS) Code for all my coding. I'm recommending it to you because I think it's a great environment for editing code. You can find the download and installation instructions for Windows, Linux, and MacOS on the VS Code website at

https://code.visualstudio.com

I like VS Code because it's lightweight, has great performance, and is configurable. It's also commonly used for Node.js and JavaScript projects. You don't need any extra plugins for this book, but it's worth noting, there is a vast range of easily installable plugins for different programming languages and tasks. You can also customize VS Code for all your development needs.

Of course, if you already have your own favorite IDE or text editor, feel free to use it, as it doesn't really make any difference. When I mention VS Code throughout the book, you'll just have to pretend it's your preferred text editor instead!

2.5.4   *Installing Node.js*

To run our microservice, we need Node.js. That's something we can't do without because the example microservices in this book are Node.js projects. All the code examples are written in JavaScript, which runs on Node.js. If you already have Node.js installed, you can open a terminal and check the version with the following commands:

```
node --version
v12.18.1

npm --version
6.14.5
```

These are the versions I currently use for node and npm. You can use these versions or later ones.

> **NOTE** We use the npm command for installing third-party packages. When you install Node.js, you get npm as well.

Installing Node.js for any platform is straightforward. To install Node.js, see the Node.js website at https://nodejs.org for download and installation instructions. It's not difficult and you shouldn't have any issues.

If you already have Node.js installed and want to get a newer version, or if you'd like to manage multiple versions of Node.js, it's worth looking at NVM described in the second sidebar that follows.

After installing Node.js, open a terminal and double-check that it installed OK. To do this, print the version numbers:

```
node --version
npm --version
```

Now that we have Node.js installed, we are ready to build and run our first microservice.

It's important to know what version you are using!

Using the `--version` argument is a good way to check if you have something installed, but it's also important to know what version you have. When you are working on a real system, it's crucial that you use the same version in development as you use in production. That's the best way to know that your code will run in production.

Need to run different versions of Node.js?

What about if you need to run multiple versions of Node.js? This can happen quite easily, actually.

Say you are maintaining or have to work on multiple production applications that are built with different versions of Node.js. Or maybe that you are just working on a single application, but it has been in development for quite some time, and different microservices are on different versions of Node.js. In these cases, I highly recommend you use nvm (the Node Version Manager) to install different versions of Node.js and switch between them.

There are actually two different applications called nvm and which one you choose depends on your operating system. See the following links for setup instructions:

- For Linux and MacOS, you want this one: https://github.com/nvm-sh/nvm.
- For Windows, use: https://github.com/coreybutler/nvm-windows.

This isn't for the faint of heart! You must be proficient at using the command line to install this software.

2.6 *Building an HTTP server for video streaming*

Now that we have our development environment, we can build our first microservice. This isn't a difficult project, and we are just building it to illustrate the process of creating a basic microservice. It's the first step in creating our example microservices application FlixTube. You can follow along with the code while reading this chapter, typing in the code as you see it, or you can read it first and then try out the example projects that are available in the chapter 2 repository on GitHub.

The microservice we are building is a simple video-streaming service. Streaming video might sound difficult and it is something that can become complicated in a real production application. But we are starting with something that's much simpler. You might be surprised at just how little code we actually need to create this.

Figure 2.5 shows the output for the end result of this chapter's project. Our microservice delivers streaming video to the web browser via port 3000 and the route *video*. We can watch the video directly through our browser by pointing it at http://localhost:3000/video.

We are running
the server on the
local computer.

Our server is
accessible via
port 3000.

Streaming video
is accessible via
the /video route.

We can watch our
streaming video
directly in Chrome.

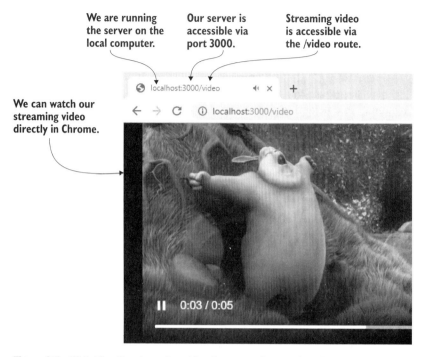

Figure 2.5 Watching the streaming video from our microservice directly in Chrome

In figure 2.5, you can see we use Chrome to watch the video. The sample video we are using was downloaded from https://sample-videos.com. Here, we used the shortest possible video, but feel free to download one of the larger sample videos for your own testing.

To create our microservice, we must go through the following steps:

1 Create a Node.js project for our microservice.
2 Install Express and create a simple HTTP server.
3 Add an HTTP GET route /video that retrieves the streaming video.

After creating this basic first microservice, we'll talk briefly about how we can configure our microservices. Then we'll cover some fundamentals for production and development setup.

2.6.1   *Creating a Node.js project*

Before we can start writing code, we need a Node.js project where our code can live. The project we'll soon create is shown in figure 2.6. This is a basic Node.js project with a single entry point: the script file index.js. You can also see package.json and package-lock.json, which are the files that track the dependencies and metadata for our project. The dependencies themselves are installed under the node_modules directory. Let's create this project!

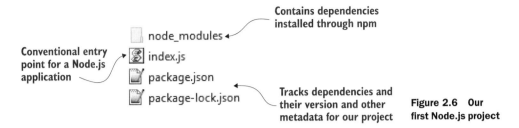

Figure 2.6   Our first Node.js project

> **DEFINITION**   A *Node.js project* contains the source code and configuration for our Node.js application. It's where we edit the code that creates the features of our microservice.

If you are creating a project from scratch (and not just running the code from GitHub), you must first create a directory for the project. You can do this from the terminal on Linux and MacOS using the `mkdir` command:

```
mkdir my-new-project
```

If you are working on Windows, you can instead use the `md` command:

```
md my-new-project
```

Now change into your new directory using the `cd` command:

```
cd my-new-project
```

You are now ready to create a *stub* Node.js project. What this means is that we are creating our package.json file. We can do this using the npm `init` command:

```
npm init -y
```

The `-y` argument means that we don't have to answer any interactive questions while initializing our project. That simply makes it a little bit faster to create our project.

After running `npm init`, we now have a package.json file with all its fields set to defaults. You can see an example of this in listing 2.1. Because the fields in this file have default values, you might want to come back later and set these to values more appropriate to your project. For the moment though, we'll leave these as they are.

Listing 2.1   The empty Node.js package file we just generated

```
{
  "name": "my-new-project"
  "version": "1.0.0",
  "description": "",
  "main": "index.js",
  "scripts": {
    "test": "..."
  },
```

The package name. It defaults to the name of the directory that contains the package; in this case, my-new-project because we initialized it in the my-new-project directory we just created.

These fields are important if you publish this package to https://www.npmjs.com.

npm scripts go here. We'll talk more about this later in the chapter.

```
"keywords": [],
"author": "",
"license": "ISC"
}
```

| These fields are important if you publish this package to https://www.npmjs.com.

After creating your Node.js project, I encourage you to open the folder in VS Code and explore your new project by opening the package.json file and examining it. With the project opened in VS Code, you are now ready to start adding some code to your project.

Package.json vs. package-lock.json

Although package.json is automatically generated and updated by npm, it can also be edited by hand. That way you can manually change the metadata and npm module dependencies for your Node.js project.

Usually, package.json doesn't specify exact version numbers for dependencies (although it can if you want it to). Instead, package.json generally sets the *minimum* version for each dependency, and it can also set a range of versions. In addition, package.json only tracks top-level dependencies for the project. You don't need to specify dependencies of dependencies; that's handled automatically for you. This makes package.json smaller, more concise, and therefore more human-readable.

The problem with package.json is that you and your colleagues can end up running different versions of dependencies. Even worse, you could be running different versions compared to what's in production. That's because package.json usually doesn't specify exact versions, so depending on when you invoke `npm install`, you can get different versions from everyone else. This is a recipe for chaos! Indeed, it makes it difficult to replicate production issues because you aren't guaranteed to be able to reproduce the exact configuration that is running in production.

Package-lock.json was introduced in npm version 5 to solve this problem. It is a generated file and is not designed to be hand edited. Its purpose is to track the *entire* tree of dependencies (including dependencies of dependencies) and the *exact* version of each dependency.

You should commit package-lock.json to your code repository. Sharing this file with teammates and the production environment is the best way to make sure that everyone has the same configuration for their copy of the project.

2.6.2 *Installing Express*

To stream video from our microservice, we'll make it an HTTP server (also known as a *web server*). That is to say that it will respond to HTTP requests from a browser, in this case, a browser's request to play streaming video. To implement our HTTP server, we'll use Express.

> **NOTE** Express is the de facto standard framework for building HTTP servers on Node.js. It's easier for us to do this using Express than it is to use the low-level Node.js API.

Express is the most popular code library for building HTTP servers on Node.js. You can find documentation and examples for it on the Express web site at http://expressjs.com/. While there, I'd encourage you to explore the many other features of Express as well. Of course, we could build an HTTP server directly on Node.js without Express, but Express allows us to do this at a higher level of abstraction, with less code, and without the nuts and bolts code we'd otherwise need using the low-level Node.js API.

Using Express is also a good excuse for us to learn how to install an npm package for use in our microservice. npm is the package manager for Node.js, and it puts at our fingertips a whole world of packages. This includes many libraries and frameworks like Express that we can use to quickly and easily do a whole range of jobs when coding. Otherwise, we'd have to write a lot more code (and probably cause a load of bugs in the process) to achieve the same effect. We can install Express from the terminal using the command `npm install` as follows:

```
npm install --save express
```

Running this command installs the express package into our project. The `--save` argument causes the dependency to be added to and tracked in the package.json file. Note that `--save` isn't actually necessary anymore. In older versions of Node.js, this was required; these days, it's the default. I've included `--save` explicitly so that I can highlight what it does, but you don't actually have to use this anymore.

You can see the result of our package install in figure 2.7 and listing 2.2. Figure 2.7 shows that an express subdirectory was created in the node_modules directory of our Node.js project. You'll also note that many other packages have been installed alongside Express. These other packages are the dependencies for Express, and npm has automatically installed these for us.

Listing 2.2 shows our updated package.json file after installing Express. The difference from listing 2.1 is that we now have a `dependencies` field that includes Express version 4.17.1. This identifies the version of Express that our Node.js project depends on.

Notice also in the title of listing 2.2 that there is a reference to the actual file that exists in the chapter-2 code repository on GitHub. This shows you where to find the working copy of that file. In this case, it's the chapter-2/example-1/package.json. If you go

Express is now installed in our node_modules directory.

Figure 2.7   Note where the express subdirectory is installed into the node_modules directory.

to the chapter-2 repository (https://github.com/bootstrapping-microservices/chapter-2) and then look in the example-1 subdirectory, you'll see the file package.json. It's the same file that is shown in this code listing. You can find this file directly by putting this link in your web browser:

https://github.com/bootstrapping-microservices/chapter-2/blob/master/example-1/package.json.

Most of the listings in this book follow this convention. They show a snippet of a file (or in this case, a complete version) that is part of a working example project on GitHub. To see this file in context, you can follow the reference to its location in GitHub or in the copy of the code repository that you cloned locally.

From there, you can either just inspect the code as it exists within its project, or rather, you can (you should) run the code because every example in this book (in this case, example-1 in chapter-2) is a working project that you can easily get running for yourself to cement into place what you are learning.

Listing 2.2   The package file with Express installed (chapter-2/example-1/package.json)

```
{
  "name": "example-1",
  "version": "1.0.0",
  "description": "",
  "main": "index.js",
  "scripts": {
    "test": "echo \"Error: no test specified\" && exit 1"
  },
  "keywords": [],
  "author": "",
  "license": "ISC",
  "dependencies": {
    "express": "^4.17.1"        Version 4.17.1 for the express package
  }                             that I installed was current when this
}                               book was written.
```

Having the dependencies tracked through the package.json file means you can easily pass your project and code to other programmers (your teammates, for example) so that they can easily replicate your work. It also means I can make this code available to you and that you can easily get it working.

For example, say you want to get example-1 working. First you need to clone the chapter-2 code repository as was shown in section 2.6.2, then from the terminal, change the directory to the code repository:

```
cd chapter-2
```

Now change the directory into the particular example that you want to get running. In this case, it's example-1:

```
cd example-1
```

Then you can use npm to install all the dependencies:

```
npm install
```

The command `npm install` by itself (not specifying any particular package) installs all the dependencies listed in package.json. In this case, it's only Express that is listed so only that is installed (plus its dependencies). For other examples in this book, there will be more dependencies. But we still only need to invoke `npm install` once per example, and that's enough to install everything you need to run each example project.

2.6.3 Creating the Express boilerplate

Before we add video streaming to our microservice, we must first create the standard Express boilerplate HTTP server. Listing 2.3 is the customary Hello World example that you get by following the official Express getting started guide (available at https://expressjs.com/).

This is only a small amount of code, but it's the simple starting point that we need for this project. You should now create an index.js file in your Node.js project and type in the code. If that's too much work, then just open example-1 from the chapter-2 repository and examine the pre-cooked index.js file you'll find there.

The code in listing 2.3 starts a web server, albeit the simplest possible web server. It uses Express', `get` function to define a route handler that returns the string `Hello World!`. The `listen` function is then called to start this HTTP server, listening for HTTP requests on port 3000.

> **Listing 2.3 A minimal Express web server (chapter-2/example-1/index.js)**

Loads the Express library for use in our code

```
const express = require('express');

const app = express();          ◁──  Creates an instance of an Express app

const port = 3000;   ◁──  Our HTTP server will listen on port 3000.

app.get('/', (req, res) => {    ◁──  Creates a handler for the main HTTP route
    res.send('Hello World!');   ◁──  The handler prints Hello
});                                   World! in the web browser.

app.listen(port, () => {        ◁──  Initiates the HTTP server
    console.log(`Example app listening
              ⇒ on port ${port}!`);   ◁──  The callback prints a message
});                                        when the server has started.
```

We called the file index.js; why is that? This is the standard name for the main entry point of a Node.js application. It's simply a convention that it is called index.js. We could just as easily have called it something else, like main.js or server.js. The choice is up to you. By calling it index.js, we are giving it a name that many other Node.js developers will immediately recognize as being the *main* file.

The port number allows us to run multiple HTTP servers on the same computer. The servers can each have their own port number so they won't conflict with each other. The choice of port 3000 is another convention. It's customary to set your Node.js application to listen on port 3000, but in production, we'll often want to set this to the standard HTTP port 80. Later on, we'll see how to set the port number as a configuration option supplied to the microservice when it's booted up.

We could have chosen another port and, if you are already running something else on port 3000, you might have to do so. For example, if port 3000 doesn't work for you, try changing it to a different number, say port 4000.

We'll use the series of port numbers starting at 4000 (4000, 4001, and so forth) later, when we run multiple microservices at the same time. Now we are ready to run this ultra simple web server.

What is index.js?
By convention, index.js is the JavaScript file that is the entry point for the Node.js application. When trying to understand an existing Node.js project, index.js is the place you should start.

2.6.4   *Running our simple web server*

To test our fledgling HTTP server, we'll run it from the terminal. First, we need to make sure we are in the same directory that contains the index.js file from listing 2.3. If you built the project yourself from scratch, you'll have to change to the directory that you created. For example

```
cd my-new-project
```

Otherwise, if you are using the code from the chapter-2 GitHub repository, you should change to the example-1 directory:

```
cd chapter-2
cd example-1
```

Now you can use Node.js to run the JavaScript code and start the HTTP server:

```
node index.js
```

What we are doing here is running Node.js with `index.js` as the argument. We are telling Node.js to run our script file. Node.js executes the JavaScript code in this file, and if successful, we'll see the following output in our terminal:

```
Example app listening on port 3000!
```

Now we can test that this has worked. Open your web browser and point it at http://localhost:3000. You should see the `Hello World` message displayed.

We can also use cURL, which you might have if you are working on Linux or MacOS (and Windows, if you have Git Bash), as a quick means for testing HTTP endpoints. With your HTTP server already running in one terminal, open a new terminal and use cURL to hit your endpoint:

```
curl http://localhost:3000
```

You should see output like this:

```
Hello World!
```

> **NOTE** Using cURL means you can run quick tests like this from the command line without having to open your web browser.

We now have a basic HTTP server running and it's time for us to add streaming video to it. When you are ready to stop your HTTP server, go back to the terminal where it is running and press Ctrl-C to quit the Node.js application.

2.6.5 *Adding streaming video*

In listing 2.3, we only had a single HTTP route handler that returned Hello World. Now we'll change this and create a REST API for streaming video to the browser.

A REST API (often just called an API) is a representational state transfer (REST) application programming interface (API). The name makes it sound complicated, but it really isn't. A REST API in its simplest sense is just a collection of HTTP route handlers that interface with systems and logic running in the backend.

Often routes in REST APIs return data, but we'll add a new route that returns streaming video. You can see what it looks like in figure 2.8. The diagram shows how our HTTP server will read the video from the filesystem and deliver it to the web browser via port 3000 and the video route.

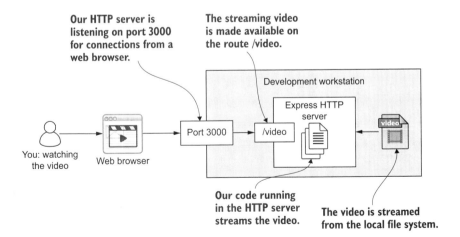

Figure 2.8   How the web browser interacts with our microservice through the video route

We define the new video route as shown in listing 2.4. If you are following along with the code, you can update the Express boilerplate HTTP server that you created earlier. Otherwise, you can open example-2 from the chapter-2 repository in VS Code to see how the updated index.js looks.

Listing 2.4 reads a video from the local filesystem and streams it to the browser. This is a simple starting point that does just what we need, which is streaming video, the core feature for our microservices application FlixTube. The video itself can be found in the videos subdirectory under example-2. Feel free to inspect the video yourself before trying to run this code. We'll use this example video throughout the book for testing so you will come to know it very well!

Listing 2.4 Simple streaming video server with Node.js (chapter-2/example-2/index.js)

```
const express = require("express");
const fs = require("fs");                      ◁──  Loads the (built-in) fs library so we
                                                     can use the Node.js filesystem API.
const app = express();

const port = 3000;
                                                     Defines the HTTP route for streaming
                                                     video. This is a REST API for streaming
app.get("/video", (req, res) => {          ◁──      video!

    const path =
        "../videos/SampleVideo_1280x720_1mb.mp4";   ◁──   The path of the video file
    fs.stat(path, (err, stats) => {        ◁──            that we'll stream to the
        if (err) {                                        browser
            console.error("An error occurred");
            res.sendStatus(500);                   Retrieves the video file size. We'll
            return;                                encode this in the HTTP header as
        }                                          a response to the web browser.

        res.writeHead(200, {               ◁──
            "Content-Length": stats.size,          Sends a response header to
            "Content-Type": "video/mp4",           the web browser, including the
        });                                ◁──      content length and mime type

        fs.createReadStream(path).pipe(res);   ◁──   Streams the video to the web
    });                                              browser. Yes it's this simple!

});

app.listen(port, () => {
    console.log(`Example app listening on port ${port}!`);
});
```

Handles any errors that may occur

The code in listing 2.4 is an example of Node.js streaming. This is a more complicated topic than we have time to get into here, but suffice it to say that here we are opening a readable stream from the video file. Then we are piping the stream to our HTTP response (look for the call to the `pipe` function).

We have created a conduit through which to stream the video byte by byte to the browser. We set up this pipeline for video streaming and then let Node.js and Express take care of the rest. Node.js and Express make this easy! To run this code, first change to the example-2 subdirectory:

```
cd chapter-2/example-2
```

Then install the dependencies:

```
npm install
```

Now start the first iteration of our streaming video microservice like this:

```
node index.js
```

We can now point our browser to http://localhost:3000/video to watch the video. It's going to look similar to what was shown earlier in figure 2.5.

> **NOTE** Don't use cURL for testing at this point; it doesn't work well with streaming video. It's going to print a massive stream of garbage into your terminal if you do that. When viewing the output of JSON REST APIs, however, cURL is really useful, so it's advantageous to have in your toolbox.

To test the code for this book, I've used the Chrome web browser. I discovered that such simple video streaming doesn't work under the Safari web browser. For details on how to make video streaming work for Safari, see my blog post on "The Data Wrangler" at http://mng.bz/11Xd. We'll talk more about ways we can test our microservices in chapter 8.

2.6.6 *Configuring our microservice*

At this point, it's worthwhile to spend a moment thinking about how we can configure our microservices. This is an important concern and will help us make better use of the microservices that we create. In future chapters, we'll see examples of how we can wire together microservices using their configurations. For now, though, let's look at a simple example to demonstrate how to configure a microservice.

We need a way to configure our microservice so it knows the port number to use when starting the HTTP server. There are a number of techniques we might use to configure our microservice, such as configuration files and command-line arguments. These techniques work, but another has emerged as the standard way to configure a microservice, and it is well supported by the tools we will be using.

We will configure our microservices using *environment variables*. Specifically, in this case, we need a single environment variable to set the port number for the HTTP server. Figure 2.9 shows how we will wire the PORT environment variable to our microservice.

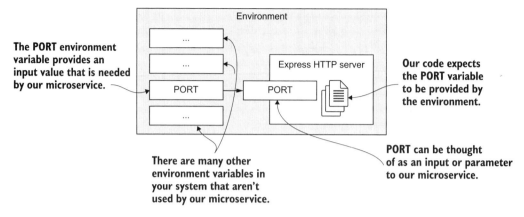

Figure 2.9 Using the PORT environment variable to configure our microservice

Using environment variables to configure our code in Node.js is quite easy. We simply access the appropriately named field of process.env. You can see how this works in listing 2.5, where our code uses process.env.PORT to get the value for the port number. The code throws an error if the PORT environment variable is not supplied. I like to add this error checking so that the microservice clearly states the configuration it is expecting. This means we can't accidentally start our microservice in production without configuring it. If we try that, the microservice will refuse to start, and it's going to tell us the reason why.

I think it's better that the microservice refuse to start rather than operate on potentially the wrong configuration simply because we forgot to configure it. The microservice then shows us how to fix the problem. This means we don't have to go rooting around in the code to figure it out.

Listing 2.5   Configuring a microservice (extract from chapter-2/example-3/index.js)

```
const express = require("express");
const fs = require("fs");

const app = express();

if (!process.env.PORT) {
    throw new Error("Please specify the port number
    ➥ for the HTTP server with the environment variable PORT.");
}

const PORT = process.env.PORT;

// ... code omitted for brevity ...

app.listen(PORT, () => {
    console.log(`Service listening on port ${PORT}!`);
});
```

Throws an error when the required environment variable isn't supplied. If not specified, you could also choose a default value.

Copies the environment variable to a global variable for easy access

Starts the HTTP server using the port number that was input to the microservice

Now let's run this code:

```
cd example-3
npm install
node index.js
```

Oops. We forgot to configure the required environment variable, and our microservice has thrown the error. How did we forget so soon about the environment variable we were supposed to configure? No problem. The error log conveniently gives us a helpful message telling us how to fix the problem:

```
chapter-2\example-3\index.js:7
    throw new Error("Please specify the port number for the HTTP server
 ➡ with the environment variable PORT.");
    ^

Error: Please specify the port number for the HTTP server
 ➡ with the environment variable PORT.
    at Object.<anonymous> (chapter-2\example-3\index.js:7:11)
```

Now we must set the PORT environment variable before trying to run the code again. On Linux and MacOS, we'll set it using this command:

```
export PORT=3000
```

If working on Windows, do this instead:

```
set PORT=3000
```

Run the file again:

```
node index.js
```

Now it should work correctly. We set the PORT environment variable so the microservice knows which port number to use for its HTTP server. To test this, we can point our browser at http://localhost:3000/video. We should see our video playing the same as before.

Now that we can configure the port for the HTTP server, we can easily start multiple separate microservices directly on our development workstation. We can only do that if they have different port numbers. Because we can set the port number, we can easily start each microservice using a different port.

Configuring our microservices through environment variables is important and is something we'll use again in future chapters. For example, we are going to need it when we add the database to our application (chapter 4) and when we connect our microservices to a message queue server (chapter 5).

We can also use environment variables to pass secret and sensitive data into a microservice (e.g., the password for our database). We need to treat this information carefully, and we shouldn't store it in the code where everyone in the company can see it. In chapter 11, we'll touch on the important issue of managing sensitive configuration such as passwords and API keys.

2.6.7   *Setting up for production*

So far, we set up our microservice to run on our development workstation. That's all well and good, but before we get to the fun stuff (Docker, Kubernetes, and Terraform), we need to know how to set up our microservice to run in the production environment.

When I say *production environment*, you might be wondering what I'm talking about. Production environment simply means our *customer-facing* environment. That's where our application is hosted so it can be accessed by our customers. For this book, our production environment is Kubernetes, and we are gearing up to run our application in a Kubernetes cluster to make it publicly accessible.

I've already said that to get an existing Node.js project ready to run, you must first install dependencies like this:

```
npm install
```

Well, to get our microservice ready to run in production, we need to use a slightly different version of this command:

```
npm install --only=production
```

We added the argument `--only=production` to install only dependencies that are required in production. This is important because when creating a Node.js project, we'll usually have a bunch of so-called *dev dependencies* that we only need for development and we don't want to install these into our production environment. You haven't seen an example of dev dependencies yet, but you will see it coming up in the next section. Up until now, we have run our HTTP server on our dev workstation like this:

```
node index.js
```

That's OK, but we'd like to run it using the following convention:

```
npm start
```

Running the command `npm start` is the conventional way to start a Node.js application. This is a special case of an npm *script* that we can use to start our application. In listing 2.6, you can see that we've updated the package.json file to include a start script under the `scripts` field. This simply runs Node.js with `index.js` as the argument.

No surprises here, but the nice thing about this convention is that for almost any Node.js project (at least those that follow the convention), you can run `npm start` and you don't have to actually know if the main file is called index.js or if it has some other name. You also don't need to know if the application takes any special command-line arguments, because these can be recorded here as well.

This gives you one command to remember regardless of which project you are looking at and how the particular application is started. It makes it much easier to understand how to use any Node.js project, even those created by other people.

Listing 2.6   Adding a start script to package.json (chapter-2/example-1/package.json)

```
{
  "name": "example-1",
  "version": "1.0.0",
  "description": "",
  "main": "index.js",
  "scripts": {
    "start": "node index.js"     ◁──┐  Adding the npm start script to
  },                                 │  package.json lets us run this
  "keywords": [],                    │  project with "npm start".
  "author": "",
  "license": "ISC",
  "dependencies": {
    "express": "^4.17.1"
  }
}
```

Try this for yourself. You'll note in listing 2.6 that I updated the example-3 package.json to include an npm start script. To try it out, change your directory to example-3 and run `npm start` (make sure you run `npm install` to get the dependencies first or execute `npm install --only=production` if you only want the production dependencies).

From now on in this book, we'll use `npm start` to run each of our microservices in production. In the future, I'll refer to this as running our microservice in *production mode*. It's worth remembering this command because so many other Node.js applications you'll encounter in the wild conform to this convention, and it's a shortcut you can remember that will help you get other people's code working.

We are going to use the commands we've just learned for getting our microservice working in production. These are the commands we'll use to get our microservice running in Docker in chapter 3, so we'll come back to these then.

Another useful command you might have heard of is `npm test`. This is the command that is conventionally used by a Node.js project to initiate automated testing. It's something we'll come back to and investigate in chapter 8.

2.6.8   Live reloading for fast iteration

Now that we have a convenient way to set up and run our microservice in production, we can also look for a better way to run it in development. Live reloading our code as we are editing helps streamline our development workflow and fosters productivity. As we change code, we can immediately see the results of executing the code. Whether the result is an error or output from a successful run doesn't matter. What matters is that we get fast feedback that shortens the cycle time for our iterations and increases the pace of our development.

In this section, we'll get set up for live reload. This way of working is illustrated in figure 2.10, and it's important because it automates the restarting of our microservice (during development). This helps us cycle more quickly through our personal coding iterations, see instant results, and become more productive. Iteration and fast feedback are crucial in my philosophy of development as I pointed out in section 2.4. (Live reload also works well with test-driven development, which we'll talk about in chapter 8.)

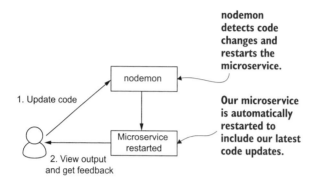

Figure 2.10   Setting up for live reload helps us to be more productive.

To create our live reload pipeline, we'll install a package called nodemon. Figure 2.10 shows how it works. We use nodemon to run our microservice, and it automatically watches for code changes in our project. When a code change is detected, nodemon automatically restarts our microservice for us, saving us the effort of doing so manually.

This might not sound like it does much at all, but I have found that it makes for a fast and fluid development cycle. Once you have tried it you might wonder how you ever did without it in the first place. We can install nodemon in our Node.js project as follows:

```
npm install --save-dev nodemon
```

Note that this time we use the `--save-dev` argument. This makes npm install this package as a *dev dependency* rather than a *normal dependency*. I mentioned this in the previous section when talking about installing production only dependencies for running in the production environment. Here you can see why it's useful for installing a dependency that you want to have in development but excluded from production.

We use nodemon during development, but there's no need to have it installed in production where, at best, it's just useless bloat and, at worst, it might be a security concern. Not that I have any reason to believe nodemon in particular has any security issues. But generally, the less we install in our production environment, the better. This is a topic we'll return to in chapter 11 when we talk about security.

This means that when we run `npm install --only=production`, then the packages we install to help with development, like nodemon, will be excluded. Normally, when we run our Node.js code, we do it like this:

```
node index.js
```

Now that we are going to be using nodemon instead, we'll replace `node` with `nodemon` and run it like this:

```
npx nodemon index.js
```

What's this `npx` command that's suddenly appeared? This is a useful command that comes with Node.js and allows us to run installed dependencies from the command line. Before `npx` was added to Node.js, we used to install modules like nodemon globally. Now we can run tools like this directly from the current project's dependencies. This really helps us use the right versions of modules and stops our system from getting cluttered up by globally installed modules.

Stopping the microservice running under nodemon is the same as when it's running under Node.js. Just type Ctrl-C at the terminal where it's running, and the microservice stops.

I usually like to wrap nodemon in an npm script called *start:dev*. This is a personal convention of mine, but I find that many other developers have something similar, often with a different name. You can see how our updated project setup looks in listing 2.7. At the bottom of the package.json, nodemon has been added as a `devDependency`, and you can see our new script, start:dev, in the `scripts` section.

Listing 2.7 Adding a start script for development (chapter-2/example-3/package.json)

```
{
  "name": "example-3",
  "version": "1.0.0",
  "description": "",
  "main": "index.js",                          Normal start script starts the
  "scripts": {                                 service in our production or
    "start": "node index.js",        <─        testing environment.
    "start:dev": "nodemon index.js"  <──┐
  },                                        Our new start:dev script starts
  "keywords": [],                           the service in our development
  "author": "",                             environment.
  "license": "ISC",
  "dependencies": {
    "express": "^4.17.1"
  },
  "devDependencies": {          <──┐
      "nodemon": "^2.0.4"           Development dependencies go here;
                                    these are dependencies that aren't
  }                         <──┘    installed in production.
}
```

The new dependency on the nodemon
package that we just added

In the previous section you learned about the convention of using `npm start`. We configured our project so that we could run our code in production mode like this:

```
npm start
```

Now that we have defined the `start:dev` command, we can run our microservice in development mode like this:

```
npm run start:dev
```

Notice the use of `npm run` to run our new script. We can use `npm run` to run any npm script that we add to our package.json file. We can omit the `run` part for `npm start` and `npm test` (which we will learn about in chapter 8) because npm has special support for these particular conventions.

Now this tells you that this start:dev script *isn't* a Node.js convention the way `start` and `test` are. That's why we have to specifically use the `npm run` command to invoke it. Using start:dev to run in development is simply my own personal convention. We'll use it throughout this book though, and I'm sure you'll also find it useful in your own development process.

With these commands in place, we can run our microservice in either production mode or development mode. It's important to make this distinction so that we can cater separately to the differing needs of each mode.

In development mode, we'd like to optimize for fast iterations and productivity. Alternately, in production mode, we'd like to optimize for performance and security. These needs are at odds with each other; hence, these must be treated separately. You'll see this become important again in chapters 6 and 7 as we approach production deployment of our application.

> **NOTE** All of the microservices that are forthcoming in this book follow the conventions that we have laid down in the last two sections.

2.6.9   *Running the finished code from this chapter*

If you get to this point and you haven't yet tried out the code in this chapter, now is the time to do so. Here's a quick summary to show you how easy it is to get the examples in this chapter running. Get a local copy of the chapter-2 code, either by downloading it or cloning the chapter-2 repository from GitHub.

- To look at the streaming video, you'll want to try out example-2.
- To see the example of configuring a microservice using environment variables, try example-3.

As an example, let's say you want to try out example-3. Open a terminal and change to the appropriate subdirectory:

```
cd chapter-2/example-3
```

Now install dependencies:

```
npm install
```

If you wanted to simulate a production deployment, you'd do this instead:

```
npm install --only=production
```

Now to run it like you would in production, type

```
npm start
```

Or to run it with live reload for fast development, you'd type this:

```
npm run start:dev
```

These are the main commands you need to remember to run any Node.js example in this book. Put a bookmark on this page and jump back to it whenever you need to remember how to do this.

2.7 Node.js review

Before we move on, we have time for a quick review of all the Node.js commands we have learned in this chapter. Table 2.3 lists these commands.

Table 2.3   Review of Node.js commands

Command	Description
`node --version`	Checks that Node.js is installed; prints the version number.
`npm init -y`	Creates a default Node.js project with a stub for our package.json, the file that tracks metadata and dependencies for our Node.js project.
`npm install --save` ➥ `<package-name>`	Installs an npm package. There are many other packages available on npm, and you can install any by inserting a specific package name.
`npm install`	Installs all dependencies for a Node.js project. This also installs all the packages that have been previously recorded in package.json.
`node <script-file>`	Runs a Node.js script file. We invoke the `node` command and give it the name of our script file as an argument. You can call your script main.js or server.js if you want, but it's probably best to stick to the convention and just call it index.js.
`npm start`	The conventional npm script for starting a Node.js application regardless of what name the main script file has or what command-line parameters it expects.
	Typically this translates into node index.js in the package.json file, but it depends on the author of the project and how they have set it up. The nice thing is that no matter how a particular project is structured, you only have to remember npm start.
`npm run start:dev`	My personal convention for starting a Node.js project in development. I add this to the scripts in package.json. Typically, it runs something like nodemon to enable live reload of your code as you work on it.

2.8   *Continue your learning*

This chapter has been a fast-paced introduction to building a barebones HTTP server with Node.js. Unfortunately, we have barely scratched the surface. But this book isn't about Node.js; that is simply the vehicle we are using to travel to the land of microservices. I do however have some references for you to learn more should you wish to drill deeper and gain more expertise in Node.js and Git:

- *Getting MEAN with Mongo, Express, Angular, and Node*, 2nd ed. by Simon Holmes and Clive Harber (Manning, 2019)
- *Node.js in Practice* by Alex R. Young and Marc Harter (Manning, 2014)
- *Node.js in Action*, 2nd ed., by Alex R. Young, Bradley Meck, and Mike Cantelon (Manning, 2017)
- *Learn Git in a Month of Lunches* by Rick Umali (Manning, 2015)

Also, see the extensive Node.js documentation that you can find online at https://nodejs.org/en/docs/.

Next, we'll move onto packaging and publishing our microservice so that it's ready for deployment to the cloud. For this, we'll use Docker, a tool that has become ubiquitous and indispensable in our industry. Docker has made microservices more accessible and has done nothing less than revolutionized the way we build and deploy our software.

Summary

- We discussed a philosophy of development: iterate, keep it working, start simple.
- We established our development environment for working on a single microservice.
- You learned how to create a new Node.js project.
- We created a simple HTTP server.
- We added video streaming to our server.
- We setup our project for use in production.
- We used live reload of our code for fast iterations in development.

Publishing your first microservice

3

This chapter covers

- Learning the difference between Docker images and containers
- Using Docker in your development environment
- Packaging your microservice as a Docker image
- Creating a private Docker registry
- Publishing your microservice to your Docker registry
- Instantiating your microservice in a Docker container

By the end of this book, we'll have deployed multiple microservices to our production environment: a Kubernetes cluster. But before we can deploy an entire microservices application, we must first be able to package and publish a single microservice! In this chapter, we'll take the video-streaming microservice we created in chapter 2 and publish it so that it's ready for deployment to our cluster.

In order to deploy a microservice to a cluster running in the cloud, we have to publish it somewhere accessible. To achieve this, we must first package our code, assets, and dependencies into a single bundle. We'll then need a location in the cloud to host this package. For that, we'll create a container registry. If you haven't heard of containers yet, this will be explained soon.

In this book, we want to emulate the building of a proprietary application for a private company. Security and privacy are important, and that's why we'll create a private container registry as opposed to a public one. We'll create this container registry manually on Azure, but later in chapter 6, we'll learn how we can build our registry with code.

At the end of this chapter, we'll test that we can instantiate our published microservice directly from the remote container registry. This allows us to test our published microservice on our development workstation (or personal computer).

3.1   New tools

This chapter introduces an important new tool: Docker. In this chapter, we lay some necessary groundwork. That's because from here on in, we'll use Docker extensively, and you will need some basic skills in place to understand how it works. That's going to help you troubleshoot when things go wrong.

Table 3.1   Tools introduced in chapter 3

Tool	Version	Purpose
Docker	19.03.12	We use Docker to package, publish, and test our microservices.

Docker works on Linux, MacOS, and Windows 10. If you are working on Windows 10 Home edition, you'll first need to install WSL2 (the Windows integrated Linux kernel), and see section 3.7.1 for a link to download it for Windows 10 Home.

3.2   Getting the code

This chapter has only one example project, which is based on example 2 from chapter 2. It's the video-streaming microservice we created in that chapter. To follow along in this chapter, you need to download the code or clone the repository.

- You can download a zip file of the code from here:
  https://github.com/bootstrapping-microservices/chapter-3
- You can clone the code using Git like this:
  ```
  git clone https://github.com/bootstrapping-microservices/chapter-3.git
  ```

For help on installing and using Git, see chapter 2. If you have problems with the code, log an issue against the repository in GitHub.

3.3 *What is a container?*

Simply put, a container (as the name implies) is something that contains something else. What does it contain? In this situation, we'll use it to contain (or host) a microservice.

DEFINITION A *container* is a way of virtualizing a server.

More formally, a container provides a way of virtualizing both the operating system and the hardware. This allows us to abstract (or *virtualize*) the resources required by our microservice. Containers provide a way to divide up the resources on one computer so that we can share these among many such services. Containers are one of the modern technologies that help make it cost-effective to run microservices.

Containers are often compared to virtual machines (VMs). Both VMs and containers allow us to isolate our microservices to prevent them from interfering with each other. Before containers were invented, we ran our services in virtual machines, and indeed, these days we can still choose to do that when appropriate. Figure 3.1 compares virtual machines to containers so you can visualize the differences.

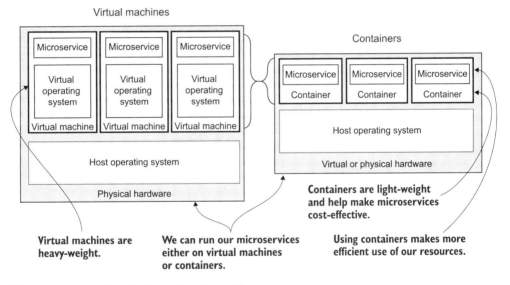

Figure 3.1 Comparing virtual machines to containers

As you can see in figure 3.1, virtual machines are more heavy-weight than containers. A virtual machine contains a complete copy of its operating system that's running on fully virtualized hardware. A container, on the other hand, virtualizes the operating system as well as the hardware. A container is therefore smaller and does less work, which makes for more efficient use of our computing resources.

Ultimately, we'll have many containers running on our Kubernetes cluster. But for now, we are aiming to instantiate just a single container to host the video-streaming microservice we created in the previous chapter.

3.4   What is an image?

An image is a snapshot of something. The word *image* is used in many different scenarios. We could be talking about an image that's a photograph, or we could be talking about an image that's a snapshot of the hard drive for a virtual machine. In this book, we are talking about Docker images.

> **DEFINITION**   An *image* is a bootable snapshot of a server (in our case, a microservice) including all the code, dependencies, and assets that it needs to run.

In the example for this chapter, we create a snapshot of our video-streaming microservice. Images are *immutable*, which means an image that has been produced cannot be modified. That's an important thing to know. We might have applied tests or security checks to an image, and because we know the image can't be tampered with, we know that our tests and security checks will remain valid.

You can think of an image as being a dormant version of a microservice, a way of storing it prior to running it. It's in a state waiting to be booted as a container, ready for when we need to instantiate it into our application.

Figure 3.2 shows how a container is booted from an image. The image itself contains everything needed to instantiate a container: the code for the microservice, its dependencies, and any other assets and resources that our microservice needs to do its job.

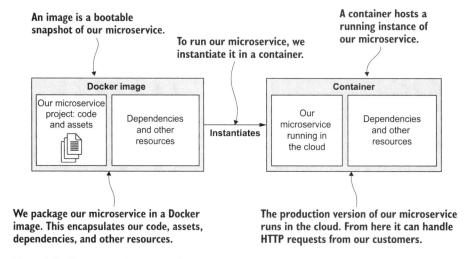

Figure 3.2   To run our microservice in the cloud, we'll instantiate its Docker image in a container.

Soon, we'll build an image for our microservice and run it as a container. Before that, let's learn more about Docker.

3.5   *Why Docker?*

Surely you have already heard about Docker? It's probably one of the reasons you bought this book. Almost everyone who is building cloud-based applications is using Docker or wanting to use it. Let's look at why this is.

Docker is quasi-ubiquitous in the software industry. There are alternatives to Docker, but Docker as a technology for packaging and deploying containers has captured mainstream attention. It's well-known and well-supported.

Docker is even making inroads in other areas. For example, I've heard of people using Docker to deploy applications to IoT devices. It does the job we need. But what exactly is the job it's doing for us?

Docker is the tool we'll use to package and publish our microservices. Although there is a lot you can learn about Docker, we'll learn the minimum we need to get this show on the road. At the end of this chapter, I'll provide references for you to dig deeper to understand Docker more broadly.

I like to think of Docker as the *universal package manager*: the one package manager to rule them all! Normally, you wouldn't think of Docker in this way, but if you think it through, it makes some kind of sense. The *package manager* part is fairly obvious; we use Docker to package and publish our work. I say that it is *universal* because it supports many different technology stacks. Docker is open source and you can find the code for the CLI tool here:

https://github.com/docker/cli

You can see other open-source projects from the makers of Docker here:

https://www.docker.com/community/open-source

> **Standardize your environment**
> Docker is also really good for standardizing your environments, ensuring that all your developers run the same development environment. This, in turn, is the same as the production environment. It maximizes the probability that code that works in development also works in production and that gives developers a better chance to find problems before the code gets to the customer.

3.6   *What are we doing with Docker?*

Let's break this question down. We will use Docker to

- Package our microservice into a Docker image
- Publish our image to our private container registry
- Run our microservice in a container

It's the last bullet point that's most important. We want to have our microservice running in our production environment, but we can only do that if we have first packaged and published it.

We aren't ready to deploy our microservice to production just yet, so instead, we'll focus on learning the Docker commands that we need to package, publish, and test our image on our development workstation.

Figure 3.3 gives you the general picture of what we need to do here. We'll take the Node.js project for our video-streaming microservice (on the left of figure 3.3), package it as a Docker image, and then publish it to our private container registry. From there, we can deploy the microservice to our Kubernetes cluster; although, that's a job we'll save for chapter 7.

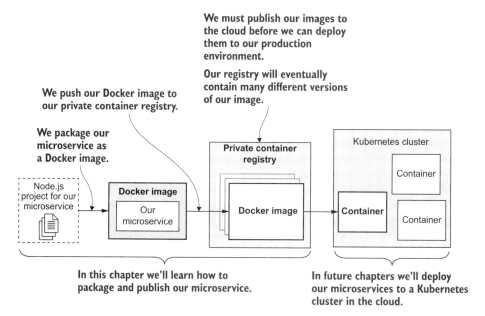

Figure 3.3   In this chapter, we will learn how to publish Docker images to our private container registry in the cloud.

3.7   *Extending our development environment with Docker*

Before we can use Docker, we must upgrade our development environment. To follow along with this chapter, you'll need to have Docker installed on your own computer. In this section, we'll install Docker and make sure it's ready to go.

Figure 3.4 shows what our development environment will look like with Docker installed. Even though you can see that we'll run our Node.js microservice under Docker, you won't always have to run your microservices this way. When you are testing an individual microservice, however, you'll just run it directly on your host operating system like we did in chapter 2.

Because we need to be able to package our microservice using Docker, it's useful to be able to test it locally, both before and after we publish it. The ability to test will be useful later for any microservice that is misbehaving on Kubernetes. We'll talk more about this in chapter 10.

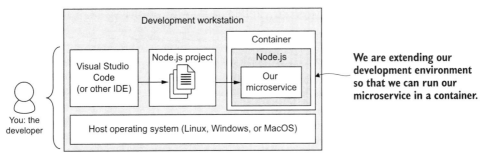

Figure 3.4　Extending our development to run our microservice in a container

3.7.1　*Installing Docker*

To install Docker, go to the Docker website at https://docs.docker.com. Once there, find the download/install link and follow the instructions to install Docker for your plat-form. Table 3.2 provides the details for installing Docker for your particular platform.

　　If you are using Windows 10, be aware that there are separate instructions for installing Docker on Home vs. the Pro/Enterprise versions. On Windows 10 Home edition, you need WSL2 (the Windows integrated Linux kernel) installed before you install Docker. Follow the instructions in table 3.2 to do that.

Table 3.2　Platforms supported by Docker

Platform	Description
Linux/MacOS/Windows 10 Pro/Enterprise	Go to the Docker website at https://docs.docker.com. Click the download/install link and follow the instructions to install Docker on your system.
Windows 10 Home	WSL2 must be installed before you can install and use Docker.
	To install WSL2 follow the instructions here:
	https://docs.microsoft.com/en-us/windows/wsl/install-win10
	After installing WSL2 you can now install Docker with the instructions here:
	https://docs.docker.com/docker-for-windows/install-windows-home/
	You can also run Docker on Windows 10 Home edition using a virtual machine as noted in the following sidebar.

3.7.2　*Checking your Docker installation*

Once you have Docker installed, you can use the terminal to check that it's OK by printing the version:

```
docker --version
```

If you have the same version installed as I do (as of this writing), the output will look like this:

```
Docker version 19.03.12, build 48a66213fe
```

But don't worry if you are using a later version of Docker. Most likely, it will be backward compatible.

Running Docker under a virtual machine (VM)

You might have noticed that the chapter 3 repository (https://github.com/bootstrapping -microservices/chapter-3) includes a Vagrantfile. This is a Vagrant script that boots a pre-configured Ubuntu Linux virtual machine (VM) that automatically has Docker installed. To use it, you must first install Vagrant and VirtualBox.

This is a convenient way for you to boot an instant and throwaway development environment. Well, it's not quite instant, but invoking `vagrant up` to build a VM for development is much quicker than creating it manually. I say that it's throwaway because invoking `vagrant destroy` removes the VM and leaves your development workstation in a clean state. This makes Vagrant a good way to try out new software (like Docker) without cluttering up your computer.

Each code repository for other chapters in the book also include a Vagrantfile. You can conveniently create a VM to try out the examples in this book if that's the way you'd like to follow along. To learn more about Vagrant, see appendix A or visit the Vagrant website:

https://www.vagrantup.com/

3.8   *Packaging our microservice*

Now that we have Docker installed, we can start to think about using it to package our microservice for deployment. Ultimately, we want to deploy our microservice to production. But first, we need everything bundled and ready to ship. We'll package our microservice with the following steps:

1 Create a Dockerfile for our microservice
2 Package our microservice as a Docker image
3 Test the published image by booting it as a container

3.8.1   *Creating a Dockerfile*

For every Docker image we want to create, we must create a Dockerfile. The *Dockerfile* is a specification for an image created by Docker. I like to think of the Dockerfile as a script file with instructions on how to construct the image. You can see this illustrated in figure 3.5.

The lines in the Dockerfile define our microservice, its dependencies, and any supporting assets. Different lines in the Dockerfile cause different files to be copied

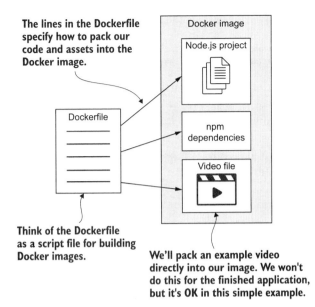

The lines in the Dockerfile specify how to pack our code and assets into the Docker image.

Docker image

Node.js project

Dockerfile

npm dependencies

Video file

Think of the Dockerfile as a script file for building Docker images.

We'll pack an example video directly into our image. We won't do this for the finished application, but it's OK in this simple example.

Figure 3.5 The Dockerfile is a script that specifies how to build our Docker image.

across to the image. To the Dockerfile, we'll add instructions for copying across our Node.js project and for installing our npm dependencies.

Also notice in figure 3.5 that we are copying an example video into our image. Baking the video into the image isn't something we'll want to do in the final production version, but it's useful in this example—we don't yet have any other way of storing this video.

Having only a single video would make for a pretty boring video-streaming application, but fixing that will have to wait until chapter 4. For now, this actually serves as a good example to show that it's not just code we can include in our image. Including other types of assets presents no problem for Docker!

Listing 3.1 shows the Dockerfile for our video-streaming microservice. There's not much to it, and it's a good example of a Dockerfile for a Node.js application. Have a read and try to visualize what each line adds to the resulting image.

Listing 3.1 A Dockerfile for our video-streaming microservice (chapter-3/example-1/Dockerfile)

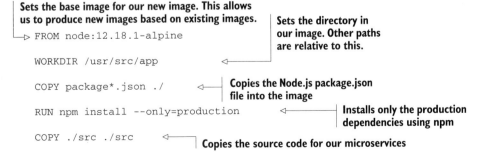

Sets the base image for our new image. This allows us to produce new images based on existing images.

```
FROM node:12.18.1-alpine

WORKDIR /usr/src/app

COPY package*.json ./

RUN npm install --only=production

COPY ./src ./src
```

Sets the directory in our image. Other paths are relative to this.

Copies the Node.js package.json file into the image

Installs only the production dependencies using npm

Copies the source code for our microservices

```
COPY ./videos ./videos      ⊲─── Copies our sample video

CMD npm start     ⊲──┐
                     │  Starts the microservice using the "npm start"
                     └  convention (see the previous chapter)
```

In listing 3.1, the first line includes the FROM instruction. This specifies the *base image* from which we derive our new image. By saying our base image is node:12.18.1-alpine, we are stating that our derived image should include Node.js version 12.18.1. (If you are wondering what alpine means, see the following sidebar.)

If you are working with languages or frameworks other than JavaScript and Node.js, then you'll choose a different base image. Choose one that is appropriate to your own tech stack.

Being able to choose the base image is extremely useful. We might choose to use any of the many public images available on Docker Hub (https://hub.docker.com), or we can even create our own custom base image. This means we can reuse existing images, and by the end of this book, we'll also have seen several examples of reusing third-party images.

Also in listing 3.1 are various lines with the COPY instruction. These lines copy files into our image. You can see that package.json, our code, and the example video are all copied into the image.

The RUN instruction is worth noting too. You can run software within the image during the build process to make changes to the image, install dependencies, and perform other setup tasks. In this example, we use RUN to install our npm dependencies and bake those into the image.

The last and most important line in listing 3.1 is the CMD instruction. This sets the command that is invoked when our container is instantiated. This is how we tell it to run our Node.js application using the npm start script we added to our package.json file in chapter 2. For a refresher on that, reread section 2.6.7.

Alpine vs. non-alpine: Part 1

When you see "alpine" in the name of an image (e.g., *node:12.18.1-alpine*), it indicates that the image is based on Alpine Linux. Alpine is a lightweight Linux distribution that includes only the bare minimum, so it is much smaller than a regular distribution. Alpine images are great for production because of the size, which makes better use of your infrastructure and cloud resources.

3.8.2 *Packaging and checking our Docker image*

Now that we have created our Dockerfile, we can package our microservice as a *ready-to-run* image. We'll build the image using the docker build command. It takes as input our Dockerfile, which contains the instructions to build the image. Figure 3.6 shows this process in action.

> **NOTE** Before we can deploy our microservice to production, we must be able to package it in a Docker image.

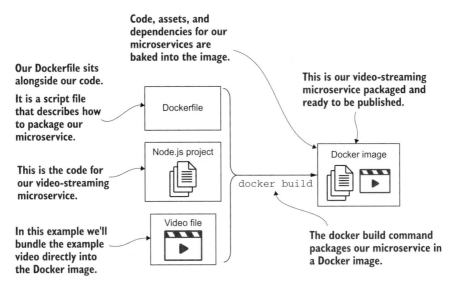

Figure 3.6   The docker build command produces a Docker image as specified by our Dockerfile.

Now comes the fun part. It's time to create an image from our microservice. To follow along, you'll need a Dockerfile like the one shown in listing 3.1 and a Node.js project. You can create your own or use example-1 from the chapter-3 code repository on GitHub (see section 3.1).

When you are ready, open a terminal and change directory to chapter-3/example-1 (or whichever directory where you have your code and Dockerfile). Now invoke docker build as follows:

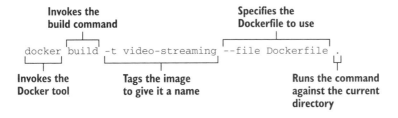

When you run this code, you'll see the various pieces of the base image being downloaded. This download only happens the first time; subsequently, you'll already have the base image cached on your workstation. It won't be downloaded again (at least not until you delete all your local images as we'll do later in section 3.9.3). Once it completes, you should see something like this at the end of the output:

```
Successfully built 9c475d6b1dc8
Successfully tagged video-streaming:latest
```

This tells you that the image was successfully built. It also gives you the unique ID for your image and displays the tag that you set for it.

> **NOTE** When you invoke this command for yourself, you will see a different output because the ID allocated to your image will be different from the ID that was allocated to my image.

Because it's a unique ID, it's going to be different for *every* new image that you create. You can take note of this ID if you want and use it to reference the image in future Docker commands. You don't really need to do that, however, because we tagged it with a meaningful name (video-streaming). We can use that name instead of the ID.

Note also in the output that the version was automatically set to latest because we didn't specify anything for it. In chapter 7, we'll set this version automatically as part of our continuous delivery process. This will distinguish each new version of the image we produce as we iteratively update our code and build new images. Some other points to note are as follows:

- *The -t argument allows us to tag or name our image.* You'll want to do this; otherwise, you'll have to reference your image by its unique ID. It's a big ugly string of numbers (as you saw in the previous output), so it's not the best option.
- *The --file argument specifies the name of the Dockerfile to use.* Technically, this is unnecessary because it defaults to the file named Dockerfile anyway. I'm including this explicitly so that you know about it, and it's something we'll make use of later in chapter 5. In that chapter, we will separate our Dockerfiles to have different versions in development and production.
- *Don't forget the period at the end!* It's easy to miss. It tells the build command to operate against the current directory. This means that any instructions in the Dockerfile are relative to the current working directory. Changing this directory makes it possible to store our Dockerfile in a different directory from our project's assets. This can be useful at times, but it's not a feature we need right now.

Here's the general format for the docker build command when building your own image:

```
docker build -t <your-name-for-the-image> --file <path-to-your-Dockerfile>
➥ <path-to-project>
```

You can plugin in the particular name of your microservice as the image name, the path to its Dockerfile, and the path to its project folder. After building our image, we should now check it to make sure it's OK. We can list our local images using this command:

```
docker image list
```

This lists the images on our local workstation. If our `docker build` command from the previous section completed successfully, we now see at least two images listed:

```
REPOSITORY        TAG             IMAGE ID       CREATED          SIZE
video-streaming   latest          9c475d6b1dc8   33 seconds ago   74.3MB
node              12.18.1-alpine  072459fe4d8a   6 months ago     70.7MB
```

You might see other images in this list if you have already been using Docker to create other images locally or if you have been exploring the many publicly available images on Docker Hub (see the sidebar entitled "Exploring other containers").

Note the columns in the preceding output. Under the `REPOSITORY` column, you can see `video-streaming` and `node`, where `video-streaming` is the image for our microservice that we just created, and `node` is the base image that we referenced in our Dockerfile in listing 3.1.

`TAG` is the next column, and it usually shows the image's version number. Because we didn't specifically choose a version for our video-streaming image, it was automatically allocated the version `latest`.

The next column is `IMAGE ID` and shows the unique ID for each image. Note here that the ID for our video-streaming image is the same as in the output from the `build` command. Again, expect the unique ID for your image to be different to what you see here. Other columns in this output include `CREATED`, which tells you when the image was created, and `SIZE`, which shows you the size of the image.

> ### Alpine vs. non-alpine: Part 2
> In this section, you can see in the output from `docker image list` that the size of our video-streaming image is 74.3 MB. This size is due to selecting an Alpine image as our base image.
>
> Want to know the size if instead we use a non-alpine image? Well, it weighs in at a whopping 902 MB for the non-alpine image. That's over 10 times the size! You can clearly see why we want to use Alpine images in production.

3.8.3 Booting our microservice in a container

Before we publish our newly created Docker image, we should do a test run on our development workstation to make sure everything is in working order. Once we have packaged our microservice as a Docker image, we can use the `docker run` command to instantiate it as a container as shown in figure 3.7. This creates an instance of our video-streaming microservice on our development workstation that we can then test using a web browser.

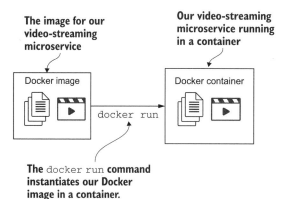

Figure 3.7 The `docker run` command produces an instance of our microservice running in a container.

When you are ready, open a terminal and invoke the following command to instantiate your microservice from the image:

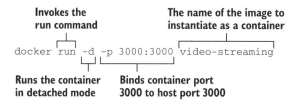

As output, you should see the unique ID for the container printed. Here is the output from when I invoked the command:

```
460a199466896e02dd1ed601f9f6b132dd9ad9b42bbd3df351460e5eeacbe6ce
```

Seeing such output means your microservice started successfully. When you run this command, you will see different output. That's because your container is going to have a different unique ID to mine. You'll still see a big long string of numbers like that shown, but again, it's going to be different. You'll need this ID to invoke future Docker commands that relate to the container.

Don't worry about trying to remember it (unless you have a photographic memory) because we can easily recall this and other details of the container on demand, as you'll soon see. More points to note here are listed next.

- *The -d argument causes our container to run in detached mode.* This means it runs in the background and we can't directly see its logs. If we omitted this, our container would run in the foreground, and we'd see its output directly; although, it would also be tying up our terminal.
- *The -p argument binds the port between the host operating system and our container.* This is like port forwarding, network traffic sent to port 3000 on our development workstation is *forwarded* to port 3000 inside our container. We set it up that way because we originally hard-coded our microservice to listen on port 3000.

The number 3000 itself isn't important here. We could have used almost any number for this, but 3000 is often used by convention when developing/testing individual HTTP servers.

- *The last argument,* `video-streaming`, *is the name we gave our image.* This is how we specify which image (we could have many) will be instantiated. This relates to the name we gave the image using `docker build` and the -t argument back in section 3.8.2.

A common error at this point is when the port we are using (e.g., port 3000) is already allocated to another application. If this happens, you'll need to either shut down the other application, or if you can't do that, you'll have to choose a port other than 3000. You can do this by using a PORT environment variable as we did in section 2.6.6 in chapter 2. Here is the general format for the `docker run` command:

```
docker run -d p <host-port>:<container-port> <image-name>
```

You can use this to boot other microservices by plugging in the particular name for each image that you create.

CHECKING THE CONTAINER

We have a running container now, but let's check to make sure it's in working order. To show the containers you have, invoke this command:

```
docker container list
```

Here's a cutdown version of the output:

```
CONTAINER ID  IMAGE            STATUS         PORTS
460a19946689  video-streaming  Up 20 seconds  0.0.0.0:3000->3000/tcp
```

Your output will look different from that shown because to make it fit, I removed the columns COMMAND, CREATED, and NAMES. But you can run the command yourself to see those.

Note the CONTAINER ID column. This shows you the unique ID of the container. It is a reduced version of the longer ID that was output from the `docker run` command in the previous section. Both are the unique IDs of your container, and as you'll see in a moment, we'll use the ID to identify the container when we run Docker commands against it.

CHECKING YOUR MICROSERVICE

We have successfully instantiated a container from our image, and we checked that it is running. But how do we know if our microservice inside the container is functional? It could be throwing up all sorts of errors and, as yet, we wouldn't know about it. Let's check the output of the microservice and see what it tells us:

```
docker logs 460a19946689
```

Whoa, hold up! You can't just invoke that command and use the unique ID for my container. Remember, the ID will be different for the container created on your workstation. You'll get an error if you invoke it exactly like this. So note the ID of *your* container as demonstrated in the previous section and invoke the command like this, plugging in your own container ID:

```
docker logs <container-id>
```

Now you should see the output from your microservice. If you run the code from example-1 in the chapter-3 code repository, you should see something like this:

```
Microservice listening on port 3000, point your browser at
➥ http://localhost:3000/video
```

Success! We built an image. We instantiated it as a container, and we confirmed that our microservice is operational. Now let's test this in the web browser. Open your browser and point it at http://localhost:3000/video. You should see the streaming video, and the result should look the same as what we tested in chapter 2.

Why does this work? It works because we used the -p argument with the docker run command to forward port 3000 on our workstation (assuming that this port wasn't already allocated) to port 3000 in the container. Our microservice was listening on port 3000 and it responded!

There's obviously more we could do to test our code. But we'll save that for later. In chapter 8, we'll look at how we can apply automated code-driven testing to our microservices. Then in chapter 10, we'll see how to monitor our microservices, how to debug them when problems are found, and what techniques we can use for building fault-tolerant systems. But now, we are ready to publish our image!

Exploring other containers

Did you know that you can easily run any public image using the docker run command? Two images we'll use later in the book are *mongodb* and *rabbitmq*. Try running these for yourself to get an *instant database* available on localhost:27017. For example

```
docker run -p 27017:27107 mongo:latest
```

There are many public images available online, and you don't need an account to access these. Search Docker Hub to find more at https://hub.docker.com.

3.9   *Publishing our microservice*

We are close now to having our first microservice ready for production deployment. We have packaged it in a Docker image, but currently, that image resides locally on our development workstation. That's great for our own testing and experimentation, but we still need to have our image published somewhere, so that we can later deploy

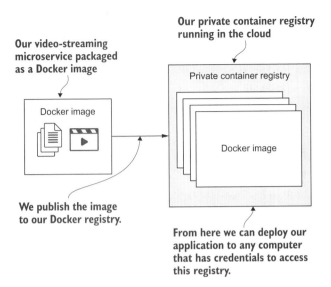

Our private container registry running in the cloud

Our video-streaming microservice packaged as a Docker image

Private container registry

Docker image

Docker image

We publish the image to our Docker registry.

From here we can deploy our application to any computer that has credentials to access this registry.

Figure 3.8 Publishing our Docker image to a private container registry in the cloud

it to our Kubernetes cluster. Figure 3.8 illustrates how we will now publish our image to a private container registry hosted in the cloud.

We'll publish our microservice with the following steps:

1 We create our own private container registry on Microsoft Azure. We only need to do this the first time we publish an image. Later, when we publish new versions of the image and images for other microservices, we'll simply reuse this same registry.

2 Before publishing, we must authenticate with the registry using the `docker login` command.

3 We use the `docker push` command to upload our image to the registry. (This is the step that actually publishes our microservice.)

4 We use `docker run` again to check that we can boot our microservice from the published image.

3.9.1 *Creating a private container registry*

Creating a private container registry turns out to be pretty simple. We'll create our registry on Microsoft Azure, but all the major cloud vendors have support for this. Why publish to a private registry? In this book, we are learning how to build proprietary applications for a private company, so it makes sense to publish our images privately instead of using a public registry such as Docker Hub.

I'm using Azure for this book because I have found it to be the simplest cloud platform to use, and it's a great starting point for learning how to build cloud-native applications. Azure provides a good deal for new signups, with free credit for your first month. That gives you some time where you can try out the cloud infrastructure demonstrated in this book for free.

Make sure you destroy all your resources later so you don't end up unnecessarily paying for them. Incidentally, this is another reason to use Azure: Microsoft has made it easy to find and destroy cloud resources so that we don't forget about something and end up paying for unused infrastructure. For now, we'll create our container registry manually. But in chapter 6, we'll return to this and learn how to create it with code.

Open your browser and load the Azure web site: https://azure.microsoft.com. Go through the steps to sign up. After signing up you should be able to sign in to the Azure portal at https://portal.azure.com.

Once in the Azure portal, you should see the Create a Resource option in the menu on the left. Click this and then in the Search input box, enter `container registry` and press Enter. You'll see matching options as shown in figure 3.9. Click the option Container Registry by Microsoft.

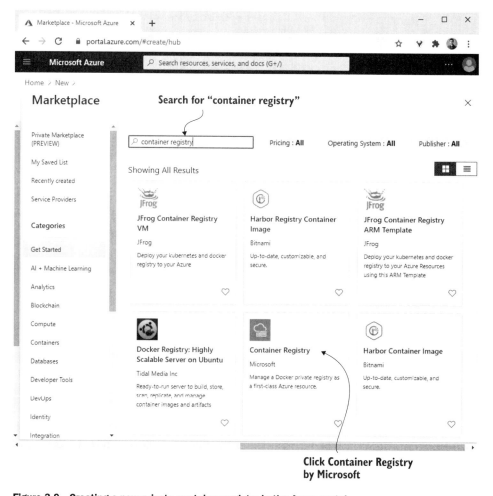

Figure 3.9   Creating a new private container registry in the Azure portal

You should now see a page that explains more about the Microsoft Container Registry. Have a read if you like before clicking the Create button.

Next, we fill in some details about the registry we are creating. Figure 3.10 shows that we first need to provide a name. The name is important because that creates a URL that we'll use later to communicate with the registry. The name I chose for my registry is bmdk1, and this results in having a URL for the container registry like this: *bmdk1.azurecr.io.*

Figure 3.10 Filling out the details for our new private container registry

Because the name chosen for the registry generates the URL, it must be globally unique. That means you can't choose a name that someone else has already taken—choose your own unique name. You should take note of the URL because you'll need that soon when you invoke Docker commands against your registry.

Before clicking Create, we need to select or create a *resource group*. As its name implies, resource groups in Azure allow cloud resources to be collected into groups for easier management. Figure 3.11 shows that I'm creating a new resource group to contain the new registry that I call bmdk1. To create a new resource group, click Create New, type a name, and click OK.

This name doesn't matter. We can use the same name as before or we can use any other name we like. It doesn't need the same name as the container registry, and it doesn't have to be globally unique. Just make sure you give it a name that's meaningful to you so that when you see it again later, you are reminded of its purpose.

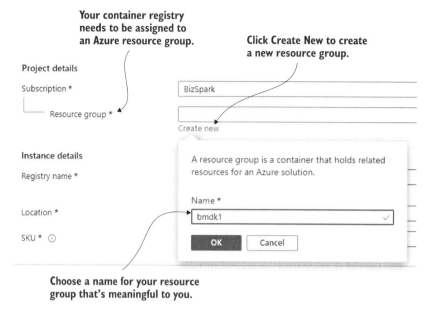

Your container registry needs to be assigned to an Azure resource group.

Click Create New to create a new resource group.

Project details

Subscription *   BizSpark

    Resource group *

                                        Create new

Instance details   A resource group is a container that holds related
                                        resources for an Azure solution.
Registry name *

                                        Name *
Location *   bmdk1

SKU * ⓘ   OK   Cancel

Choose a name for your resource group that's meaningful to you.

There's no need to use the same name that I use!

Figure 3.11   Creating a new resource group to contain the private container registry

Now click the Review + Create button. On the next page, click Create to create your registry.

To follow up on the creation of our registry, we'll need to watch the notifications in the Azure Portal. Click the Notification icon to open the Notifications sidebar and watch the progress of our deployment. This might take some time, but when completed, we'll see a Deployment Succeeded notification in the sidebar as figure 3.12 shows.

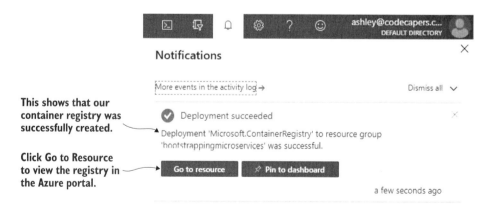

                                        ashley@codecapers.c...
                                        DEFAULT DIRECTORY

Notifications   ✕

More events in the activity log →   Dismiss all ∨

This shows that our container registry was successfully created.

    ✓ Deployment succeeded   ✕

    Deployment 'Microsoft.ContainerRegistry' to resource group
    'bootstrappingmicroservices' was successful.

Click Go to Resource to view the registry in the Azure portal.

    Go to resource   ⚲ Pin to dashboard

                                        a few seconds ago

Figure 3.12   The deployment of our new container registry was successful!

From the Deployment Succeeded notification, we can click Go to Resource to view details of the new registry. Otherwise, if we need to find our registry again later, click All Resources on the left-hand menu. Figure 3.13 shows that this lists all our resources (if you have created any others), along with our new container registry.

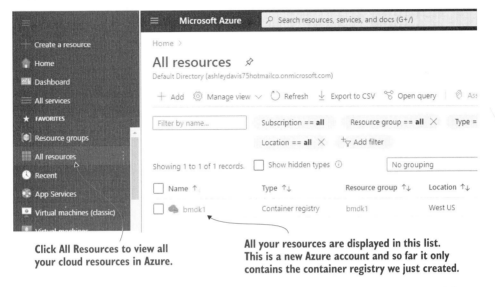

Click All Resources to view all your cloud resources in Azure.

All your resources are displayed in this list. This is a new Azure account and so far it only contains the container registry we just created.

Figure 3.13   You can find your container registry in the All Resources list. At this stage we only have a single resource, the registry itself.

Next, click your container registry in the list to drill down to see its details, then click Access Keys in the menu on the left. You can see what this looks like in figure 3.14. Note here that we can see the registry's URL.

> **NOTE**   It's important that we enable the Admin User option. We need this enabled to authenticate with our registry when pushing and pulling our images.

Now take note of your registry's username and password (you only need the first password). Don't bother noting the ones you see in figure 3.14. These are the details for my registry, and it won't exist by the time you read this. Be sure to use the details for your own registry!

That's all there is to it! If you followed these instructions, you now have your own private container registry. You can push your images to the registry, and from there, you can deploy these to production. So let's get our first image published!

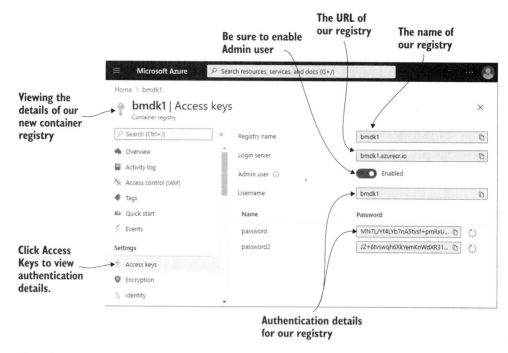

Figure 3.14   Viewing the authentication details of our new private container registry

Public vs. private

For this book, we are only interested in publishing private Docker images. But you might also be interested to know that you can also publish public images.

For example, let's say you create an open-source microservice. Create a Docker image for it and then publish it publicly to Docker Hub. That can help your users get it running quickly!

To publish to Docker Hub, you'll have to sign up at https://hub.docker.com. Then you can use the `docker push` command to push your image to Docker Hub.

Docker Hub also allows you to publish private images. Although to publish more than one of those, you'll need to upgrade to a paid account.

3.9.2   *Pushing our microservice to the registry*

Now that we have a private container registry, we have a place to publish our first microservice. We'll publish our image by invoking the `docker push` command as shown in figure 3.15.

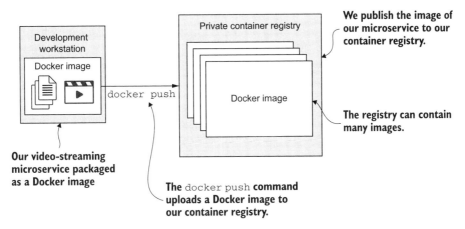

Figure 3.15 The `docker push` command uploads our Docker image to our private container registry.

Authenticating with the Registry

Before we can push to our registry, we must first login. We have authentication enabled because we don't want just anyone to be able to publish images to our registry.

In the last section, you created your private container registry, and you took note of its details. To communicate with the registry, you must know its URL. To push and pull images, you need the username and password. If you can't remember those, refer back to section 3.9.1 to find your registry in the Azure portal and recall these details. To authenticate, we'll invoke the `docker login` command:

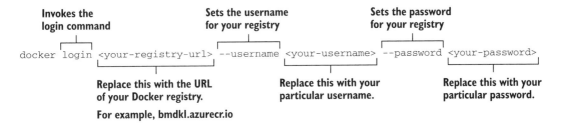

I could have shown you the full command I used complete with the URL, username, and password of my own registry. But that won't fit on the page! Also, it wouldn't help you because, at this point, you have to use the details of your own registry. When you invoke `docker login`, be sure to use your own URL, username, and password. After authenticating with `docker login`, you can now invoke other Docker commands against your registry.

TAGGING OUR IMAGE

Before we can publish our image to the registry, we must tell Docker where the image is being pushed. We do this by tagging the image with the URL of the registry with the command `docker tag` as follows:

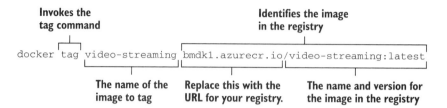

Of course, you can't just type that command verbatim. You have to use the URL for your own registry! The `docker tag` command has the following general format:

```
docker tag <existing-image> <registry-url>/<image-name>:<version>
```

We set the name of an existing image to be tagged and then the new tag to apply to it. We are tagging in this case, only because we want to push to our registry. For this reason, we are including the registry's URL in the tag we are applying.

We can check that our new tag was applied by invoking `docker image list`. Try doing that after applying the new tag. You should see a new entry in the table for the new tag. Note that Docker hasn't created a new image; it has simply applied a new tag to the existing image. We can check that this is the case by inspecting the image's unique ID, and we see that it is the same for both of the tagged versions.

PUSHING OUR IMAGE TO THE REGISTRY

Finally, we are ready to publish our image to the registry. To do that, we'll invoke the `docker push` command:

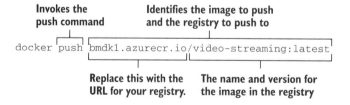

Again, make sure that you use the URL of your own registry here; otherwise, this command won't work for you. Here is the general format for `docker push`:

```
docker push <registry-url>/<image-name>:<version>
```

The part of the command after the `docker push` identifies the image to push. And it's also that part that identifies the registry to push to.

If you are thinking this is a bit awkward, then I'd agree with you. It seems to me, there should be a one-step process for pushing an existing image to a registry without having to go through the malarky of tagging it first. But there isn't, and this is the way it's done. After starting the image uploading, sit tight and wait for it to complete.

CHECKING THAT OUR IMAGE MADE IT TO THE REGISTRY

After we've pushed our image to the registry, we now want to check that it made it there OK. How do we know that it was successful? The first clue was in the output. It should have said that the push was successful, and we can trust that's correct. But let's go back to the registry in the Azure portal anyway and see what it looks like now.

In the Azure portal, navigate to All Resources, find your registry, and click it. Click Repositories from the menu on the left. As you can see in figure 3.16, you should be able to see your video-streaming image in the list of repositories. If you look inside the repository (on the right of figure 3.16), you can see a list of versions here. There's only a single version at the moment (tagged as *latest*), but in the future, after you have pushed updates to this image, you can return here and see the other versions that are listed as well.

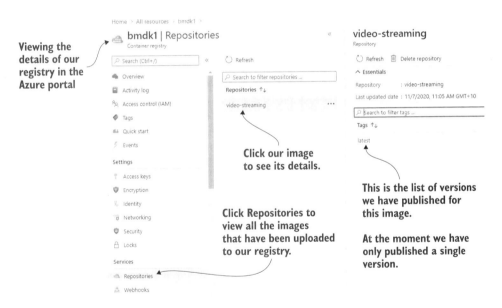

Figure 3.16   Viewing the image pushed to the container registry via the Azure portal

You can drill down even further through the latest tag to see the details about the image, including a manifest of its files. I encourage you to explore this interface more to see what you can find out about the image you just published.

3.9.3   *Booting our microservice from the registry*

Congratulations, you just published your first image to your very own private registry. We could now deploy this image to our production environment, although we can't do that because we haven't yet built our Kubernetes cluster. We'll build that in chapter 6. But before then, we still have more work to do and more things to learn.

Before moving on, we should confirm that our published image works. What I mean is that we should be able to instantiate the image as a container directly from the registry in the cloud. Just because we don't have a production environment yet doesn't mean we can't simulate a deployment on our development workstation. This isn't difficult, and it actually isn't anything different to what we already learned in this chapter.

Running a container from an image is basically the same regardless of whether the image is one we built locally or one that is available in a remote registry. We'll return to the docker run command to test our published image as shown in figure 3.17.

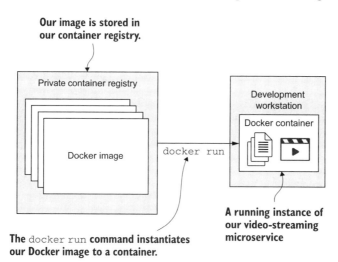

Our image is stored in our container registry.

Private container registry

Docker image

docker run

Development workstation

Docker container

A running instance of our video-streaming microservice

The docker run **command instantiates our Docker image to a container.**

It pulls the image from our registry if we don't already have it on our development workstation.

Figure 3.17   We can test our published image by running it on our development workstation; in this case, the docker run command must first *pull* the image from the registry.

CLEANING UP OUR MESS

Before we can test our image from the registry, there's one thing standing in our way. We must first remove the local versions of our image. We have to do this; otherwise, when we invoke docker run, it will boot the container from the local version of the image that we already have. This isn't what we want!

Instead, we want to test that we can *pull* the image from the remote registry. If we have a version of the image already cached locally it doesn't need to pull the remote version. This is also a good excuse for us to learn how to remove local containers and images.

Containers don't go away by themselves. When we create containers for long-lived servers, the containers usually hang around! We need to shut them down when we are done so they don't continue to consume our system resources.

NOTE Before we can remove images, we must first remove any containers instantiated from them. Attempting to remove images that have running containers will result in an error.

We'll invoke `docker ps` from our terminal. It's like `docker container list`, but it shows *both* running and stopped containers. If you see your video-streaming microservice in the list of containers, that's the one you want to remove. Take a note of its container ID. You'll remember from earlier that the ID for my own container was 460a19946689. Yours will be different, of course, so don't expect to see that particular ID in your list of containers. I removed my container with the following commands:

```
docker kill 460a19946689
docker rm 460a19946689
```

Just remember to use the container ID for your container. Here's the general format:

```
docker kill <your-container-id>
docker rm <your-container-id>
```

After removing the container, we can invoke `docker ps` again and check that the container is no longer in the list. After removing any container(s), we can now proceed with removing the image(s).

Invoke `docker image list`. We can see at least three images in the list. There are the Node.js base image and the two tagged versions of our video-streaming microservice. We only need to remove the image for our microservice. There's no need to remove the Node.js base image because that doesn't really matter for this test run.

Note that both tagged versions of our image have the same image ID, and these are actually just the same image referenced multiple times. We can remove both by invoking the `docker rmi` command with the `--force` argument as follows:

```
docker rmi 9c475d6b1dc8 --force
```

Of course, you need to run this with your particular image ID (which you can find from the output of `docker image list`). The general format is

```
docker rmi <your-image-id> --force
```

We use `--force` here because, otherwise, we'd be stopped with an error message like `Image is referenced in multiple repositories`. That's because we have multiple tagged versions of our image. We can use `--force` to make sure these are all removed.

After removing the image, invoke `docker image list` again to check that this worked properly and that our image is no longer in the list. It's OK to see the Node.js base image in the list because there's no need to remove that for this test run.

RUNNING A CONTAINER DIRECTLY FROM THE REGISTRY

With local containers and images cleaned up, we can now instantiate a new container directly from the image in the remote registry. We'll use `docker run` again like this:

```
docker run -d -p 3000:3000  bmdk1.azurecr.io/video-streaming:latest
```

As always, you must use the URL for your own registry. Here's the general format:

```
docker run -d -p <host-port>:<container-port> <registry-url>/<image-name>:
➡ <version>
```

This time when we invoke `docker run`, we use all the same arguments that we did back in section 3.8.3. There's `-d` for detached mode and `-p` to bind the port. The only thing we have changed here is the tag that we use to identify the image. In this case, the tag also identifies the remote registry from which to pull the image.

When you invoke `docker run` in your terminal give it some time to download. It first has to pull your image. You probably already have the Node.js base image cached locally (unless you decided to remove it in the previous section), and in that case, it shouldn't take long.

When this process has completed, you should have a running container. But this time, the image for it has been pulled *on-demand* from your private container registry in the cloud. When the `docker run` command has completed, you should see the container ID printed. We can also check that the container is running using the steps outlined earlier in section 3.8.3. Or we can test it directly by pointing our web browser at http://localhost:3000/video to see the video.

3.10 *Docker review*

Wow! What a trip. Docker seems simple until you try and explain it in a single chapter! What did we just do?

- We created a Dockerfile for our microservice that instructs Docker how to build an image for it.
- We invoked `docker build` to package our microservice as an image.
- After creating our private container registry on Azure, we then invoked `docker tag`, `docker login`, and `docker push` to publish our image.
- We finished with a test run of our published image using `docker run`.

The complete pipeline we pieced together is shown in figure 3.18. Peruse this diagram with care and revel in what you have learned so far.

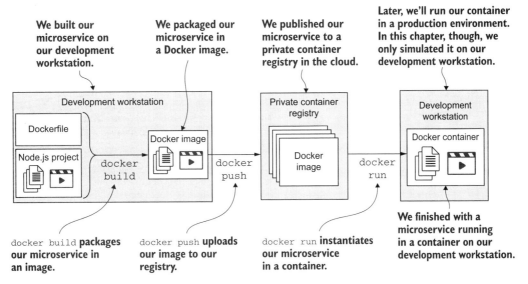

We built our microservice on our development workstation.

We packaged our microservice in a Docker image.

We published our microservice to a private container registry in the cloud.

Later, we'll run our container in a production environment. In this chapter, though, we only simulated it on our development workstation.

`docker build` **packages our microservice in an image.**

`docker push` **uploads our image to our registry.**

`docker run` **instantiates our microservice in a container.**

We finished with a microservice running in a container on our development workstation.

Figure 3.18 A complete Docker build pipeline showing where *build*, *push*, and *run* fit within the process.

Before moving on, let's do a quick review of the commands we added to our toolbelt in this chapter. Table 3.3 shows these.

Table 3.3 Review of Docker commands

Command	Description
`docker --version`	Checks that Docker is installed and prints the version number
`docker container list`	Lists running containers
`docker ps`	Lists all containers (running and stopped)
`docker image list`	Lists local images
`docker build -t <tag> --file` `⇨ <docker-file> .`	Builds an image from assets in the current directory according to the instructions in `docker-file`. The `-t` argument tags the image with a name you specify.

`docker run -d -p <host-`
`⇨ port>:<container-port>`
`⇨ <tag>`
	Instantiates a container from an image. If the image isn't available locally, it can be pulled from a remote registry (assuming the tag specifies the URL of the registry).
	
	The `-d` argument runs the container in detached mode, so it won't be bound to the terminal and you won't see the output. Omit this argument to see output directly, but this also locks your terminal.
	
	The `-p` argument allows you to bind a port on the host to a port in the container.

`docker logs <container-id>`	Retrieves output from a particular container. You need this to see the output when running a container in detached mode.

Table 3.3   Review of Docker commands *(continued)*

Command	Description
`docker login <url>` `--username <username>` `--password <password>`	Authenticates with your private Docker registry so that you can run other commands against it.
`docker tag <existing-tag> <new-tag>`	Adds a new tag to an existing image. To push an image to your private container registry, you must first tag it with the URL of your registry.
`docker push <tag>`	Pushes an appropriately tagged image to your private Docker registry. The image should be tagged with the URL of your registry.
`docker kill <container-id>`	Stops a particular container locally.
`docker rm <container-id>`	Removes a particular container locally (it must be stopped first).
`docker rmi <image-id>` `--force`	Removes a particular image locally (any containers must be removed first). The `--force` argument removes images even when they have been tagged multiple times.

3.11   Continue your learning

This chapter moved quickly. The aim is to give you the minimum you need to bootstrap your application, but there's so much more you could learn about Docker. Here are some references to other books that will help you go deeper into Docker:

- *Learn Docker in a Month of Lunches* by Elton Stoneman (Manning, 2020)
- *Docker in Practice* by Aidan Hobson Sayers and Ian Miell (Manning, 2016)
- *Docker in Action* by Jeff Nickoloff (Manning, 2016)

Docker also has good online documentation. It's worth having a browse at

- https://docs.docker.com/engine/reference/commandline/docker/

In this chapter, we explored how to use Docker to build and publish a single microservice. We'll build on these skills in future chapters as we roll out more microservices and create our application. In the next chapter, we will scale up to multiple microservices, and we'll learn how we can easily run multiple Docker-based microservices on our development workstation.

Summary

- We learned about Docker images and containers and how they relate to virtual machines.
- You installed Docker into your development environment and checked the version number

- We created a Dockerfile and used the `docker build` command to package our microservice in a Docker image.
- We instantiated our microservice in a Docker container using the `docker run` command.
- You created your own private Docker registry in the cloud.
- You published your microservice to your Docker registry.
- You cleaned up all your local containers and images before instantiating your microservice from the published image in the registry using the `docker run` command.

Data management
for microservices

When building any application, typically, we'll need to deal with data or files and sometimes both. Microservices are no different. We need a database to store dynamic data that's generated and updated by the application, and we need a place to store assets that are served by the application or uploaded to it.

In this chapter, we add both file storage and a database to our FlixTube example application. First, we'll add file storage so FlixTube has a location to store its videos. We want to have distinct areas of responsibility in our application for streaming and video storage. That implies that we'll need to add another microservice to our application, and in this chapter, we will indeed create our second microservice.

Then we'll add a database. At this point, we add a database so that we have a place to record the path to each video, but this is really just an excuse to get a database in place. Because once we have it, we can easily use it to store all the metadata for our videos and to provide for the on-going data storage needs of all our microservices.

By adding a database server and a second microservice to our application, we are taking an important step. In chapter 2, we built our first microservice; in chapter 3, we used Docker to instantiate our first microservice in a container. In this chapter, we scale up our application to host multiple containers, and for this, we need a new tool!

4.1 New tools

This chapter introduces two ways of storing data for microservices: file storage and database. Typically there are many different ways of doing this, and many different tools we could choose for the job. The tools you choose for each project will be the ones that work best for the particular project, your team, your company, and your customer.

As for any example in the book, I need to make a choice, so starting in this chapter, we'll use MongoDB for our database and Azure Storage for our file storage. We will also upgrade our development environment to run multiple containers at the same time. We could do this with Docker's `build` and `run` commands as we learned in the previous chapter. But then, we'd end up having to run the commands repeatedly for each container.

This isn't a big problem when only working with a few containers, but it doesn't scale to a larger application. Imagine trying to build and run just 10 microservices this way! So we need a better way to manage multiple microservices. For that, this chapter introduces Docker Compose. Table 4.1 lists the new tools we'll learn about in this chapter.

Table 4.1   Tools introduced in chapter 4

Tool	Version	Purpose
Docker Compose	1.26.2	Docker Compose allows us to configure, build, run, and manage multiple containers at the same time.
Azure Storage	SDK version 2.10.3	Azure Storage is a service to store files in the cloud. We can manage the assets through the Azure Portal, through the APIs, or from the command line. We'll upload a video through the Azure Portal and then use the Node.js Azure Storage SDK to read it back.
MongoDB	4.2.8	MongoDB is a popular NoSQL type of database. It's lightweight, easy to setup and use, and it's convenient for microservices.

4.2 Getting the code

To follow along with this chapter, you need to download the code or clone the repository.

- You can download a zip file of the code at
  https://github.com/bootstrapping-microservices/chapter-4
- You can clone the code using Git like this:
  `git clone https://github.com/bootstrapping-microservices/chapter-4.git`

For help on installing and using Git, see chapter 2. If you have problems with the code, log an issue against the repository in GitHub.

4.3 *Developing microservices with Docker Compose*

At the end of the previous chapter, we created a single microservice running in a container on our development workstation (or personal computer). We were able to test it using our web browser. Figure 4.1 illustrates our current situation.

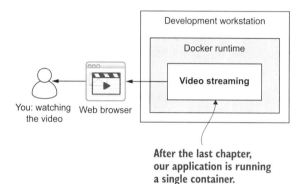

After the last chapter, our application is running a single container.

Figure 4.1 Our single microservice runs under Docker on our development workstation, which we created in chapter 2.

A microservices application, however, is *not* a microservices application if it only consists of a single microservice! The time has come to scale up our application and add more containers to it. To develop a microservices application, in this chapter, we'll use Docker Compose to make the move to multiple microservices.

We are scaling up to multiple containers in this chapter because we'd like to add a database (that's one container), and we'd also like to add a new microservice to handle our file storage (that's another container). So given that we started with one container (our video-streaming microservice), by the end of this chapter, we'll have three containers as depicted in figure 4.2.

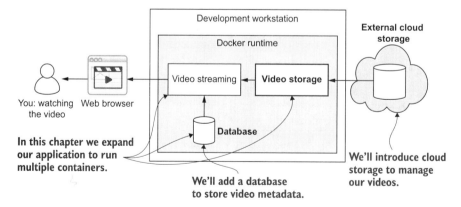

In this chapter we expand our application to run multiple containers.

We'll add a database to store video metadata.

We'll introduce cloud storage to manage our videos.

Figure 4.2 We expand our application to multiple containers.

To build, run, and manage our growing application, we could get by running the various Docker commands multiple times (repeated for each image or container). But this quickly becomes tedious during development because we'll need to stop and restart our application many times during our working day. And this only gets worse! As our application continues to grow, we'll add even more containers to it. We need a better tool.

4.3.1 *Why Docker Compose?*

Managing multiple containers in development can be painstaking; in chapter 6 you'll see how we'll use Kubernetes to manage containers in production. However Kubernetes is a big and complex system designed to run on multiple computers (you need at least one master and one node). It's not easy to "simulate" Kubernetes on a development workstation. You could use Minikube to do this, that's like a cut-down version of Kubernetes. But there's an easier way, and you might even already have it installed—Docker Compose.

Why Docker Compose? In the same way that Docker allows us to build, run, and manage a single microservice, Docker Compose gives us a convenient way to build, run, and manage multiple microservices in development.

Docker Compose, another tool from the developers of Docker, builds on top of Docker to more easily manage a multi-container application. During development and testing, we must boot and reboot our entire application frequently. And after each small increment of development, we must test the changes to our code. We can do this through the methods already covered in earlier chapters:

- Opening multiple terminals (one for each microservice) and then running each microservice separately using Node.js or whatever our tech stack is (as covered in chapter 2)
- Using Docker to build and run each container separately (as covered in chapter 3)

Each of these methods has been an important stepping stone for us in our quest to build a microservices application, and indeed, we will often go back to these when working with individual microservices. But when it comes to working with a whole microservices application, these are less effective.

Using these methods to manage our growing application means that we spend more and more time on managing the running application. That comes at the expense of development time. This slows down our iterative progress, saps our productivity, and ultimately, drains our motivation.

We need a more effective way of managing our application during development. That's where Docker Compose comes in. Docker Compose is an open-source tool written in Python, and you can find the code here: https://github.com/docker/compose.

4.3.2   *Installing Docker Compose*

The good news is that you probably already have Docker Compose installed on your development workstation. If you followed along with chapter 3 and installed Docker then, you might already have Docker Compose because it comes bundled with the standard installers for Windows and MacOS. If you are working on Linux, you might have to install Docker Compose separately. To check if you already have it, open a terminal and print the version number as follows:

```
docker-compose --version
```

If you have it installed, you'll see the version number printed out. This is the output I see for the version I'm running at the time of writing:

```
docker-compose version 1.26.2, build eefe0d31
```

> **NOTE**   It's OK if you are running a later version than this because, most likely, it will be backward compatible.

If you find that you don't have Docker Compose installed, then you should invoke `docker --version` to double-check that you have the base Docker tool installed. If you don't have that installed, return to section 3.7.1 in chapter 3 to install it.

You might already have Docker installed, but not Docker Compose. This can happen, for example, if you are working on Linux and you followed the command-line installation instructions for Docker. If you need to install Docker Compose in addition to Docker, see the Docker Compose installation instructions on the Docker website at:

https://docs.docker.com/compose/install/

Follow the instructions there. When finished, use `docker-compose --version` to check that it is ready to go.

4.3.3   *Creating our Docker Compose file*

Docker Compose revolves around the Docker Compose file. I like to think of this as a script file for automatically building a microservices application.

> **DEFINITION**   The *Docker Compose file* is a script that specifies how to compose an application from multiple Docker containers.

Recall the Dockerfile we created in section 3.8. That was a script for building a single image. The Docker Compose file scales this up and allows us to orchestrate the creation of a whole application from a collection of Dockerfiles. Docker Compose reads the Docker Compose file and produces a running application as figure 4.3 shows.

Before we learn how to use Docker Compose to create an application composed of multiple containers, let's keep it simple and create an application with just a single container. We'll do some experiments on that so you can get comfortable with Docker Compose. After that, we'll add more containers into the mix.

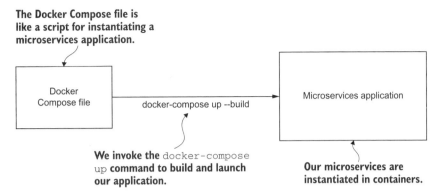

Figure 4.3   The Docker Compose file is like a script for building and launching a microservices application.

Our first step in learning Docker Compose is to get our video-streaming microservice from chapter 2 working with it. The next example for this chapter is a direct follow up from example-1 in the chapter 3 code repository. You can start with that example and make updates to it if you like, or you can follow along with the pre-made examples in the chapter 4 code repository.

The first thing we need to do is to move the Dockerfile and code for our microservice into a new subdirectory. In this case, we call it video-streaming to match the name of the microservice. The reason we do this is that we are now building an application that will soon have more than one microservice. We must therefore put each microservice into its own separate subdirectory. Our convention will be that each subdirectory is named after its microservice.

Now let's create our Docker Compose file. This file is actually called docker-compose.yaml. Because it doesn't belong to any single microservice, it lives in the root directory of our microservices application. Listing 4.1 shows our first Docker Compose file. You can type this code in yourself or just load it into Visual Studio (VS) Code from the example-1 directory in the chapter 4 code repository.

Listing 4.1   Docker Compose file for our microservice (chapter-4/example-1/docker-compose.yml)

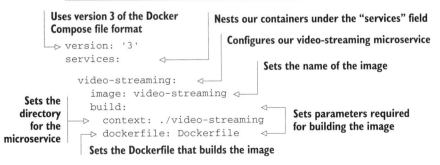

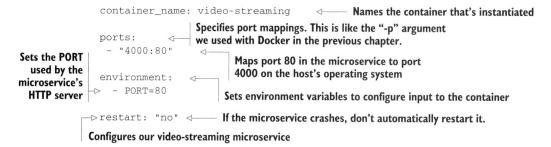

Listing 4.1 is a Docker Compose file that creates a single container: our video-streaming microservice. Note the build section. The fields here set the subdirectory that contains the microservice's project and the name of its Dockerfile. This is how Docker Compose finds the information to build the image for our video-streaming microservice.

Also note that Dockerfile is the default name of this file. We could have omitted this, but I've specified this explicitly because in the next chapter, we'll separate our Dockerfiles. That way, we can have separate versions for use in development and production. Also configured are various options (see the code annotations) that you might remember from chapter 2:

- Setting the image name to video-streaming
- Binding the port
- Setting environment variables to configure the microservice

In listing 4.1, we are starting the port numbers for our containers from 4000. Once we have multiple containers, they'll be numbered 4000, 4001, 4002, and so on. This is just so that port numbers for multiple microservices don't conflict.

> **NOTE**   The choice of port numbers is arbitrary, and for your own application, you can use a different set of numbers if you like.

You might be wondering why we set the restart option to no in listing 4.1. When working in development, we don't want our microservices to automatically restart when these crash. If they did that, we could easily miss problems!

Instead, if these crash, we want them to stay that way so that we will notice the problem. This is the opposite of how we'd usually like our microservices to work in production. We'll see later in chapter 10 how we can have Kubernetes automatically restart our production microservices that crash.

Even though our first Docker Compose file is simple, it is already pretty useful. This Docker Compose file only creates a single container, but it encodes all the information we need to build and run our microservice. Recording these configuration details already makes things a bit easier. Otherwise, we would have to type this configuration into the terminal every time we invoke the Docker build and run commands. Even at this early stage, we are seeing how Docker Compose can improve our development process.

> ### YAML
>
> You might have noticed that the Docker Compose file is a YAML format file. According to Wikipedia, YAML is a recursive acronym for "YAML Ain't Markup Language."
>
> YAML, although not actually a markup language, is probably best described as a data format or a configuration language. YAML's purpose is similar to JSON, but the language itself is structured to be more human-readable.
>
> That's why you see YAML being used by tools like Docker Compose and Kubernetes. These are configuration files designed to be edited by humans, while still being easily machine-readable.

4.3.4 *Booting our microservices application*

So far, we've created a Docker Compose file to build and run our video-streaming microservice from chapter 2. We reused the entire project for this microservice, including the Dockerfile from chapter 3. We will now test the work we have done.

In this section, we use Docker Compose to boot a single service. This doesn't yet give us much advantage over just using Docker, but sit tight. This is just a starting point, and soon we'll extend our Docker Compose file to include multiple containers. We'll use the Docker Compose file we just created so we can boot up our application using Docker Compose.

Open a terminal and change to the directory that contains your Docker Compose file. If you are following along with the code from the chapter 4 code repository on GitHub, then you should change to the directory chapter-4/example-1. Now invoke the Docker Compose up command:

```
docker-compose up --build
```

The up command causes Docker Compose to boot our microservices application. The --build argument makes Docker Compose build each of our images before instantiating containers from these.

Technically, at this point, the --build argument is not necessary because the first time you invoke the up command it builds your images anyway. At other times (without the --build argument), the up command just starts our container from the image that was previously built. This means that if you change some code in your microservice and invoke the up command again, it won't include your changes *unless* you use the --build argument. Unfortunately, this makes it all too easy to accidentally omit the code changes you are trying to test.

When this happens, and you don't realize it, you end up wasting time testing changes that aren't even there. I don't like wasting my time; that's why I make it a point to always use the --build argument every time I run the up command. It means I don't have to think about it. I know my code changes will always get through to the running application.

When you invoke the up command, you'll see the various layers of your base image being downloaded. After that, you'll start to see the (by now familiar) output from your video-streaming microservice. It should look something like the following:

```
video-streaming    |
video-streaming    | > example-1@1.0.0 start /usr/src/app
video-streaming    | > node ./src/index.js
video-streaming    |
video-streaming    | Microservice online
```

You can see on the left of the output that it shows the name of the container. This is what identifies the output as coming from our video-streaming microservice. The name of the container isn't really important at the moment, because at this point, we are only running a single container in our application—all the output is coming from just that one container.

Now that we have our microservice running, we can test that everything is OK. Point your browser to http://localhost:4000/video to watch the video that you should know well from earlier chapters.

With just a single microservice, this isn't much of a microservices application. But now that we are set up to use Docker Compose, we can easily add new containers to our application. But before we do that, let's take some time to learn some more about managing our application with Docker Compose.

Although we haven't yet scaled up to multiple containers, you might already recognize that Docker Compose has given us a more efficient process for working with a single container. Using the up command saves us from invoking separate Docker build and run commands.

That's only a small savings in time right now, but as you'll soon see, the Docker Compose up command is scalable to many containers. You can imagine how much time it's going to save when you have, say, 10 microservices and you can use a single up command to *build and run* all of these at once! That's one command (the up command) instead of 20 commands (10 build commands and 10 run commands).

The Docker Compose up command is *probably the most important command you will learn in this book!* You will invoke it time after time as you develop and test your application, and I'm going to make sure you don't forget about it!

4.3.5   *Working with the application*

After starting your application, Docker Compose continues to print output to the terminal while it is running. This locks up your terminal, so we can't do anything with it now except watch the output. We could use the -d argument with the up command to run in detached mode, just like we did with the Docker run command in chapter 3. But using the -d argument hides the application's output. We don't want that because being able to view the live output is useful for understanding what is going on.

NOTE The output can be recovered, of course, with the Docker Compose `logs` command. Still, I tend not to use the `-d` argument because I like the output to be visible front and center to see what's happening in real time.

Even though our terminal is locked up with Docker Compose, we can always simply open a new terminal and use it to invoke other commands. Let's try that now. Open a new terminal, change the directory to where the Docker Compose file is located, and invoke the following command:

```
docker-compose ps
```

The `ps` command shows a list of our running containers. Because we only have one microservice running in our application, you should see output like this:

```
Name              Command                              State    Ports
------------------------------------------------------------------------
video-streaming   docker-entrypoint.sh ...     Up       .0.0.0:4000->80/tcp
```

It's useful to note again at this point that Docker Compose is simply a layer on top of the regular Docker command. That means that all our regular Docker commands work as well. As an example, you can try `docker ps` to get a list of containers or `docker push` to upload an image to your private Docker registry.

The output of Docker commands like `docker ps` can be different from the output of `docker-compose ps`. That's because Docker commands relate to all images and containers on your development workstation, whereas Docker Compose commands only relate to the images and containers specified in your Docker Compose file.

In this sense, we are using Docker Compose like a scoping mechanism. It constrains the commands so these only apply to images and containers in your current project. Essentially, it restricts the scope of these commands to the current working directory. This is another useful aspect of Docker Compose.

More specifically, `docker-compose ps` shows us only the containers that are listed in our Docker Compose file, whereas, `docker ps` shows us all containers on our development workstation. If you invoke the `docker ps` command and find that it shows more containers than `docker-compose ps`, that's because you have previously created other containers on your computer, possibly from when you were following along with chapter 3.

There are many other Docker Compose commands for you to explore in the official documentation. See the end of this chapter for a link.

4.3.6 *Shutting down the application*

You can stop your application in either of two ways. If you opened a second terminal in the previous section, you can use that to invoke the `stop` command:

```
docker-compose stop
```

The other way to stop your application is by typing Ctrl-C at the terminal where you invoked the up command in the first place. However, there are some problems with this approach.

The first problem is that you have to be careful to press Ctrl-C only once. If you press it just a single time, then the application will stop gracefully and patiently wait for all your containers to stop. But if you are like me (impatient), then you will tend to press Ctrl-C repeatedly until the process completes and gives you back your terminal. Unlike when you are at a traffic intersection and furiously pound the walk button, this actually works. But unfortunately, it aborts the shutdown, and it can leave some or all of your containers in a running state.

The second problem is that stopping the application doesn't remove the containers. Instead, it leaves these in place in the *stopped* state so you can inspect these. That's a handy way to debug a crashed container! We'll talk more about debugging containers in chapter 10. Right now, though, it's more useful that we can remove our containers and return our development workstation to a clean state. For that, we can use the down command:

```
docker-compose down
```

I actually think we are better off always using the down command. Although Ctrl-C is needed to unlock our terminal, it's unreliable, and the down command makes the stop command redundant.

TIP   Get into the habit of using the down command after pressing Ctrl-C.

We can use both the up and down commands in combination to easily reboot our application when we want to get updated code or dependencies into it. We can chain these commands as follows:

```
docker-compose down && docker-compose up --build
```

If you are starting to tire of all these complicated commands, well, I'm hearing you. You might want to invest some time in creating shell scripts for the commands you use most often. See the following sidebar for some examples.

We now have some good fundamentals in place for Docker Compose that will serve us well for development and testing of our microservices application. We'll learn more about using Docker Compose in chapter 5 and chapter 8.

> **Shell scripts**
>
> During the daily development grind, you might find that typing some of these commands becomes onerous. For example, typing docker-compose up --build gets old quickly, so I usually encapsulate it in a shell script called up.sh.

Typically, when I write such long commands, I'll create shell scripts that are easier to run; at least I do this when I have to run a command many times per day. Other shell scripts I use are

- down.sh for `docker-compose down`
- reboot.sh for `docker-compose down && docker-compose up --build`

We'll talk more about shell scripts in chapter 7.

4.3.7 Can we use Docker Compose for production?

At this point, we might pause to consider why we are using Docker Compose for development but not for production. Docker Compose seems like a great way to define a microservices application, so why can't we use it in production? Why would we choose to use Kubernetes instead?

Rolling your own Docker Compose stack for production is easy at the outset but difficult to scale. You could deploy to Docker Swarm, but then that locks you into that particular platform. Kubernetes is a robust and flexible platform for running microservices in production. It's supported by all the major cloud vendors, but it's also independent, so it doesn't lock you in.

The fact is that we could use Docker Compose for production. Here are at least two ways to achieve this:

- Create a virtual machine (VM) in the cloud and install Docker and Docker Compose. Then copy your application to the VM and boot it using Docker Compose.
- Use the Docker Swarm hosted service (from the makers of Docker) to deploy your application defined by the Docker Compose file.

Both of these options could be desirable in the short term, especially if you don't want to go to the trouble of learning Kubernetes. But neither is ideal in the long term.

Option 1 is vertically scalable, but not horizontally scalable, and this is extremely limiting. (If you haven't heard of the concepts of horizontal and vertical scaling, don't be concerned. I'll explain these in chapter 11, where we learn about scaling our application.)

Option 2 could be a good option, but unfortunately, it locks us into this *paid* service from Docker. One good thing about Kubernetes is that it is independent of any particular cloud vendor and, yet, it is supported by all of them. This means we aren't being locked in!

Even though this book gives examples using Microsoft Azure, you can indeed run Kubernetes on both AWS and Google Cloud, not to mention with other vendors. So anything you learn about Kubernetes is transferable knowledge, and any application you build on Kubernetes is generally portable between cloud vendors. I prefer to remain vendor neutral as much as possible, and that's why I prefer Kubernetes for production.

We'll learn more about Kubernetes in chapter 6, but for now, I wanted to explain why Docker Compose is the best option for development, but probably not the best option for production. Of course, the strategy you choose depends on your situation, your project, and your company. Please don't take this as gospel!

4.4 *Adding file storage to our application*

Now that we are using Docker Compose, we can easily run multiple containers. This gives us the tools we need to move on to the real topic of this chapter—data management.

We'd like to add file storage and a database to our application. We are adding file storage so that we have a location to store the videos used by our application. A common approach is to use a storage solution provided by one of the big cloud vendors. Because we are using Azure in this book, we'll use Azure Storage as our storage provider.

> **NOTE** Many applications, including our example application, FlixTube, need to store files. There are various ways to do this, but one of the most common is to use external cloud storage such as Azure Storage, AWS S3, or Google Cloud Storage.

We could add cloud storage by directly connecting our video-streaming microservice to the storage provider. We won't do that. Instead, we'll employ good design principles, namely, *separation of concerns* and *single responsibility principle*; and we'll create a new microservice whose purpose is to be an abstraction of our file storage provider. Figure 4.4 illustrates what our application will look like once we have added the new video-storage microservice to it.

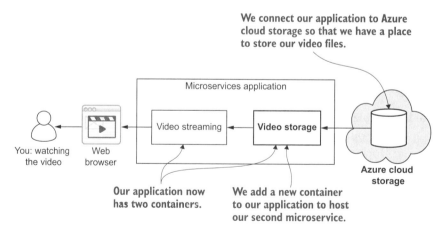

Figure 4.4   **We add a second microservice and external cloud storage to our application.**

Figure 4.4 shows how the video-storage microservice will be an intermediary between the video-streaming microservice and the external cloud storage. At the end of this section, we'll talk more about the reasoning behind the separation of these microservices. For now, just be satisfied with this excuse: this is as good a reason as any to introduce our second microservice, and we will, thus, officially be running a microservices application (albeit a small one).

4.4.1 Using Azure Storage

Azure Storage is a cloud storage service provided by Microsoft. We'll use it to add storage capability to our application. You should already have an Azure account from the work we did in chapter 3, and in this section, we'll go back into Azure, create a storage account, and upload our test video. We'll then create a new microservice whose purpose is to retrieve the video from storage.

> **DEFINITION** *Azure Storage* is a Microsoft Azure service for hosting private or public files in the cloud. You upload your files to Azure Storage and can then access these through the Azure Storage API.

Although we can host both private and public files on Azure Storage, we'll use the private option. We don't want just anyone to be able to go and download our videos from storage. Instead, we'd like them to go through the front end. The code we write for our new microservice authenticates with Azure and retrieves videos using the official Azure Storage SDK for JavaScript, available via npm.

WHY AZURE STORAGE?

We have plenty of options for file storage, so why choose Azure Storage? The truth is we could have just as easily have used AWS S3 or Google Cloud Storage. For our purposes in this book, it doesn't make much difference. The code we write would be different, of course, because if we used a different cloud vendor, we'd have to use a different storage API.

> **NOTE** The example for this chapter demonstrates external cloud storage using Azure. There's nothing particularly special about Azure in this case. The code will look different using a different API, but the structure of the microservices will be essentially the same.

It's convenient for us to use Azure because you have already signed up for it from the last chapter. However, there's no need to be locked into Azure.

One of the advantages of the architecture we are putting into place is that we could easily swap out our Azure storage microservice and replace it with an alternative. We can even do this while our application is running in production! In this sense, you can think of this video-storage microservice as *hot-swappable*.

CREATING AN AZURE STORAGE ACCOUNT

Before we get our test video into storage, we must create an Azure storage account. To do this, you'll need to login to the Azure Portal at https://portal.azure.com/ as you did in chapter 3. Then in the left-hand menu, click Create a Resource and search for "storage account" as shown in figure 4.5.

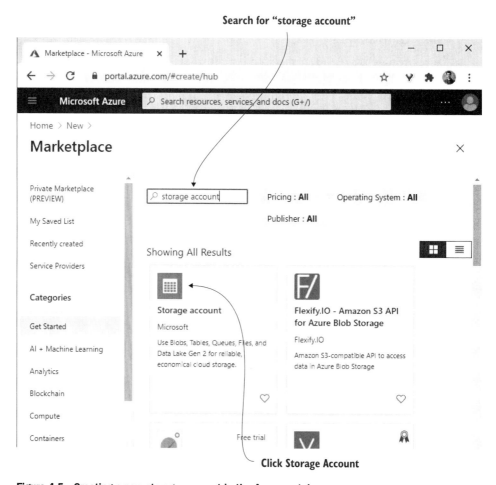

Figure 4.5   Creating a new storage account in the Azure portal

Click Microsoft's Storage Account option, then click Create. You can now fill out the details of your new storage account as shown in figure 4.6.

You'll need to choose a resource group. For that, you can use the resource group you created in chapter 3, or you can click Create New to create a new resource group. Then you'd need to choose a name for your storage account.

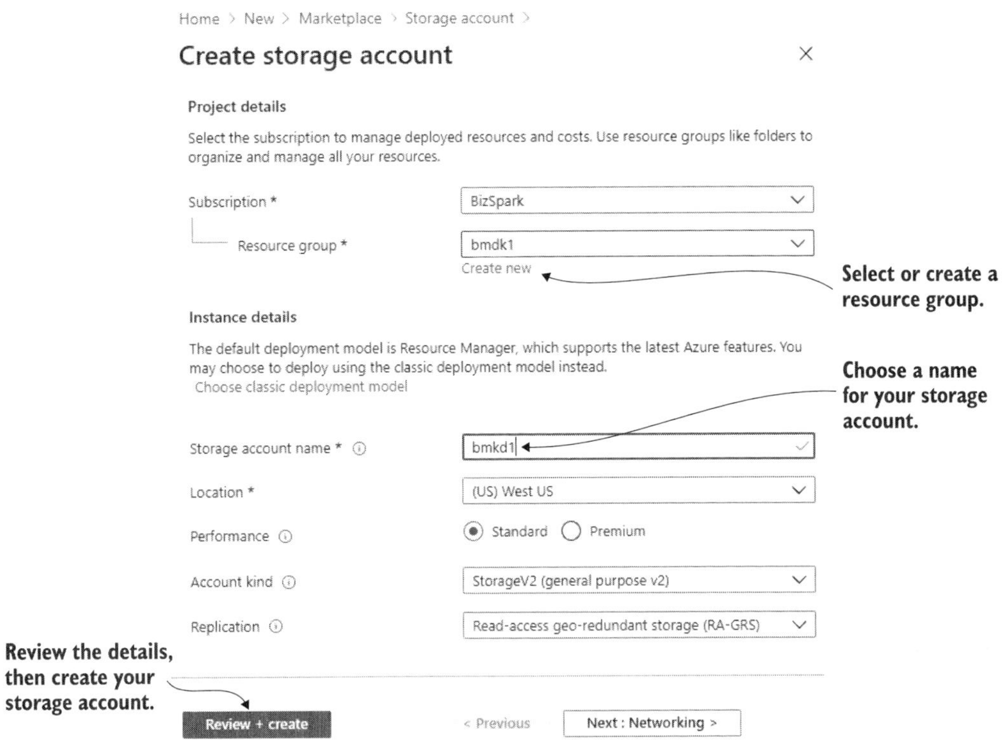

Figure 4.6   Filling out details for the new storage account

The other settings can be left at their defaults. After filling out the details, click Review + Create. If the details pass validation, you can then click Create to create the storage account. If they don't validate, then you'll need to follow the instructions to fix the problem.

Now, wait until you get the notification saying your storage account has been deployed. At that point, you can click Go to Resource in the notification, or you can find your resource in the global list like you did in chapter 3.

Once you open the storage account in the Azure portal, click Access Keys in the left-hand menu. Here you'll see the access keys for your storage account like figure 4.7 shows. These are the details you need to authenticate with your storage account. Make a note of your storage account name and one of the keys. You only need the value for one of the keys. You don't need the connection string.

Note that figure 4.7 shows the keys from my account. You'll need to look up the keys for your own account. These will be different from my keys, of course, and my keys won't even work anymore by the time you read this.

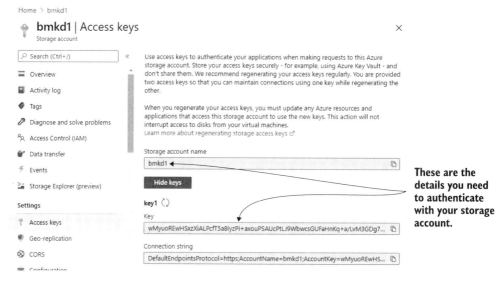

Figure 4.7   Viewing the authentication details of our new storage account

UPLOADING YOUR VIDEO TO AZURE STORAGE

With our storage account created, we can now upload our test video. In the Azure portal, with your storage account open, click Containers in the menu on the left. You should see a message like figure 4.8 shows, saying you don't have any containers yet.

By the way, just to avoid confusion, I need to say that the container we are talking about here is *not* the same as the containers we are running in our microservices application. A container in Azure Storage is like a directory; it's a location to store files.

Figure 4.8   Navigating to Containers and creating our videos container

Click the + Container button in the toolbar to create your first container. Now type in a name for your container. You can call it anything you like at this point, but to make it work with the example code coming up, let's call it videos. Here you can also choose the access level, but we'll stick with the default, which is Private Access Only. Next, click OK to create the container.

You should see the videos container in the list now. Click it to drill down. When viewing the contents of your new container, you'll see a message like in figure 4.9. In case you are wondering what a *blob* is, it is simply a file, and we don't have any of those yet. Let's upload one now.

Click the Upload button in the toolbar to upload your video file, and select a file on your disk to upload. You can use the test video that is included in either of the code repositories for chapter 2 or 3; otherwise, use a video of your own choice.

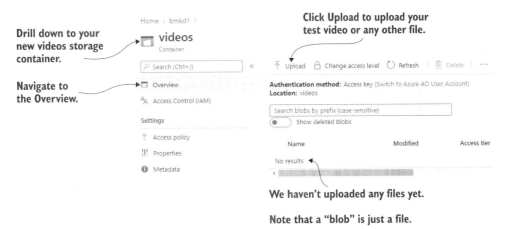

Figure 4.9   Drilling down into the videos container and clicking Upload to upload a video file

After the video has uploaded, it will appear in the list as shown in figure 4.10.

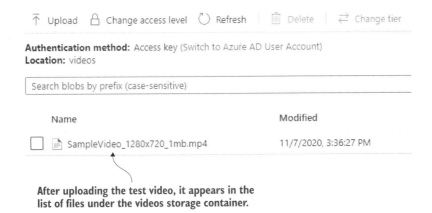

Figure 4.10   After the video is uploaded, you will see it in the list under the videos container.

CREATING A MICROSERVICE TO READ AZURE STORAGE

We now have a test video uploaded to Azure Storage, so it's time to create our new video-storage microservice. This is our second official microservice, and it will be a REST API to retrieve videos from our storage provider.

> **NOTE** We could directly integrate our video-streaming microservice with cloud storage, but instead, we'll *abstract* this connection behind another microservice. This makes it trivial to later replace the storage mechanism and can pave the way for our application to support multiple storage providers.

The first thing we need to do is to create a new directory for our second microservice. You should either create a new subdirectory or just load example-2 from the chapter-4 code repository into VS Code. We'll name the subdirectory for the new microservice as azure-storage. We name this new project specifically to indicate that its purpose is related to Azure Storage. If we were to add different storage providers, we would call these something different (for example, aws-storage or google-storage).

A quick note: in case you were thinking of porting the code presented here over to AWS or GCP, converting from the Azure store microservice over to another provider is not a simple task. The APIs to interface with AWS and GCP storage will be quite different to Azure, and you'll need to read their docs separately to figure out how to use these. Make sure you finish learning about the Azure storage microservice in this chapter before you attempt to convert to any other provider.

Now open a terminal and change into the azure-storage directory. If you are creating the new microservice from scratch, you'll need to create a new package.json and install the express package like we did in chapter 2. You'll then need to install the azure-storage package like this:

```
npm install --save azure-storage
```

If you are following along with example-2 in the chapter 4 code repository, everything you need is already there:

- The package file
- The code
- The Dockerfile

To run the new microservice directly under Node.js, you'll first need to change directory to azure-storage and then install the dependencies:

```
npm install
```

Listing 4.2 presents the code for our new microservice. Before we run this code, let's read it and understand what it's doing.

Listing 4.2 A microservice to retrieve videos from Azure storage (chapter-4/ example-2/azure-storage/src/index.js)

```
const express = require("express");
const azure = require('azure-storage');          Loads the azure-storage package so our code
                                                  can interact with the Azure Storage API
const app = express();
                                                  Gets the name of the storage account
const PORT = process.env.PORT;                    from an environment variable
const STORAGE_ACCOUNT_NAME =
    process.env.STORAGE_ACCOUNT_NAME;             Gets the name of the access key
const STORAGE_ACCESS_KEY =                         from an environment variable
    process.env.STORAGE_ACCESS_KEY;
                                                  Helper function that connects
function createBlobService() {                    to the azure-storage API
    const blobService = azure.createBlobService(STORAGE_ACCOUNT_NAME,
        STORAGE_ACCESS_KEY);
    return blobService;                           HTTP GET route for retrieving
}                                                 a video from Azure storage

app.get("/video", (req, res) => {                 Specifies the path to the video in
                                                  storage as an HTTP query parameter
    const videoPath = req.query.path;
    const blobService = createBlobService();      Connects to the azure-storage API

    const containerName = "videos";               Hard-coded container name.
    blobService.getBlobProperties(containerName,  Later we can vary this for some
        videoPath, (err, properties) => {         purpose (say, by user ID so we
        if (err) {                                can keep videos for each user
            // ... error handling ...             separately).
            res.sendStatus(500);
            return;
        }
                                                  Writes content length and mime
        res.writeHead(200, {                      type to the HTTP response headers
            "Content-Length": properties.contentLength,
            "Content-Type": "video/mp4",
        });

        blobService.getBlobToStream(containerName,
            videoPath, res, err => {              Streams the video from Azure
            if (err) {                            storage to the HTTP response
                // ... error handling ...
                res.sendStatus(500);
                return;
            }
        });
    });
});

app.listen(PORT, () => {
    console.log(`Microservice online`);
});
```

Retrieves the video's properties from Azure storage

In listing 4.2, we use `azure-storage`, which is the official Azure Storage SDK installed via npm. We also created an HTTP server using Express in the same way as we did in chapter 2.

There are two new environment variables to configure this microservice; STORAGE _ACCOUNT_NAME and STORAGE_ACCESS_KEY set the authentication details for our Azure Storage account. Note that you will have to set these environment variables to the authentication details from your own storage account. You'll do that in the next section. The authentication details are used in the helper function `createBlobService` to create the API object that we need to access the storage SDK.

The most important thing in listing 4.2 is the HTTP GET route /video, by which we can retrieve a video from storage. This route streams a video from Azure Storage to the HTTP response.

TESTING OUR NEW MICROSERVICE INDEPENDENTLY

Before we try and integrate this microservice into our application, it's best if we test it independently. In this case, we could easily integrate it first and then test it later. Working that way is feasible when our application is this small. However, as our application grows larger and more complicated, integration testing becomes more difficult.

Testing microservices individually works better because we can start or reload a single microservice quickly. But doing the same isn't as easy for the application as a whole. Let's therefore get into a habit of testing our microservices individually before integration testing the application as a whole.

Before running (and testing) the new microservice, we need to set the environment variables to configure it. We will do this from the terminal. On MacOS and Linux, we do it like this:

```
export PORT=3000
export STORAGE_ACCOUNT_NAME=<the name of your storage account>
export STORAGE_ACCESS_KEY=<the access key for your storage account>
```

On Windows, we do it like this:

```
set PORT=3000
set STORAGE_ACCESS_KEY=<the name of your storage account>
set STORAGE_ACCESS_KEY=<the access key for your storage account>
```

Note that you must insert the name and key for the storage account that you created earlier. When running the microservice, we can choose to run it in either production mode or in development mode as we discussed in chapter 2. We can run it in *production mode* like this:

```
npm start
```

Alternatively, we can run it in *development mode* with nodemon for live reload like this:

```
npm run start:dev
```

Live reload is really important to fast development because we can make changes to our code and have our microservice automatically restart. In the next chapter, you'll learn how to extend live reload to the *entire* microservices application. For now, we'll settle for using it during development and testing of an individual microservice.

With your microservice running, you can now open your browser and navigate to http://localhost:3000/video?path=SampleVideo_1280x720_1mb.mp4. If you used a different name for your video, you'll need to adjust the name of that video in this URL to fit. You should now see the familiar video playing, but this time, it's streamed from your Azure storage account.

We'll talk more about testing microservices in chapter 8. For the moment though, let's move on and integrate our new microservice into the application.

4.4.2 *Updating the video-streaming microservice*

The first step of integrating the new microservice with our application is to update our video-streaming microservice. As a reminder, we ended chapter 3 with a video-streaming microservice that loaded the test video from the filesystem. Now, we are going to update that microservice so that it instead delegates the loading of the video to our new Azure Storage microservice.

Here we update our video-streaming microservice to delegate storage to another microservice. We are *separating our concerns* so that the video-streaming microservice is solely responsible for streaming video to our user and so that it doesn't need to know the details of how storage is handled.

Listing 4.3 shows the changes we'll make to the video-streaming microservice. Read through the code in the listing to see how we are forwarding the HTTP request for a video through to the new video-storage microservice.

> **Listing 4.3 Updated video-streaming microservice (chapter-4/example-2/video-streaming/src/index.js)**

```
const express = require("express");        Loads the (built-in) http library
const http = require("http");       ◁──┘   so we can forward HTTP requests


const app = express();

const PORT = process.env.PORT;
const VIDEO_STORAGE_HOST =
➥ process.env.VIDEO_STORAGE_HOST;              Configures the connection to
const VIDEO_STORAGE_PORT =                      the video-storage microservice
➥ parseInt(process.env.VIDEO_STORAGE_PORT);

app.get("/video", (req, res) => {       Forwards the HTTP GET request to the video
    const forwardRequest = http.request(  ◁── route to the video-storage microservice
        {
            host: VIDEO_STORAGE_HOST,       Sets the host and port
            port: VIDEO_STORAGE_PORT,       we are forwarding to
            path:'/video?path=
            ➥ SampleVideo_1280x720_1mb.mp4',   ◁── Sets the route we are forwarding to
            method: 'GET',
```
Forwarding
as an HTTP
GET request

```
            headers: req.headers           Forwarding the HTTP headers as they are
        },
        forwardResponse => {               Gets the response from the forwarded request
            res.writeHeader(forwardResponse.statusCode,
              forwardResponse.headers);    Returns the status code and header of the forwarded request
            forwardResponse.pipe(res);     Pipes the response stream using Node.js streams
        }
    );

    req.pipe(forwardRequest);              Pipes the request stream using Node.js streams
});

app.listen(PORT, () => {
    console.log(`Microservice online`);
});
```

In listing 4.3, we use the Node.js built-in http library to forward an HTTP request from one microservice to another. The response that is returned is then streamed to the client. The way this works might be difficult to understand, but don't worry too much about it right now. In the next chapter, we'll explore this more because communication between microservices is so important that it deserves its own chapter.

Note that we have hard-coded the path to the video in storage at this point. This is just a stepping stone, and we'll soon fix that. But for this code to work in the meantime, you must have uploaded the test video to this path. If you've uploaded a different video, you should change the code accordingly.

After updating our video-streaming microservice, we should test it independently. That's kind of difficult given that it depends on the video-storage microservice. We could do this if we had the tools and techniques in place to *mock* our dependencies.

Mocking is a technique used in testing where we replace the dependency with a fake or simulated alternative. We don't have those techniques yet, but this is something we'll explore in chapter 8, and you'll see an example of a mock microservice in chapter 9. Right now, let's just press on and finish the integration. Then we can check that the application works as expected.

4.4.3 Adding our new microservice to the Docker Compose file

We've done quite a lot of work to get to this point. We created an Azure Storage account, and we uploaded our test video. Then we created our second microservice, the Azure Storage microservice, which is a REST API that abstracts our storage provider. After that, we updated our video-streaming microservice so that instead of loading the video from the filesystem, as it did in chapters 2 and 3, it now retrieves the video via the video-storage microservice.

NOTE The beauty of the Docker Compose file is that it makes it easier to define and manage a whole suite of containers. It's a convenient way to manage a microservices application!

To integrate the new microservice into our application and test it, we now must add it as a new section to our Docker Compose file. You can see what this looks like in figure 4.11, which shows what the Docker Compose file will look like later, after we add our second microservice and the database server. You can see that the Docker Compose file on the left has three sections that map to the three containers on the right.

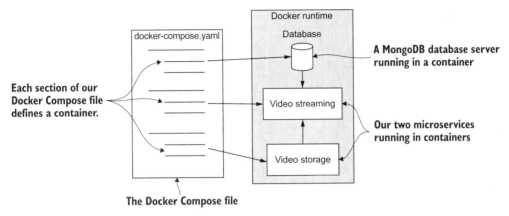

Figure 4.11   Each section in our Docker Compose file defines a separate container.

You can think of the Docker Compose file as a kind of *aggregate* Dockerfile that we use to describe and manage multiple containers at once. It's an aggregate because we use it to tie together the multiple Dockerfiles for each of our microservices.

Listing 4.4 shows our updated Docker Compose file with the addition of the Azure Storage microservice. Before we get to testing this, make sure you set the values of STORAGE_NAME and STORAGE_ACCESS_KEY to the values you noted down earlier from your own Azure Storage account.

Listing 4.4   Adding a new microservice to our Docker Compose file (chapter-4/example-2/docker-compose.yaml)

```
version: '3'
services:                          Adds the new microservice
                                   to our application
  azure-storage:        ◁─┘
    image: azure-storage      ◁──── Sets the name of the image
    build:
      context: ./azure-storage
      dockerfile: Dockerfile         The container's name connects
    container_name: video-storage  ◁─┘ these two microservices!
    ports:
      - "4000:80"                              Configures the microservice to
    environment:                               connect to our Azure storage
      - PORT=80                                account. Make sure you add
      - STORAGE_ACCOUNT_NAME=<your storage account>  your own details here.
      - STORAGE_ACCESS_KEY=<your storage access key>
    restart: "no"
```

```
video-streaming:
  image: video-streaming
  build:
    context: ./video-streaming
    dockerfile: Dockerfile
  container_name: video-streaming
  ports:
   - "4001:80"
  environment:
    - PORT=80
    - VIDEO_STORAGE_HOST=video-storage
    - VIDEO_STORAGE_PORT=80
  restart: "no"
```

Configures the microservice to connect to the video-storage microservice

The container's name connects these two microservices!

There are some questions you might have on your mind at this point: why is the container name set to `video-storage` instead of `azure-storage`? We called the microservice azure-storage, but we called the container video-storage; why is that? This is an intentional abstraction. It's a part of our design that the video-streaming microservice doesn't care where it retrieves its videos from! It's not interested in the fact that the videos are stored in Azure. From its point of view, these could just as easily be stored anywhere else, such as AWS S3 or Google Cloud Storage.

By naming our container as video-storage, we are now able to connect our microservices to it using a name that is independent of the underlying storage provider. This is good application structure put into practice. We have given ourselves the flexibility of later being able to swap out azure-storage and replace it with aws-storage or google-storage. And we can do this without interrupting the video-streaming microservice. From its point of view, nothing will have changed. This kind of freedom to effect change in the future without knock-on effects is important, and it shows that we are making the most of our microservices architecture.

4.4.4 Testing the updated application

We have updated our Docker Compose file to include both of our microservices. Now we are finally ready to boot our application and test it with our additional microservice. For this, we run our application the same as before:

```
docker-compose up --build
```

The difference now is that we have booted up two containers, rather than just the one. You can see an example of the output in the following:

```
video-streaming   | > example-1@1.0.0 start /usr/src/app
video-streaming   | > node ./src/index.js
video-streaming   |
video-storage     |
video-storage     | > example-1@1.0.0 start /usr/src/app
video-storage     | > node ./src/index.js
```

```
video-storage      |
video-streaming    | Forwarding video requests to video-storage:80.
video-streaming    | Microservice online.
video-storage      | Serving videos from...
video-storage      | Microservice online.
```

Note in the output how the name of each container is printed on the left. This is an aggregate stream of logging from all containers. The name on the left allows us to differentiate the output from each microservice.

> **NOTE** We are booting our application with multiple containers using a single command so we can test our application with multiple microservices.

Now that we have added our second microservice, this is where we start to see the real value of Docker Compose. We could have booted up the application without Docker Compose in either of the following ways:

- *Open two terminals and use Node.js directly to run the video-streaming microservice in one terminal and the Azure storage microservice in the other.* That's two terminals and two commands to run our application.
- *Use Docker to run two containers.* In this case, we have to run `docker build` and `docker run` once for each microservice. That's one terminal and four commands.

No one wants to spend all day repetitively typing commands. Instead, Docker Compose allows us to boot our application with a *single* command, and this is scalable to any number of containers.

Just imagine down the track a bit; we have built our application with up to 10 microservices. Without Docker Compose, you will have to type at least 20 commands to build and start your application. With Docker Compose, we can build and run our 10 microservice applications with just one command! No matter how many containers we need, it's still just one command.

At this point, we have two opportunities for testing. At a minimum, we must test the video-streaming microservice because, currently, that's the only customer-facing endpoint we have. To do that, open a browser and navigate to http://localhost:4001/video.

Yet again, you'll see the familiar test video. Testing the video-streaming microservice actually tests both microservices because the video-streaming microservice depends on the video-storage microservice. These both get tested at the same time. We could stop here, but we can also independently test the video-storage microservice.

If you glance back to listing 4.4, you'll see that we have bound its port to 4000. We can navigate our browser to that port and see video streaming directly from the video-storage microservice. The video-storage microservice, however, expects us to tell it the path where the video is located. We do that via the URL. Let's navigate our browser to http://localhost:4000/video?path=SampleVideo_1280x720_1mb.mp4 and test the video-storage microservice.

Note that testing an internal microservice from the *outside* like this is only possible in development. Once we move this microservice to production, its REST API is only available within the Kubernetes cluster. In this case, we'll make it private because we don't want the outside world having direct access to our video storage. This is a security feature of microservices! We can control which microservices are exposed to the outside world, and we can use that to restrict access to parts of the application that should not be directly accessible by outsiders. We'll talk more about security in chapter 11.

Well, there we have it. We added external file storage to our application, and in the process, we scaled it up to two microservices. Before we congratulate ourselves, however, let's consider some design theory.

4.4.5   *Cloud storage vs. cluster storage*

At this point, if you know anything about Kubernetes, you might be wondering why we haven't used Kubernetes volumes for file storage as opposed to cloud storage. That's an important design decision, and again, it's the kind of thing that depends on the needs of your project, your business, and your customers.

We used cloud storage instead of cluster storage because it's simple, it works when we run in development, it's cheap, and it's managed for us. These are the benefits of cloud storage and why it's in common use by many companies. Besides, we haven't learned anything about Kubernetes yet, so we definitely couldn't have used Kubernetes volumes at this point in the book. However, there's another important reason why I generally choose to use cloud storage over cluster storage.

We could store the files and data for our application in the Kubernetes cluster, but I prefer my production cluster to be *stateless*. That means I can destroy and rebuild the cluster at will without risk of losing the data. Later, this enables us to use *blue-green deployment* for our production rollouts, which we'll talk about in chapter 11. This makes it easy to build a new and updated instance of our application that runs in parallel with the previous version.

To upgrade our customers to the new version, we can then switch the DNS record so that the hostname now refers to the new instance. This gives us a low-risk way to do major upgrades to our application. It's low risk not because problems won't happen, but because if problems do happen, we can quickly switch the DNS back to the old instance so that our customers are (almost) immediately reverted to the previous (and presumably working) version.

4.4.6   *What did we achieve?*

Congratulations! We now have a small microservices application running! That's a big deal. Using Docker Compose, we created a scaffold into which we can easily add new microservices and grow our application. Take a moment to pat yourself on the back. This is a big milestone!

What did we achieve? We added file storage capability to our application. Our microservice now has the capability to store files in external cloud storage, and this gives our application a place to host its videos.

We also added a second microservice. With Docker Compose in place, we can now continue to expand our application by adding new containers to it. We'll make use of this capability again in a moment when we add a database server to our application.

We added the second microservice as an abstraction over our storage provider. This is a design decision with benefits. We can now swap out and replace our video-storage microservice with a different storage provider with minimal impact on our application. We could even do this while the application is running in production! It's even possible in the future that we might want to have multiple storage microservices running in parallel. If it suited our product, we could upgrade it to support Azure Storage, AWS S3, and Google Cloud Storage all at the same time!

The details of how storage works have been restricted to the internals of the video-storage microservice. That means we can change the details independently from the rest of the application without causing knock-on problems. This kind of protection might seem superfluous right now, but it becomes more important as our application grows.

> **NOTE** Eventually, our application will become a spider's web of communication among many microservices. Changes in one will have the potential to cause an exponential ripple of problems across the application. Careful construction of the interfaces between microservices to minimize their coupling helps us make the most of our microservices architecture.

Separating our microservices, the so-called separation of concerns (mentioned in chapter 1), is important—each microservice should look after its own separate area of responsibility. We are also following the single responsibility principle (also mentioned in chapter 1) that says each microservice should look after one single thing. Our microservices now look after their own areas of responsibility:

- The video-streaming microservice is responsible for streaming a video to a user.
- The video-storage microservice is responsible for locating videos in storage and retrieving these.

The separation of the microservices in this way helps to ensure that each microservice is small, simple, and manageable.

4.5 *Adding a database to our application*

The other half of data management relates to the database. Most applications need some kind of database to store their dynamic data, and FlixTube is no exception.

The first thing we need is metadata storage for each video. We'll start using our database by storing the path to each video. This will fix the problem we encountered earlier of having a hard-coded path to the video file in our video-streaming microservice.

> **NOTE** Practically all applications need some kind of database to store the data that is to be updated by the application.

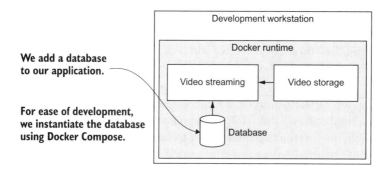

Figure 4.12   Adding a database to our application

Figure 4.12 shows what our application will look like after we add the database. In addition to the two containers for our two microservices, we will have another container that hosts a MongoDB database. You can see in the diagram that only the video-streaming microservice connects to the database; the video-storage microservice doesn't require a database.

4.5.1   Why MongoDB?

MongoDB is one of the most popular of the so-called NoSQL variety of databases. Using Docker allows us to have an almost *instant database*. We only need to specify the name of a database image, and Docker will pull it from DockerHub and instantiate it on our development workstation.

> **NOTE**   MongoDB is easy to use, provides a flexible database that stores schema-free structured data, and has a rich query API.

But there are many different databases that we could easily boot up with Docker, so why MongoDB? In my experience, even manually downloading and installing MongoDB is easy compared to older and more traditional databases; now that we have Docker it's even easier still. Like any database, we can use MongoDB to store rich structured data. MongoDB is also known to have high performance and is extremely scalable.

I work with a lot of unpredictable data, and it's hard to tell what's going to be thrown at me next. I like the fact that MongoDB doesn't force me to define a fixed schema! Although, it's certainly possible to define a schema with MongoDB if you use an object-relational mapping (ORM) library like Mongoose (https://www.npmjs.com/package/mongoose).

MongoDB is also easy to query and update in many different programming languages. It's well supported, has great documentation, and there are many examples in circulation. MongoDB is open source. You can find the code here: https://github.com/mongodb/mongo.

4.5.2   Adding a database server in development

We are going to add a database to our application in development using Docker Compose in the same way that we added our video-storage microservice earlier in this chapter. We will add one new container to our application to host a single database server. We only need a single server, but we can host many databases on that server. This means we'll be set up for the future to easily create more databases as we add more microservices to our application.

ADDING THE DATABASE SERVER TO THE DOCKER COMPOSE FILE

To add the database server to our application, we must update our Docker Compose file. Docker Compose makes it easy to add a database to our application. We just add a few lines to the Docker Compose file to specify the public Docker image for the database and set some configurations. Abracadabra, instant database!

Listing 4.5 shows the updated Docker Compose file. We are adding a new section to the top of the file with the name db (short for database). The configuration for this container is different from the configuration for the microservices we added earlier. That's because now we don't need to build the image for the new container. Instead, we use the publicly published mongo image from Docker Hub.

> **Listing 4.5 Adding a MongoDB database (chapter-4/example-3/docker-compose.yaml)**

Adds a MongoDB database server to our microservices application

Sets the image name and version. This is a public MongoDB image retrieved from Docker Hub.

Sets the name of the container that's instantiated in our application. Our microservices use this name to connect to the database.

Maps the MongoDB standard port 27017 to 4000 on our host OS. We can interact with and check the database on our host using port 4000.

Sets the restart policy to always. If MongoDB ever crashes (which hardly ever happens), this automatically restarts it.

```
version: '3'
services:

  db:
    image: mongo:4.2.8
    container_name: db

    ports:
     - "4000:27017"
    restart: always

  azure-storage:
    image: azure-storage
    build:
      context: ./azure-storage
      dockerfile: Dockerfile
    container_name: video-storage
    ports:
     - "4001:80"
    environment:
      - PORT=80
      - STORAGE_ACCOUNT_NAME=<your Azure storage account name here>
      - STORAGE_ACCESS_KEY=<your Azure storage account key here>
    restart: "no"

  video-streaming:
    image: video-streaming
    build:
      context: ./video-streaming
      dockerfile: Dockerfile
    container_name: video-streaming
    ports:
     - "4002:3000"
```

```
environment:
  - PORT=80
  - DBHOST=mongodb://db:27017      ◄──
  - DBNAME=video-streaming         ◄──
  - VIDEO_STORAGE_HOST=video-storage
  - VIDEO_STORAGE_PORT=80
restart: "no"
```

Configures the microservice to connect to the database

Sets the name the microservice uses for its database

In our updated application, the video-streaming microservice will be connected to the database. Notice that we now have new environment variables, DBHOST and DBNAME, which configure the microservice's connection to its database.

It's also worth noting in the configuration for the db container how we have mapped the container's ports. Here we have mapped the standard MongoDB port of 27017 to 4000. What does this mean? Within the Docker runtime, other containers can access the database using 27017. That's the conventional port for MongoDB, so we'll stick with that.

On our host operating system (OS), we have mapped the port to 4000. That's an arbitrary choice. We could have given it any number, including 27017. I prefer not to give it the standard MongoDB port because that would conflict with an instance of MongoDB that we might have running on our host OS.

This is a good setup. Our application can interact with MongoDB via the standard port, but we can also use tools (as we'll soon see) to directly query and edit our database from our development workstation. This is great for development as it gives us the ability to directly interact with and query our database.

UPDATING THE VIDEO-STREAMING MICROSERVICE TO USE A DATABASE

We added environment variables to our Docker Compose file to connect our video-streaming microservice to its database. Now we need to update the code for this microservice to make use of these environment variables to establish the database connection.

Listing 4.6 shows the updated code for the video-streaming microservice that allows it to query and read data from its database. Browse this code and notice how it differs from the previous incarnation.

Listing 4.6   Updating the microservice to use the database (chapter-4/example-3/video-streaming/src/index.js)

```
const express = require("express");
const http = require("http");
const mongodb = require("mongodb");      ◄──

const app = express();

const PORT = process.env.PORT;
const VIDEO_STORAGE_HOST = process.env.VIDEO_STORAGE_HOST;
const VIDEO_STORAGE_PORT = parseInt(process.env.VIDEO_STORAGE_PORT);
const DBHOST = process.env.DBHOST;      ◄──
const DBNAME = process.env.DBNAME;      ◄──
```

Loads the MongoDB library so the microservice can connect to its database

Sets the name that this microservice uses for its database

Specifies the database server to connect to

```
function main() {

    return mongodb.MongoClient.connect(DBHOST)
        .then(client => {
            const db = client.db(DBNAME);
            const videosCollection =
            ➥ db.collection("videos");

            app.get("/video", (req, res) => {
                const videoId =
                ➥ new mongodb.ObjectID(req.query.id);
                videosCollection
                ➥ .findOne({ _id: videoId })
                    .then(videoRecord => {
                        if (!videoRecord) {
                            res.sendStatus(404);
                            return;
                        }

                        const forwardRequest = http.request(
                            {
                                host: VIDEO_STORAGE_HOST,
                                port: VIDEO_STORAGE_PORT,
                                path:`/video?path=${videoRecord
                                ➥ .videoPath}`,
                                method: 'GET',
                                headers: req.headers
                            },

                            forwardResponse => {
                                res.writeHeader(forwardResponse.statusCode,
                                ➥ forwardResponse.headers);
                                forwardResponse.pipe(res);
                            }
                        );

                        req.pipe(forwardRequest);
                    })
                    .catch(err => {
                        console.error("Database query failed.");
                        console.error(err && err.stack || err);
                        res.sendStatus(500);
                    });
            });

            app.listen(port, () => {
                console.log(`Microservice online.`);
            });
        });
}

main()
    .then(() => console.log("Microservice online."))
    .catch(err => {
```

Connects to the database server

Retrieves the database that this microservice uses

Retrieves the videos collection where we store metadata for each video

Specifies the video ID via an HTTP query parameter. This is a MongoDB document ID.

Queries the database to find a single video by the requested ID

The video was not found! Responds with an HTTP 404 error code

When forwarding the HTTP request to the video-storage microservice, maps the video's ID to the video's location

Wraps the body of this microservice in a main function. This is the main entry point for this microservice. Can you tell that I'm a recovering C++ programmer?

Starts the microservice

```
        console.error("Microservice failed to start.");
        console.error(err && err.stack || err);
    });
```

Listing 4.6 queries its database by video ID to retrieve the location of a video in storage. It then passes that location to the video-storage microservice to retrieve the video that is stored there. The rest of the code here should be familiar. We are forwarding HTTP requests for videos to the video-storage microservice.

This update to the video-streaming microservices has removed the hard-coded video path. Instead, we now refer to videos by their database ID. We could have fixed this without using IDs. We could simply refer to videos by their path in storage. But as you might suspect, that's not a good idea. Let's consider why.

If we use *paths* to identify our videos, that makes it difficult to later move videos to a different location if in the future we decide we'd like to restructure our storage filesystem. The reason this is a problem is that various other databases and records will need to refer to our videos. This includes a metadata database for recording information about a video such as its genre. And we'll later want a database for recording recommendations and views of each video.

Each of these databases must have a way to refer to a video. If we only record the ID for each video, we give ourselves much more freedom to make independent changes to our storage without causing any nasty problems to ripple through our microservices and databases.

This also makes it a bit simpler because the location of the video could potentially be a long path, and internal details like this are not something we'd usually like to let leak out of our application. Why? Exposing such details that hint at the internal structure can give a potential attacker an advantage. It's better to keep a lid on this kind of information.

LOADING SOME TEST DATA INTO OUR DATABASE

We've added a database to our Docker Compose file and we've updated the video-streaming microservice to use that database. We are almost ready to test our changes!

In order to test our updated code, we must now load some test data into our database. Later, we'll have a way for our users to upload their own videos and populate the database with relevant details, but we don't yet have any way to do this in our application.

We could test our code by replacing the database with some kind of simulated version of it. I'm talking about mocking the database. (We first talked about mocking earlier in this chapter.) Another way we can do this is to use a *database fixture*, which is a piece of test data that we load into our database purely for testing.

There are various ways we can load some data in our database. The simplest way to do this is to use Robo 3T (formerly known as Robomongo). This is a fantastic UI tool for working with MongoDB. I use it all the time myself, which you already know if you read my first book, *Data Wrangling with JavaScript* (Manning, 2018). It's available for Windows, MacOS, and Linux.

For download and install instructions for Robo 3T, see https://robomongo.org/. Robo 3T allows you to view the collections and documents in your database. You can easily create databases, collections, and data records.

But before we can use Robo 3T to load example data into our database, we first must have our database up and running. We can do that by booting our application. If you haven't yet done so, open a terminal and start your application:

```
docker-compose up --build
```

> **NOTE** You should run this command from the same directory as the updated Docker Compose file in listing 4.5. You can find this file in the example-3 sub-directory of the chapter 4 code repository.

After starting our application, we now have a MongoDB database server running in a container. Because we mapped the standard MongoDB port 27017 to port 4000 on our development workstation, we can now access the database from Robo 3T by connecting to localhost:4000.

Listing 4.7 shows the test data we'll add to our database using Robo 3T. This is a single JSON document that is available under the example-3 directory and is suitable for a copy and paste insert using Robo 3T.

To load this data using Robo 3T, open that application, create a new database called video-streaming, create a collection called videos, and then insert a document into that collection. For our purposes, use the content from this listing.

Listing 4.7   Loading a data record with Robo 3T (chapter-4/example-3/db-fixture/ videos.json)

The data record to load into the database
```
{
    "_id" : { "$oid": "5d9e690ad76fe06a3d7ae416" },   ⟵──  Special syntax that
                                                             sets the video's ID as a
                                                             MongoDB document's ID

    "videoPath" : "SampleVideo_1280x720_1mb.mp4"   ⟵──  Sets the location
                                                             of the video
}
```

We'll come back to mocking and database fixtures in chapter 8. For now, let's look at how to test our application.

TESTING OUR UPDATED APPLICATION

At this stage, you can first test the microservice directly under Node.js if you like. It's always a good idea to test your microservices independently before you integrate them. If you are putting this code together by yourself and testing directly under Node.js, don't forget to install the mongodb driver package from npm:

```
npm install --save mongodb
```

There's no need for me to walk you through individual testing for each new microservice. In the interest of expediency, we'll skip that and go straight to running our integrated code in the application under Docker Compose.

You should already have the application running from the last section. We needed it there for the database, so we could load our test data. If the application isn't running, start it now:

```
docker-compose up --build
```

We can now test the application in the usual way with a web browser. This time, though, we must provide the ID of the video we'd like to watch. The ID that we specified in our test data was a big long string of numbers, and that's what we must now add to our URL to test the updated application. Open your browser and navigate to this link:

http://localhost:4002/video?id=5d9e690ad76fe06a3d7ae416

If you change the ID in the test data, you also need to update the ID in this URL. You should now see the test video playing. You must know this video very well by now!

4.5.3   *Adding a database server in production*

So far we have only covered the case of adding a database server to the development version of our application. This works well enough for the moment because we haven't yet learned how to deploy our application to production; that's coming in chapters 6 and 7. What we can do now though is to briefly consider how we might deploy a database server for use by our production environment.

Docker Compose makes it easy to add a database server to our application for development, but what about production? For production, I recommend using a database external to the Kubernetes cluster. This keeps the cluster stateless, which, as we discussed in section 4.4.5, means that we can tear down and rebuild our cluster at any time without risk to our data.

Once we have built our production Kubernetes cluster, we can easily deploy a MongoDB database in a way that is similar to what we've just done with Docker Compose. In fact, that's what we will do in chapter 7 because that's the easiest way for us to get our database server into production.

Beyond that though, I recommend that you keep your database separate to your cluster. You can run it on a separate VM, or you could use an external managed database. The reason for this is to keep the production cluster stateless.

Another advantage to using a managed database is security. The database provider takes care of maintenance for us; it takes care of protecting and backing up our data! If we work for a big company, our company will probably manage this in-house. But if we work for a small company or startup, we need all the help we can get.

4.5.4 *Database-per-microservice or database-per-application?*

At this point, we have only created a single database on our database server. But we are now set up to create many more additional databases.

You probably noticed that we named the database video-streaming to coincide with the microservice that uses it! This alludes to a rule we'll be following throughout the book: *each microservice should have its own database.* We do this because we'd like to encapsulate our data within the microservice in the same way we'd encapsulate data within an object in object-oriented programming.

Should we have one database per microservice or one per application? Definitely aim to have only one database per microservice. Your databases can be hosted on a single server, but make sure each individual microservice has its own database. If you share databases or make a database the integration point between microservices, you are inviting architectural and scalability problems.

We are restricting our data from all but the code that directly encapsulates it. This helps us to safely evolve the structure of our data over time because changes to it can be *hidden* within the microservice. This is another technique that, if we structure our REST APIs carefully, allows us to avoid propagating breakages and problems from one microservice to other parts of the application. Care applied when designing these REST APIs equates to better design for our application.

You might think that sharing a database between microservices is a good way for them to share data. But using a database as an integration point or interface between microservices is a bad idea because it makes for a more fragile and less scalable application.

At some point, you might find yourself wanting to share a database for performance or some other reason. After all, rules sometimes have to be broken to achieve a difficult goal. Carefully consider why you want to do this and if it's truly necessary. Bringing such anti-patterns into our application is not something we should do blindly. We'll talk more about databases and scalability in chapter 11.

4.5.5 *What did we achieve?*

We have added a database to our application. We now have two different methods at our disposal to manage our application's data: we can store files in external cloud storage and we can store data in a database. We made good use of Docker Compose to run an application composed of multiple containers, and we upgraded our application to two microservices and a database.

We have hidden our storage provider behind a video-storage microservice. Its job is to retrieve videos from storage. The abstraction we put in place allows us to easily change our storage provider later without much disruption to our application.

We created a database server and added a database for use by our video-streaming microservice. We are following the rule that each microservice should have its own database, and in the future, we can easily add more databases to our server and continue to satisfy this rule.

We have also briefly seen how one microservice can communicate with another. The HTTP GET request received by the video-streaming microservice was forwarded to the video-storage microservice. This is the first and simplest form of communication that one microservice can use to request or delegate tasks to another. In the next chapter, we'll more deeply explore this and other methods of communication between microservices. In addition, we'll further extend our skills with Docker Compose and learn how to apply automated live reload to our entire microservices application.

4.6   *Docker Compose review*

Throughout this chapter, we have seen increasing value from Docker Compose, using it to help manage the complexity of our growing application on our development workstation. Even when running just a single container, it was useful because it allowed us to capture and record configuration details. At that early stage, it magically turned two commands into one.

As we progressed through the chapter, we added two more containers to our application, and the value of Docker Compose became even clearer. We can add as many containers as we want to our application, we can record all their configuration details, and no matter how many containers we have, we can manage these all as an aggregated entity using single commands.

Figure 4.13 shows the simple lifecycle of our application running under Docker Compose. We use the up command to boot our application and all of its microservices. We use the down command to destroy our application and return our development workstation to a clean state.

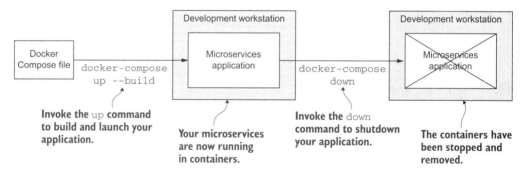

Figure 4.13   The lifecycle of your microservices application when using Docker Compose

Before you finish this chapter, scan table 4.2 for a quick review of the Docker Compose commands you have learned. Put a bookmark on this page so you can return here quickly when you need help working with Docker Compose.

Table 4.2   Review of Docker Compose commands

Command	Description
`docker-compose --version`	Checks that Docker Compose is installed and prints the version number
`docker-compose up --build`	Builds and instantiates an application composed of multiple containers as defined by the Docker Compose file (docker-compose .yaml) in the current working directory
`docker-compose ps`	Lists running containers that are part of the application specified by the Docker Compose file
`docker-compose stop`	Stops all containers in the application, but persists the stopped containers for inspection
`docker-compose down`	Stops and destroys the application, which leaves the development workstation in a clean state

4.7   *Continue your learning*

This chapter skimmed the surface of two big topics. We added a new microservice to our application and connected it to our Azure Storage account. We also added a MongoDB database to our application. Both Azure and MongoDB are technologies that each have a world of their own, so now I'll leave you with some references to dig deeper in these areas:

- *Azure in Action* by Brian H. Prince and Chris Hay (Manning, 2010)
- *Learn Azure in a Month of Lunches* by Iain Foulds (Manning, 2018)
- *MongoDB in Action*, 2nd ed. by Kyle Banker, Peter Bakkum, et al (Manning, 2016)

To learn more about Docker Compose, read the documentation online:

- https://docs.docker.com/compose/
- https://docs.docker.com/compose/compose-file/
- https://docs.docker.com/compose/reference/

In this chapter, we scaled up to multiple microservices using Docker Compose. We also added data management capability to our application. In the next chapter, we will learn in more detail how to make our microservices talk to each other. We'll also improve our skills with Docker Compose and learn how to extend *live reload* so that it works across the entire application.

Summary

- We created a Docker Compose file that specifies the microservices in our application.
- You learned how to use the Docker Compose commands `up` and `down` to run your microservices application in development.

- You learned how to create an Azure storage account and upload videos to it.
- We added a second microservice to our application to retrieve videos from Azure storage.
- We modified our video-streaming microservice to forward requests to the new video-storage microservice.
- We included a MongoDB database in our application to store information about videos.
- We modified our video-streaming microservice to use the database to determine the location of the video.

Communication
between microservices

This chapter covers

- Using live reload at the application level for faster iterations

- Sending direct messages between microservices with HTTP requests

- Sending indirect messages between microservices with RabbitMQ

- Choosing between using direct and indirect messages

A microservices application is composed of many microservices, each looking after its own area of responsibility. Because each microservice by itself is small, simple, and doesn't do much, our microservices must collaborate to create the complex behaviors needed to implement our application's feature set. To work together, our microservices need ways to communicate. If they can't talk to each other, then they won't be able to coordinate their activities, and they won't achieve much.

In this chapter, we examine the different ways that microservices can communicate so that these can collaborate and fulfill the higher-level requirements of the application. In the process, we'll also revisit Docker and Docker Compose to set up live reload for our entire application. Moving forward, that's essential so that we aren't constantly rebuilding and restarting our application as we update our code.

We already saw in earlier chapters that HTTP requests are one way that microservices communicate. In this chapter, we'll expand on using HTTP requests for direct messaging, and we'll also look at using RabbitMQ for indirect messaging. Throughout the chapter, you'll learn how to decide what type of messaging to use for a given situation.

5.1   *New and familiar tools*

This chapter introduces the RabbitMQ software for queuing messages. This will help us decouple our microservices. We'll use the npm package, amqplib, to connect our microservices to RabbitMQ so these can send and receive messages. We'll also revise some familiar tools, and we'll explore in more detail how we can use HTTP requests to send messages and upgrade our development environment to support application-wide live reload.

Table 5.1   New and familiar tools in chapter 5

Tool	Version	Purpose
Docker Compose	1.26.2	Docker Compose lets you configure, build, run, and manage multiple containers at the same time.
HTTP	1.1	Hypertext Transfer Protocol (HTTP) is used to send direct (or synchronous) messages from one microservice to another.
RabbitMQ	3.8.5	RabbitMQ is the message queuing software that we'll use to send indirect (or asynchronous) messages from one microservice to another.
amqplib	0.5.6	This npm package allows us to configure RabbitMQ and to send and receive messages from JavaScript.

5.2   *Getting the code*

To follow along with this chapter, you need to download the code or clone the repository.

- Download a zip file of the code from here:
  https://github.com/bootstrapping-microservices/chapter-5
- You can clone the code using Git like this:
  ```
  git clone https://github.com/bootstrapping-microservices/chapter-5.git
  ```

For help on installing and using Git, see chapter 2. If you have problems with the code, log an issue against the repository in GitHub.

5.3 *Getting our microservices talking*

At this point in the book, we have an application with two microservices: video streaming and video storage. In the previous chapter, we added data storage capability; the video-streaming microservice has a database, and the video-storage microservice uses external cloud storage to store the video files. Figure 5.1 shows what our application looks like now.

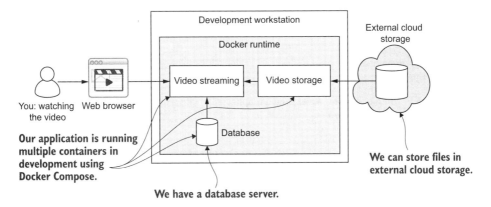

Figure 5.1   We finished the last chapter with two microservices and a database running under Docker Compose on our development workstation. In that chapter, we also added a connection to Azure cloud storage to store our videos.

A microservices application can only be built from services that collaborate to provide the application's features. Our application can't do much if we have microservices that can't communicate! Communication between microservices is therefore a crucial part of building with microservices, and it's essential that we have communication techniques at our disposal.

   Actually, we wouldn't have gotten this far without having already used HTTP requests for communication between the video-streaming and video-storage microservices like we did in chapter 4. We glossed over it there, but it was really quite important. Without it, we would have stumbled at the first hurdle: separating out the streaming and storage capabilities for our application.

> **NOTE**   Our microservices must work together to implement the features of our application, so it's crucial that they be able to communicate for collaboration.

In this chapter, we add a third microservice to our application: the history microservice. The purpose of adding this new microservice is to demonstrate communication among microservices. You can see in figure 5.2 how the video-streaming microservice is sending a stream of messages to the history microservice.

   Figure 5.2 shows conceptually what our application will look like at the end of this chapter, but it doesn't show the full technical details of what we'll add. To get the full picture, we need to know the various styles of communication we can make use of, and

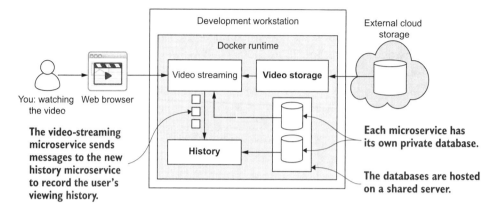

Figure 5.2   In this chapter, we expand our application with a new microservice and explore methods of communication between our microservices.

the technologies that underpin these. Before that though, let's better understand the history microservice.

5.4   *Introducing the history microservice*

We are using the history microservices in this chapter as an example of how microservices can send and receive messages to each other. Actually, this new microservice really does have a proper place in FlixTube, and as the name suggests, it records our user's viewing history.

There are multiple ways our application can make use of this history. For starters, our user might want to look at their own history to remember a video they watched in the past. They might like to resume watching a video later, or we might use it to provide recommendations for other users.

To keep the examples in this chapter simple, we'll drop out the video-storage microservice from the last chapter, which simplifies the video-streaming microservice. In fact, for our starting point in this chapter, we'll revert back to an earlier version of the video-streaming microservice that has the example video baked into its Docker image. We'll use the video-streaming microservice like it was after chapter 3. This simplification is just while we get our heads around the communication techniques. After this chapter, we'll reinstate the video-storage microservice and restore the video-streaming microservice to its former glory.

The message we'll transmit between microservices is the *viewed* message. This is how the video-streaming microservice informs the history microservice that the user has watched a video. Figure 5.3 shows you what the history microservice is doing. It receives a stream of messages from the video-streaming microservice, and it records them in its own database.

We haven't yet discussed the styles of messaging we could use—that's coming soon. For the moment, know that we have multiple techniques we can use to send the

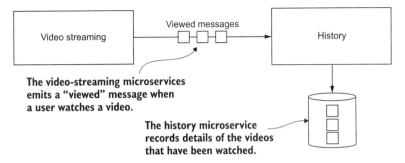

The video-streaming microservices emits a "viewed" message when a user watches a video.

The history microservice records details of the videos that have been watched.

Figure 5.3 As a way to explore communication methods, we'll have the video-streaming microservice send a viewed message to the history microservice to record our user's viewing history.

viewed message. Through this chapter, we'll explore our options, and we can decide later which one is best suited for this particular situation. Before that though, let's upgrade our development environment for faster development cycles.

5.5   *Live reload for fast iterations*

In section 2.4, we talked about our philosophy of development and how small, fast increments are essential for a tight feedback loop and for maintaining a fast development pace. In chapter 2, when directly running our first microservice under Node.js, we were able to use the npm package, nodemon, to make our microservice *live reload*. This means our microservice automatically reloads when we make changes to its code. Having an efficient live reload mechanism is even more important at the application level than it is at the microservice level. That's because building and booting up the whole application is much slower than it is for each individual microservice.

In chapter 3, we used Docker and began to "bake" the code for our microservice into the Docker image. Docker is an incredibly useful way for us to package, publish, and deploy our microservices. That's why we use it, even though we've yet to see the deploy part of this puzzle. To see deployment in action, however, we need a production environment (which is coming in chapter 6) and by chapter 7, we'll see our Docker images deployed to production.

In chapter 4, we used Docker Compose in our development environment as a convenient way to structure and manage our growing application. This is all well and good, but unfortunately, in transitioning from direct use of Node.js to running our microservices in Docker containers, we lost our ability to automatically reload our code.

Because we are baking our code into our Docker images, we aren't able to change it afterward! This is great for production because, for security reasons, we really don't want any *man-in-the-middle* able to mess with that code. The problem now is that during development, we don't want to constantly rebuild our images and reboot our application to include updated code. Doing this is quite slow. And for repeated rebuilds and restarts, the time really adds up, especially as our application grows in size.

NOTE Not being able to quickly update the code in a running application is a terrible thing for our development process and can be a huge drain on our productivity. We'll address this early and find a way to restore our live reload capability.

In this section, we'll upgrade our Docker Compose file to support sharing code between our development workstation and our containers. Figure 5.4 shows you how the source code directory for the new history microservice is shared from our development workstation into the microservice's container.

Again, we'll use nodemon for this, and we'll use it across the board for all our microservices. It automatically restarts each microservice when the code changes. This configuration might seem onerous to put in place, but it really is worthwhile to get this right because it's going to have a big impact on our pace of development!

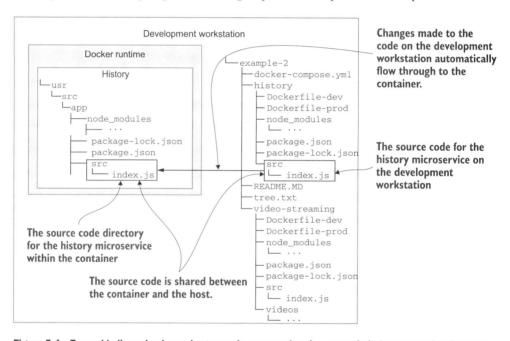

Figure 5.4   To enable live reload on a larger scale, we synchronize our code between our development workstation and the container so that changes to the code automatically propagate through into the container.

5.5.1 Creating a stub for the history microservice

We'll create the live reload configuration only for the new history microservice, but after that, we'll need to apply this same configuration to each and every microservice. This way live reload is supported for all the microservices in our application.

Before we get started, read through listing 5.1 and familiarize yourself with the newly born history microservice. This doesn't do anything yet. It's just a stub and is waiting to have features added. Once we have live reload working for this microservice, we'll be able to boot our application using Docker Compose. Then, we'll make live updates and incremental changes to evolve this new microservice without having to restart the application.

Listing 5.1 A stub for the history microservice (chapter-5/example-1/history/src/index.js)

```
const express = require("express");

function setupHandlers(app) {

}

function startHttpServer() {
    return new Promise(resolve => {
        const app = express();
        setupHandlers(app);

        const port = process.env.PORT &&
        ➥ parseInt(process.env.PORT) || 3000;
        app.listen(port, () => {
            resolve();
        });
    });
}

function main() {
    console.log("Hello world!");

    return startHttpServer();
}

main()
    .then(() => console.log("Microservice online."))
    .catch(err => {
        console.error("Microservice failed to start.");
        console.error(err && err.stack || err);
    });
```

This is a stub microservice. Later, we'll add HTTP routes and message handlers here!

5.5.2 *Augmenting the microservice for live reload*

We don't need to do anything else to the basic code for our microservice, other than what we already learned in chapter 2, where we set up our first microservice and installed nodemon for live reload. Each microservice needs nodemon installed like this:

```
npm install --save-dev nodemon
```

The npm package, nodemon, is what we'll use to watch our code and to automatically restart our microservice when the code changes. The package.json file for the microservice includes an npm script called start:dev, according to the convention we started in chapter 2. You can see what this looks like in listing 5.2.

Listing 5.2   Setting up package.json for live reload with nodemon (chapter-5/example-1/history/package.json)

```
{
  "name": "history",
  "version": "1.0.0",
  "description": "",
  "main": "./src/index.js",
  "scripts": {
    "start": "node ./src/index.js",
    "start:dev":
      ➥ "nodemon --legacy-watch ./src/index.js"   ⟵
  },
  "keywords": [],
  "author": "",
  "license": "MIT",
  "dependencies": {
    "express": "^4.17.1"
  },
  "devDependencies": {
    "nodemon": "^1.19.1"
  }
}
```

Uses nodemon to enable live reload for this microservice. When the code changes, nodemon automatically restarts the microservice.

With the start:dev npm script in place, we can run our microservice like this:

```
npm run start:dev
```

This invokes nodemon for our microservice like this:

```
nodemon --legacy-watch ./src/index.js
```

Obviously, you could always type out the full nodemon command, but using `npm run start:dev` is shorter, and it's always the same for all our microservices, assuming that we apply the convention to each and every microservice. If you just started the history microservice, now exit with Ctrl-C. Soon, we'll run our entire application again using Docker Compose.

You are probably wondering why I used the `--legacy-watch` argument with nodemon. I used this argument because I often run Docker and Docker Compose under a Linux virtual machine (VM). It's a convenient way to work with Linux on your Windows Home PC. (Prior to WSL2, Windows Home wasn't capable of directly running Docker.)

The `--legacy-watch` argument disables the filesystem watch and, instead, uses a frequent polling mechanism to monitor for code changes. If you do your development on a VM, you need this because the automatic file watch required by live reload doesn't translate changes through from the host operating system.

If you are not doing your development under a VM, you can safely remove the `--legacy-watch` argument and your live reload will work with slightly better performance. You can read more about using VMs for development in appendix A.

5.5.3 *Splitting our Dockerfile for development and production*

In chapter 2, we talked about being able to run our microservices in either development mode or production mode. We made this distinction so that we can optimize separately for the differing needs of development and production. In this section, you'll see this separation start to come to fruition.

> **NOTE** At this point, we'll create separate Dockerfiles for our development and production modes. In each case, our needs differ. For development, we prioritize fast iteration. For production, we prioritize performance and security.

For all microservices, henceforth, we'll create not just one but two Dockerfiles. We now need one for development and another for production. We'll call the development one Dockerfile-dev and the production one Dockerfile-prod.

These names are chosen to avoid confusion. Naming is so important in software development that we should aim to select clear names to help avoid ambiguity. We are separating our Dockefiles at this point so that we can enable live reload in development. That isn't something that we want to be enabled in production!

Listing 5.3 shows a production Dockerfile for the new history microservice. There's nothing new here as this is a fairly standard Node.js Dockerfile. It's similar to the Dockerfile we created in chapter 3.

Listing 5.3 Creating the production Dockerfile (chapter-5/example-1/history/ Dockerfile-prod)

We use the alpine Linux image for production because it makes the image for our microservice much smaller.

```
FROM node:12.18.1-alpine

WORKDIR /usr/src/app                  Installs just the production dependencies
COPY package*.json ./
                                      Copies the source code into the image.
RUN npm install --only=production     We can say that the code is baked into
COPY ./src ./src                      the image.

CMD npm start            Starts the microservice in production mode
```

We won't actually make use of the production Dockerfiles in this chapter, but we'll definitely need these in chapter 7, when we deploy to our production environment. It's a good idea to maintain our development and production Dockerfiles side by side so that the development version doesn't get too far ahead of the production one.

Listing 5.4 shows the development Dockerfile for the history microservice. Read through it and compare it to the production Dockerfile in listing 5.3. Notice the differences between development and production for yourself.

Listing 5.4   Creating the dev Dockerfile (chapter-5/example-1/history/Dockerfile-dev)

Instead of the alpine version, we could choose to use the non-alpine version of Linux here. A non-alpine distribution is bigger, but it has more debugging tools that can be handy during development.

```
FROM node:12.18.1-alpine

WORKDIR /usr/src/app
COPY package*.json ./

CMD npm config set cache-min 9999999 && \

    npm install && \

    npm run start:dev
```

Copies the package.json file into the image. Note that we don't copy the code into the image.

Enables caching for npm installs, making subsequent npm installs faster

Does the npm install when the container starts. This means we can make use of npm caching so it's much faster to install at container startup than if we installed it during the build process.

Starts the microservice in development mode, using nodemon for live reload

Did you pick up the differences between the two different Dockerfiles? In listing 5.3, we installed production only dependencies, whereas in listing 5.4, we installed all dependencies, including our dev dependencies. But did you spot the most important change? In listing 5.3, we baked our code into the production Docker image using the COPY instruction:

```
COPY ./src ./src
```

That command copies our code into the image. What's most interesting in the development version of the Dockerfile is what's missing. You'll note there is *no* COPY instruction for our code in listing 5.4 (although there is one for the package.json), and we are, thus, excluding our code from the development Docker image! If we bake our code into the image, then we can't easily change it later. If we can't change our code, then we can't use live reload.

But if we aren't copying code into our development image, then how will it get into the container? We'll find an answer to this in the next section. For now, we still have one more big difference to look at between our development and production Dockerfiles.

Note the CMD instruction that specifies how to start our microservice within the container. In the production Dockerfile, we simply start the microservice using the npm start convention that was described in chapter 2:

```
CMD npm start
```

The CMD instruction in the development Dockerfile is different and does a lot more work:

```
CMD npm config set cache-min 9999999 && \
    npm install && \
    npm run start:dev
```

This command is separated over three lines using the backslash (\) line continuation character. The first line configures the npm cache, and the second installs the npm. The third line starts the microservice.

In the production Dockerfile, we invoke `npm install` during the Docker build process, which means our dependencies are baked into the image, just as they should be in production. In the development version, though, we do the `npm install` at container startup. The reason for the difference in development is for better performance in doing subsequent rebuilds.

The `npm install` can take significant time. When we do it at container startup, we are able to cache the npm packages on the host operating system. That's why we configured the cache on the first line. Caching our npm packages in this way makes subsequent npm installs much faster, and this in turn, makes container startup faster. We'll learn more about how this works in the next section.

The third line of the `CMD` instruction in the development Dockerfile is what actually starts the microservice. It invokes `npm script start:dev` to start our microservice in development mode with live reload enabled.

5.5.4 *Updating the Docker Compose file for live reload*

The final part of getting our application-wide live reload working is to make some necessary changes to our Docker Compose file to share our code and the npm cache between the host operating system and the containers. In this section, we use Docker volumes to share the filesystem between our development workstation and the container. This means we can edit code in Visual Studio (VS) Code and see the changes appear almost immediately in our microservice running in the application under Docker Compose.

Listing 5.5 is an extract from the example-1 Docker Compose file that shows the configuration for our new history microservice. This is similar to the Docker Compose files we created in chapter 4, but there are some differences and new additions.

> **Listing 5.5 Updating the Docker Compose file for live reload (extract from chapter-5/ example-1/docker-compose.yaml)**

```
version: '3'
services:

    # ... other services defined here ...

    history:                          Defines the container     Defines volumes that are shared
        image: history                for our new history       between the host operating
        build:                        microservice              system and the container
            context: ./history
            dockerfile: Dockerfile-dev
        container_name: history                                 Shares the npm cache from the host
                                                                 to the container. This is what allows
        volumes:                                                 npm modules to be cached, making
            - /tmp/history/npm-cache:/root/.npm:z                subsequent installs faster.
```

Uses the development version of the Dockerfile

```
      - ./history/src:/usr/src/app/src:z
    ports:
      - "4002:80"
    environment:
      - PORT=80
      - NODE_ENV=development
    restart: "no"
```

> **Shares the source code directly from the host to the container. You can make changes on your development workstation (e.g., using VS Code), and those changes are automatically visible within the container.**

The first thing that is new in listing 5.5 is that we now use `Dockerfile-dev`, which is the development version of our Dockerfile. I mentioned back in chapter 4 that we could omit the `dockerfile` field and that it would default to `Dockerfile`. In chapter 4, we didn't leave it at the default value; instead, we explicitly set it to `Dockerfile`. I indicated that we'd need to explicitly set this in the near future. Well, this is where we are at now, and we are explicitly setting it to `Dockerfile-dev` to use the development version of our Dockerfile.

The next thing that is new is the addition of the `volumes` field, where we create some Docker volumes to connect the filesystem on our development workstation with the filesystem of the container. This links our source code directly into the container. It's the reason why we didn't bake our code directly into the image.

To share the code, we use one Docker volume. The other volume creates a shared directory for the npm cache. This allows npm packages that are installed in the container to be cached on the host operating system so that, if we destroy and recreate the container, subsequent npm installs are faster because we have retained the cache outside of the container.

In case you were wondering about the z flag used in the volume configuration in listing 5.5, that simply indicates to Docker that the volume is to be shared (potentially among multiple containers). If you like, you can read more about it here:

https://docs.docker.com/storage/bind-mounts/

This has been quite a lot to take in, and so far, it's only for the history microservice! We'll need to make these changes to all our microservices. Fortunately, we can just use the same pattern and apply it to each microservice as follows:

- Install nodemon for each microservice.
- Update package.json and implement the start:dev script to start the microservice with nodemon (as in listing 5.3).
- Create development and production versions of our Dockerfiles. The development Dockerfile should not copy the code into the image (as in listing 5.4).
- Do the `npm install` on container startup; only for development, not production (this is for performance, as in listing 5.4).
- Update the Docker Compose file so that it uses the development Dockerfile (as in listing 5.5).
- Add Docker volumes to the Docker Compose file so that the source code and npm cache are shared into the container (as in listing 5.5).

I've gone ahead and done this already for all examples in the chapter 5 repository so you don't have to worry about it. But you should at least start example-1 and then make some code changes to the history microservice so that you can see live reload in action! So let's do that now.

5.5.5 *Trying out live reload*

Enough looking at code listings! It's time to see live reload in action so you can truly appreciate how useful it is. Open a terminal and change directory to the example-1 subdirectory under the chapter-5 code repository. Then use Docker Compose to start the application:

```
docker-compose up --build
```

This example contains the simplified video-streaming microservice and the new stub history microservice. Check the output from Docker Compose. You should see "Hello world!" printed out by the stub history microservice as it starts up. To test live reload, we'll change the message that is printed by the history microservice:

1 Open the example-1 directory in VS Code.
2 Find and open the index.js file for the history microservice.
3 Search for the line of code that prints the "Hello world!" message and change this line of code to print "Hello computer!" instead.
4 Save the index.js file and then switch back to the Docker Compose output.

If you switched over quickly enough, you'll see the history microservice being reloaded and printing your updated message. If you weren't quick enough, you should see that this has already happened. When you do this, note that the video-streaming microservice didn't reload. That's because we didn't change its code. Only the history microservice was updated so only it reloaded.

This is the promise of live reload. We can update our code in quick iterations and receive fast and direct feedback. We don't have to wait to build and start the entire application. Instead, we can *hot reload* the code for each microservice that needs to be updated.

So what happens if we introduce an error in our code? What do we see when a microservice reloads with an error? The error is displayed in the Docker Compose output. We can then correct the error and save the code file. The microservice automatically reloads, and assuming our change actually fixes the error, we should see clean output from the updated microservice.

At this point, I'll actually recommend that you try and break the history microservice to see what happens. Go on. Open the index.js file for it and type some random gibberish that's sure to break it. Save the file and switch back to the Docker Compose output to see the result.

Ask yourself what the error message means and what did I do that caused it? Now I hear you say, "But Ash, we'd like to keep our code working, so why are we trying to break it?"

It's actually good to practice breaking and fixing your code in a controlled and safe environment. That way, when it comes to encountering real problems in the wild, you'll be more experienced and have a better understanding of the error messages and how to deal with these. Spend some time now breaking the code; cause problems and try to have some fun while you're at it.

Forcing a container to restart

Every so often we might want to force a reload of a microservice that hasn't changed. Say the microservice has hung or crashed and is now stuck. With our live reload system, we can make a container restart simply by changing the code, for example, adding some whitespace and then saving the file.

Actually, we don't even need to go that far. We can simply save the file in VS Code, and that's enough to make the container restart. We don't need to make the change!

If you have access to the `touch` command from your terminal, you can also trigger live reload from the command line for the history microservice as follows:

```
cd chapter-5/example-1
touch history/src/index.js
```

If you don't have live reload set up for a particular container (you only really need live reload for microservices whose code changes frequently), then you can use the Docker Compose `restart` command to make a container restart; for example, to force the history microservice to restart, type

```
docker-compose restart history
```

5.5.6   *Testing production mode in development*

So far, in this chapter, we've split our Dockerfiles into separate files so that we can have different versions for development mode and production mode, but we aren't making use of the production Dockerfiles yet. This will change in chapter 7, when we deploy to production. For now, just be aware that we won't test our application in production mode quite as frequently as we test it during development.

During development, we'll constantly make small incremental code changes and then test that our application still works. Even though we aren't making quite as frequent use of our production Dockerfiles as the development version, we should still keep these updated alongside the development versions. We should also regularly test in production, albeit less frequently than we test in development.

For example, you might be testing in development mode every few minutes as you make code changes. You still want to test production mode, but maybe, you'll only do that every few hours after substantial code changes have been accumulated. The main point is that you also need to test your production Dockerfiles even before you deploy these to production. What you don't want is to unwittingly bank up hidden problems that will only be revealed *after* deployment to production.

You can easily and preemptively solve this problem by testing regularly in production mode on your development workstation. Usually, what I do to make this easier is to have two separate Docker Compose files: one for development and the other for production.

When you invoke Docker Compose, you can use the `-f` argument to specify the Docker Compose file. For instance, if you want to run your application in production mode on your development workstation, you might like to create a separate *production* version of your Docker Compose file and run it like this:

```
docker-compose -f docker-compose-prod.yml up --build
```

You can get away with having a single Docker Compose file that is parameterized by an environment variable, but generally, I keep separate versions for testing development and production. That's because I like to have my production Docker Compose file mimic the real production environment as much as feasible. Also, usually my development version will replace various microservices with mock versions for easier and faster testing.

We'll talk about mocking microservices in chapter 9. And in chapter 8, we'll cover automated testing, which is another thing that can enhance your productivity.

5.5.7　*What have we achieved?*

In section 5.5, we configured our microservices for live reload. We started with the history microservice and applied the same pattern to the video-streaming microservice. From now on, we'll use this for all our microservices.

We did this because it takes significant time to build and start our application. We don't want to build and restart our application for each line of code that we change. Instead, we want to be able to quickly change code to experiment and iterate quickly and have the application automatically update itself. Now, we can edit code and our microservices will automatically restart. That's why this is called *live reload*—it reloads automatically while you are coding.

This makes for a very efficient and effective workflow. We can now continuously evolve our microservices application while receiving a constant stream of feedback. Browse the code in example-1 and make sure you understand how the live reload configuration is applied across the entire application.

5.6　*Methods of communication for microservices*

After that interlude of upgrading our development environment to support application-wide live reload, let's now return to the main topic of this chapter: exploring mechanisms for communication between microservices. But before we dive into the technology for communication, we'll start with a high-level overview of the two styles of communication used by microservices: direct messaging and indirect messaging, also commonly known as *synchronous* and *asynchronous* communication.

I prefer to use the terms direct and indirect messaging rather than synchronous and asynchronous messaging because the words "synchronous" and "asynchronous" have a different meaning in normal computer programming. Also, the concept of asynchronous programming, especially, can be difficult to learn and has sent chills down the spines of many aspiring coders. Don't be concerned; we will avoid using the word asynchronous.

5.6.1   *Direct messaging*

Direct messaging simply means that one microservice directly sends a message to another microservice and then receives an immediate and direct response. Direct messaging is used when we'd like one microservice to directly message a particular microservice and immediately invoke an action or task within it.

Direct messaging is also used for triggering a direct action in another microservice. We can also use it to sequence a strict series of behaviors across multiple microservices. You can think of this as sending commands or instructions to another microservice (e.g., *do this* or *do that* and then *tell me* if you were successful).

The recipient microservice can't ignore or avoid the incoming message. If it were to do so, the sender will know about it directly from the response. Figure 5.5 shows how the video-streaming microservice directs the viewed message to the history microservice, which provides a direct and immediate response.

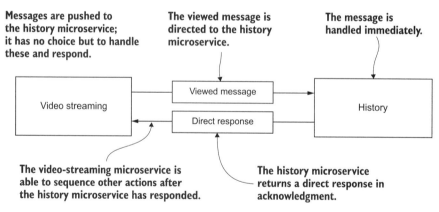

Figure 5.5   A direct message is sent to the history microservice explicitly by its name and is handled immediately.

Direct messaging is often required for certain use cases. It has the major drawback that it requires the tight coupling of the two microservices that are at either end of the communication. Often, we'd prefer to avoid the tight coupling between our microservices, and for that reason, we'll make frequent use of indirect messaging instead of direct messaging.

5.6.2 *Indirect messaging*

Indirect messaging introduces an intermediary between the endpoints in the communication process. We add a middleman to sit between our microservices. For that reason, the two parties of the communication don't actually have to know about each other. This style of communication results in a much looser coupling between our microservices. It means two things:

- *Messages are sent via an intermediary so that both sender and receiver of the messages don't know which other microservice is involved.* In the case of the sender, it doesn't even know if any other microservice will receive the message at all!
- *Because the receiver doesn't know which microservice has sent the message, it can't send a direct reply.* This means that this style of communication can't be applied in situations where a direct response is required for confirming success or failure.

We should use indirect messages when the sending microservice doesn't care if any subsequent action has been taken or not. We can also use it to broadcast messages to the entire application (e.g., a notification of an important event that other microservices would like to know about).

> **NOTE** We use indirect messaging to announce important events that don't need a direct response. This kind of messaging allows a more flexible communication structure than direct messages and makes for less coupling between our microservices.

Figure 5.6 shows how the video-streaming microservice (on the left) sends an indirect message through a message queue (the intermediary) to the history microservice (on the right). Note that there is no direct connection between the video-streaming and history microservices. This is why we can say they are *loosely coupled.*

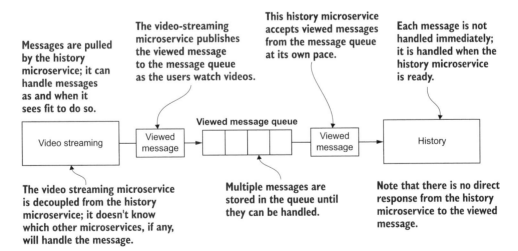

Figure 5.6 An indirect message isn't explicitly sent to a microservice; instead, the message is placed in a queue and can be handled later.

Indirect messaging can help us to build flexible messaging architectures to solve many complicated communication problems. Unfortunately, with this flexibility comes increased complexity. And as your application grows, you will find it more difficult to map the communication pathways precisely because these are not direct and, therefore, not as obvious. With this overview of direct and indirect messaging out of the way, we can dive head first into actually trying out each of these communication methods.

5.7   *Direct messaging with HTTP*

In the previous chapter, we used HTTP for data retrieval, which retrieved our streaming video from storage. In this chapter, we use HTTP for a different purpose: sending direct messages from one microservice to another.

> **NOTE**   Messages sent with HTTP requests have direct responses. We can know immediately if the handling of the message succeeded or failed.

Specifically, in this section, we'll use HTTP POST requests to send messages directly from the video-streaming microservice to the history microservice. Figure 5.7 shows this process.

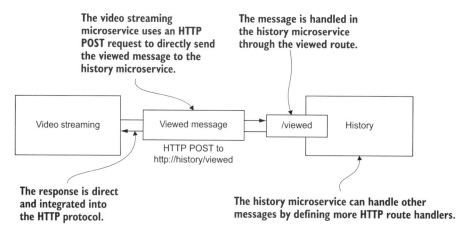

Figure 5.7   An HTTP POST request explicitly targets another microservice by name.

5.7.1   *Why HTTP?*

Hypertext transfer protocol (HTTP) is the language and foundation of the world wide web and is the defacto standard when creating a *web service*. It's well understood by everyone, and it's something we can depend on.

HTTP is already ubiquitous for creating representational state transfer (REST) APIs, and we don't need to think too hard about why we should use it. It was made for this kind of thing, and it's supported by every programming language we would care to work with. We also have easy access to huge amounts of learning resources related to it, and ironically, this information will most likely be delivered to us via the HTTP protocol that is underlying the world wide web.

5.7.2 *Directly targeting messages at particular microservices*

Before we can send a message to a microservice, we need a way to locate it. Accompanying HTTP is another internet protocol called *domain name system* (DNS). This gives us a simple and almost automatic means by which to direct messages at microservices using their names.

A key question with microservices communication is how do we direct a message to another microservice? The simplest answer to this question is the ubiquitous DNS, which translates hostnames to IP addresses. This works automatically with Docker Compose (the container name is the hostname) and doesn't require much effort to have it work within our production Kubernetes cluster.

Figure 5.8 shows how we can send an HTTP POST message to a particular hostname. A lookup of the DNS is done automatically when sending an HTTP request, and it translates our hostname to the internet protocol (IP) address of the microservice.

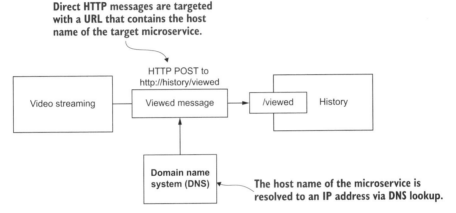

Figure 5.8 HTTP requests are routed through the DNS lookup to translate the hostname of the target microservice to an internet protocol (IP) address.

The IP address is the string of numbers that represents the unique internet location for our microservice. Note that just because it's an IP address doesn't necessarily mean we are talking about the public internet. The IP address, in this case, actually represents a private server that is located in a private network, either operating under the Docker runtime on our development workstation or operating within our production Kubernetes cluster. It is the IP address that we need to direct a message at a recipient using an HTTP request, and DNS operates automatically and almost magically under the hood when we make the request.

Using Docker and Docker Compose for development as we have been doing means that DNS works automatically, and we can rely on it. When we deploy to our production Kubernetes cluster, we'll have some more work to make our microservices accessible via DNS, but we'll address that in chapter 7.

5.7.3   *Sending a message with HTTP POST*

There are two sides to the messaging equation: one microservice sends a message and another receives it. In this section, we examine how to send a message using an HTTP POST request.

In section 4.4.2, we looked at an HTTP GET request that was forwarded from one microservice to another. We did that then using the builtin Node.js http library. We'll use that library again to make a request from one microservice to another.

Listing 5.6 is an extract from an updated index.js file from the example-2 video-streaming microservice that shows how to send an HTTP POST message. It implements a new function, `sendViewedMessage`, that sends the viewed message to the history microservice whenever a user starts watching a video.

> **Listing 5.6   Sending a direct message with HTTP POST (extract from chapter-5/ example-2/video-streaming/index.js)**

A helper function that sends the viewed message to the history microservice

```
function sendViewedMessage(videoPath) {         Configures options
    const postOptions = {                       for the HTTP request
        method: "POST",
        headers: {                              Sets the HTTP method to POST
            "Content-Type": "application/json",
        },                                      Sets the content type for the
    };                                          body of the HTTP request

    const requestBody = {
        videoPath: videoPath                    The body of the HTTP request defines the message
    };                                          payload; this is the data we send with the message.

    const req = http.request(        Sends the HTTP request to the history microservice
        "http://history/viewed",
        postOptions                  Sets the URL for the HTTP request, which identifies
    );                               the history microservice and the viewed message

    req.on("close", () => {
        ...
    });                    This function is called when the request completes.

    req.on("error", (err) => {
        ...
    });                    Handles any errors that might have occurred
                                                 Writes the body
    req.write(JSON.stringify(requestBody));      to the request
    req.end();
}            Finalizes the request
```

We call the function `http.request` to create the HTTP POST request. We direct the request to the history microservice using the URL http://history/viewed. This URL incorporates both the hostname (`history` in this case) and the route (`viewed` in this case). It is this combination that identifies the target microservice and the message we send to it.

Separate callback functions handle the success and the failure of the request. It is here where we can detect an error and take subsequent remedial action. Otherwise, if it succeeds, we might want to invoke follow up actions.

5.7.4 Receiving a message with HTTP POST

On the other side of the equation, we receive HTTP POST messages by creating an Express route handler in the receiving microservice. Listing 5.7 shows an extract of the index.js file for the history microservice, which demonstrates this.

The updated `setupHandlers` function adds an HTTP POST handler for the `viewed` route to receive incoming messages. In this listing, we simply store the received messages in the database to keep a record of the viewing history.

Listing 5.7 Receiving a direct message with HTTP POST (extract from chapter-5/example-2/history/index.js)

```
function setupHandlers(app, db) {

    const videosCollection = db.collection("videos");    Handles the viewed
                                                         message received via
    app.post("/viewed", (req, res) => {    ◀──────────  an HTTP POST request
        const videoPath = req.body.videoPath;
        videosCollection
            .insertOne({ videoPath: videoPath })    ◀──── Records the view in the database
            .then(() => {
                console.log(`Added video ${videoPath} to history.`);
                res.sendStatus(200);
            })
            .catch(err => {
                console.error(`Error adding video ${videoPath}
                 to history.`);
                console.error(err && err.stack || err);
                res.sendStatus(500);
            });
    });
}
```

Extracts data from the JSON body of the HTTP request (annotation pointing to `const videoPath = req.body.videoPath;`)

Did you notice in the HTTP POST handler how we access the body of the request through `req.body`? We treated the body of the request as the message *payload*. The body variable was automatically parsed from the JSON format because we used the body-parser middleware for Express, installed like this:

```
npm install --save body-parser
```

If you are interested in seeing how the body-parser middleware is added to Express, look at the code file chapter-5/example-2/history/index.js.

5.7.5   *Testing the updated application*

Now it's time to test our latest code and see for yourself how this kind of messaging operates. Open a terminal, change to the example-2 directory, and start the application in the usual way:

```
docker-compose up --build
```

If you get any errors about containers already created, it might be because you left the previous example running. When moving on from each example, be sure to shut it down using

```
docker-compose down
```

Wait for the microservices to come online and then point your browser to http://localhost:4001/video. The test video will play.

Switch back to the terminal to see the Docker Compose output. You should see output confirming that the video-streaming microservice sent a viewed message, followed up by some text that shows the history microservice received the message.

At this point, we can directly check to make sure that the "view" was stored in the database. You'll need a database viewer installed. If you have Robo 3T installed from chapter 4, you can use that.

Connect your database viewer to the database (connect on localhost:4000 as the port that is configured in the Docker Compose file), then look at the videos collection of the history database and confirm that a new record is created each time you refresh your browser. Checking the database is a practical way to test the end result of this code.

5.7.6   *Sequencing direct messages*

A potential benefit of direct messaging is the ability to have one controller microservice that can orchestrate complex sequences of behavior across multiple other microservices. Because direct messages have a direct response, this allows a single microservice to coordinate or orchestrate the activities of multiple other microservices.

The reason this type of messaging is called *synchronous communication* is that we are able to coordinate messages as shown in figure 5.9. In the figure, Microservice A is coordinating the activities of the other microservices.

> **NOTE**   Direct messaging can be useful to coordinate behaviors in an explicit way or well-defined order.

With direct messages, it's easy to follow the code and understand the sequence of messages. You'll see in a moment that tracing the sequence of indirect messages isn't as easy.

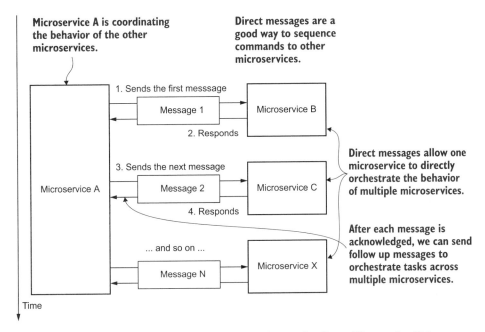

Figure 5.9   Direct messaging allows one controller microservice (here, Microservice A) to orchestrate complex behaviors across multiple other microservices.

5.7.7   *What have we achieved?*

In section 5.7, we explored using HTTP POST requests to directly send a viewed message from microservice to microservice. This is called *direct messaging* because we can direct these messages to particular microservices by their name. We can also know immediately if the message was handled successfully or if it failed.

It's best to think of this type of message more as a command or a call to action and less as a notification. Due to the synchronous nature of direct messages, we can sequence multiple coordinated messages. This is useful when we want a controller microservice that orchestrates complex behaviors in other microservices.

Although direct messages can be useful and are sometimes necessary, these also have some major downsides. For a start, we can only target a single other microservice at a time. Direct messages, therefore, don't work easily when we'd like to have a single message received by multiple recipients.

In addition, direct messages are a point of high coupling between microservices. Sometimes high coupling is necessary, but we'd prefer to avoid it where possible. The ability to centrally orchestrate multiple microservices from a controller microservice might seem like an advantage, and it certainly can make it easier to work out what's going on in your application.

But the biggest problem is that this creates a single point of failure for what could be a large and complex operation. What happens if the controlling microservice crashes while in the middle of the orchestration? Our application might now be in an inconsistent state, and it may have lost data. The problems that arise from direct messaging can be solved with indirect messaging, and that's why we now turn to RabbitMQ.

5.8   *Indirect messaging with RabbitMQ*

Now that we have a handle on using HTTP POST requests for direct messages, it's time to look at indirect messaging, which can help us decouple our microservices. On the one hand, it can make the architecture of our application more difficult to understand. On the other hand, it has many positive side effects for security, scalability, extensibility, reliability, and performance.

> **NOTE**   RabbitMQ allows us to decouple message senders from message receivers. A sender doesn't know which, if any, other microservices will handle a message.

Figure 5.10 shows the structure of our application after the addition of a RabbitMQ server. The video-streaming microservice is no longer directly coupled to the history microservice. Instead, it is publishing its viewed messages to a message queue. The history microservice then pulls messages from the queue in its own time.

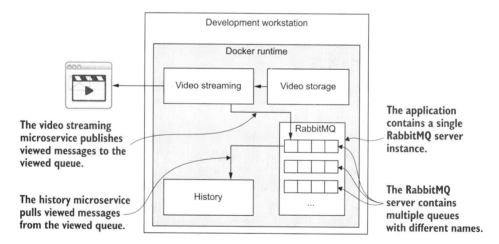

Figure 5.10   Using RabbitMQ to indirectly send messages to other microservices through message queues

5.8.1   *Why RabbitMQ?*

RabbitMQ is well known and established software for queuing messages. It is in common use by many companies, and it's my go-to solution for indirect messaging. RabbitMQ is stable and mature. It was developed over a decade ago, and among other protocols, it implements the Advanced Message Queueing Protocol (AMQP), which is an open standard for message-broker communication.

> **NOTE** RabbitMQ is well-known for indirect communication between micros-
> ervices, and it allows for complex and flexible messaging architectures.

RabbitMQ has libraries for all the popular programming languages, so you'll have no
problems using it whatever your tech stack. We are using Node.js, so we'll use the
amqplib library available on the npm registry. RabbitMQ is open source and fairly easy
to get started with. You can find the code for the server here:

https://github.com/rabbitmq/rabbitmq-server

5.8.2   *Indirectly targeting messages to microservices*

With indirect messaging, we aren't directly targeting any particular microservice, but
we do still need to direct our messages to something. And that something will be a
RabbitMQ server. In that server is either a named queue or a message exchange. The
combination of queues and exchanges gives us a lot of flexibility in how we structure
our messaging architecture.

> **NOTE** The message sender uses DNS to resolve the IP address of the RabbitMQ
> server. It then communicates with it to publish a message on a particular named
> queue or exchange. The receiver also uses DNS to locate the RabbitMQ server
> and communicate with it to retrieve the message from the queue. At no point
> do the sender and receiver communicate directly.

To publish a message to a queue or an exchange, we must first add a RabbitMQ server
to our application. Then we can use the AMQP code library (called amqplib) to send
and receive messages.

Under the hood, DNS resolves the RabbitMQ hostname to an IP address. Now,
rather than directing our message to a particular microservice, as we did when sending messages via HTTP POST requests, we are instead directing these to a particular
queue or exchange on our RabbitMQ server with the server located by DNS.

The transferal of an indirect message is conducted in two parts, so I'll use two dia-
grams to explain it. We'll first consider using queues, and later we'll look at using an
exchange. Figure 5.11 shows the video-streaming microservice *pushing* its message to
the *viewed* queue. Then in figure 5.12, we can see the history microservice *pulling* the
message from the queue.

I've used the verbs *pushing* and *pulling* here because that's a good way to visualize
this transaction. Earlier with HTTP POST, we can imagine the video-streaming microservice is pushing its message onto the history microservice, which has no choice in
the matter. The message is forced on to the history microservice with no regard for
whether it actually has the capacity to handle it.

With indirect messaging, more control is given to the history microservice. It now
pulls messages from the queue when it is ready to do so. When it is overwhelmed and
has no capacity to accept new messages, it is free to just ignore these, letting those pile
up in the queue until it is able to handle them.

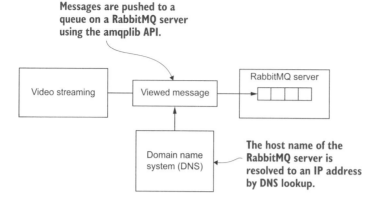

Figure 5.11   A message is sent by pushing it into a RabbitMQ queue.

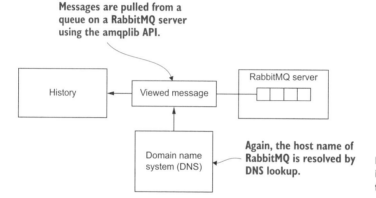

Figure 5.12   A message is received by pulling it from a RabbitMQ queue.

5.8.3   *Creating a RabbitMQ server*

Let's add a RabbitMQ server to our application. Believe it or not, RabbitMQ is programmed in the Erlang language. There might have been a day when it was difficult to set up, but not anymore! These days, it's a no brainer, thanks to the skills we have already learned with Docker and Docker Compose.

Listing 5.8 is an extract from the example-3 Docker Compose file that shows adding a RabbitMQ server to our application. This is another example of instantiating a container from an image on Docker Hub, as we did in chapter 4 for our MongoDB database.

Listing 5.8   Adding a RabbitMQ server to the Docker Compose file (extract from chapter-5/example-3/docker-compose.yaml)

```
version: '3'
services:

    # ... other services defined here ...
                                                    Defines the container that
                                                    hosts our RabbitMQ server
    rabbit:
```

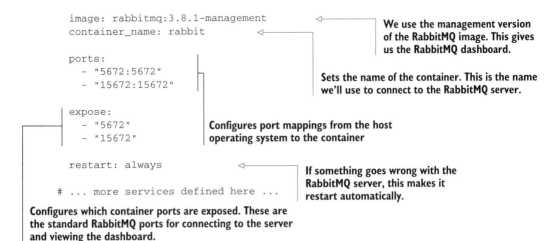

```
image: rabbitmq:3.8.1-management
container_name: rabbit

ports:
  - "5672:5672"
  - "15672:15672"

expose:
  - "5672"
  - "15672"

restart: always

# ... more services defined here ...
```

We use the management version of the RabbitMQ image. This gives us the RabbitMQ dashboard.

Sets the name of the container. This is the name we'll use to connect to the RabbitMQ server.

Configures port mappings from the host operating system to the container

If something goes wrong with the RabbitMQ server, this makes it restart automatically.

Configures which container ports are exposed. These are the standard RabbitMQ ports for connecting to the server and viewing the dashboard.

5.8.4 *Investigating the RabbitMQ dashboard*

You might have already noticed in listing 5.8 how the RabbitMQ ports were configured. Port 5672 is the port number we'll soon use with amqplib to send and receive messages through RabbitMQ. We'll use port 15672 to access the RabbitMQ management dashboard.

> **NOTE** RabbitMQ's dashboard is a great way to learn about how RabbitMQ works and to better understand the messages that are being passed around your application.

We booted our RabbitMQ server from the image named rabbitmq:3.8.1-management because this one comes with a built-in management dashboard. The dashboard is pictured in figure 5.13 and serves as a graphical way to explore message flow in our application. Let's have a look at that now. Start the application for yourself so you can try it out!

Open a terminal and change to the example-3 directory. Start the application in the normal way (if nothing else, I'm going to make sure you remember this command!):

```
docker-compose up --build
```

In addition to the output from the database and your microservices, you should also see a stream of output from your RabbitMQ server. Give it some time to start and then point your web browser at http://localhost:15672/. You can login with the default user name, *guest*, and the default password, *guest*.

You should now see the RabbitMQ dashboard. But unlike figure 5.13, you won't yet see any queues or exchanges. I took the figure's screenshot after the viewed queue was created. We'll trigger the queue to be created in a moment and then you can come back to the dashboard to see what it looks like.

The RabbitMQ management dashboard
is a great way to debug the messages
being sent within your application.

Click here to view
your message queues.

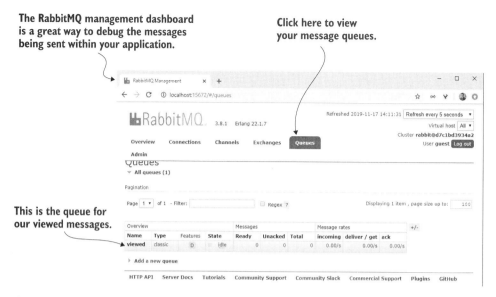

This is the queue for
our viewed messages.

Figure 5.13   The RabbitMQ management dashboard

The RabbitMQ dashboard is a useful tool for debugging. I believe it's always better to be able to visualize what's happening rather than just assuming we know what's happening. The dashboard is one of those great visual tools that make it obvious what our application is actually doing!

You might note that we don't have to include the RabbitMQ dashboard. We could, instead, use the image rabbitmq:3.8.1. This is a version of the image that doesn't include the dashboard. This might be your preference if you are building a lean, mean production application or if you have particular security concerns. But generally, I prefer to leave the dashboard in place for production (behind a private network, of course) because it's so valuable to have these tools to help us understand what's happening in our production environment.

5.8.5   *Connecting our microservice to the message queue*

With our RabbitMQ server in place, we can now update our microservices to connect to it. If you are coding this from scratch, you must first install the amqplib npm package into each microservice that needs to connect to RabbitMQ:

```
npm install --save amqplib
```

If you are running the code from example-3 directly under Node.js, you must first install all dependencies:

```
npm install
```

The next listing is an extract from the index.js file for the history microservice. It shows how we make the connection to the RabbitMQ server.

Listing 5.9   Connecting to the RabbitMQ server (extract from chapter-5/example-3/ history/index.js)

```
// ... other package imports here ...
                                         Imports the amqplib library. This is the
const amqp = require("amqplib");    ⊲──┘ API for talking to the RabbitMQ server.

const RABBIT = process.env.RABBIT;  ⊲──── Gets the URI for connecting to RabbitMQ

// ... code omitted here ...

function connectRabbit() {    ⊲──── A helper function to create the connection

    return amqp.connect(RABBIT)         ⊲──── Connects to the RabbitMQ server
        .then(messagingConnection => {
            return messagingConnection
            ➥ .createChannel();    ⊲──── Creates a RabbitMQ messaging channel
        });
}


// ... code omitted here ...

function main() {
    return connectDb()    ⊲──── Connects to the database
        .then(db => {
            return connectRabbit()    ⊲──── Connects to the RabbitMQ server
                .then(messageChannel => {
                    return startHttpServer(db,
                    ➥ messageChannel);    ⊲──── Starts the HTTP server
                });
        });
}

main()
    .then(() => console.log("Microservice online."))
    .catch(err => {
        console.error("Microservice failed to start.");
        console.error(err && err.stack || err);
    });
```

One of the most important parts of listing 5.9 and listing 5.10 (which follows) is how the RABBIT environment variable configures the connection to the RabbitMQ server. Listing 5.10 is an extract from the example-3 Docker Compose file. It sets the RABBIT environment variable to include the user name (guest), the password (also guest), the hostname for the server (rabbit), and the port number (5672) for the connection.

```
version: '3'
services:

  # ... other services defined here ...

  history:
    image: history
    build:
      context: ./history
      dockerfile: Dockerfile-dev
    container_name: history
    volumes:
      - /tmp/history/npm-cache:/root/.npm:z
      - ./history/src:/usr/src/app/src:z
    ports:
      - "4002:80"
    environment:
      - PORT=80
      - RABBIT=amqp://guest:guest@rabbit:5672     <--| Sets the URI for
      - DBHOST=mongodb://db:27017                      connecting to RabbitMQ
      - DBNAME=history
      - NODE_ENV=development
    depends_on:                       The history microservice now
      - db                            depends on the rabbit container
      - rabbit           <----------  that we defined in listing 5.8.
    restart: "no"
```

There's yet another piece to this puzzle that may not have occurred to you until you try and start this version of our application. The RabbitMQ server is fairly heavyweight, and it takes time to start up and get ready to accept connections. Our tiny microservices, on the other hand, are lightweight and ready in just moments.

What happens when our microservice attempts the connection to RabbitMQ and it's not ready yet? It will error and abort! We now have a problem because we have startup dependencies in our application that need to be resolved in a particular order.

To be a fault-tolerant and well-behaved microservice, it should really wait until the RabbitMQ server is ready before it tries to connect. Better yet, if RabbitMQ ever goes down (say because we are upgrading it), we'd like our microservices to handle the disconnection and automatically reconnect as soon as possible. We'd like it to work that way, but that's more complicated. For the moment, we'll solve this with a simple workaround. In chapter 10, we'll learn a more sophisticated way to handle this.

What's the simplest way to solve this problem? We'll add an extra command to our Dockerfile that delays our microservice until the RabbitMQ server is ready. We'll use the handy wait-port command installed using npm:

```
npm install --save wait-port
```

Listing 5.11 shows the history microservice's updated Dockerfile with the addition of the `wait-port` command. We use this to delay the start of the microservice until after RabbitMQ has started.

Listing 5.11　Updated Dockerfile for the history microservice, which waits for RabbitMQ (chapter-5/example-3/history/Dockerfile-dev)

```
FROM node:10.15.2-alpine

WORKDIR /usr/src/app
COPY package*.json ./

CMD npm config set cache-min 9999999 && \
    npm install && \
    npx wait-port rabbit:5672 && \      ◁
    npm run start:dev
```

> Uses npx to invoke the locally installed wait-port command to wait until the server at hostname rabbit is accepting connections on port 5672

> After wait-port has completed, this starts the history microservice

---

At the same time, we should update the production version of the Dockerfile. It's good to keep both versions in sync as we work.

Using `wait-port` is a simple and effective way to get up and running when we first start building our microservices application. It's not very robust though. The startup ordering problem isn't the only problem. We generally want our microservice to be fault-tolerant and able to survive the inevitable outages of other servers and microservices. We'll come back to this in chapter 10.

At this point, you might be wondering why we didn't have this startup order problem in chapter 4 when we started using the MongoDB database? Surely the database also takes time to start up, but we didn't have to wait for it to be ready before we connected to it.

Well, this is simply down to good software engineering in the MongoDB library. It is already programmed for automatic reconnections, so thank the MongoDB engineers for going to this level of effort for you. This should give you some pause for thought. When writing code libraries, a little time considering the perspective of our users translates into a much better experience for them.

5.8.6　*Single-recipient indirect messaging*

There are many ways we can configure message routing in RabbitMQ to achieve various messaging architectures. We will focus on just two simple configurations that will handle many of the communication problems you will face when building your application.

The first is a setup for single-recipient messages that we'll use to create a one-to-one, but still indirect, messaging conduit between microservices. Although, in this configuration you are allowed to have multiple senders and receivers participating, you are guaranteed that only a single microservice will receive each individual message. This is great for when you are distributing a job to a pool of microservices, but the job should be handled only by the first one that is capable of dealing with it.

> **NOTE** Single-recipient messages are *one-to-one*: a message is sent from one microservice and received by only a single other. This is a great way of making sure that a particular job is done only once within your application.

RECEIVING SINGLE-RECIPIENT MESSAGES

Let's add code to the history microservice so that it can receive single-recipient messages. We already added code in section 5.8.5 to connect to our RabbitMQ server. Once connected, we can now *assert* a message queue and start pulling messages from that queue. Note the new terminology I've used here.

I said "assert" a message queue and not "create" a message queue. The difference is that multiple microservices can assert a queue, so it's like checking for the existence of the queue and then only creating it when it doesn't already exist. That means the queue is created once and shared between all participating microservices. Don't get this confused with the other kind of assert that is commonly used in programming—these are two separate concepts.

Listing 5.12 is an extract of the index.js from the history microservice that asserts the viewed queue and calls `consume` to start receiving messages. This causes our function `consumeViewedMessage` to be called each time a new message arrives. This is it! There really isn't very much code needed to receive messages from RabbitMQ.

Listing 5.12   Consuming viewed messages from a RabbitMQ queue (extract from chapter-5/example-3/history/index.js)

```
// ... code omitted here ...

function setupHandlers(app, db, messageChannel) {

    const videosCollection = db.collection("videos");

    function consumeViewedMessage(msg) {        ⟵— A function to handle incoming messages

        const parsedMsg = JSON                                   Parses the JSON message
            .parse(msg.content.toString());      ⟵┘            to a JavaScript object

        return videosCollection.insertOne({ videoPath: parsedMsg.videoPath })
            .then(() => {                        ⟵
                messageChannel.ack(msg);         ⟵┐  If there is no error ...
            });                                     └─ ... acknowledges the message.
    };

    return messageChannel.assertQueue("viewed", {})   ⟵┐ Asserts that we have
        .then(() => {                                   └ a viewed queue
            return messageChannel.consume("viewed",
                consumeViewedMessage);           ⟵┐
        });                                         │ Starts receiving messages
}                                                   └ from the viewed queue

// ... code omitted here ...
```

Records the view in the history database

The code in listing 5.12 is only slightly complicated by the fact that we'd like to send messages in the JSON format, but RabbitMQ doesn't natively support JSON. We must therefore manually parse the incoming message payload.

RabbitMQ is actually agnostic about the format for the message payload, and from its point of view, a message is just a blob of binary data. This can be useful in performance-critical cases where we'd probably like to replace JSON with a more efficient binary format.

SENDING SINGLE-RECIPIENT MESSAGES

Sending a simple message with RabbitMQ is even easier than receiving a message. Listing 5.13 is an extract of the index.js file from the video-streaming microservice. Assume that we've already added code like that in listing 5.9 and connected this microservice to the RabbitMQ server. We now call `publish` by specifying the name of the queue (viewed) and providing the message payload.

> **Listing 5.13 Publishing viewed messages to a RabbitMQ queue (extract from chapter-5/example-3/video-streaming/index.js)**

A helper function to send the viewed message

```
// ... code omitted here ...

function sendViewedMessage(messageChannel,
    videoPath) {
    const msg = { videoPath: videoPath };      ← Defines the message payload. This is the data we send with the message.

    const jsonMsg = JSON.stringify(msg);       ← Converts the message to the JSON format

    messageChannel.publish("", "viewed",
        Buffer.from(jsonMsg));                 ← Publishes the message to the viewed queue
}

// ... code omitted here ...
```

Again, listing 5.13 is only slightly complicated by the fact that we have to manually *stringify* (or serialize) our message payload to JSON before sending the message. Other than that, it's pretty straightforward. Now we have the video-streaming microservice publishing a viewed message whenever a user watches a video.

TESTING SINGLE-RECIPIENT MESSAGES

We have everything we need in place to do another test run. We have a RabbitMQ server. The video-streaming microservice is sending the viewed message, and the history microservice is receiving it. If you haven't already, start the example-3 application:

```
docker-compose up --build
```

Wait for the database and RabbitMQ to start and the microservices to establish their connections. Now point your web browser at http://localhost:4001/video. Check the output to see that the message has been sent and received. You can use Robo3T to check that the history microservice has created a new record for the view in its database.

5.8.7   *Multiple-recipient messages*

Sending single-recipient messages is the first common use case for RabbitMQ. It's also the simplest to understand—that's why we started with it. Potentially, even more useful are multiple-recipient (or broadcast-style) messages. Put simply, one microservice sends the message, but many others can receive it.

We use this type of message for *notifications* (e.g., messages that indicate an important event has occurred in the application, such as the event that a video has been viewed). This is the kind of message that multiple other microservices would like to know about.

> **NOTE**   Multiple-recipient messages are *one-to-many*: a message is sent from only a single microservice but potentially received by many others. This is a great way of publishing notifications within your application.

To make this work with RabbitMQ, we must now use a message exchange. Figure 5.14 shows the video-streaming microservice publishing its message to the viewed exchange. From the exchange, the message is routed to multiple anonymous queues to be handled by multiple microservices simultaneously.

When you look at figure 5.14, you might wonder where the recommendations microservice came from? No, you didn't miss anything! I've literally just snuck a new microservice in while you weren't looking. I had to do this; otherwise, I don't have a way to show you how these broadcast-style messages work.

The recommendations microservice will later suggest videos to watch to our users. It's appearance here and now is only so that we can see multiple-recipient messages in action.

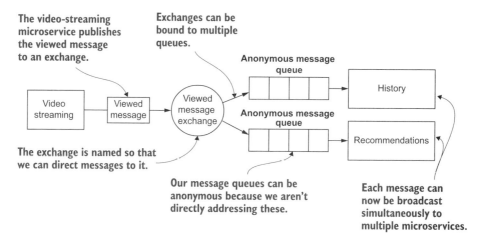

Figure 5.14   Broadcasting a message to be handled by multiple recipients

RECEIVING MULTIPLE-RECIPIENT MESSAGES

Receiving multiple-recipient messages is not much different than receiving single-recipient messages. The following listing is an extract of the index.js file from the history microservice.

Listing 5.14 Consuming viewed messages from a RabbitMQ exchange (extract from chapter-5/example-4/history/index.js)

```
// ... code omitted here ...

function setupHandlers(app, db, messageChannel) {

    const videosCollection = db.collection("videos");

    function consumeViewedMessage(msg) {                       ◁── A function to handle incoming messages
        const parsedMsg = JSON.parse(msg                       ◁─┐ Parses the JSON message
            .content.toString());                                │ to a JavaScript object

        return videosCollection.insertOne({ videoPath: parsedMsg
                            .videoPath })                      ◁── Records the view in the history database
            .then(() => {                                      ◁── If there is no error ...
                messageChannel.ack(msg);                       ◁── ... acknowledges the message.
            });
    };

    return messageChannel
        .assertExchange("viewed", "fanout")                    ◁── Asserts that we have a viewed exchange
        .then(() => {
            return messageChannel
                .assertQueue("", { exclusive: true });         ◁── Creates an anonymous queue. The option exclusive is set to true so that the queue will be deallocated automatically when the microservices disconnects from it (otherwise, our application will have a memory leak).
        })

        .then(response => {                                        Assigns the anonymous queue an automatically generated unique identifier for its name
            const queueName = response.queue;
            return messageChannel
                .bindQueue(queueName, "viewed", "")            ◁── Binds the queue to the exchange
                .then(() => {
                    return messageChannel
                        .consume(queueName, consumeViewedMessage);  ◁── Starts receiving messages from the anonymous queue that's bound to the viewed exchange
                });
        });
}

// ... code omitted here ...
```

The difference between listing 5.14 and listing 5.12 is that we are now *asserting* the viewed exchange (there's that assert terminology again) rather than the viewed queue. After that, we assert an anonymous queue. By creating an unnamed queue, we get one that was created uniquely for this microservice. The viewed exchange is shared among all microservices, but the anonymous queue is owned solely by this microservice. That detail is an important part of how this works.

In creating the unnamed queue, we are returned a random name generated by RabbitMQ. The name that RabbitMQ assigned to our queue is only important because we must now bind the queue to the viewed exchange. This binding connects the exchange and the queue, such that RabbitMQ messages published on the exchange are routed to the queue.

Every other microservice that wants to receive the viewed message (e.g., the recommendations microservice that I snuck in here) creates its own unnamed queue to bind to the viewed exchange. We can have any number of other microservices bound to the viewed exchange, and these will all receive copies of messages on their own anonymous queues as messages are published to the exchange.

SENDING MULTIPLE-RECIPIENT MESSAGES

Sending multiple-recipient messages is, again, similar to sending single-recipient messages. Listing 5.15 is an extract of the index.js file for video-streaming microservice. I've included more code in this extract because it's important to see how the connection to the RabbitMQ service is different in this situation. It's different because we are asserting the existence of the viewed exchange when the microservice starts.

Doing this once at start up means we can rely on the existence of the exchange for the lifetime of the microservice. In the listing, we are still sending the message with the `publish` function, except now we are specifying that the message is published to the viewed exchange rather than the viewed queue.

> **Listing 5.15 Publishing viewed messages to a RabbitMQ exchange (extract from chapter-4/example-3/video-streaming/index.js)**

```
// ... code omitted here ...

function connectRabbit() {

    return amqp.connect(RABBIT)
        .then(connection => {
            console.log("Connected to RabbitMQ.");

            return connection.createChannel()
                .then(messageChannel => {
                    return messageChannel.assertExchange(      ⟵ Asserts that we have
                    ➡ "viewed", "fanout")                         a viewed exchange
                        .then(() => {
                            return messageChannel;
                        });
                });
        });
}

function sendViewedMessage(
➡ messageChannel, videoPath) {
    const msg = { videoPath: videoPath };        ⟵ Defines the payload of the message
    const jsonMsg = JSON.stringify(msg);         ⟵ Converts the message to the JSON format
    messageChannel
```

A helper function to send the viewed message

```
    .publish("viewed", "", Buffer.from(jsonMsg));        ◄─┐  Publishes the message
}                                                          │  to the viewed exchange

// ... code omitted here ...

function main() {                        ┌─  Connects to the
    return connectRabbit()           ◄──┘   RabbitMQ server
        .then(messageChannel => {
            return startHttpServer(messageChannel);    ◄───  Starts the HTTP server
        });
}

// ... code omitted here ...
```

TESTING MULTIPLE-RECIPIENT MESSAGES

Let's test our updated code. It is for this test that I added the recommendations microservice to our application. The new microservice is really just a stub; it does nothing except print out the messages it receives. That's just enough to show that multiple microservices can handle these messages. Open a terminal, change to the example-4 directory, and do the usual thing:

```
docker-compose up --build
```

When you hit http://localhost:4001/video in your web browser, you should see messages being printed to the console to show that both the history microservice and the recommendations microservice are receiving the viewed message.

This works because we have one exchange that is bound to two queues: we have one queue for each receiving microservice. We can't achieve this behavior with only a single queue. When we publish a message to a single shared queue, the receiving microservices compete to be the first one that pulls the message and handles it. You can view this as a kind of load balancing. That's a useful technique, sometimes, but broadcast-style messages are more generally useful.

5.8.8 *Sequencing indirect messages*

Indirect messages have plenty of positive benefits, but these can make it harder to understand and control the behavior of our application. There's no way to get a direct response for an indirect message, and from the sender's point of view, the receiver may as well not even exist! The sender has no way of knowing if there is a receiver out there waiting to pick up its message.

> **NOTE** Because there is no "central control" over indirect messages, these allow for much more flexible, extensible, and evolvable messaging architectures. Each separate microservice is in charge of how it responds to incoming messages and can generate many other messages in response.

With indirect messaging, unlike direct messaging, there is no single microservice in charge of orchestrating the others. This isn't necessarily a bad thing. Consider that having a single controlling microservice means we have a single point of failure, and that's undoubtedly a bad thing. If that controlling microservice crashes in the middle of a complex orchestration, what happens? Whatever was in progress will be lost! That can be the terrible side effect of direct messages.

Sometimes direct messaging is useful, but generally speaking, indirect messaging allows for much more complex and resilient networks of behaviors. We might struggle to understand how it all fits together in its complexity, but at least we know that it's reliable! That's because there is no single point that can fail, and the connections between microservices are implemented by reliable and fault-tolerant message queues (well, RabbitMQ can fail, but it's much less likely to do so than one of our own microservices).

Any particular microservice can fail, but even if it does so while handling a message, we know that the message won't be lost. Because messages aren't acknowledged when a microservice crashes, these will eventually be delivered to another microservice to be handled. It's the sum of small techniques like this that contribute to us building a rock-solid and reliable microservices application. Cast your eyes over figure 5.15 for a more visual understanding of how indirect messages can be sequenced into a dynamic flow of messages within your application.

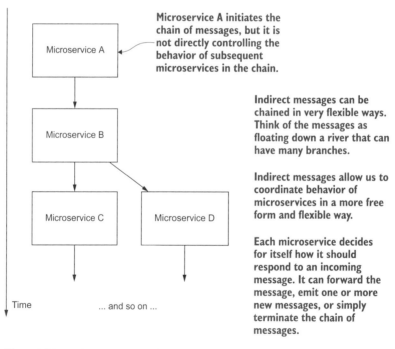

Figure 5.15   Indirect messages allow for more freeform and flexible orchestration of microservices, resulting in emergent behavior.

5.8.9 *What have we achieved?*

In the section, we have learned how to use RabbitMQ to send indirect messages between our microservices. First, we tried sending single-recipient messages. Then we changed to multi-recipient messages so that we can broadcast application-wide messages.

> **NOTE** Using indirect multi-recipient messages seems like the right way to go for the viewed message, and our microservices are less coupled as a result. That's a good win.

We could have easily planned ahead and headed straight for the indirect broadcast-style messages, but that's the benefit of experience. Now that we have worked through all the options, you have that experience and are better placed to decide for yourself what style of messaging you'll need case by case as you add more messages to your application.

5.9 *Microservices communication review*

You now have at your disposal two different styles of messaging that you can use to make your microservices talk to each other. You've learned how to send direct messages with HTTP requests and indirect messages with RabbitMQ. With RabbitMQ, you can send single-recipient and multiple-recipient (or broadcast) messages.

We have a flexible structure for messaging that can be extended in the future. Later, we'll add more microservices to this application, and each one may or may not care about the viewed message. But those that do can simply handle it without us having to modify the original sender of the message.

We've talked through various reasons why you might want to choose one style of messaging over the other. For your convenience, this information is summarized in table 5.2. You can refer back to this table later when you are deciding what style of messaging you need in particular situations.

Table 5.2   When to use each type of communication

Situation	What to use
I need to direct a message to a particular microservice by name.	Direct messaging: HTTP
I need confirmation that the message handling was successful or that it failed.	Direct messaging: HTTP
I need to be able to sequence subsequent messages after completion of the first.	Direct messaging: HTTP
I want one microservice to be able to orchestrate the activity of other microservices.	Direct messaging: HTTP
I need to broadcast a message across the application to notify zero or more microservices of an event in the system (and I don't care if the messages are handled or not).	Indirect messaging: RabbitMQ

Table 5.2   When to use each type of communication *(continued)*

Situation	What to use
I want to decouple the sender and the receiver (so these can more easily change and evolve independently).	Indirect messaging: RabbitMQ
I want the performance of sender and receiver to be independent (the sender can emit as many messages as it likes, the receiver will process these in its own time).	Indirect messaging: RabbitMQ
I want to be sure that if message handling fails that it will automatically be retried again later until it succeeds (so no messages are lost due to intermittent failures).	Indirect messaging: RabbitMQ
I need to load balance handling of a message so it is handled by one out of a pool of workers.	Either HTTP or RabbitMQ
I need to distribute handling of a message to multiple workers who can act in parallel.	Indirect messaging: RabbitMQ

5.10   *Continue your learning*

This chapter has been a tour through the various ways we can make our microservices communicate. We've used HTTP for direct messages and RabbitMQ for indirect messages. As usual, we only briefly touched on each of these subjects, and there is a whole lot more you can learn. Here are some great resources for you to learn more:

- *API Design Patterns* by JJ Geewax (Manning, est. Spring 2021)
- *The Design of Web APIs* by Arnaud Lauret (Manning, 2019)
- *RabbitMQ in Depth* by Gavin M Roy (Manning, 2017)
- *RabbitMQ in Action* by Alvaro Videla and Jason J.W. Williams (Manning, 2012)

To learn more about the amqplib package, read the documentation here:

- http://www.squaremobius.net/amqp.node/

To learn more about the `wait-port` command, see:

- https://github.com/dwmkerr/wait-port

We've come a long way to this point. After building our first microservice, we quickly scaled up to developing multiple communicating microservices. Each microservice can have its own database and/or file storage. We are now using live reload to efficiently reload our whole application while we are coding.

What's next? We have a fledgling app. It can't do much yet, but that's no reason to avoid moving to production. Getting our application to run in a production environment can be a difficult affair, and it's best done while the application is small and simple. So without further ado, in chapters 6 and 7, we'll take our application to production!

Summary

- We can use Docker volumes to share code between our development workstation and the containers in our application.
- Using nodemon for live reload means we can update our code and have the relevant microservices in our application automatically reload without having to rebuild and restart the entire application.
- There are two styles of communication between microservices: direct and indirect.
- Direct or synchronous messaging is most useful when we want to explicitly sequence the flow of messages or carefully orchestrate the behavior of other microservices.
- With direct messages, we know immediately if the message handling succeeded or failed.
- Indirect or asynchronous messaging helps us to decouple our microservices from each other, which helps promote the development of flexible and evolvable applications.
- With indirect messages, we can broadcast a message throughout the application to notify other microservices of important events in the system.
- HTTP POST requests are useful for sending direct messages between microservices.
- RabbitMQ is software for queuing messages. We can use it to send indirect messages between microservices.
- Although we used the wait-port npm package to wait until the RabbitMQ server was ready before our microservice connected to it, in chapter 10, we'll learn a better way of waiting for other services that aren't currently available.
- Deciding to use either HTTP or RabbitMQ depends on the needs of the situation. Refer to table 5.2 in section 5.9 for help deciding which to use based on your needs.

Creating your
production environment

This chapter covers

- Building production infrastructure for your application
- Working with Terraform to script the creation of infrastructure
- Creating a Kubernetes cluster to host microservices
- Interacting with your Kubernetes cluster

Finally, we arrive at the most exciting chapters of the book! The next two chapters are also probably the hardest so far, but do follow along with the examples. That's how you'll learn the most and gain real experience bringing your own application to production.

In this chapter and the next, we will create a Kubernetes cluster and deploy containers to it: a MongoDB database, a RabbitMQ server, and of course, our video streaming microservice. In the next chapter, we'll also build a continuous delivery (CD) pipeline that automatically deploys our updated code to production.

The examples in these two chapters are designed for you to follow along with step by step to build our infrastructure and application. This closely emulates the real process of prototyping new infrastructure and is close to what I really do in my own development.

These chapters are two parts of what we need for production deployment. In chapter 6, this chapter, we'll build our production infrastructure. By the end of this chapter, we'll have a fresh container registry and an empty Kubernetes cluster ready and waiting to host our application. In chapter 7, we'll continue the effort and learn how to deploy our microservices through an automated deployment pipeline. Let's begin!

6.1 New tools

This chapter introduces two new tools: Kubernetes and Terraform. These tools are so important that they made it into the title of the book! We'll use Terraform to create the infrastructure for our microservices application, including our Kubernetes cluster.

Table 6.1 New tools in chapter 6

Tool	Version	Purpose
Kubernetes	1.18.8	Kubernetes is the computing platform that we use to host our microservices in production.
Terraform	0.12.29	Terraform allows us to script the creation of cloud resources and application infrastructure.
Kubectl	1.18.6	Kubectl is the command-line tool for interacting with a Kubernetes cluster.
Azure CLI	2.9.1	We'll use the Azure command-line tool to authenticate with Azure and give Terraform access to our Azure account. This tool is generally useful for managing Azure accounts and cloud resources.

6.2 Getting the code

To follow along with this chapter, you need to download the code or clone the repository.

- Download a zip file of the code from here:
  https://github.com/bootstrapping-microservices/chapter-6
- You can clone the code using Git like this:
  ```
  git clone https://github.com/bootstrapping-microservices/chapter-6.git
  ```

For help on installing and using Git, see chapter 2. If you have problems with the code, log an issue against the repository in GitHub.

6.3 Getting to production

The day has arrived. We are taking our application to production. It might seem like it is too early to take this small application to production, but actually, in normal development situations, I really do advocate going to production as early as possible. Maybe not as early as this, but I do believe it's a good idea to go to production while your application is still small. Why is that?

Going to production means putting our application where our customers can see it and use it. Putting our product in front of users is essential to getting feedback, adapting to their needs, and building valuable features. If we don't go to production, we won't get that feedback. Having a deployment pipeline that allows for rapid and reliable updates is the best tool we have for experimenting and figuring out how to make a great product.

Also, while our application is still small, this is the best time to build a CD pipeline and to go to production. When our application is small, it's easier to deploy. But this task becomes progressively more difficult as our application grows larger.

Figure 6.1 shows what we'll do in this chapter. We'll use Terraform on our development workstation (or personal computer) to build infrastructure in the cloud. We'll use code to create our container registry and our Kubernetes cluster. Then, in chapter 7, we'll learn how to put this on automatic with continuous delivery (CD). But for now, we'll learn to evolve our development infrastructure by manually invoking Terraform.

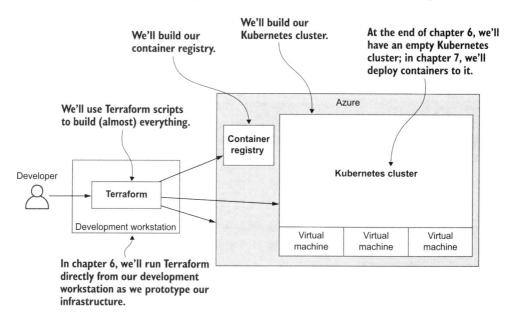

Figure 6.1   Prototyping our infrastructure with Terraform

6.4 *Infrastructure as code*

Infrastructure as code is the name of the technique we'll use in this chapter to bring our application to production. It's called *infrastructure as code* because rather than manually creating infrastructure (say, through a GUI, as we did with our private container registry in chapter 3), we will write code that creates our infrastructure.

Not only will this code describe our infrastructure, but we will also execute it to actually create our infrastructure. Using code to create infrastructure means that we can reliably and repeatedly create and recreate our infrastructure on demand and as often as we like.

The fact that this code both describes and builds our infrastructure makes it a form of *executable documentation*. It's a statement about how we want our infrastructure to look, and unlike normal (i.e., non-executable) documentation, it's a form of documentation that's never going to go out of date.

Through infrastructure as code, creating and updating our infrastructure becomes a kind of coding task. The best form of infrastructure as code uses a declarative language instead of a procedural one. This means it describes the configuration and layout of the infrastructure instead of the step-by-step instructions for building it. We prefer the declarative format because we can let our tools do the heavy lifting, and these can figure out the best way to make changes to our infrastructure.

Figure 6.2 illustrates the concept of infrastructure as code. The code for our infrastructure lives in a code repository such as Git. From there, we execute it to create, configure, and maintain our cloud-based infrastructure.

Infrastructure as code is not just important because we can use our well-tested code to reliably and repeatedly create our infrastructure. It's also important because it's what allows us to automate the creation and maintenance of our infrastructure. As such, it's a crucial enabler for continuous delivery, which we'll see in the next chapter where we build our automated deployment pipeline.

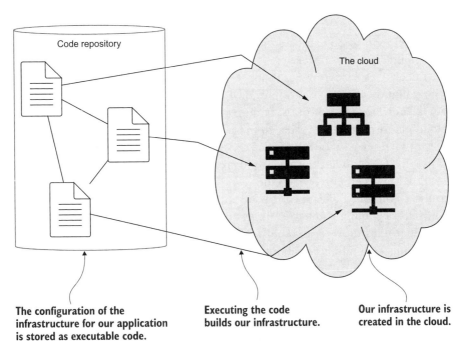

The configuration of the infrastructure for our application is stored as executable code.

Executing the code builds our infrastructure.

Our infrastructure is created in the cloud.

Figure 6.2 Infrastructure as code uses executable code to create infrastructure.

6.5   *Hosting microservices on Kubernetes*

By the end of the next chapter, we'll run multiple containers in the production environment for our application. These containers are hosted on a managed version of Kubernetes that is running in the cloud (you can think of this as Kubernetes as a *service*).

> **NOTE**   Kubernetes is a computing platform for managing container-based applications. It was originally created by Google but is now managed by the Cloud Native Computing Foundation, a committee that has huge industry support and is also responsible for many other interesting projects.

Kubernetes is commonly known as a container orchestration platform. This tells us all we need to know. Kubernetes can manage and automate the deployment and scaling of our containers. Kubernetes is the production backbone of our microservices application. I like to think of it as *a platform for microservices*.

6.5.1   *Why Kubernetes?*

There are many reasons to use Kubernetes. The simplest reason is to avoid vendor lock-in. All the main cloud vendors offer their own container orchestration services that are good in their own right. But each of these also offers a managed Kubernetes service, so why use a proprietary service when you can instead use Kubernetes? Using Kubernetes means our application can be portable to any cloud vendor.

I believe it's worthwhile to learn Kubernetes (at least the basics) because the knowledge is transferable. Although, in this book, we host our Kubernetes cluster on Microsoft Azure, you can take the Kubernetes skills with you and use them on whichever cloud you most prefer.

Kubernetes has a reputation for being complicated. And certainly, it is if you want to install it on your own hardware or if you want to deep dive and become an expert. Fortunately, for the rest of us, building a managed Kubernetes cluster in our favorite cloud platform is much easier, to the point where (at least on Azure) we can create it in the GUI in a handful of clicks. We won't create our infrastructure manually through a GUI though. Instead, we'll create our cluster through Terraform code.

Kubernetes emerged from the vast experience of Google, then it was turned over to the community. This means you can fork the code and contribute to Kubernetes yourself—assuming you have a desire to be lost down that particular rabbit hole!

Kubernetes allows us to build applications that are scalable in multiple ways. That's something we'll talk more about in chapters 10 and 11. In this chapter and the next, however, we'll learn the absolute basics. That's enough to build a production cluster to which we can deploy our small microservices application.

Most importantly, Kubernetes has an automatable API. This is what will allow us to build our automated deployment pipeline in chapter 7. Kubernetes is becoming an industry standard for microservices, and I expect it to continue in that direction. It's well supported and has a great community and a large ecosystem of tools.

To me, Kubernetes is the *universal computing platform.* It's supported by all the major cloud players. No matter where we end up, we can take Kubernetes with us. Kubernetes is open source and you can find the code here:

https://github.com/kubernetes/kubernetes

6.5.2 *How does Kubernetes work?*

A Kubernetes cluster is composed of multiple computers. Each computer is called a *node.* Each node is actually a virtual machine (VM). We can add as many VMs as we need to our cluster to control the amount of computing power available to our application. And, each node can host multiple pods. A *pod* is the basic unit of computation in Kubernetes.

Figure 6.3 illustrates an example of the arrangement of nodes and pods. The depicted cluster has three nodes (it is powered by three VMs). However, the cluster we create in this chapter only has a single node. That's because our simple application doesn't need much computing power. It also means we won't pay for more VMs than we actually need. Scaling up to more nodes is easy though, and we'll look at a real example in chapter 11.

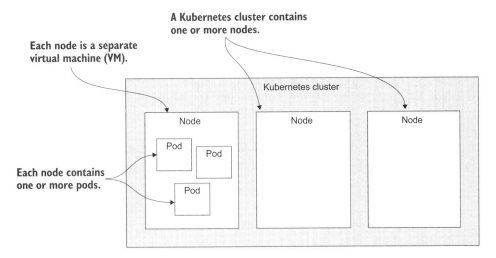

Figure 6.3   The structure of a Kubernetes cluster

Each pod can actually host multiple containers, as figure 6.4 shows. This can be the basis for many interesting architectural patterns (such as the well-known sidecar pattern for proxies and authentication).

In this book, though, we are keeping things simple. Each pod will host only a single container or microservice. Even though figure 6.4 shows a pod with multiple containers, for the purposes of this book, you can think of a pod as a container or as a microservice if that's a simplification that is helpful for you.

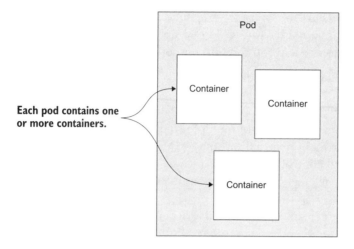

Figure 6.4   The structure
of a Kubernetes pod

6.6   Working with the Azure CLI

Before we can start working with Terraform, we need the Azure CLI up and running. That's the simplest way for us to authenticate Terraform so that it has access to our Azure account and to give it permission to create infrastructure on our behalf in Azure. It's also really handy to have the Azure CLI because it's a useful way to interact with our Azure account and manage our cloud resources.

6.6.1   Installing the Azure CLI

You can find the instructions for installing the Azure CLI here:

https://docs.microsoft.com/en-us/cli/azure/install-azure-cli

Choose your platform and follow the instructions to install it. After installing the Azure CLI, you can test it from your terminal with the following command:

```
az --version
```

At the time of writing, I'm using version 2.9.1. Future versions should be backward compatible.

Azure CLI is preinstalled in the Vagrant VM

If you are using the Vagrant VM included in the chapter 6 code repository, you'll find all the tools you need already installed. This includes the Azure CLI.

If you are working on Linux, take a look at the shell script scripts/provision-dev-vm.sh in the chapter 6 code repository. This shell script installs the tools in the VM so you can use it as an example of how to install the Azure CLI on a Linux computer.

See appendix A for more information on using Vagrant.

6.6.2   *Authenticating with Azure*

The main reason we install the Azure CLI is simply to authenticate with our Azure account. We can do that from the terminal by running the following command:

```
az login
```

Running this command opens a browser so you can sign in to your Azure account. If it doesn't automatically open your browser, you'll have to manually check the output, open the URL, and then enter the code. The output of the command gives instructions:

```
To sign in, use a web browser to open the page https://microsoft.com/devicelogin
➥ and enter the code XXXXXX to authenticate.
```

After entering the code, click Next. Now sign in to your Azure account with your user-name and password. After signing in, you will see a message in your browser like this:

```
You have signed in to the Microsoft Azure Cross-platform Command Line
➥ Interface application on your device. You may now close this window.
```

You can now close your browser and return to the terminal. The `az login` command completes and displays a JSON formatted list of your Azure subscriptions. If you only just signed up for Azure for this book, you should see only one subscription. If you already use Azure for work you might see multiple subscriptions listed.

The authentication is saved locally, and from now on, you can issue other commands against your Azure account without having to sign in each time. We can test which Azure subscription we are working with using this command:

```
az account show
```

The output from this command shows us the current default subscription. We can view a list of all subscriptions with this command:

```
az account list
```

The output is a JSON formatted list of subscriptions. Each subscription has an `id` field that is a unique ID for the subscription. You'll also notice that the current default sub-scription is marked by having its `isDefault` field set to `true`. This field is set to `false` for any other subscriptions in the list.

At this point, you should verify that you are using the right subscription to follow along with the examples in this book. For example, if you have access to subscriptions from your employer, you probably shouldn't use those for your own learning and experimentation (or at least, check with your boss first). If you need to change the current working subscription, you can set a new default with the following command:

```
az account set --subscription=<subscription-id>
```

Replace <subscription-id> with the ID of the subscription that you want to set as the default. After changing the default subscription, double-check it again with this command:

```
az account show
```

This is just to be absolutely sure that we are using our own subscription to follow along with the examples. We don't want to accidentally use an Azure subscription from our employer.

6.6.3   *Which version of Kubernetes?*

Let's do something practical with the Azure CLI to understand how it can be useful. Toward the end of this chapter, we'll create our managed Kubernetes cluster. It will be helpful to know in advance which versions of Kubernetes are available in the location where we are creating it.

To interact with the Azure Kubernetes service via the Azure CLI, we'll use the aks subcommand. Here's an example that lists versions of Kubernetes in the West US region:

```
az aks get-versions --location westus
```

The output is a JSON formatted list that shows the available versions of Kubernetes in that location. The output will be more readable for us if use the *table style* of output like this:

```
az aks get-versions --location westus --output table
```

You should now see something like this:

```
KubernetesVersion    Upgrades
-------------------  -------------------------------
1.18.4(preview)      None available
1.18.2(preview)      1.18.4(preview)
1.17.7               1.18.2(preview), 1.18.4(preview)
1.16.10              1.17.7
1.15.12              1.16.10
1.15.11              1.15.12, 1.16.10
```

From this list, you should select the most recent stable (non-preview) version of Kubernetes. That's 1.18.8 at the time of writing. But by the time you read this, there will be a more recent version. It's quite possible that version 1.18.8 will have also been expired (no longer available through Azure). *Be sure to choose a version number that's currently available!*

Make a note of the version number. We'll need it soon to create our cluster. You could choose a preview version of Kubernetes, say, if you wanted to evaluate the latest release. But normally for production use, we'd prefer to use the latest stable version.

6.6.4 *What have we achieved?*

We've installed the Azure command-line tool (Azure CLI). This is a useful tool for interacting with our Azure account from the terminal. We used it to authenticate with our Azure account.

> **NOTE** Terraform needs to be authenticated with Azure so that it can create infrastructure on our behalf.

As a practical example, we used the Azure CLI to query for the versions of Kubernetes that are available for use in our chosen location. We noted the most recent version number of Kubernetes, and we'll use that later to create our cluster.

6.7 *Creating infrastructure with Terraform*

Now we are coming to the point where we'll actually start to create our infrastructure! We could build our infrastructure manually, either using the GUI from our cloud vendor (e.g., the Azure portal) or via the command line (e.g., the Azure CLI). In this book, though, we'll build our infrastructure in an automated fashion using code.

From here on in, we'll use infrastructure as code to automate the process of infrastructure creation and, hence, make it reliable and repeatable. Automation allows us to later scale up our application without scaling up our manual workload. We'll do this with Terraform, an amazingly flexible tool for executing Hashicorp Configuration Language (HCL) code.

HCL is the declarative configuration language in which we'll define our infrastructure. Executing this code with Terraform actually creates our infrastructure in the cloud.

> **NOTE** In the future, I'll refer to HCL simply as *Terraform code.*

Terraform supports multiple cloud vendors through plugin providers as figure 6.5 illustrates. For the examples in this chapter, we use Terraform to create infrastructure on Microsoft Azure.

If learning HCL seems in any way daunting, remember this: HCL is actually just like YAML or JSON, but it's a different format. Hashicorp created HCL to be a human-readable configuration format that is also machine-translatable to YAML and JSON. Think of it as YAML or JSON but structured so that it's more friendly for humans.

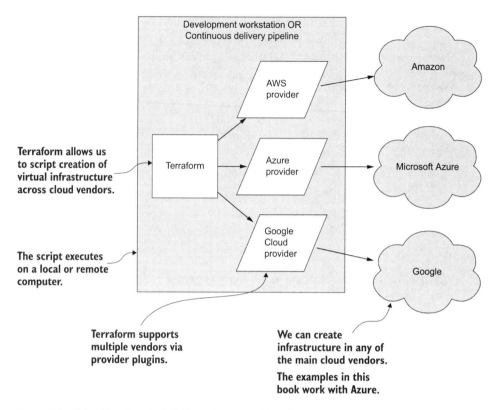

Figure 6.5   Using Terraform to build infrastructure with various cloud vendors

6.7.1   *Why Terraform?*

Terraform is a tool and a language for configuring infrastructure for cloud-based applications. Terraform makes it easy to reliably and repeatedly configure cloud infrastructure. It's incredibly flexible, as its functionality is extended through plugin providers. This is how it supports multiple cloud vendors! Terraform already has robust providers implemented for Azure, AWS, and Google Cloud.

Just like with Kubernetes, we'll again learn transferable skills that can be used with all the major cloud vendors. No matter which cloud we use, we can make use of Terraform to build our infrastructure. We can even create our own providers and extend Terraform to work with platforms that it doesn't yet support. To seal the deal, Terraform supports Kubernetes, and we'll also use it to deploy containers to our cluster.

Terraform does just about everything we need to create our application's automated deployment pipeline. It's an all-in-one tool for scripting infrastructure because, even for the things it can't do, we can fill the gaps ourselves. In the next chapter, you'll see one simple method we can use to extend the functionality of Terraform to cover those areas that it can't yet handle.

To me, Terraform seems like the *universal configuration language*. It's one language we can use to create all of our infrastructure. Terraform is open source, and you can find the code here:

https://github.com/hashicorp/terraform

6.7.2 *Installing Terraform*

Installing Terraform is simply a matter of downloading the binary executable for your operating system and moving it to a directory that's included in your system's PATH environment variable. Download the latest version of Terraform from here:

https://www.terraform.io/downloads.html

After installing Terraform, test it from your terminal with the following command:

```
terraform --version
```

At the time of writing, I'm using version 0.12.29. Future versions should be backward compatible.

> **Terraform is preinstalled in the Vagrant VM**
>
> If you are using the Vagrant VM included in the chapter 6 code repository, you'll find that all the tools you need, including Terraform, are already installed.
>
> If you are working from Linux, take a look at the shell script scripts/provision-dev-vm.sh in the chapter 6 code repository. This shell script installs the tools in the Vagrant VM, and it contains an example of how to install Terraform on a Linux computer.

6.7.3 *Terraform project setup*

Before we get started with Terraform, let's become familiar with what a Terraform project looks like. Figure 6.6 shows a fleshed out Terraform project. This is what example-3 from chapter 7 looks like. You don't have to look at chapter 7 yet or even open that particular code example right now. We are just looking at the structure of that project in figure 6.6 to become familiar with what a Terraform project looks like.

As you can see in figure 6.6, a Terraform project is composed of a number of Terraform code files; those are the files ending in the .tf extension. These files contain the Terraform code that, when executed by Terraform, creates the infrastructure for our application.

There are a lot of files here. That's because we are looking at a more complex example from the next chapter. Don't be concerned! In a moment, we'll start with example-1 from this chapter (chapter 6), which is much simpler.

You should be able to read the filenames in figure 6.6 and get an idea of their purpose. That's because I've used a naming convention where each script file is named according to the piece of infrastructure that it creates. When you read through the filenames in figure 6.6 (or any project in chapters 6 and 7), you should read it like this: *resource-group.tf* is responsible for creating an Azure resource group; *database.tf* is responsible for deploying the database; and so on.

Let's try this now. Read through the filenames in figure 6.6 and have a go at guessing the purpose of each one. Mostly, it should be obvious; although, there are a couple of files that are outside the naming convention. Don't be concerned if you can't figure it all out; all will be explained throughout this chapter and the next.

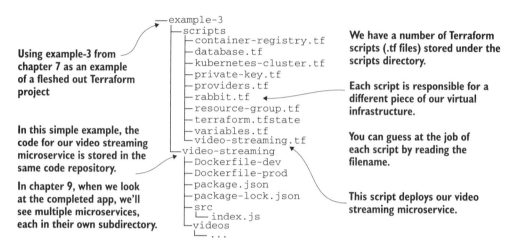

Figure 6.6   The structure of a more complete Terraform project (we have jumped forward to see example-3 from chapter 7).

Note in figure 6.6 that we have co-located the code for the video streaming microservice alongside the Terraform code files. It lives under the video-streaming subdirectory in the same code repository. This should explain why we are storing the Terraform code files under the scripts subdirectory. That keeps our infrastructure code separate from the code for our microservices.

The structure and filenames in this example project are not dictated by Terraform. It just happens to be the convention we'll use in these examples. For your own projects, a different structure might be better, so feel free to experiment and find the best structure for your own project.

To keep things simple while learning, and because this is a good way to start a new microservices project, we'll co-locate our infrastructure and microservices code. You might already realize that this monolith-like project structure eliminates some of the benefits of using microservices in the first place. Don't worry too much about that right now. Just know that this simple structure is only for the early days of our new application. As we grow our application, we'll need to convert it to a more scalable structure, but that's something we'll discuss in chapter 11. For the moment, let's stick with this simple project structure.

6.8   *Creating an Azure resource group for your application*

After looking at the advanced project structure of example-3 from the next chapter, let's now dial back the complexity and look at the much simpler example-1 from this chapter. We need to start our Terraform journey somewhere, and our starting points should always be simple. This is the case with example-1, which contains the simplest Terraform code from which we can start to create our deployment pipeline.

The first thing we do is to create an Azure resource group that groups together all the other Azure resources we'll build throughout this chapter. Back in chapter 3, we manually created a resource group through the Azure Portal GUI. Now, we create a resource group again, but this time, we aren't doing it manually. We'll build it through code using Terraform.

Figure 6.7 shows what we'll do in this section. Example-1 contains two Terraform code files: providers.tf and resource-group.tf. The script file, resource-group.tf, is the one that actually creates the resource group. The other file, providers.tf, contains configurations for the Terraform provider plugins.

We will use the `terraform apply` command to execute our Terraform code. Figure 6.7 shows how our code files are input to Terraform, which executes our code and creates a FlixTube resource group in Azure (shown on the right of figure 6.7).

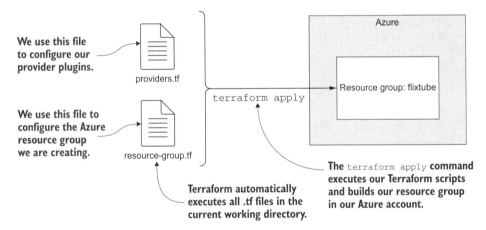

Figure 6.7   Using Terraform to create an Azure resource group

The file providers.tf isn't technically necessary to this process. We could delete it, and this example would still work. It's useful to have this file, though, because this is where we can put our code for configuring the providers that we use. In a moment, we'll talk about providers.tf in more detail.

6.8.1   *Evolutionary architecture with Terraform*

Terraform is a tool for building our infrastructure in an iterative fashion—something we call *evolutionary architecture*. In this chapter, you can experience this iterative method of building infrastructure for yourself.

At this point, we will start to write Terraform code. You have a choice about how to follow along with the examples in this chapter and the next one:

- Start with example-1 and then iteratively update your example project to evolve your infrastructure as you read through this chapter and the next
- Start each example fresh and build new infrastructure for each example in this chapter and the next

All of the examples in chapters 6 and 7 can run standalone, so you can easily start your infrastructure from any point by jumping ahead to any of the examples and invoking Terraform for that code. However, the best way for you to follow along, the way that is most like "real" development, is to iteratively update your code and evolve your infrastructure in a step-by-step manner (that's the first option mentioned). To follow along in this way, you should create a separate working directory for your evolving project, for example:

```
mkdir working
```

Then copy the example-1 code to it:

```
cp -r chapter-6/example-1/* working
```

Now you can follow along with the examples in chapters 6 and 7. Each time you get to a new example, copy over the new code to your working project like this:

```
cp -r chapter-6/example-2/* working
```

To execute these commands on Windows, you should consider installing Git for Windows. It comes with many Linux commands compiled to work under Windows. Here's the link:

https://gitforwindows.org

Alternatively, on Windows you can use WSL2 or Linux running under a Vagrant VM. See chapter 3 and appendix A for more details.

The example code in chapters 6 and 7 is designed to be used in this evolutionary way, and thus, emulates the real iterative process of infrastructure development. Figure 6.8 shows this process. Note how we use multiple iterations of the `terraform apply` command as we edit our infrastructure code. Through this, we progressively add to and update our growing infrastructure.

> **TIP** It's best to use Git to keep track of the updated code that you copy into your working project.

After copying the code from example-1, create a new Git code repository and commit the code. Then, after you copy each new example to your working project, you can use `git diff` to understand the new changes that are going in. At each iteration, commit the updated code and continue with the next example.

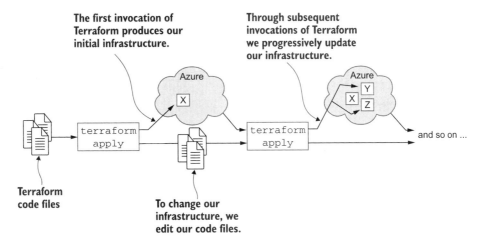

The first invocation of Terraform produces our initial infrastructure.

Through subsequent invocations of Terraform we progressively update our infrastructure.

Terraform code files

To change our infrastructure, we edit our code files.

Figure 6.8   Iterative evolution of infrastructure with Terraform

This might all seem like a lot of work. I understand you are busy, and you might not have time to follow along using the evolutionary method. If that's the case, feel free to jump directly to any example in this chapter that you might like to run. These are all designed to run standalone, so you can follow along whichever way you like.

I will say this, though, if you do want to follow along with every example, then the iterative evolutionary approach is actually more efficient. That's because at each step of the iteration, Terraform only creates those resources that don't already exist.

If instead, you run each example on its own, you will end up running Terraform to create a complete infrastructure for each example. That's the least efficient way to do this. Creating a Kubernetes cluster from scratch is slow, but updating an existing Kubernetes cluster is much quicker! Following along with the evolutionary approach can actually save you some time!

6.8.2   *Scripting infrastructure creation*

Listing 6.1 shows our first Terraform code file. It doesn't get much simpler than this. Using the Azure provider, we will create an Azure resource group simply by declaring it in three lines of Terraform code.

Listing 6.1   Creating an Azure resource group (chapter-6/example-1/scripts/ resource-group.tf)

```
resource "azurerm_resource_group" "flixtube" {

    name = "flixtube"

    location = "West US"
}
```

Declares an Azure resource group. This resource group will contain all the resources we create, so it's a fundamental beginning for our new infrastructure.

Sets the name of the resource group

Sets the location (data center) where the resource group will be created

Through Terraform code, we are defining the components of our infrastructure. In listing 6.1, we have defined the first piece of our infrastructure. We have declared an Azure resource group called `flixtube` that has the type, `azurerm_resource_group`. This is a Terraform resource type that comes from the Azure provider and gives us the ability to create a resource group on Azure. Soon we'll run Terraform, and it will create this resource group in our Azure account just how we have configured it.

6.8.3   *Initializing Terraform*

We have taken the first steps in creating our infrastructure. We wrote a simple script that creates an Azure resource group. But before we invoke Terraform and execute this script, we must first initialize Terraform.

When we initialize Terraform, it downloads the provider plugins required for our script. At this point, we only need the Azure provider. To initialize Terraform, first change directory to the location of the Terraform code:

```
cd chapter-6/example-1/scripts
```

Now run the `terraform init` command:

```
terraform init
```

You should see some output indicating that the Azure provider plugin is downloaded; for example,

```
Initializing the backend...

Initializing provider plugins...
- Checking for available provider plugins...
- Downloading plugin for provider "azurerm" (hashicorp/azurerm) 1.43.0…

Terraform has been successfully initialized!
```

Once this completes, we are now ready to execute our Terraform code. We must always run the `terraform init` command at least once for each Terraform project before we execute any Terraform code in that directory. You must also run it at least once for each new provider that you use. Each time you invoke `terraform init`, it only downloads those providers that it has not yet cached.

If you are following along with the examples in chapters 6 and 7 in the evolutionary way proposed in section 6.8.1, then you only need to do the initialization for each example that includes a new provider. Otherwise, if you run each example standalone, you'll just need to remember to run `terraform init` for each example.

Don't worry if you forget to run `terraform init`, it won't cause you any problem. When you forget, Terraform reminds you that you need to do that first.

6.8.4   *By-products of Terraform initialization*

With Terraform initialized, we can now inspect the files that the `init` command has created or downloaded in the scripts subdirectory. Have a look through the scripts

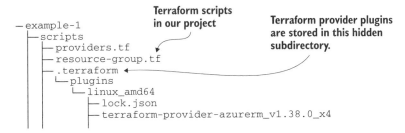

Figure 6.9 Files downloaded or created while running `terraform init`.

directory and see what you can find. Figure 6.9 shows the example-1 project after running `terraform init`.

You'll notice there's a hidden subdirectory, `.terraform`, that was created, and it contains a bunch of files. This is the place where Terraform stores the provider plugins that it has downloaded. These are cached here so they can be reused each time we invoke Terraform.

6.8.5 *Fixing provider version numbers*

Before we invoke Terraform for the first time, let's talk about that other file in our project. Listing 6.2 shows the code for providers.tf. This is the file where we define and configure all of our Terraform provider plugins.

Listing 6.2   Configuring Terraform provider plugins (chapter-6/example-1/scripts/ providers.tf)

```
provider "azurerm" {        ◁──── Sets the name of the provider plugin

    version = "1.38.0"      ◁──┐ Sets the version of the provider
}                              │ plugin to download and use
```

Technically, we don't need this file yet, and we don't need to declare our providers ahead of time. We can simply invoke `terraform init`, and it is smart enough to figure out which providers we need and download those for us.

This is convenient when starting a new project. We can simply start writing Terraform code to create our cloud infrastructure, and we don't have to declare our providers upfront. Then, when we invoke `terraform init`, it downloads the latest versions of the providers we need. Terraform lists the versions of the plugins it downloads in the output, like this extract from the earlier output:

```
- Downloading plugin for provider "azurerm" (hashicorp/azurerm) 1.43.0…
```

This is a great way to get started, but it can lead to unexpected problems down the road. For example, in the future, you might find yourself unwittingly upgraded to a new version of the Azure provider that isn't 100% backward compatible with the version you originally used (yes, that happened to me). As a result, your Terraform code can break in ways that are often difficult to predict or understand.

Fortunately, we can preemptively solve this by fixing our versions to those that we have tested and that we trust. You can see the current version of any provider by inspecting the output from `terraform init` and then hard-code this version number into your providers.tf file (as shown in listing 6.2).

Eventually, our Terraform code must run completely unattended in our automated CD pipeline (which we'll create in chapter 7). Our code must be bullet-proof and fixing our version numbers makes our Terraform code more reliable. This means that in the future, we won't be exposed to having our dependencies changed underneath us.

We can also use the providers.tf as a place to configure other parameters to providers. We'll see an example of this in the next chapter.

6.8.6 *Building your infrastructure*

After initializing our Terraform project, we are ready to invoke the `terraform apply` command to execute our Terraform code and build the first iteration of our infrastructure. If you need to, refer back to figure 6.8 for a graphical depiction of the `apply` command. From the same directory where you invoked the `init` command, run this command:

```
terraform apply
```

The `apply` command gathers together and executes all of our Terraform code files. (So far we only have two code files, but soon we'll have more.) When you invoke the apply command you'll see output like this:

```
An execution plan has been generated and is shown below.
Resource actions are indicated with the following symbols:

  + create

Terraform will perform the following actions:

  # azurerm_resource_group.flixtube will be created
  + resource "azurerm_resource_group" "flixtube" {
      + id       = (known after apply)
      + location = "westus"
      + name     = "flixtube"
      + tags     = (known after apply)
    }

Plan: 1 to add, 0 to change, 0 to destroy.

Do you want to perform these actions?
  Terraform will perform the actions described above.
  Only 'yes' will be accepted to approve.

  Enter a value:
```

This output describes the planned update to our infrastructure. Terraform is telling us the changes that it is about to make. (You can also use the `terraform plan` command to get this output separately.)

Terraform is now waiting for us to approve the plan before it continues and actually makes the update to our infrastructure. It's a good idea at this point to scan the output and double-check that the upcoming changes are OK and what we expect. Once happy with the plan, type `yes` and press Enter to allow Terraform to proceed.

Terraform now creates the infrastructure we requested. In this case, on our first invocation of Terraform, the flixtube resource group is created in our Azure account. This should happen pretty quickly (because at the moment it's still a small script and doesn't do much). Then you'll see a success message like this:

```
azurerm_resource_group.flixtube: Creating...
azurerm_resource_group.flixtube: Creation complete after 5s
    [id=/subscriptions/219aac63-3a60-4051-983b-
    45649c150e0e/resourceGroups/flixtube]

Apply complete! Resources: 1 added, 0 changed, 0 destroyed.
```

The output gives a quick summary of what was added, changed, and deleted. In this case, it confirms what we already know, that we have created one cloud resource, our Azure resource group.

Now let's manually check what the change looks like. Open your web browser and navigate to the Azure portal at https://portal.azure.com/. You can check for yourself that an Azure resource group has indeed been created in your Azure account. In the portal, click Resource Groups and verify that the flixtube resource group is now in the list. This is what your first Terraform code just created!

Of course, you don't always need to check that every resource has been created by manually inspecting the Azure portal. We are only doing this in the first instance so that you can connect the dots about what just happened.

6.8.7 *Understanding Terraform state*

At this point, after invoking `terraform apply` in our project for the first time, Terraform will have generated its state file terraform.tfstate. You should see this file in the same directory as your Terraform code files.

It's important that we understand Terraform's persistent state management; although, most of the time we won't care what's in the state file. But it's good to know why it's there and how to deal with it.

Let's take a look at our Terraform state file and see what it looks like after we have created our first piece of infrastructure. This is a good time to look at the state file: while it's still small and easily understandable. Invoke the `cat` command to display the state file:

```
cat terraform.tfstate
```

Your output will look something like this:

```
{
 "version": 4,
 "terraform_version": "0.12.29",
 "serial": 1,
 "lineage": "dc5cb51c-1ab4-02a5-2271-199538b7655a",
 "outputs": {},
 "resources": [
   {
     "mode": "managed",
     "type": "azurerm_resource_group",
     "name": "flixtube",
     "provider": "provider.azurerm",
     "instances": [
       {
         "schema_version": 0,
         "attributes": {
             "id": "/subscriptions/219aac63-3a60-4051-983b-
             ➥ 45649c150e0e/resourceGroups/flixtube",
          "location": "westus",
          "name": "flixtube",
          "tags": {}
         },
         "private": "bnVsbA=="
       }
     ]
   }
 ]
}
```

You can see that our Terraform state file has one item in the resources field. The details of the resource group we just created were recorded in this state file.

The first time we invoked terraform apply, the state file is generated. Subsequent invocations of terraform apply use the state file as input. Terraform loads the state file and then *refreshes* it from the live infrastructure. Figure 6.10 shows how successive invocations of Terraform are connected by both the live infrastructure and the state file.

You might like to know at this point what exactly is the point of the state file? If our infrastructure is defined in our Terraform code, and Terraform can know the current state directly from the live infrastructure, why must it persist the state in a separate file? There are two points to consider to understand why the state file is necessary:

- This Terraform project doesn't *own* all the infrastructure in your Azure account.
- As we make changes to our Terraform code (to change our infrastructure), it becomes out of sync with the live infrastructure. (We are relying on Terraform to change the live infrastructure to make it look like our declared infrastructure.)

Let's consider the first point. An Azure subscription may well be shared among multiple projects. Infrastructure in that account can have been created by other Terraform

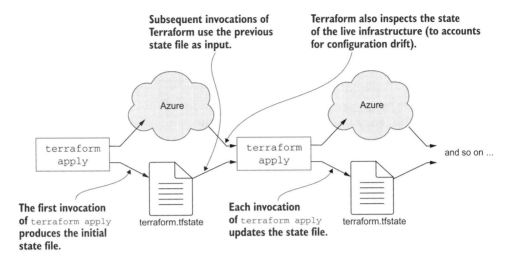

Figure 6.10   Understanding Terraform state is crucial to working with Terraform.

projects or even by entirely different means (e.g., created manually in the Azure portal or with the Azure CLI tool).

As you follow the examples in this book, you most likely have an entire Azure subscription dedicated to it. But this won't be the case if you are working for a company that is managing multiple projects or if you are managing multiple projects yourself. In that case, an Azure subscription is shared between projects, with the subscription containing multiple sets of infrastructure.

The point I'm making is that Terraform *can't* and, indeed, *doesn't* assume that it owns everything in the Azure account that it is allowed to access. What this means is that Terraform can't simply read the live infrastructure and assume that it owns everything. It can only assume ownership of infrastructure that is either declared in our infrastructure code or that is recorded in the state file. The first thing that Terraform does is load your code and your state file. That's how it *knows* which set of infrastructure it owns.

Terraform always wants to be up to date though, so after loading the state file, it refreshes the state directly from the live infrastructure. This allows Terraform to handle configuration drift when the actual state has changed (e.g., because someone tweaked it manually) from the previously recorded state.

You can see how this might affect performance as well. Terraform only queries those parts of the live infrastructure for which it is responsible; those parts which it knows about because of the recorded state. If, instead, it queried *all* live infrastructure, that could be an expensive and time-consuming operation, depending on the total amount of infrastructure that exists in our Azure account.

Now, let's consider the second point mentioned. As we change our Terraform code (to change our infrastructure), it becomes out of sync with our live infrastructure.

That's because we are leading changes to the infrastructure with changes in the code. That's why we call it *infrastructure as code*.

We can add, update, and delete infrastructure by modifying our code. How does Terraform know what's changed? Terraform compares its recorded state with what's in our code. Terraform then automatically figures out the precise set of changes it needs to update our infrastructure. It's amazing when you think it through, just how smart Terraform is and how much work it can do on your behalf.

Now you know more than you probably wanted to about Terraform state, but honestly, it's crucial that we have a good understanding of Terraform state before we can implement it properly in our CD pipeline. We'll come to that in the next chapter. As you proceed through the examples in this chapter and the next, feel free to look at the state file again to see how it grows and changes.

6.8.8   *Destroying and recreating your infrastructure*

We have bootstrapped our infrastructure! It's not much yet, but it's a good start. Before we continue evolving our infrastructure, let's take some time out to experiment with destroying and rebuilding it.

The reason we are choosing this moment to experiment is that it's more efficient to do this experimentation while our infrastructure is small. At the end of this chapter, we'll have added a Kubernetes cluster, and that will take much more time to destroy and rebuild.

Not to mention that eventually, you'll need to clean up these Azure resources anyway. You don't want to end up paying for those (unless, of course, you are developing a real product). *It costs money to run this infrastructure*; although, I hope you are starting with the free credit from Azure. But don't leave it running longer than you need it!

Now, go ahead and destroy your current infrastructure with the Terraform `destroy` command like this:

```
terraform destroy
```

Your output will look something like this:

```
An execution plan has been generated and is shown below.
Resource actions are indicated with the following symbols:
  - destroy

Terraform will perform the following actions:

  # azurerm_resource_group.flixtube will be destroyed
  - resource "azurerm_resource_group" "flixtube" {
      - id       = "/subscriptions/219aac63-3a60-4051-983b-
  ➡ 45649c150e0e/resourceGroups/flixtube" -> null
      - location = "westus" -> null
      - name     = "flixtube" -> null
      - tags     = {} -> null
    }
```

```
Plan: 0 to add, 0 to change, 1 to destroy.

Do you really want to destroy all resources?
  Terraform will destroy all your managed infrastructure, as shown above.
  There is no undo. Only 'yes' will be accepted to confirm.

  Enter a value:
```

Just like the `apply` command, `destroy` shows us its plan. These are the changes it will make. To continue, we must type `yes` and press Enter. Terraform does the work and displays a summary:

```
azurerm_resource_group.flixtube: Destroying... [id=/...
azurerm_resource_group.flixtube: Still destroying...
    [id=/subscriptions/219aac63-3a60-4051-983b-
    45649c150e0e/resourceGroups/flixtube, 10s elapsed]
[id=/subscriptions/219aac63-3a60-4051-983b-
    45649c150e0e/resourceGroups/flixtube, 50s elapsed]
azurerm_resource_group.flixtube: Destruction complete after 54s

Destroy complete! Resources: 1 destroyed.
```

When you have finished with each example in the book, you should invoke `destroy` to clean up the infrastructure that you created. If you are evolving your infrastructure using the iterative method from section 6.8.1 and following this all the way to the end of chapter 7, then you won't need to invoke `destroy` again until the end.

You could also manually delete Azure resources through the Azure portal or the Azure CLI tool. But it's easier to do this with the `destroy` command. It also means you won't accidentally delete other infrastructure, say, if you are sharing the Azure subscription with other projects.

After your practice run with `terraform destroy`, it's simple to rebuild your infrastructure. For that, we'll simply invoke `terraform apply` again:

```
terraform apply
```

Practice this as many times as you want. This process of destroying and rebuilding your infrastructure helps you comprehend the fact that you are actually managing infrastructure with executable code! You can destroy and create your infrastructure at will with no manual effort. At this early stage, this doesn't seem like much, but the significance of this increases as your infrastructure and application grow larger and more complex.

In fact, you may have already realized that we can use our Terraform code to create multiple copies of our infrastructure! In chapter 11, we'll learn how to parameterize our Terraform code to create separate instances for development, testing, and production. If that doesn't excite you, I don't know what will.

6.8.9   What have we achieved?

We now have Terraform installed and we have built our fledgling infrastructure. Terraform is the tool we use for *infrastructure as code*. This is the technique where we store our infrastructure configuration as executable code (e.g., in Terraform code files) that we can use to create, manage, and destroy our infrastructure.

We also created our first Terraform code files and initialized our project using `terraform init`. Then we invoked `terraform apply` to create an Azure resource group. And we learned how to destroy and recreate our infrastructure using `terraform destroy` followed by `terraform apply`.

6.9   Creating your container registry

The next step for our infrastructure is to create a private container registry. We'll use this registry in the next chapter to publish Docker images for our microservices.

If you remember back in chapter 3, we learned how to build and publish Docker images. In that chapter, we manually created a container registry through the GUI in the Azure portal. Now that we have a basic understanding of Terraform, we will revisit that territory and create our registry with code.

6.9.1   Continuing the evolution of our infrastructure

We are now moving to example-2 in the chapter 6 code repository. At this point, if you are working in an iterative manner and continuing onward from example-1, you should copy the example-2 code to the working directory you created earlier in section 6.8.1:

```
cp -r chapter-6/example-2/* working
```

If you are instead working with each example as a separate project, you should destroy the infrastructure you created from example-1:

```
cd chapter-6/example-1/scripts
terraform destroy
```

After destroying the example-1 infrastructure, you can move to example-2 and initialize it:

```
cd chapter-6/example-2/scripts
terraform init
```

6.9.2   Creating the container registry

Listing 6.3 shows the newest Terraform code file that creates our container registry. To get this code to work you need to change the name of the registry. That's because Azure container registry names must be unique. It won't let you use the same name I have chosen (flixtube).

If you are following along, go into container-registry.tf now. Change the name of the registry to something else.

Declares the container registry resource

```
resource "azurerm_container_registry"
 ➥ "container_registry" {

    name = "flixtube"
    resource_group_name = azurerm_resource_group
     ➥ .flixtube.name
    location = "westus"
    admin_enabled = true
    sku = "Basic"
}

... code omitted here ...
```

Sets the name of the container registry. This has to be unique, so you must change this to something else.

Sets the location of the container registry

Sets the name of the resource group and creates a link to another resource

Enables the admin account so we can remotely authenticate with the registry

Using the basic SKU costs less and is easier because storage is managed automatically.

> **NOTE** In case you were wondering, a SKU or *stock keeping unit* is a different version of a product. What this means here is that we are using the Basic version of the container registry.

Take note of how the value of resource_group_name is set from the properties of a resource that is defined in another file (the file resource-group.tf that we looked at in figure 6.1). These two resources are now linked via the Terraform *resource graph*. This is how Terraform manages the dependencies between resources. It's how Terraform knows the order in which it should execute our script files.

Terraform must create the resource group *before* it can populate our Azure account with other resources (such as the new container registry). Let's invoke the apply command to add this new piece of infrastructure:

```
terraform apply -auto-approve
```

Note that we use the -auto-approve argument this time. That means we don't have to type yes each time to approve the changes. This is convenient while we are prototyping our infrastructure, but it becomes essential in the next chapter, when we create our CD pipeline. At that point, we will need to invoke Terraform in an automated and unattended manner. There will be no person there to do the approval! Because of this, we'll now start using -auto-approve to run Terraform in *non-interactive* mode.

We start to create more complex infrastructure now, so you might have to wait a bit longer than last time. Once it's finished, you'll see output similar to before; Terraform is showing us what's changed in our infrastructure. Tacked on the end, though, you'll see some new output. This gives us the details we need to authenticate with our new container registry. We'll learn more about this new output in the next section.

```
Outputs:

registry_hostname = flixtube.azurecr.io
registry_pw = +2kGfgthObeCHPh+VIf9fqJhAf7zEqX6
registry_un = flixtube
```

6.9.3   *Terraform outputs*

Terraform (or the underlying plugin providers) often produces configuration information that we need to know. In the previous section, we created our new container registry. In listing 6.3, you saw that we enabled the admin user for the registry. This allows us to authenticate and interact with our registry (pushing and pulling Docker images).

> **NOTE** Enabling the admin user causes Terraform to generate a username and password. We need to take note of these details so we can later use those to login to our registry.

We can use *Terraform outputs* to extract generated configuration details from our Terraform code. In listing 6.4, you can see multiple outputs declared. This causes these values to be displayed in the terminal when we execute this code. We'll also use outputs in multiple other code files, so look for these in future code listings.

> **Listing 6.4   Terraform outputs (extract from chapter-6/example-2/scripts/ container-registry.tf)**

```
... code omitted here ...

output "registry_hostname" {
    value = azurerm_container_registry.
    ➥ container_registry.login_server      ◁─────┐
}                                                 │
                                                  │
output "registry_un" {                            │   Sets the values
    value = azurerm_container_registry.           │   to be output
    ➥ container_registry.admin_username   ◁───────┤
}                                                 │
                                                  │
output "registry_pw" {                            │
    value = azurerm_container_registry.           │
    ➥ container_registry.admin_password   ◁───────┘
}
```

Creates an output

6.9.4   *What have we achieved?*

We have continued to evolve our infrastructure by creating a container registry. This is something we'll need in the next chapter, when we publish Docker images for our microservices.

In this section, we added a new Terraform code file and executed it. This created the new container registry in our Azure account. Finally, we learned about how we can use Terraform outputs to display pertinent information about the resources and infrastructure that was created.

6.10 *Refactoring to share configuration data*

You might have noticed in recent code listings that we are starting to repeat certain configuration values from file to file. This can be a problem when it comes to changing these values. Ideally, we'd like to be able to change important values in one place and have these shared between all our Terraform code files. We can achieve this with *Terraform variables*, so now we'll refactor our code to share configuration data.

6.10.1 *Continuing the evolution of our infrastructure*

We now move to example-3 in the chapter 6 code repository. At this point, if you are working in an iterative manner and continuing from earlier examples, you can now copy the example-4 code to the working directory you created earlier in 6.8.1:

```
cp -r chapter-6/example-3/* working
```

Otherwise, you can jump directly to example-3 and run `terraform init` in the chapter-6/example-3/scripts directory. If you do this, don't forget to first destroy any infrastructure you created for earlier examples.

6.10.2 *Introducing Terraform variables*

Example-3 in the chapter 6 code repository is a refactoring of example-2, modified to share configuration values between code files, adding a new file called variables.tf. Listing 6.5 shows the new code file.

In the listing, you can see how Terraform global variables are defined for some of our most important configuration values. We have variables defined for the name of our application (flixtube), the location of our data center (West US), and more like that.

Listing 6.5 Setting Terraform global variables (chapter-6/example-3/scripts/variables.tf)

```
variable "app_name" {
    default = "flixtube"         ⊲── Sets default values for
}                                    global variables that
                                     we use across multiple
variable location {              ⊲── Terraform code files
  default = "West US"
}
```

At this point, if you are following along, you should edit variables.tf and set a *unique* name for your application. In listing 6.5, the name is set to `flixtube`. There are various

Azure resource names that will be set from this variable and some will need to be unique for your own version of this project (e.g., the name of your container registry).

Listings 6.6 and 6.7 show how we use our new variables. You can see that the name of our resource group and the name of our container registry are both set from the value of the `app_name` variable. We can also set the locations of these resources from the `location` variable.

Listing 6.6   Resource group configuration with variables (chapter-6/example-3/scripts/resource-group.tf)

Sets the name of the resource group from the app_name variable

```
resource "azurerm_resource_group" "flixtube" {

  name = var.app_name

  location = var.location
}
```

Sets the location from the location variable

Listing 6.7   Container registry configuration with variables (extract from chapter-6/example-3/scripts/container-registry.tf)

```
resource "azurerm_container_registry" "container_registry" {
  name = var.app_name
  resource_group_name = azurerm_resource_group.flixtube.name

  location = var.location
  admin_enabled = true
  sku = "Basic"
}
```

Sets the name of the container registry from the app_name variable

Sets the location from the location variable

```
... code omitted here ...
```

We have refactored our Terraform code and shared some pertinent configuration values between our code files using Terraform variables. We now have one convenient place to go to change these values. For example, let's say that we want to change the location of our application. We can do this simply by changing the `location` variable in variables.tf.

6.11   Creating our Kubernetes cluster

Now we arrive at our most vital piece of infrastructure. We need a platform on which to host our microservices in production, and for this, we'll use Terraform to create a Kubernetes cluster in our Azure account.

6.11.1   Scripting creation of your cluster

Continuing with example-3, now let's look at the code to create our Kubernetes cluster. Listing 6.8 is a new Terraform code file that defines the configuration of our cluster.

We are making continued use of our Terraform variables here, and some of these fields will already be familiar to you. Fields such as `name`, `location`, and `resource _group_name` require no new explanation. However, there are other fields that will be completely new.

Listing 6.8 Creating our Kubernetes cluster (chapter-6/example-3/scripts/ kubernetes-cluster.tf)

```
resource "azurerm_kubernetes_cluster" "cluster" {          ◁──┐  Declares the resource for
    name = var.app_name                                        │  our Kubernetes cluster
    location = var.location
    resource_group_name = azurerm_resource_group.flixtube.name
    dns_prefix = var.app_name
    kubernetes_version = "1.18.8"          ◁──────  Specifies the version of Kubernetes we
                                                    are using. By the time you run this code,
                                                    this version may no longer be available
                                                    on Azure. See section 6.6.3 for how to
                                                    choose a version number.

    linux_profile {
        admin_username = var.admin_username

        ssh_key {
            key_data = "${trimspace(tls_private_key.key.public_key_openssh)}
              ↪ ${var.admin_username}@azure.com"
        }
    }

    default_node_pool {          ◁──┐
        name = "default"             │  Configures the nodes
        node_count = 1               │  for our cluster
        vm_size = "Standard_B2ms"    │
    }                            ◁──┘

    service_principal {          ◁──┐  Configures authentication
        client_id = var.client_id    │  details to allow the cluster
        client_secret = var.client_secret   │  to interact with Azure
    }                            ◁──┘
}

output "cluster_client_key" {
  value = azurerm_kubernetes_cluster.cluster.kube_config[0].client_key
}

output "cluster_client_certificate" {
  value = azurerm_kubernetes_cluster.cluster.kube_config[0]
    ↪ .client_certificate
}

output "cluster_cluster_ca_certificate" {
  value = azurerm_kubernetes_cluster.cluster.kube_config[0]
    ↪ .cluster_ca_certificate
}

output "cluster_cluster_username" {
  value = azurerm_kubernetes_cluster.cluster.kube_config[0].username
```

Sets authentication details for our cluster

```
}

output "cluster_cluster_password" {
  value = azurerm_kubernetes_cluster.cluster.kube_config[0].password
}

output "cluster_kube_config" {
  value = azurerm_kubernetes_cluster.cluster.kube_config_raw
}

output "cluster_host" {
  value = azurerm_kubernetes_cluster.cluster.kube_config[0].host
}
```

Notice in listing 6.8 how we specify which version of Kubernetes to use. If you'll recall, we decided on this back in section 6.6.3. Then we provide an SSH key that we can use to interact with our cluster. We are linking to the `tls_private_key` resource that is defined in the file private-key.tf. In this code file, we use a different Terraform provider to generate an SSH key. You haven't seen this yet in a code listing. But if you are curious and want to understand how the SSH key is generated, take a look for yourself in the file example-3/scripts/private-key.tf.

Listing 6.8 is also where we define the nodes and VM size that powers our cluster. Note here that we are building our cluster on only a single node. Although we could easily add more, but we'll save that for chapter 11. For now, configuration of the service principal is what we must focus on next. Repeated here from listing 6.8, we link Azure authentication details into the configuration of our cluster:

```
service_principal {
    client_id     = var.client_id
    client_secret = var.client_secret
}
```

A *service principal* is an authentication mechanism for Azure. It allows our cluster to authenticate with Azure so that it can create Azure load balancers as external endpoints for our customer-facing microservices (e.g., our front-end gateway).

We use two new Terraform variables, `client_id` and `client_secret`, which are defined in the latest version of variables.tf. We didn't give these variables default values. That's because these contain sensitive authentication details, and for security reasons, we'd prefer not to include their values in our codebase.

6.11.2 *Cluster authentication with Azure*

We can't create our cluster just yet. If we invoke the `apply` command at this point, Terraform will ask us to provide values for the variables `client_id` and `client_secret` (because we didn't supply default values for these in the code).

These variables provide our Kubernetes cluster with the authentication details for our Azure subscription. To fulfill these variables, we must first create a service principal in Azure. That's like a separate access account that allows our cluster to interact with Azure on our behalf.

It is possible to create the service principal completely in Terraform, and it would be ideal if we could do that. After all, the service principal is only another aspect of our infrastructure, and we'd prefer to have our entire infrastructure created by Terraform.

Unfortunately, at the time of writing, this doesn't work reliably. Although the Azure provider does cater to creating service principals, for some reason, it doesn't deal with the timing of creation properly. It takes time for the service principal to propagate through Azure, and there is no way of delaying the creation of the cluster until the service principal is ready. If we attempt this in Terraform, we will end up creating a cluster before the service principal exists. This results in an error because the creation of the cluster requires the service principal to already be in place.

Due to this problem with the Azure provider (which might be fixed by the time you read this), we can't reliably create the service principal from Terraform. Instead, we'll resort to using the Azure CLI tool for this task. This is actually OK because we only have to create the service principal once, and thereafter, we will simply continue using it. Before you can create the service principal, you must know the ID of your Azure subscription, which you can do with the following command:

```
az account show
```

Pick out the value from the `id` field and use it create your service principal:

```
az ad sp create-for-rbac --role="Contributor"
➥ --scopes="/subscriptions/<subscription-id>"
```

When you run that command, you should replace `<subscription-id>` with your own subscription ID. The output from the command will look something like the following:

```
{
  "appId": "a2016492-068c-4f37-a32b-6e6196b65488",
  "displayName": "flixtube",
  "name": "http://flixtube",
  "password": "deb781f5-29e7-42c7-bed8-80781411973a",
  "tenant": "f88afda7-7b7b-4fb6-a093-6b254e780c4c"
}
```

We have created a service principal for our cluster to authenticate with Azure. Jot down your own values for the fields `appId` and `password` (these will be different than mine!). You'll need these in a moment to input the values for the Terraform variables `client_id` and `client_secret`.

6.11.3 *Building your cluster*

We are now ready to run our latest Terraform code to create our Kubernetes cluster. Invoke the `apply` command:

```
terraform apply -auto-approve
```

Terraform prompts you to enter the variables that don't have values. The first is `client _id`:

```
var.client_id
  Enter a value:
```

Here you should enter the `appId` value for your service principal. Then Terraform prompts you for `client_secret`:

```
var.client_secret
  Enter a value:
```

Now enter the `password` value for your service principal. Terraform now creates your Kubernetes cluster. This can take some time; you might like to grab a cup of coffee.

> **NOTE** If you have a problem with the version number I've used (1.18.8), it is probably because that version is no longer available on Azure. See section 6.6.3 for instructions on how to choose an available version.

At the end, you'll see a load of Terraform outputs that give you configuration and authentication details for your new cluster. Take note of these following values. These are the credentials we need to interface with our new Kubernetes cluster.

- `cluster_client_certificate`
- `cluster_client_key`
- `cluster_cluster_ca_certificate`

6.11.4 *What have we achieved?*

Well done! We just created a Kubernetes cluster. If you had previously been convinced that Kubernetes is complicated, you might now be surprised at just how simple this was!

This is a significant achievement on the road to production. Again, we continued the evolution of our architecture, adding a Kubernetes cluster to our existing infrastructure. Along the way, we did some refactoring and used Terraform variables to share important values between our various Terraform code files.

We also created a service principal for authentication with Azure. The Kubernetes cluster uses this when it needs to create Azure load balancers. We'll talk about those in the next chapter.

6.12 *Interacting with Kubernetes*

Now that we have a Kubernetes cluster, how do we interact with it? Figure 6.11 shows the methods of interaction we have at our disposal. Briefly, these are

- The Kubernetes CLI tool, Kubectl
- Terraform, the primary method we use in this book
- The Kubernetes dashboard

In this chapter, we created a Kubernetes cluster using Terraform. In the next chapter, we'll expand on this and learn how to interact with the cluster to deploy containers. Once again, we'll use Terraform.

In this book, the primary way we interact with Kubernetes is with Terraform. But it's also useful for us to understand the other methods of interaction so we can test the cluster we just created. We'll round out this chapter by interacting with our cluster using Kubectl and the Kubernetes dashboard.

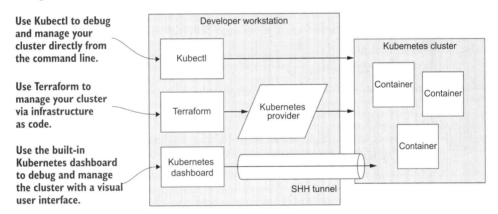

Use Kubectl to debug and manage your cluster directly from the command line.

Use Terraform to manage your cluster via infrastructure as code.

Use the built-in Kubernetes dashboard to debug and manage the cluster with a visual user interface.

Figure 6.11   Methods of interacting with Kubernetes

6.12.1 *Kubernetes authentication*

Before interacting with your Kubernetes cluster, we must first authenticate with it. In section 6.11.3, you took note of the following outputs from Terraform. These are the credentials you need to authenticate with your cluster.

- `cluster_client_certificate`
- `cluster_client_key`
- `cluster_cluster_ca_certificate`

At this point, you could try and manually set up your authentication details. To do this, you would create the file .kube/config under your home directory and then type into it your Kubernetes credentials. Unfortunately, this setup is not a trivial exercise! But happily, we are using Azure and the Azure CLI tools to automate this set up for us with the following command:

```
az aks get-credentials --resource-group flixtube --name flixtube
```

When you invoke `aks get-credentials`, be sure to replace both instances of `flixtube` with the name of your own application. This is the name that you set for your `app_name` variable back in section 6.10. Invoke the command according to this template:

```
az aks get-credentials --resource-group <your-app-name>
    --name <your-app-name>
```

After running this command, the Azure CLI tool creates your Kubectl config file. You can take a look at it with the following command:

```
cat ~/.kube/config
```

You can learn more about the manual setup of the Kubectl config file here:

http://mng.bz/op8D

6.12.2 *The Kubernetes CLI*

With the configuration in place, we can now use the Kubernetes CLI (Kubectl) to interact with our cluster.

INSTALLING THE KUBERNETES CLI

Instructions for installing Kubectl can be found here:

https://kubernetes.io/docs/tasks/tools/install-kubectl/

Installation is simply a matter of downloading the correct binary executable for your operating system and adding it to your system path. When you have installed Kubectl, you can test it with the following command:

```
kubectl version
```

This shows you the version numbers for both Kubectl on your local computer and for your Kubernetes cluster, which might look something like this:

```
Client Version: version.Info{Major:"1", Minor:"19", GitVersion:"v1.19.3",
    GitCommit:"1e11e4a2108024935ecfcb2912226cedeafd99df",
    GitTreeState:"clean", BuildDate:"2020-10-14T12:50:19Z",
    GoVersion:"go1.15.2", Compiler:"gc", Platform:"windows/amd64"}
Server Version: version.Info{Major:"1", Minor:"18", GitVersion:"v1.18.8",
    GitCommit:"73ec19bdfc6008cd3ce6de96c663f70a69e2b8fc",
    GitTreeState:"clean", BuildDate:"2020-09-17T04:17:08Z",
    GoVersion:"go1.13.15", Compiler:"gc", Platform:"linux/amd64"}
```

This is a little hard to read! But if you scan across from `Client Version`, you'll find `GitVersion`, which shows you the version of Kubectl. You can see that I am using version 1.19.3. You can then scan across from `Server Version` to find `GitVersion`, which shows you the version of Kubernetes. You can see that my cluster is on version 1.18.8 of Kubernetes.

USING KUBECTL

Kubectl is the official and primary method of interaction with Kubernetes. Anything that can be done with Kubernetes can be done from Kubectl—configuration, deployment of containers, and even monitoring live applications.

In this book, we mostly control Kubernetes through Terraform code. That's a higher level and more expressive way to work with Kubernetes. It's also nice that we can maintain a simple deployment pipeline and keep all of our infrastructure and deployment code in Terraform. But that's not always possible in real-world production systems; although, we are able to achieve that for the simple examples in this book.

We should, however, learn the basics of Kubectl because it is the official interface to Kubernetes, and it is also what underlies the Kubernetes provider for Terraform. We need to know it at least because it's the best way to debug our Kubernetes cluster, which is something we'll look at in chapter 10. With that in mind, let's test the authenticated connection to our Kubernetes cluster with the following command:

```
kubectl get nodes
```

The get nodes command shows the list of the nodes that are powering our cluster. We have created a cluster with a single node, so the output will be quite short; something like this:

```
NAME                            STATUS   ROLES   AGE   VERSION
aks-default-42625609-vmss000000  Ready    agent   21m   v1.15.7
```

That's it for now. We'll return to Kubectl and learn more commands in upcoming chapters. If you desire, you can continue to learn and experiment with Kubectl here:

https://kubernetes.io/docs/reference/kubectl/overview/

6.12.3 *The Kubernetes dashboard*

Kubectl is one way to interact with Kubernetes. Another is through the Kubernetes dashboard, and once we have Kubectl setup and authenticated, we can use it to access the dashboard.

INSTALLING THE KUBERNETES DASHBOARD

The Kubernetes dashboard is not installed by default. Although, we can install it easily with the following command:

```
kubectl apply -f
  https://raw.githubusercontent.com/kubernetes/dashboard/v2.0.4/aio/deploy/
  recommended.yaml
```

CONNECTING TO THE KUBERNETES DASHBOARD

We can't directly connect to the Kubernetes dashboard. It's simply not exposed to the public. However, given that we have already authenticated Kubectl to connect to our cluster, we can use Kubectl to create a proxy that allows us to access the dashboard from our development workstation:

```
kubectl proxy
```

If you are running the proxy within a Vagrant VM and want to access it from your host operating system, you need to change its bound IP address so that it's externally accessible:

```
kubectl proxy --address=0.0.0.0
```

The proxy allows us to use the full Kubernetes REST API, which is accessible at http://localhost:8001. You can open that URL in your browser and see what it returns.

   If you'd like to explore the Kubernetes HTTP API, you can do so using the `curl` command, Postman, or Visual Studio Code REST Client. You can learn more about the proxy command here:

https://kubernetes.io/docs/reference/generated/kubectl/kubectl-commands#proxy

Now with the REST API available, we can go through the proxy to get to the dashboard. Open this rather long and awkward URL in your web browser:

http://localhost:8001/api/v1/namespaces/kubernetes-dashboard/services/https:kubernetes-dashboard:/proxy/

After opening the dashboard, we come to its authentication screen. We can authenticate by selecting our Kubeconfig file as shown in figure 6.12. This config file is the one we looked at earlier in section 6.12.1, which you can find in your home directory at ~/.kube/config.

   NOTE If you are working under a Vagrant VM, you must copy this file out of the VM to your host operating system so that you can select it and authenticate with the dashboard.

To learn more about installing and connecting to the Kubernetes dashboard, read the information on this web page:

https://kubernetes.io/docs/tasks/access-application-cluster/web-ui-dashboard/

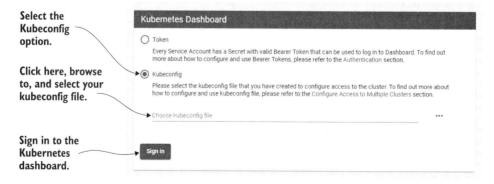

Figure 6.12   Authentication for the Kubernetes dashboard

EXPLORING THE KUBERNETES DASHBOARD

With the Kubernetes dashboard open in our browser, we can graphically inspect our cluster using the GUI. This is a great way to understand our cluster and learn about Kubernetes! I encourage you to spend some time exploring this dashboard by yourself before moving on. As you work through the next chapter, you'll be able to return to this dashboard and see the containers that we will soon deploy.

Figure 6.13 shows you the overview page of the dashboard. This is where you will start your exploration. The dashboard is the first place to come, especially in the early days, when something is wrong with your cluster or any of the containers it is hosting. We'll learn more about how the dashboard can help with debugging in chapter 10.

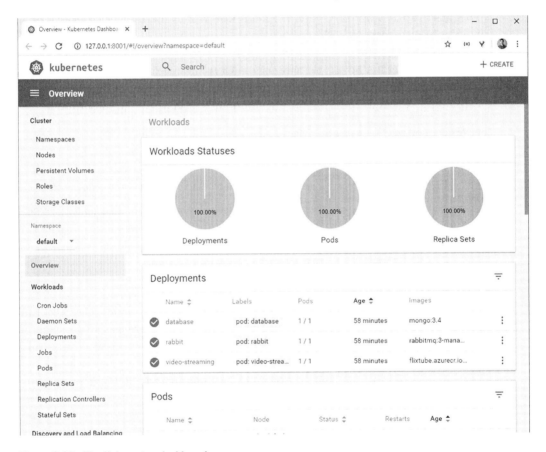

Figure 6.13 The Kubernetes dashboard

6.12.4 *What have we achieved?*

We have our Kubernetes cluster online and are ready to start deploying our microservices to it. In this book, we mostly use Terraform code to interact with our cluster, but we just learned about two other ways of interacting with it: the Kubernetes CLI and the Kubernetes dashboard.

- *The Kubernetes CLI (known as Kubectl) is used to configure and query our cluster from the terminal.* It gives us a lower-level API for administration and debugging.
- *The Kubernetes dashboard is a visual GUI for interacting with our cluster.* It allows us to visually explore the variety of resources that are available to use with Kubernetes. As well as being a good tool for debugging, it's also a great educational tool to better understand Kubernetes.

In the next chapter, we'll continue to learn about interacting with Kubernetes through Terraform code.

6.13   *Terraform review*

This has been another big chapter! I bet it now makes the Docker chapter look a lot simpler in retrospect.

To review, Terraform is a universal tool for the creation and configuration of cloud-based infrastructure. So far, we have used it to create the entire infrastructure for our microservices application (with the exception of the Azure service principal). Before continuing, let's review the Terraform commands we have added to our toolkit.

Table 6.2   Review of Terraform commands

Command	Description
`terraform init`	Initializes a Terraform project and downloads the provider plugins
`terraform` ➧ `apply -auto-approve`	Executes Terraform code files in the working directory to incrementally apply changes to our infrastructure
`terraform destroy`	Destroys all infrastructure that was created by the Terraform project

6.14   *Continue your learning*

In this chapter, we learned how to create a production environment based on Kubernetes. To build our production environment, we used Terraform and the technique called infrastructure as code. We'll continue to learn more about both Terraform and Kubernetes in the next chapter.

Kubernetes itself is a deep and complex technology, definitely the most complex we will talk about in this book. You might spend many months working with it before you dig all the way to the bottom! In this book, we barely scratched the surface, but we covered enough to get our application deployed to production. To dive deeper into these topics, I recommend the following books:

- *Core Kubernetes* by Jay Vyas and Chris Love (Manning, est. Summer 2021)
- *Kubernetes in Action* by Marko Lukša (Manning, 2017)
- *Terraform in Action* by Scott Winkler (Manning, est. Spring 2021)
- *GitOps and Kubernetes* by Billy Yuen, Alexander Matyushentsev, et. al. (Manning, est. Spring 2021)

- *Kubernetes Quickly* by William Denniss (Manning, est. Summer 2021)
- *Learn Kubernetes in a Month of Lunches* by Elton Stoneman (Manning, est. February 2021)

You can learn more about Kubernetes by reading the Kubernetes documentation here:

- https://kubernetes.io/docs/home/

The documentation for Terraform is available here:

- https://www.terraform.io/docs/index.html

To find out what else you can do with the Azure CLI tool, read the documentation here:

- https://docs.microsoft.com/en-us/cli/azure/

You can read more about the managed Kubernetes service on Azure here:

- https://docs.microsoft.com/en-au/azure/aks

Summary

- Infrastructure as code is a technique where we store our infrastructure configuration as code. Editing and executing that code is how we update our infrastructure.
- We use Terraform to script the creation of cloud resources and application infrastructure from code.
- Terraform must be initialized before it can be used, and we should fix our provider version numbers to avoid nasty surprises.
- Terraform state maintains a record of the system we created and makes future modifications to the system more efficient.
- We created production infrastructure for our application on Azure: a container registry and a Kubernetes cluster.
- We can use Terraform outputs to find out key details of the infrastructure that was created.
- The Terraform resource graph ensures that resources created by Terraform are created in the correct order.
- Kubernetes is a computing platform with support for multiple cloud vendors.
- Kubernetes has an automatable API. This allows us to build a continuous delivery pipeline (more in the next chapter).
- We interact with our cluster not only using Terraform, but also with the Kubernetes CLI (kubectl) and the Kubernetes dashboard.

Getting to
continuous delivery

7

This chapter covers

- Deploying containers to your Kubernetes cluster
- Working with Terraform to configure Kubernetes
- Creating an automated deployment pipeline for your application
- Using Bitbucket Pipelines for continuous delivery

In this chapter, we bring an early version of our microservices application to production. Having just created an empty Kubernetes cluster in the previous chapter, we are now ready to deploy containers to it.

First, we'll deploy our MongoDB database and RabbitMQ servers. Then, we'll deploy our first microservice to the Kubernetes cluster: the video-streaming microservice we created way back in chapter 2 (you've come such a long way since then).

After learning how to use Terraform to deploy containers to Kubernetes, we'll wrap up our deployment process in an automated continuous delivery (CD) pipeline. At that point, updating our infrastructure and application will be achieved by pushing code changes to our hosted code repository. Exciting times!

If you find this chapter difficult to follow, don't worry. This chapter and the previous one are probably the most difficult chapters in the book, so please push through! Following along with the examples is the best way to gain experience. At the end of this chapter, your application will be *live* in production, and you need to know for yourself how good that feels!

7.1 New and familiar tools

This chapter revisits both Kubernetes and Terraform. But now, we'll use Terraform to deploy containers and microservices to our Kubernetes cluster. We are also introduced to Bitbucket Pipelines, a hosted service we'll use to create a CD pipeline for our microservices application.

Table 7.1 New and familiar tools in chapter 7

Tool	Version	Purpose
Kubernetes	1.18.6	Kubernetes is the computing platform that we'll use to host our microservices in production.
Terraform	0.12.29	Terraform allows us to script the creation of cloud resources and application infrastructure.
Bitbucket Pipelines	N/A	The hosted service from Atlassian that we'll use for CD to automate the deployment of our application.

7.2 Getting the code

To follow along with this chapter, you need to download the code or clone the repository.

- Download a zip file of the code from here:
  https://github.com/bootstrapping-microservices/chapter-7
- You can clone the code using Git like this:
  ```
  git clone https://github.com/bootstrapping-microservices/chapter-7.git
  ```

For help on installing and using Git, see chapter 2. If you have problems with the code, log an issue against the repository in GitHub.

7.3 Continuing to evolve our infrastructure

In the previous chapter, you had a choice for following along with the examples. It went like this:

- *Iteratively evolve our infrastructure while following the examples in chapters 6 and 7.* We started with chapter-6/example-1 and then progressively copied in the code from each new example.
- *Build fresh infrastructure for each example.* The examples in chapters 6 and 7 can also be run standalone, so we can easily start our infrastructure from any point by jumping into any examples and invoking Terraform.

You might have chosen to follow along using the iterative and evolutionary approach (the first option). If so, you can continue to do that in this chapter, where the examples are designed to follow on directly from the previous chapter. Continue to copy files from each new example into your working directory as you did in chapter 6. If, instead, you are running each example by itself or jumping directly to particular examples that interest you (the second option), you can also continue to do that in this chapter.

Whichever way you work, be sure to change the value of the app_name variable at the top of variables.tf to a name that is unique to you. This must be unique! If you call your application FlixTube, it's going to overlap with resources that myself or other readers of this book have created.

Figure 7.1 illustrates what we'll implement in this chapter. We'll create an automated deployment pipeline to deploy a MongoDB database server, to deploy a RabbitMQ server, and most importantly, to deploy our first microservice.

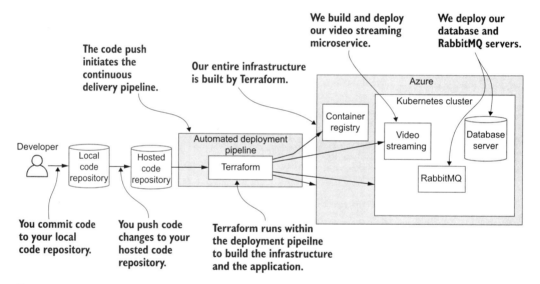

Figure 7.1   The continuous delivery (CD) pipeline and application we build in this chapter

7.4   *Continuous delivery (CD)*

Continuous delivery (CD) is a technique in software development where we do frequent automated deployments of our updated code to a production (or testing) environment. This is an important aspect of our application because it's how we reliably and frequently deliver features into the hands of our customers. Getting feedback from customers is vital to building a product that's relevant. CD allows us to quickly and safely get code changes into production and promotes a rapid pace of development.

So far, we have managed to keep our entire deployment process scripted with Terraform. That won't always be the case with more complex production systems, but it suffices for our example application and helps to keep things simple. It also makes it easier for us to instantiate our deployment process within the CD pipeline.

Figure 7.2 shows you what our CD pipeline will look like by the end of this chapter. Pushing code changes to our Bitbucket code repository initiates automated deployment. This executes our Terraform code and updates our application that is hosted in the Kubernetes cluster.

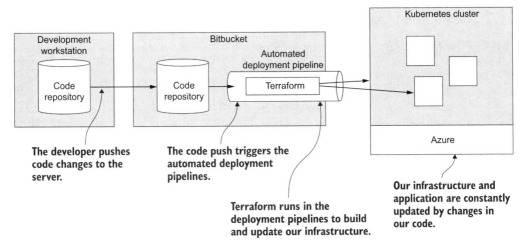

Figure 7.2 With infrastructure as code, we can use code to create our infrastructure.

The Terraform code that we write must be simple and as bullet-proof as possible. That's because, ultimately, it's more difficult to debug code running in a hosted CD pipeline! This is why our deployment code should be simple, have minimal moving parts, and be well tested.

Like any other code, we'll test our deployment code on our development workstation (or personal computer) before it goes to production. A large part of this chapter (and the previous chapter) consists of prototyping and testing our deployment pipeline before we get anywhere near CD.

If CD in any way sounds complex or difficult, let me reassure you that it is not. Continuous delivery, in fact, is little more than the ability to host an automatically invoked shell script in the cloud. Our deployment shell script will be invoked automatically when we push code changes to our code repository.

> **NOTE** If you can write a shell script (it's not difficult), then you can build a CD pipeline. As mentioned, CD isn't difficult; although, what you put in the shell script might be.

For the examples in this chapter, we'll create a deployment shell script and invoke Terraform from it to do our deployment. Before we tackle creating the deployment shell script and moving it to our CD pipeline, we will first learn how to deploy containers to Kubernetes using Terraform. Once we are through that, setting up our CD pipeline will be relatively easy.

7.5   *Deploying containers with Terraform*

In the previous chapter, we learned how to create infrastructure with Terraform. We created a private container registry and a Kubernetes cluster. In this chapter, we use Terraform again, but this time to deploy containers to our cluster. Before we can do that, we must first configure the Kubernetes provider for Terraform.

7.5.1   *Configuring the Kubernetes provider*

We are now moving to example-1 in the chapter 7 code repository. Depending on how you were working in chapter 6 (see section 6.8.1), you can either update your working project with the new code or just start fresh with example-1 for this chapter. The following listing shows the new code we'll add to providers.tf to configure the Kubernetes provider.

> **Listing 7.1   Setting up the Kubernetes provider (extract from chapter-7/example-1/scripts/providers.tf)**

```
... code omitted ...

provider "kubernetes" {   ⟵── Configures the Kubernetes provider

    version = "1.10.0"   ⟵── Fixes the version number of the provider

    host = azurerm_kubernetes_cluster
    ➥ .cluster.kube_config[0].host                          ⟵

    client_certificate = base64decode(azurerm_kubernetes_cluster
    ➥ .cluster.kube_config[0].client_certificate)           ⟵
                                                    Sets the connection
                                                    and authentication
    client_key = base64decode(azurerm_kubernetes_cluster     details for our
    ➥ .cluster.kube_config[0].client_key)              Kubernetes cluster

    cluster_ca_certificate = base64decode(azurerm_kubernetes_cluster
    ➥ .cluster.kube_config[0]
    ➥ .cluster_ca_certificate)                              ⟵

}
```

You might be interested to know that this is where we configure the connection and authentication details for our Kubernetes cluster. In this code file, those values are automatically pulled from the other Terraform code file that created our cluster (see kubernetes-cluster.tf).

You could just as easily replace these values with the details for a cluster that you created separately. For instance, you might have created your cluster manually in the Azure portal GUI or with the Azure CLI tool. You may have used a completely separate Terraform project to create your cluster as well. (We'll talk about separating our code in this way in chapter 11.) Either way, as long as you have the connection details for your cluster (like the ones we noted in section 6.11.3), then you can use them here to connect to it.

If you are following along, you now need to invoke `terraform init`. You need to do this regardless of whether you are evolving your working project or starting fresh with example-1. We added a new provider to our Terraform project and the `init` command is what downloads the plugin for it.

7.5.2 Deploying our database

The first container we'll deploy to Kubernetes is for our MongoDB database server. Eventually, this is where we'll host separate databases for each of our microservices.

Listing 7.2 shows the Terraform code to deploy a database server to our cluster. This script creates a Kubernetes deployment that instantiates a container from the public Docker image for MongoDB. It then creates a Kubernetes service that makes the deployment accessible by other containers via DNS. This is how other containers can connect to our database. You can learn more about Kubernetes concepts like deployments and services in the Kubernetes documentation at https://kubernetes.io/docs/concepts/.

Listing 7.2 Deploying your database (chapter-7/example-1/scripts/database.tf)

```
resource "kubernetes_deployment" "database" {          ◁──┐  Declares a Kubernetes deployment
                                                             for our MongoDB database server,
    metadata {            ◁──┐  Sets metadata for          causing the MongoDB container to
      name = "database"        the deployment               be instantiated into our Kubernetes
                                                            cluster
      labels = {
        pod = "database"      ◁──┐  Labels the deployment
      }
    }

    spec {                      ┌──  Sets the number of replicas (or copies)
      replicas = 1       ◁──┘       to create for pods in this deployment

      selector {         ◁──┐
        match_labels = {        Attaches the deployment
          pod = "database"      to its pods by matching
        }                       labels
      }                  ◁──┘

      template {         ◁──┐  Template for pods that are
        metadata {            created by this deployment
          labels = {
            pod = "database"   ◁──┐
          }                       Labels the pod
        }

        spec {                 ┌──  Specifies details for the single
          container {    ◁──┘       container instantiated in the pod
```

Sets the name of the deployment → (points to `name = "database"`)

Sets metadata for each pod → (points to `metadata {`)

```
                         image = "mongo:4.2.8"        ◁
        Sets the    ┌─▷  name  = "database"                Sets the image from which to
      name of the   │                                      instantiate the container
        container   │      port {
                    │          container_port = 27017  ◁    Shows the ports in the container to be
                    │      }                                exposed; in this case, the default port for
                    │   }                                   MongoDB (optional, primarily informational)
                    │  }
                    │ }
                    }

        resource "kubernetes_service" "database" {    ◁
            metadata {                                     Declares a Kubernetes service
        Sets the   ┌─▷  name = "database"                  that creates a DNS record so the
        name of    │   }                                   database is accessible by other
      the service  │                                       containers within the cluster
                   │  spec {
                       selector = {
                           pod = kubernetes_deployment.database
                      ➥    .metadata[0].labels.pod   ◁
        Sets the   │   }                                   Attaches the service to the
       port that is│                                       deployment by matching labels
       exposed by  │   port {
      this service └─▷    port = 27017
                       }
                                                      Exposes the service to the external world using an
                       type = "LoadBalancer"   ◁      Azure load balancer. This allocates an externally
                   }                                  accessible IP address for the database. We can use
                                                      this to test our deployment.
               }
```

You can see toward the end of listing 7.2 that we attached an Azure load balancer to the Kubernetes service to expose our database to the outside world. The real purpose of a load balancer is something we'll talk about in chapters 10 and 11, but here, we simply use it to access the database in our cluster from our development workstation. This is something we couldn't do if the container was hidden within the cluster.

From a security perspective, exposing our database like this is a big no-no. This means that anyone (including those with nefarious intent) could make changes to our database. Be assured that this situation is only temporary! We have only exposed our database for testing (which we'll do in a moment) at this early stage in our infrastructure. After testing, we'll lock it down so that it's accessible only from within the cluster.

7.5.3   *Preparing for continuous delivery*

We are in the middle of prototyping and testing our deployment code on our development workstation. In the process, we'll prepare to run this code in our CD pipeline. That means we need our code to run in a fully automated fashion, so we should now factor out any human interaction.

If you remember back to section 6.11.2, we created an Azure service principal that allows our Kubernetes cluster to authenticate with Azure. It needs this so that it can create load balancers for our services such as in listing 7.2, where we requested an external endpoint for our database service. Then, in section 6.11.3, when invoking `terraform apply`, we manually supplied values for the `client_id` and `client_secret` variables. For that, we typed in the values from the `appId` and `password` fields from our service principal.

Manually typing in values like this doesn't work in a CD pipeline. This has to be automated! It's also kind of annoying having to constantly type these values while we are prototyping our Terraform code.

Now we will set these values through command-line arguments. First, though, you must remember the details for your service principal. If the one you created in section 6.11.2 is still operational, and you have the details noted down, you can reuse that. Otherwise, run through the instructions in section 6.11.2 again to create or update your service principal. Then take note of the `appId` and `password` fields. Now invoke `terraform  apply` for example-1 while setting `client_id` and `client_secret` as command-line arguments:

```
terraform apply -var="client_id=a2016492-068c-4f37-a32b-6e6196b65488"
  -var="client_secret=deb781f5-29e7-42c7-bed8-80781411973a" -auto-approve
```

Just remember to *replace* the values for `client_id` and `client_secret` with the values for your own service principal according to this template:

```
terraform apply -var="client_id=<your-client-id>"
  -var="client_secret=<your-client-secret>" -auto-approve
```

You can see we also continue to use the `-auto-approve` command-line option that we started using in section 6.9.2. Setting the variables and enabling automatic approval puts our Terraform project in a fully automatic mode. No human intervention is required, and this means we'll be able to execute this code completely unattended in our CD pipeline.

7.5.4   *Testing the new database server*

After invoking `terraform apply` in the previous section, you should now have a database server running in your Kubernetes cluster. In order to test that our database is up, we have attached an Azure load balancer to it (as shown in listing 7.2). This is a temporary measure so that we can make our database externally accessible and test it to be sure that it is working.

FINDING THE EXTERNAL IP ADDRESS

To find out the external IP address that's been allocated to the database service, we can either use the Kubernetes CLI tool (Kubectl) or the Kubernetes dashboard that we set up earlier (section 6.12). We can use Kubectl to list the services we have in our cluster:

```
kubectl get services
```

If you have trouble using Kubectl and connecting to your cluster, refer back to section 6.12.1. The output looks something like this:

```
NAME       TYPE         CLUSTER-IP    EXTERNAL-IP    PORT(S)
database   LoadBalancer 10.0.226.64   168.62.216.232 27017:30390/TCP
kubernetes ClusterIP    10.0.0.1      <none>         443/TCP
```

Pick out the database service (e.g., the name we gave it in listing 7.2) and note the IP address in the `EXTERNAL-IP` column. You can also see the MongoDB default port 27017 listed in the `PORT(S)` column. This is the IP address and port to access our database from outside the cluster. Alternatively, we can open the Kubernetes dashboard (as per section 6.12.3) and navigate to the Services section to find these details.

TESTING THE CONNECTION

Now using Robo 3T (like in section 4.5.2) or another database viewer, connect to your database server with the external IP address that you jotted down for it. Make sure you use port number 27017 to connect. If all is well, you should be able to connect to your database and view its default content (we haven't added anything specific yet, however).

7.5.5   *Deploying and testing RabbitMQ*

In the same way as with our database server, but with a slightly different configuration, we now move to example-2. In that, we deploy a RabbitMQ server to our Kubernetes cluster.

Listing 7.3 is similar to listing 7.2. It creates a Kubernetes deployment that instantiates a RabbitMQ server in a container. It creates a Kubernetes service that makes the container accessible via DNS within the cluster. Again, we attach an Azure load balancer to the Kubernetes service so that we can make it accessible from outside the cluster for testing. Then, we can use the RabbitMQ dashboard to check that RabbitMQ is functional.

> **Listing 7.3   Deploying your RabbitMQ server (chapter-7/example-2/scripts/rabbit.tf)**

```
resource "kubernetes_deployment" "rabbit" {     ◁─── Declares a Kubernetes deployment to
  metadata {                                           deploy our RabbitMQ server. This is
    name = "rabbit"                                    what instantiates the RabbitMQ
                                                       container in our Kubernetes cluster.
    labels = {
      pod = "rabbit"
    }
  }

  spec {
    replicas = 1

    selector {
      match_labels = {
        pod = "rabbit"
      }
    }
```

```
    template {
      metadata {
        labels = {
          pod = "rabbit"
        }
      }


      spec {
        container {
          image = "rabbitmq:3.8.5-management"    ◁──┐  Instantiates the container from
          name  = "rabbit"                            the public RabbitMQ image

          port {
            container_port = 5672
          }
        }
      }
    }
  }
}

resource "kubernetes_service" "rabbit" {                              ◁───────────────┐
    metadata {
        name = "rabbit"
    }

    spec {
        selector = {
            pod = kubernetes_deployment.rabbit.metadata[0].labels.pod
        }
                                                    Declares a Kubernetes service
        port {                                      that creates a DNS record so the
            port = 5672                             RabbitMQ server is accessible by
        }                                           other containers within the cluster
    }
}

resource "kubernetes_service" "rabbit_dashboard" {                    ◁───────────────┘
    metadata {
        name = "rabbit-dashboard"
    }

    spec {
        selector = {
            pod = kubernetes_deployment.rabbit.metadata[0].labels.pod
        }

        port {
            port = 15672
        }                       Creates an Azure load balancer for the service, which
                                allocates an externally accessible IP address for the
        type = "LoadBalancer"   ◁── dashboard. We can use this to test the deployment.
    }
}
```

Now run `terraform apply` (with the same command-line arguments as earlier in section 7.5.3). Then deploy RabbitMQ to your Kubernetes cluster.

Again, we have configured our service (the service that exposes the RabbitMQ dashboard) to be externally accessible using an Azure load balancer. Now we can use Kubectl or the Kubernetes dashboard to find the external IP address that has been allocated. Refer back to section 7.5.4 to remember how we did this for our database. Take note of the external IP address, and use your browser to open the RabbitMQ management dashboard. You can login with the default user name *guest* and the default password *guest*.

For example, if the IP address for your RabbitMQ dashboard is 40.112.161.104, then you would point your browser at http://40.112.161.104:15672/. The port number for the dashboard is 15672. However, the IP address for your own service *will be different from mine*. Make sure you replace it with the one that was allocated to your RabbitMQ instance.

7.5.6   *Tightening our security*

We have tested our MongoDB and RabbitMQ servers through external endpoints. Exposing these servers to the world is like asking for trouble! Now that we have tested, let's remove the external access and tighten our security. This is as simple as removing the following line from our scripts:

```
type = "LoadBalancer"
```

That's exactly what we'll do from example-3 onward. When you update your working project with the example-3 code and next invoke `terraform apply`, external access to MongoDB and RabbitMQ will be removed, tightening the security for our application.

7.5.7   *What have we achieved?*

After creating our Kubernetes cluster in the previous chapter, in this chapter, we have now started populating it with containers. After setting up the Kubernetes provider for Terraform, we created new Terraform scripts to deploy a MongoDB database and a RabbitMQ server.

We temporarily exposed our servers to the outside world for testing. After testing, we tightened our security by removing those external IPs—for security's sake, we don't want the outside world able to access our internal infrastructure.

7.6   *Deploying our first microservice with Terraform*

We have already deployed some publicly available Docker images to our cluster (MongoDB and RabbitMQ). Now, let's move on to example-3 and deploy our first microservice to the cluster.

Although we are still deploying a container from a Docker image, this time the image is built from our own private code. Before we can deploy a container from it, we must be able to build an image and publish it (just like we practiced in chapter 3) to the private container registry that we created in section 6.9 of the previous chapter.

7.6.1   *Using local variables to compute configuration*

To make things easier and to keep our Terraform code a bit more compact, we'll make use of Terraform *local variables* to compose and share some common configuration values within our newest code file video-streaming.tf. This new file is responsible for building, publishing, and deploying our video-streaming microservice.

The next listing is an extract from the new code file. It shows the declaration of multiple local variables that we'll use in the rest of the script.

> **Listing 7.4   Using local variables for configuration (extract from chapter-7/example-3/scripts/video-streaming.tf)**

```
locals {                                    Sets the name of this deployment service
    service_name = "video-streaming"   ◁    that we use throughout this code file
    login_server = azurerm_container_registry.container_registry
    ⟶ .login_server
    username = azurerm_container_registry        Sets the connection details for our
    ⟶ .container_registry.admin_username         private container registry. These details
    password = azurerm_container_registry        are pulled from the Terraform file that
    ⟶ .container_registry.admin_password         creates the registry.

    image_tag = "${local.login_server}/${local.service_name}:${
    ⟶ var.app_version}"          ◁
}                                      Composes the tag for the video-streaming
                                       microservices' Docker image
# ... code omitted here ...
```

Note how the image_tag local variable is composed of multiple other variables, especially the app_version variable, which we use to tag each successive image with a new version number. The image_tag variable is also how we tag our images to publish these to our container registry.

7.6.2   *Building and publishing the Docker image*

Now, let's look at the Terraform code that builds and publishes the Docker image for our video-streaming microservice. This code has three tasks:

- Building the image
- Logging into the container registry
- Pushing the image to the container registry

You learned how to do all these things in chapter 3. Here, we'll automate this with Terraform.

In listing 7.5, we continue to look at the code in video-streaming.tf. While there is a Docker provider available to use with Terraform, unfortunately, it doesn't have the ability to do the tasks we need. That's why we are making use of Terraform's catch-all `null_resource` and its `local-exec` feature to invoke the Docker commands that we need.

We can use `null_resource` to create Terraform resources that don't have any particular resource type. We use `local-exec` to invoke commands on the local computer. If this listing looks like a big dirty hack, especially the use of `timestamp` to force the Docker image to build, well that's because it is a big dirty hack!

We are using this as a workaround to keep things simple and keep our entire deployment process in Terraform. Long term, we don't want code like this in production. Eventually, we'll migrate away from this hacky starting point and implement a much cleaner solution. But you'll have to wait until chapter 11 to see what that looks like.

Listing 7.5   Build and publish a Docker image (extract from chapter-7/example-3/ scripts/video-streaming.tf)

```
# ... code omitted here ...

resource "null_resource" "docker_build" {

    triggers = {
        always_run = timestamp()
    }

    provisioner "local-exec" {
        command = "docker build -t ${local.image_tag} --file
        ../${local.service_name}/Dockerfile-prod
        ../${local.service_name}"
    }
}

resource "null_resource" "docker_login" {

    depends_on = [ null_resource.docker_build ]

    triggers = {
        always_run = timestamp()
    }

    provisioner "local-exec" {
        command = "docker login ${local.login_server}
        --username ${local.username}
        --password ${local.password}"
    }
}

resource "null_resource" "docker_push" {

    depends_on = [ null_resource.docker_login ]

    triggers = {
        always_run = timestamp()
    }
}
```

Builds our Docker image

Forces our commands to always be invoked

Declares our Docker commands using Terraform's null_resource

Invokes a command to authenticate with our container registry

Authenticates with our registry

Sets a dependency on the previous command because we can't publish our image until after we build it

```
    provisioner "local-exec" {                              ◁─┐ Pushes the image
        command = "docker push ${local.image_tag}"            │ to our registry
    }
}

# ... code omitted here ...
```

I'll be the first to admit that our use (some would say, abuse) of `null_resource` in listing 7.5 is not ideal. If only the Docker provider supported build and push operations directly (why doesn't it?), we wouldn't need this ugly code! Unfortunately, this is the way it is at the moment, but maybe in the future, there will be a more elegant solution. In chapter 11, we'll talk about fixing this when we move away from the *mono-repo* (single code repository) structure towards a *multi-repo* (many code repositories) structure.

7.6.3 *Authentication with the container registry*

After building and publishing the Docker image for our microservice, we must now give the cluster permission to pull the image from the container registry. You can see how this is accomplished in listing 7.6 as we continue to look at video-streaming.tf. In the listing, we create a Kubernetes secret to contain our Docker credentials. This is a secure way to store sensitive data in our cluster.

Listing 7.6   Authentication with the container registry (extract from chapter-7/ example-3/scripts/video-streaming.tf)

```
# ... code omitted here ...                   Defines more local variables
                                              for use in this code file
locals {                           ◁──────┘
    dockercreds = {
        auths = {                                                           ◁──────
            "${local.login_server}" = {
                auth = base64encode("${local.username}:${local.password}")
            }                                          Creates a variable that contains the
        }                                              authentication details for our container registry
    }                                                                         ◁──────
}

resource "kubernetes_secret" "docker_credentials" {   ◁─┐
    metadata {                                           │ Declares a Kubernetes
        name = "docker-credentials"                      │ secret to securely store
    }                                                    │ our authentication
                                                         │ credentials
    data = {
        ".dockerconfigjson" =
        ➡ jsonencode(local.dockercreds)   ◁────── Sets the data for the secret
    }

    type = "kubernetes.io/dockerconfigjson"   ◁────── Sets the type of the secret
}

# ... code omitted here ...
```

Again, we have written code that feels rather awkward. It would be nice if the Docker providers had a more elegant way to express this, and maybe in the future, they will provide that.

7.6.4   *Deploying the video-streaming microservice*

We now have the Terraform code to build and publish our video-streaming microservice. We also have a Kubernetes secret that contains our registry credentials. Now we can write the code to deploy our microservice.

Listing 7.7 shows the remainder of the code in video-streaming.tf. The rest of the file is similar to the code we saw in listings 7.2 and 7.3, which deploy containers for MongoDB and RabbitMQ. We have a Kubernetes deployment that instantiates a container for our video-streaming microservices and a Kubernetes service to make it accessible by DNS within the cluster. Also, yet again, we attach an Azure load balancer to the Kubernetes service to make it externally accessible so we can test our microservice in the cluster from our development workstation.

The major difference here is that the image for our microservice is private and pulled from our own private container registry, whereas MongoDB and RabbitMQ are public images. To facilitate this, we have added an explicit dependency (using `depends_on` that you can see in the listing). This dependency causes our Docker image to be built and published prior to the creation of the Kubernetes deployment. Also, note how the registry credentials are provided via `image_pull_secrets`.

> **Listing 7.7   Deploying the video-streaming microservice (extract from chapter-7/ example-3/scripts/video-streaming.tf)**

```
# ... code omitted here ...                    Declares a Kubernetes deployment to deploy our video-
                                               streaming microservice. This instantiates the container
resource "kubernetes_deployment"               for the microservice into our Kubernetes cluster.
  "service_deployment" {

    depends_on = [ null_resource.docker_push ]    Creates a dependency that causes
                                                   our Docker image to be built and
    metadata {                                     published before the container is
        name = local.service_name                 deployed

    labels = {
            pod = local.service_name
        }
    }

    spec {
        replicas = 1                           Uses local variables to
                                               share configuration
        selector {                             across this code file
            match_labels = {
                pod = local.service_name
            }
        }
```

```
            template {
                metadata {
                    labels = {
                        pod = local.service_name
                    }
                }

                spec {
                    container {
                        image = local.image_tag       ◄─┐  The image is pulled from our
                        name  = local.service_name       │  private container registry.

                        env {
                            name = "PORT"
                            value = "80"
                        }
                    }
```

Specifies authentication
credentials for our container
registry so Kubernetes can
pull the image
```
                    image_pull_secrets {
                        name =
                ➡  kubernetes_secret.docker_credentials.metadata[0].name
                    }
                }
            }
        }
```

Declares a Kubernetes service that creates
a DNS record to make the microservice
accessible within the cluster

```
        resource "kubernetes_service" "service" {  ◄─┘
            metadata {
                name = local.service_name
            }

            spec {
                selector = {
                    pod =
            kubernetes_deployment.service_deployment.metadata[0].labels.pod
                }

                port {
                    port = 80
                }
```

Uses the Azure load balancer to create an external
IP address for this service. We can use this to test
that the deployed microservice is working.

```
                type = "LoadBalancer"   ◄─┘
            }
        }
```

At the end of listing 7.7, you can see that we have attached an Azure load balancer to the Kubernetes service to create an external endpoint. We have *temporarily* exposed a container to the outside world for testing purposes. This allows us to check our video-streaming microservice from the web browser to verify that it is functional. Be assured that the final FlixTube example application has restricted external endpoints! You'll have to wait until chapter 9 to see that.

7.6.5   *Testing your microservice*

Let's get this microservice deployed already! Invoke `terraform apply` and deploy the video-streaming microservice to your Kubernetes cluster:

```
terraform apply -var="app_version=1" -var="client_id=<your-client-id>"
⮡ -var="client_secret=<your-client-secret>" -auto-approve
```

Note that we are now setting the `app_version` variable. We'll set this to version 1 initially and increment it each time we publish a new version of the image for our microservice. Remember to replace the values for `client_id` and `client_secret` with those for your own service principal as shown in sections 6.11.2 and 7.5.3.

After this has completed, look up the external IP address for the video-streaming microservice as you did for the database service in section 7.5.4. Now open your web browser at that IP address and navigate to the /video route. For example, if your IP address is 40.112.161.104, then point your browser at http://40.112.161.104/video. Just remember to use your own external IP address. You should now see the familiar video playing in your browser.

7.6.6   *What have we achieved?*

After first deploying containers for MongoDB and RabbitMQ, we've now packaged, published, and deployed our first microservice! Along the way, we learned how to use Terraform local variables to compose and share configuration details for use in multiple places. This saved us from having to type in those details many times and will be convenient later, when we need to change these.

We used Docker to build and publish the image for our microservice. Authentication from the cluster to the container registry (to pull the image) was a bit tricky, but we created a Kubernetes secret to handle that.

Ultimately, we deployed and tested our video-streaming microservice, and we finished prototyping our deployment pipeline. It's now time to put the deployment process on automatic by creating our CD pipeline.

7.7   *Continuous delivery with Bitbucket Pipelines*

Up until this point in chapters 6 and 7, we have manually invoked Terraform to execute our infrastructure code and build the infrastructure for our application. Doing this is a part of the normal process of prototyping our deployment code.

Like any coding task, we need to develop and test our code locally before we can run that code in production. It's especially important in this situation because this code runs in a hosted service, and it can be quite difficult to debug problems that occur there. We'd like this code to be as bulletproof as possible before it leaves our development workstation.

Running Terraform locally is also the best way to learn it and understand infrastructure as code. But the whole point of using Terraform and infrastructure as code is to automate our deployment pipeline. We don't want to manually invoke Terraform for every change to our infrastructure or microservices. We'd like to deploy changes frequently, and we want it to be automated and streamlined so that we can spend the majority of our time building features rather than deploying our software. In addition, automation also greatly reduces the potential for human error.

Now we'll create our CD pipeline with Bitbucket Pipelines. This is a hosted service from Atlassian that we'll use to run our deployment process in an automated fashion. It makes our deployment process as simple as a code push. Pushing code changes to our hosted code repository will automatically invoke our deployment pipeline.

7.7.1 Why Bitbucket Pipelines?

There are many good hosted services for CD, and these are all quite similar. If you learn one, you'll find that the others aren't that different.

Bitbucket Pipelines is convenient because it's included with Bitbucket from Atlassian so we can have our code and CD pipeline together. You can't complain about the price! Atlassian provides a good starter tier with free private repositories and a limited amount of *free build minutes* per month to spend on your CD pipeline. This gives us some space to host a small build pipeline completely for free.

> **NOTE** It doesn't really matter which hosted service we use. For example, GitHub and GitLab both offer similar services that are configured in a similar way. Bitbucket Pipelines appears in this book because it is what I currently use in production, even though I have used GitLab in the past, and I continue to use GitHub for most of my open source coding.

I like to think of CD simply as a way to automatically run a shell script in the cloud. That's a simplification of course, but it might help you understand that CD is not particularly complex or mysterious. Creating a shell script for our deployment is also useful because we can easily test it locally.

7.7.2 Importing the example code to Bitbucket

To use Bitbucket Pipelines, we must first have our code committed to a Bitbucket code repository. We'll now move onto code example-4. This is the same as example-3, but it includes the extra configuration we need for our CD pipeline.

Also, at this point, you should destroy your previously created infrastructure with `terraform destroy` (if you haven't done that already). The infrastructure you created previously was our *prototype* infrastructure. From here on in, we'll use our CD pipeline to create *production* infrastructure, and we don't want these to overlap.

SIGNUP FOR BITBUCKET

To start, you need to sign up for a Bitbucket account, assuming you don't have one already. Sign in or sign up here: https://bitbucket.org.

CREATE THE HOSTED CODE REPOSITORY

When signed into your account, click the button to create a new code repository. Choose a name for your new repo and fill out the details (an example is shown in figure 7.3).

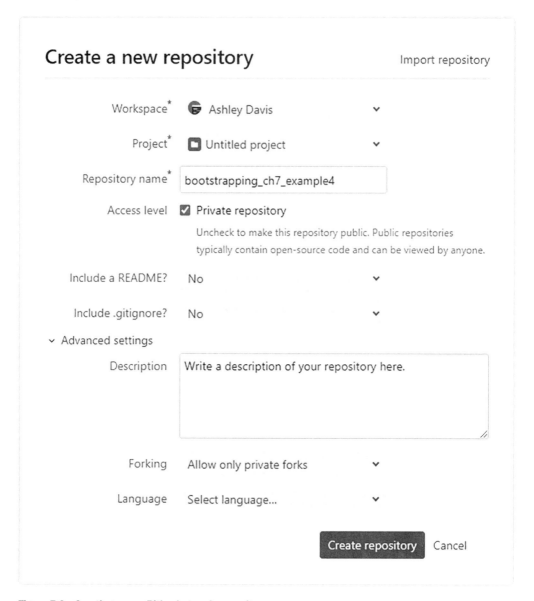

Figure 7.3   Creating a new Bitbucket code repository

After creating your code repository, you are presented with a page like figure 7.4. This gives instructions to get code into the repository. These are just standard Git com-

Let's put some bits in your bucket

SSH ⌄ | git clone git@bitbucket.org:ashleydavis75/bootstrapping_ch7_example4.git | 📋

Get started quickly

Creating a README or a .gitignore is a quick and easy way to get something into your repository.

Create a README   Create a .gitignore

Get your local Git repository on Bitbucket

Step 1: Switch to your repository's directory

```
1   cd /path/to/your/repo
```

Step 2: Connect your existing repository to Bitbucket

```
1   git remote add origin git@bitbucket.org:ashleydavis75/bootstrapping_ch7_example4.git

2   git push -u origin master
```

Need more information? Learn more

Figure 7.4 Instructions from Bitbucket to get your code into the new repository

mands, but it's convenient that these give us the exact commands we need to import our code.

CREATE A LOCAL REPOSITORY

Before importing the example-4 code to our new repo, let's make a fresh copy of it so that we don't mess up the chapter-7 repo:

```
cp -r chapter-7/example-4 bootstrapping_ch7_example4
```

Go into the new directory and initialize a new empty Git repository:

```
cd bootstrapping_ch7_example4
git init
```

Now commit all the files to the new repo:

```
git add .
git commit -m "First commit"
```

PUSH TO THE HOSTED REPOSITORY

Now we can follow the instructions given by Bitbucket (as shown in figure 7.4). The commands that are given to you will be different because we have different Bitbucket accounts. The first command is to add the remote repo as the origin for the local one. For example

```
git remote add origin
    git@bitbucket.org:ashleydavis75/bootstrapping_ch7_example4.git
```

Remember to replace the URL for the remote repository with your own details. Here is the template you should use:

```
git remote add origin git@bitbucket.org:<your-user-name>/<your-repo-name>.git
```

Now push your code to your hosted repository:

```
git push -u origin master
```

At this point, you need to enter your credentials. To avoid doing that for every push, I recommend that you set up an SSH key, which is fairly easy to do on every platform, following these instructions from Bitbucket Support:

https://confluence.atlassian.com/bitbucket/ set-up-an-ssh-key-728138079.html

In the future, you can push code changes with the shortened command:

```
git push
```

ENABLING BITBUCKET PIPELINES

We have created our hosted code repository and pushed the example code to it. Now, we can enable Bitbucket Pipelines for this repository. Navigate to the Pipelines page (as in figure 7.5).

The example code includes a bitbucket-pipelines.yaml configuration file. Bitbucket detects this file, and you can now click the Enable button (as shown in figure 7.6), which enables Bitbucket Pipelines for this code repository. (Note that you may need to scroll down so you can see the Enable button.)

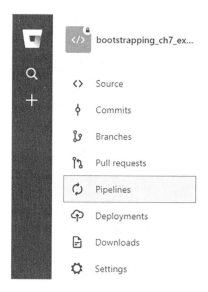

Figure 7.5   Navigating to the Pipelines page for your repository

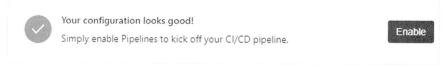

Figure 7.6   Click the Enable button to enable Bitbucket Pipelines

7.7.3   *Creating a deployment shell script*

Most CD pipelines can be boiled down to a shell script with inputs provided by environment variables. Taking this approach is useful for two reasons:

- Our deployment pipeline is somewhat portable between CD providers.
- We can easily test our deployment pipeline locally by executing the shell script.

Creating a deployment shell script gives us some freedom. That's nice, but it's also essential for local testing of our deployment pipeline. We need to make sure this code is bulletproof before we try to execute it unattended in the cloud.

We've spent most of this chapter prototyping and testing our deployment code, so we are already quite sure that it works. We just need to wrap it up in a shell script. The shell script included in example-4 is shown in the following listing. It's simple, and that's because we've been able to keep our deployment code entirely in Terraform. Our shell script simply invokes Terraform.

Listing 7.8   A shell script for deployment (chapter-7/example-4/scripts/deploy.sh)

**Initializes Terraform and
download providers**

```
set -u
: "$VERSION"                                      ◁─────┐
: "$ARM_CLIENT_ID"                                      │  Checks that expected input
: "$ARM_CLIENT_SECRET"                                  │  environment variables are provided
: "$ARM_TENANT_ID"                                      │
: "$ARM_SUBSCRIPTION_ID"                          ◁─────┘

                                                        ┌─ Invokes Terraform from the directory
cd ./scripts                                      ◁─────┘   that contains our deployment scripts

export KUBERNETES_SERVICE_HOST=""         ◁──────  Workaround for a problem
                                                   with the Kubernetes provider
└─▷ terraform init                                 (an explanation follows)
┌─▷ terraform apply -auto-approve \
│       -var "app_version=$VERSION" \        ◁──────┐
│       -var "client_id=$ARM_CLIENT_ID" \           │  Sets Terraform variables
│       -var "client_secret=$ARM_CLIENT_SECRET"  ◁──┘  from environment variables
Invokes Terraform apply
```

One interesting thing to note in this script is how it checks for the input environment variables. These are the current version number for our application (used to tag our Docker images) and the authentication details for our Azure account. We'll soon see where these variables come from.

You are probably wondering why we are setting the KUBERNETES_SERVICE _HOST environment variable. This is a workaround for a problem that occurs when attempting to use the Kubernetes provider for Terraform within a Kubernetes pod. (Did I just short circuit your brain?) It appears that Bitbucket Pipelines quietly runs our CD pipeline in a pod within Bitbucket's own Kubernetes cluster. This makes sense, and it's an awesome use case for Kubernetes. The problem that results from this shouldn't happen, but it does. We empty out the KUBERNETES_SERVICE_HOST environment variable to fool the Kubernetes provider and to avoid the issue.

We shouldn't have to care about things like this, but sometimes working with early tools (Terraform is pre-version 1), we sometimes have to cope with unusual issues in Terraform or its provider plugins. Possibly, by the time you read this, the problem will have been corrected, and this workaround won't be needed. If you are curious and want to learn more, you can read about it here:

https://github.com/terraform-providers/terraform-provider-kubernetes/issues/679

7.7.4 Managing Terraform state

Now we return to the tricky issue of managing Terraform state. Cast your mind back to section 6.8.7 in the previous chapter. You'll recall that Terraform has a state file so that it has a memory of the infrastructure it created.

The question now is how do we persist the state file in our CD pipeline? The nature of CD pipelines is that each invocation happens in a fresh container instance. That's why we must invoke `terraform init` in our deployment shell script for each and every deployment.

How do we manage the Terraform state file? We must persist it between instances of the CD pipeline so that subsequent invocations of Terraform have a memory of what was created earlier. That's so it isn't blindly trying to recreate infrastructure that it already created. Terraform has a solution to this. We can provide external storage in which Terraform can store its state file. This allows the state file to be stored separately to the CD pipeline.

The following listing shows our configuration for the Azure backend. Through this configuration, we set an Azure storage account as the backend for the storage of our Terraform state.

Listing 7.9 Configuring backend storage (chapter-7/example-4/scripts/backend.tf)

```
terraform {
    backend "azurerm" {

        resource_group_name  = "terraform"
        storage_account_name = "terraform"
        container_name       = "terraform"
        key = "terraform.tfstate"

    }
}
```

Sets configuration for the Azure storage backend → (points to `backend "azurerm" {` and `}`)

Sets the name of the resource group, storage account, and container for use by Terraform → (points to resource_group_name, storage_account_name, container_name)

Names the storage blob where the Terraform state is stored → (points to key = "terraform.tfstate")

Before Terraform will work in your CD pipeline, we have to create a separate Azure storage account for it to use. First, choose a name to use for your storage account. I have used the name `terraform` as you can see in listing 7.9. Unfortunately, you can't use that because the names of storage accounts must be globally unique (which is kind of annoying).

Open the Azure portal in your browser and create a new storage account with the name you have chosen under a resource group with that same name. (See section 4.4.1 in chapter 4 for a refresher on creating a storage account.)

In your new storage account, also create a container (a storage container, not a Docker container) with the same name. You can use any name you want for this (although, there are restrictions for names of storage accounts). I used the name `terraform` for the resource group, storage account, and container names. I used that name just to indicate that these are all purely for use by Terraform running in our CD pipeline. This new storage account isn't otherwise used by our infrastructure or application.

Once you have created the storage account and container, edit backend.tf (shown in listing 7.9) and replace each instance of `terraform` with the name that you have selected. At this stage, you can commit these changes to your local code repository, but don't push them to Bitbucket yet! We still have some configuration to do before our CD pipeline will work.

7.7.5 The Bitbucket Pipelines script

The final piece of our CD pipeline is the bitbucket-pipelines.yaml configuration file. This YAML file is what we use to configure our CD pipeline. To use Bitbucket Pipelines, you must have this file in the root of your code repository. It simply doesn't work without it.

Listing 7.10 shows bitbucket-pipelines.yaml from example-4. You can see that we use this file simply as a wrapper for our shell script from listing 7.8. There's a bit more to it than this, of course, but not much! With Bitbucket Pipelines enabled for our Bitbucket code repository, this YAML file now invokes our deployment shell script when code is pushed to the hosted code repository.

> **Listing 7.10   Configuring our Bitbucket Pipelines automated deployment pipeline (chapter-7/example-4/bitbucket-pipelines.yaml)**

Sets the base image for the container within which the CD pipeline is executed. We use the Terraform base image so that we have access to the Terraform tool within our CD pipeline.

```
image: hashicorp/terraform:0.12.6

pipelines:
    default:
        - step:
            name: Build and deploy
            services:
              - docker
            script:
              - export VERSION=$BITBUCKET_BUILD_NUMBER
              - chmod +x ./scripts/deploy.sh
              - ./scripts/deploy.sh
```

Configures the default pipeline for our repo. We can also have separate pipelines for each branch.

Defines a step in our deployment pipeline (here, it's only a single step)

Enables the Docker service. This lets us use Docker from within our Terraform code.

Sets the VERSION environment variable to the Bitbucket build number

Ensures that our deployment script is executable

Executes our deployment script. This is the core of our deployment pipeline.

Note in listing 7.10 how the first line of the file sets the base image for the CD pipeline's container. Bitbucket instantiates a new container from this image each time our CD pipeline is triggered. We automatically have access to the Terraform tool because it's pre-installed in the base image. If we weren't using Terraform, we could select a different base image. Check out the following line of code from listing 7.10:

```
export VERSION=$BITBUCKET_BUILD_NUMBER
```

This is one method of passing environment variables into our deployment shell script, and here we have set the version number for our application. We are setting this from Bitbucket Pipeline's BITBUCKET_BUILD_NUMBER environment variable, which simply counts the number of times the CD pipeline has been triggered. This is a convenient way to generate version numbers for the images created within our CD pipeline. Bitbucket Pipelines also has many other built-in environment variables that can be useful. For more information, see

https://confluence.atlassian.com/bitbucket/variables-in-pipelines-794502608.html

7.7.6   *Configuring environment variables*

In the previous section, you saw one example of how to input an environment variable to our deployment shell script. There are still other environment variables we have yet to provide.

We could set these inline in bitbucket-pipelines.yaml as we did with the VERSION environment variable in listing 7.10, but we shouldn't do that for our Azure credentials. These are sensitive, and for security reasons, we don't want to include those in our code repository. Instead, we'll configure these as *repository variables* through the Bitbucket GUI. Navigate to the Repository Variables page under the Settings option for your code repository (shown in figure 7.7).

Now create repository variables and enter their values as shown in figure 7.8. Feel free to check the Secured option for an extra layer of security for these sensitive values. These values are passed to our CD pipeline as environment variables.

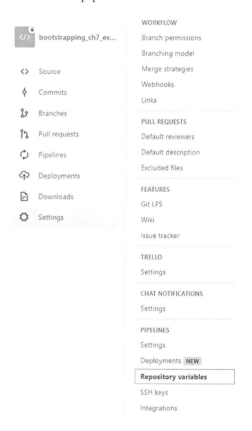

Figure 7.7   Navigating to Repository Variables for your code repository

When creating these variables, you must enter authentication credentials for your own Azure account and Azure service principal. The values for ARM_CLIENT_ID and ARM_CLIENT_SECRET are the `appId` and `password` fields from your service principal you created back in section 6.11.2. The values for ARM_TENANT_ID and ARM_SUBSCRIPTION_ID are the details for your Azure account that you can see using the command `az account show` like we also did in section 6.11.2.

These authentication details must be set somewhere. If you recall, back in section 6.6.2, we used the command `az login` on our development workstation to authenticate with Azure. This command doesn't work in our CD pipeline because no human interaction is possible. To allow Terraform to authenticate with Azure to build and update our infrastructure, we must pass these authentication details into our pipeline.

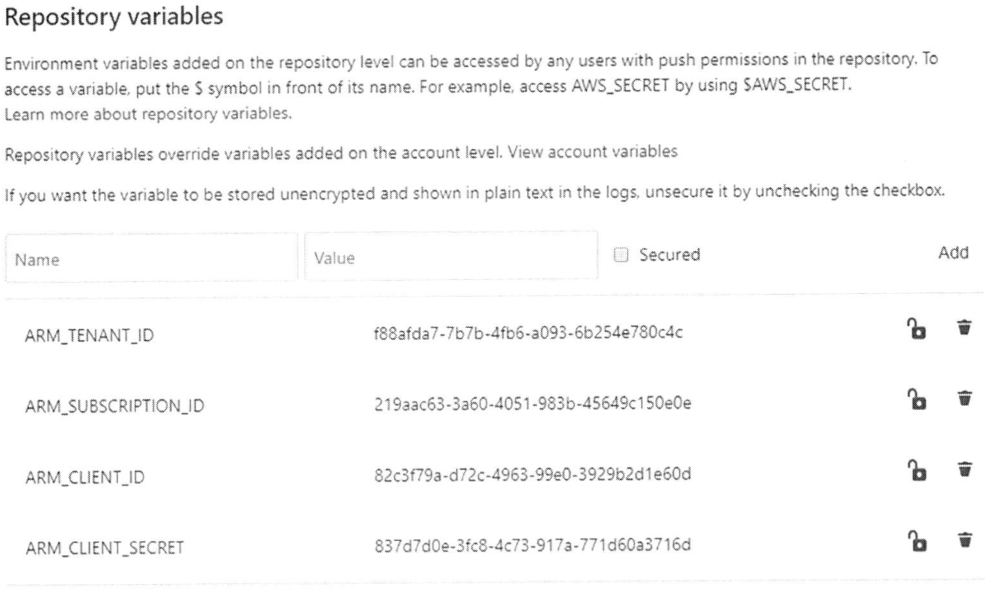

Repository variables

Environment variables added on the repository level can be accessed by any users with push permissions in the repository. To access a variable, put the $ symbol in front of its name. For example, access AWS_SECRET by using $AWS_SECRET. Learn more about repository variables.

Repository variables override variables added on the account level. View account variables

If you want the variable to be stored unencrypted and shown in plain text in the logs, unsecure it by unchecking the checkbox.

Name	Value	☐ Secured	Add
ARM_TENANT_ID	f88afda7-7b7b-4fb6-a093-6b254e780c4c		🔓 🗑
ARM_SUBSCRIPTION_ID	219aac63-3a60-4051-983b-45649c150e0e		🔓 🗑
ARM_CLIENT_ID	82c3f79a-d72c-4963-99e0-3929b2d1e60d		🔓 🗑
ARM_CLIENT_SECRET	837d7d0e-3fc8-4c73-917a-771d60a3716d		🔓 🗑

Figure 7.8   Creating repository variables to specify Azure authentication credentials

7.7.7   *Testing your deployment pipeline*

OK, we are finally ready to test our CD pipeline! We have created a Bitbucket code repository and pushed to it a copy of the example-4 code. We have enabled and configured Bitbucket Pipelines for the repository, and we have a CD pipeline; we just need to trigger it!

We can trigger the pipeline simply by pushing code to it. You probably already have an unpushed code change ready to go. If you were following along, you committed changes to backend.tf earlier in section 7.7.4. Go ahead now and push those changes:

```
git push
```

If you pushed those code changes earlier, that's not a big deal. Make a simple change now (e.g., add a blank line to one of the code files) and then commit it and push it to trigger the CD pipeline. You can repeat this process as many times as you like while testing and debugging your CD pipeline.

You can monitor pipeline invocations in the Pipelines page under your Bitbucket repository (like that in figure 7.9). You can see in this example that my first pipeline invocation failed and that the second invocation has just started (denoted by the word "Pending").

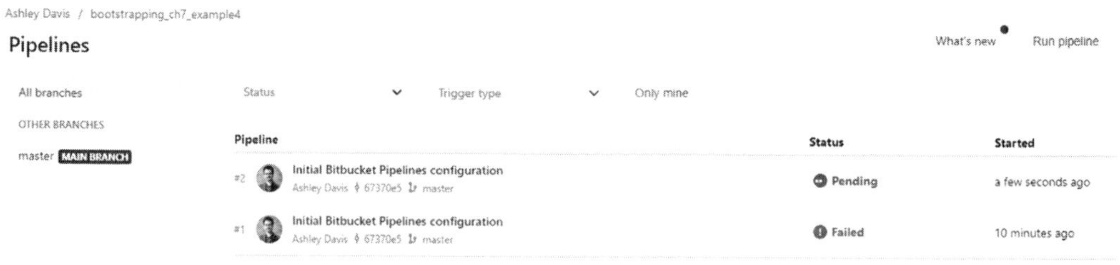

Ashley Davis / bootstrapping_ch7_example4

Pipelines   What's new   Run pipeline

All branches   Status   ⌄   Trigger type   ⌄   Only mine

OTHER BRANCHES

master **MAIN BRANCH**   **Pipeline**   **Status**   **Started**

                    #2   Initial Bitbucket Pipelines configuration   ⏳ Pending   a few seconds ago
                          Ashley Davis ⎇ 67370e5 ⎇ master

                    #1   Initial Bitbucket Pipelines configuration   ⛔ Failed   10 minutes ago
                          Ashley Davis ⎇ 67370e5 ⎇ master

Figure 7.9   Monitoring pipeline invocations from the Pipelines page

You can drill down into any of the pipeline invocations to find out what happened. Of course, you will need to do this in the future to find out what went wrong after it fails.

As an example, I clicked down into my second invocation (the one that completed successfully). You can see what it looks like in figure 7.10. You'll note that the complete output from the deployment shell script is displayed here. This should be familiar to you by now because it's the same output we saw earlier when testing our Terraform code locally.

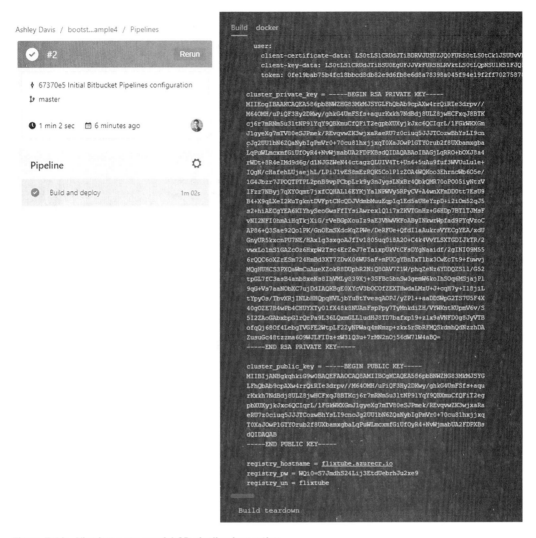

Figure 7.10 Viewing a successful CD pipeline invocation

7.7.8 Debugging your deployment pipeline

We now have a CD pipeline. Changing our infrastructure and deploying our application is now synonymous with changing our code: what we call *infrastructure as code.*

You probably have a new question now: how do I debug my deployment pipeline? You might be wondering about this after seeing my failed pipeline from figure 7.9. Or, possibly, because you might already have had your own failed pipeline!

The first step is to thoroughly test any changes to your deployment code locally on your own development workstation. Then, we can catch many issues before our deployment code gets to the CD pipeline.

When you do get a failed pipeline, you'll need to drill down into it, read the output, and try to understand the problem. Understanding the problem is the hard bit; fixing the problem is usually easy once we know what it is.

You can see an example of a problem in figure 7.11, when I drilled down to figure out why my first pipeline invocation failed. I read the error message here and realized it failed because I hadn't provided the required environment variables. I had invoked this pipeline prior to configuring the repository variables as we did in section 7.7.6. That's an easy mistake to make, and you might have made it yourself if you were a bit too gung-ho in pushing the changes we made in section 7.7.4.

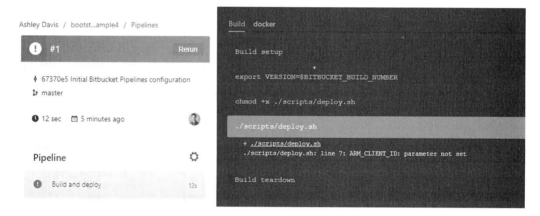

Figure 7.11   Viewing a failed CD pipeline and reading the error message

When debugging your pipeline, you should note that you can use any of the common commands to help you. Commands such as `cd`, `ls`, `pwd`, and `cat` can be used to navigate and inspect the filesystem within the CD pipeline's container. This gives you a variety of ways to understand what's going on in there. Hopefully, this small but invaluable tip will assist your future CD pipeline debugging!

7.7.9   *What have we achieved?*

You just created your first CD pipeline, and you used it to deploy production infrastructure and containers. This is real progress!

There are many services for CD, but we used Bitbucket Pipelines from Atlassian. We created a repository on Bitbucket and imported the code from example-4. We then created a shell script to wrap up our deployment.

Although there are many vendors for CD, building a CD pipeline usually amounts to not much more than invoking a shell script. That's useful because a shell script is something we can test locally before we try to run it in our CD pipeline. The deployment shell script we created is simple. That's because our entire deployment process is in Terraform code, so we simply invoked Terraform to create our infrastructure and deploy our containers.

7.8   *Continue your learning*

In this chapter, we deployed our fledgling microservices application to the Kubernetes cluster that we created in the previous chapter. In future chapters, we'll continue to flesh out the FlixTube application into a complete application.

As always, there is so much more to be learned than we can cover here. As we get deeper into development, you will undoubtedly need to dive deeper while you are working. Here are the books that will help you do that:

- *Core Kubernetes* by Jay Vyas and Chris Love (Manning, est. Summer 2021)
- *Kubernetes in Action* by Marko Lukša (Manning, 2017)
- *Terraform in Action* by Scott Winkler (Manning, est. Spring 2021)
- *GitOps and Kubernetes* by Billy Yuen, Alexander Matyushentsev, et. al. (Manning, est. Spring 2021)
- *Kubernetes Quickly* by William Denniss (Manning, est. Summer 2021)
- *Learn Kubernetes in a Month of Lunches* by Elton Stoneman (Manning, est. February 2021)

To learn about Atlassian Bitbucket, see the Bitbucket website:

- https://bitbucket.org/

See the Bitbucket overview at

- https://bitbucket.org/product/guides/getting-started/overview

To learn more about CD with Bitbucket Pipelines, see

- https://bitbucket.org/product/features/pipelines

Learn more about Kubernetes concepts in the Kubernetes documentation at

- https://kubernetes.io/docs/concepts/

Summary

- Continuous delivery (CD) is a technique where production infrastructure and software are continuously updated as changes are made to the code.
- We used Terraform to script the configuration and deployment of multiple containers onto our Kubernetes cluster.
- We deployed a MongoDB database server and a RabbitMQ server for use by our microservices.
- We used Terraform to build and publish the Docker image for our first microservice, the video-streaming microservice, which we then deployed to our Kubernetes cluster.
- We created a shell script to wrap up our deployment pipeline.
- We moved our code to a private Bitbucket code repository and configured Bitbucket Pipelines to create a CD pipeline for our application.

- Our Bitbucket Pipelines file was simple; it only invoked our deployment shell script.
- Having the shell script is important because it allows us to test and debug our deployment pipeline on our development workstation. Doing testing and debugging within the CD pipeline is more difficult.
- We learned how to use the Bitbucket interface to configure environment variables as input to our deployment pipeline.
- We learned how to persist Terraform state using Azure storage.

Automated testing
for microservices

To this point in the book while building microservices, we have tested our code manually. In this chapter, though, we'll shift up a gear and learn how to apply automated testing to our microservices.

So far, we have primarily done our testing by running our code and visually inspecting the output. In various chapters, we used our web browser, the output from the command line, or changes in the local filesystem to check the results of our code. In other chapters, we used more specific tools like Robo3T in chapter 3 or the RabbitMQ dashboard in chapter 5.

Methods of manual testing are many and varied. I want you to know that manual testing is OK and perfectly valid. You should start with manual testing and continue with it until you are comfortable enough to use automated testing, and your product is well enough understood that it's worth making the investment in that. I can recommend tools for manual testing like Postman or REST Client for Visual Studio Code. These will help you to manually test your REST APIs.

At a point, though, manual testing becomes tedious and time-consuming. You will want to turn to automated testing. Of course, automated testing is generally useful in the realm of software development, but with microservices, it becomes essential as we grow our application. It's also important for small teams because, at some point, the burden of manual testing becomes overwhelming to the point that all you'll be doing is testing. There's no reason you should carry a heavy testing burden when great testing tools are within easy reach!

Think of this chapter as a guided tour through the testing landscape as it applies to microservices. We'll start with an introduction to testing, then we'll look at more advanced examples of unit testing, integration testing, and end-to-end testing.

Automated testing is an advanced topic. I've included it in this book because I believe it really is essential for scaling microservices. If you haven't done automated testing before, you might find this chapter a little overwhelming. Hopefully not, but otherwise, feel free to skip this chapter and come back to it again later. Just know that automated testing is important and that even though you don't need it in the early days, eventually you will definitely need it.

8.1 New tools

As modern developers, we are spoiled with great testing tools that are free, easily available, and straightforward to learn. In this chapter, we'll learn automated testing with two popular and important testing tools. We'll use Jest and Cypress to test our microservices to ensure these are robust.

Jest is a tool for testing JavaScript code; Cypress is a tool we'll use for end-to-end testing. Both Jest and Cypress are written in JavaScript. If you are building microservices in a different language than JavaScript, then you probably wouldn't pick Jest. Instead, you'd pick the best testing tool for your particular language.

Cypress is a great tool for testing web pages regardless of what language you use in the backend. If you aren't using JavaScript as the language for your microservices, Cypress is still a great choice for your end-to-end testing.

Toward the end of the chapter, we'll learn how to add automated testing to the continuous delivery (CD) pipeline we started in the previous chapter. This means our tests will be invoked automatically as we push code changes to our hosted code repository. That's important because it makes the testing process a checkpoint before production. Broken code or failing tests will automatically halt deployment and alert us to problems as these are automatically detected.

Table 8.1 New tools in chapter 8

Tool	Version	Purpose
Jest	26.2.2	Jest is a tool for automated testing of JavaScript code.
Cypress	4.12.1	Cypress is a tool for automated testing of web pages.

8.2 Getting the code

To follow along with this chapter you need to download the code or clone the repository.

- Download a zip file of the code from here:
  https://github.com/bootstrapping-microservices/chapter-8
- You can clone the code using Git like this:
  `git clone https://github.com/bootstrapping-microservices/chapter-8.git`

For help on installing and using Git, see chapter 2. If you have problems with the code, log an issue against the repository in GitHub.

8.3 Testing for microservices

Like any code that we write, microservices need to be well tested so we can know the code is robust, difficult to break, and can gracefully handle problems. Testing gives us peace of mind that our code functions in both normal and unexpected circumstances.

Effective testing emulates production as closely as possible. This includes both the environment, the configuration of the code, and the test data that we use. Using Docker and Docker Compose allows us to configure our testing environment to be like the production environment.

This makes the "it worked on my computer" excuse for broken code much less useful in modern development. Usually, when it works on your computer (in a correctly configured Docker environment), you can be fairly sure it's going to work in the production environment. Having a stable environment for our code is a crucial factor for reliable testing.

Manual testing is a good starting point and is a skill worth cultivating. But at a certain point, automated testing is necessary to scale up our application. As the number of microservices grows, we will rely more and more on automation to keep the application running and to help us maintain a rapid pace of development. In the previous chapter, we created our CD pipeline to automate deployment. Now, let's turn our attention to bringing automated testing online.

8.4 Automated testing

Automated testing, put simply, is *code-driven* testing. We write code to exercise our code and verify that it works correctly. This sounds like circular logic, but we break out of it after a single iteration. We have our application code or *code under test* and then we have our test code (or just *tests*).

Often the test code directly invokes the code under test, but it can also be invoked indirectly, for example, through HTTP requests or RabbitMQ messages. The test code then verifies that the result is correct, either by checking the output or checking the behavior.

Throughout this chapter, you'll learn a handful of automated testing techniques. You'll be able to apply these techniques over and over again to create a comprehensive suite of tests for your application.

Testing for microservices can be applied at multiple levels. We can test individual functions, we can test whole microservices, we can test groups of microservices together, or we can test the whole application (until the application grows too large; more about that later). These levels of testing are related to the following three types of automated testing:

- *Unit testing*—Tests isolated code and individual functions
- *Integration testing*—Tests whole microservices
- *End-to-end testing*—Tests groups of microservices and/or the entire application including the front end

You may have heard of these types of testing before. If not, don't worry because we'll look at each in turn.

Figure 8.1 shows a diagram that is called the *testing pyramid*. It relates the types of automated testing to each other and gives you an idea of how many of each type of test you should have in your test suite.

Unit tests run quickly, so you can afford to have many of these. These are, therefore, at the foundation of the testing pyramid. Integration testing and end-to-end testing are higher in the pyramid. These types of tests are slower to run, so you can't afford to have as many of those. (The diminishing area as we go up the pyramid indicates that we'll

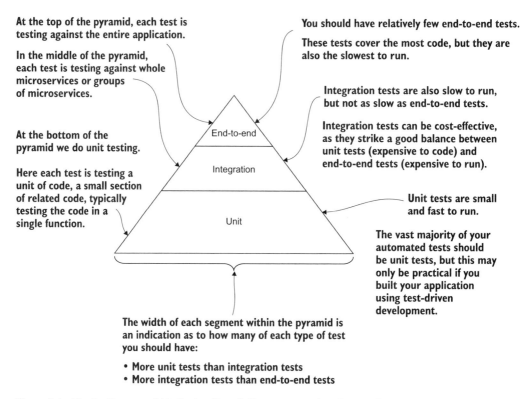

Figure 8.1   The testing pyramid indicates the relative amounts of each type of test we should have.

have less and less of these types of tests.) This means we should have fewer integration tests than unit tests and fewer end-to-end tests than integration tests.

Figure 8.2 illustrates what end-to-end testing looks like for a cut-down version of FlixTube. In that figure, I show end-to-end testing first, because it's the type of testing most like manual testing; that is, we test against the whole application in a manner similar to how our customer would use it.

End-to-end testing is the easiest type of testing to understand, even though it's actually quite involved, and we don't get to it until near the end of this chapter. End-to-end testing is closest to manual testing because we have to load the entire application to test it, just like we do when testing manually. Figure 8.2 shows running Cypress tests against a cut-down version of our whole application that is running on Docker Compose.

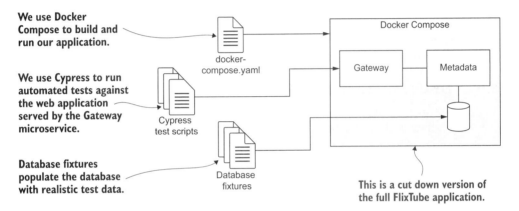

Figure 8.2   End-to-end testing of a simplified version of FlixTube using Cypress

Automated testing coupled with CD is like an early warning system. When the alarm goes off, we can be thankful, as it gives us the opportunity to stop problems going into production and potentially impacting our customers. Automated testing (like automated deployment) is best started early in the project because trying to bolt automated testing onto a legacy application (one not designed to be tested) can be extremely difficult.

But don't start automated testing too early in the development lifecycle. It's a balancing act. When starting a new product, you should first begin with a prototyping phase prior to adding automated testing. *Prototyping* allows you to experiment with your product before committing to it. If you aren't sure exactly what your product is yet (e.g., you are still experimenting) or if you are still trying to validate your business model, then you might want to hold off on automated testing and stick with manual testing for a bit longer.

Building infrastructure for testing is a significant investment in your product. For the purpose of this chapter, let's imagine that we are ready to make the automated testing commitment for FlixTube.

NOTE   The true payoff with automated testing is that it will save you from countless hours of routine testing, not to mention that it can stop deployment of broken code that might have otherwise gone into production and caused havoc.

As amazing as automated testing is, it is not a panacea! It is not a replacement for good exploratory testing (e.g., manual testing) by actual humans. That still needs to happen because it's the only way to find the bugs that the development team couldn't even imagine.

Automated testing isn't just about proving that your code works. It also serves as an invaluable communication tool, a kind of *executable documentation* that demonstrates how the code is intended to be used. It also gives you a safe framework in which to refactor and restructure your application. This allows you to continuously move towards a simpler and more elegant architecture. Let's now work through each type of testing and look at examples of tests applied to the metadata microservice and then to the FlixTube application.

8.5   *Testing with Jest*

Testing is a huge topic, so let's start by looking at some simpler examples that aren't directly related to microservices. The code we'll look at in this section is generally applicable for testing JavaScript code, regardless of whether that code is in a front end, a backend, or even in a mobile or desktop application.

If you can already write an automated test with Jest, and you understand mocking, feel free to skip this section and move directly to section 8.6. In that section, we'll start to relate automated testing to microservices.

For this section, imagine we are creating a JavaScript math library for use in our microservices. We'll use Jest to do our testing. That's a JavaScript testing tool and framework. Figure 8.3 gives you an idea of how we'll use it.

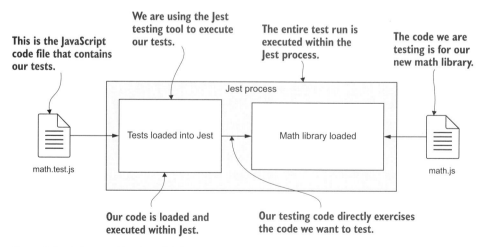

Figure 8.3   Automated testing with Jest

In the figure, on the left, we have math.test.js. This is a file that contains the tests that we'll run against our math library. On the right, we have math.js. This is the file that contains the code for our math library. When we run Jest, it loads our test code, which in turn, runs the code we are testing. From our tests, we can directly invoke our code to test it and then verify in the result that everything went as expected.

8.5.1 Why Jest?

Jest is arguably the most popular testing tool and framework for JavaScript. It is easy to set up with minimal configuration, so it's great for beginners. It's fast, and it can run tests in parallel. Jest also has great support for live reloading; you can run it in *watch* mode, where it reloads by itself while you are coding.

Jest was created by Facebook, so you know it has great support behind it. But it also has a huge following and many contributors outside of Facebook. The API is extensive, supports multiple styles of testing, and has various ways of validating tests and creating mocks. And Jest has great support for creating mock objects.

There are other great features that we won't even touch on in this chapter. (At the end of the chapter, you'll find a link to learn more about Jest.) Jest is open source and free to use. You can find the code here:

https://github.com/facebook/jest

8.5.2 Setting up Jest

We'll start by looking at example-1 in the chapter-8 code repository. This example is small enough that you can type it out directly if you like. If you don't want to do that, you can get the code from GitHub to follow along.

You can run these tests for yourself and make changes to those to see what happens. Example-1 already has Jest in its package.json, so we'll simply install dependencies for the project:

```
cd chapter-8/example-1
npm install
```

You can install Jest into a new Node.js project like this:

```
npm install --save-dev jest
```

We used the --save-dev argument to save Jest as a dev dependency in package.json. Jest is something we'll only use in our development or testing environment, so we save it as a dev dependency so that it's excluded from our production environment.

If you look in the package.json file, you'll see that I've installed Jest version 26.2.2. When you install Jest in the future, you will see a later version. Much of what you learn here will still be valid because Jest is stable (it's up to version 26!).

The following listing shows the Jest configuration from example-1. This is actually the default configuration that was generated by Jest. I didn't change it except to remove comments.

Listing 8.1   Configuration file for Jest (chapter-8/example-1/jest.config.js)

```
module.exports = {                    Automatically clears mocks between
                                      every test (I'll explain mocks soon)
  clearMocks: true,        ◁───┘
  testEnvironment: "node",   ◁─────── This is the environment for testing Node.js.

};
```

When starting a fresh project, create your own Jest configuration file like this:

```
npx jest --init
```

When you initialize your Jest configuration, it asks you a few questions. If you accept all the defaults, then your configuration file will look similar to listing 8.1. I only changed `clearMocks` to `true` (default is `false`) to help stop tests from interfering with each other.

Just to remind you, `npx` is a command that comes with Node.js and allows us to run npm modules as command-line applications. There are many npm installable modules that work this way, including Jest. You might recall the `wait-port` command we used with `npx` back in chapter 5.

When you generate the configuration file as in the listing, you'll see it contains many options that are commented out. Reading through the generated configuration file is a great way to understand what's possible with Jest. Because it's not necessary for this example, I removed the comments to have a minimal configuration.

Figure 8.4 shows the structure of the example-1 Node.js project with Jest installed. You can see the familiar package.json and package-lock.json files that are in every Node.js project that we learned about in chapter 2. As for Jest, note that this project

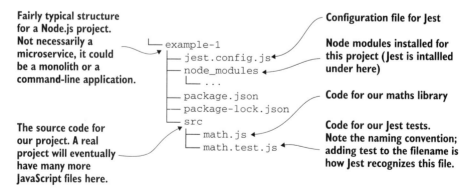

Figure 8.4   The structure of a fairly typical Node.js project with Jest installed

contains the Jest configuration file (content shown in listing 8.1) and the files for our code and tests. The code for our maths library is in math.js, and the code for our tests is in math.test.js. As with any other npm module, Jest itself is installed under the node_modules directory.

Note that the test file is named after the code that it tests. When creating math.test.js, we simply appended .test.js to the name of our library. This naming convention is how Jest locates our test code. Jest automatically loads code with *.test* in the name. This is a default convention with Jest, but we can configure it differently if we want a different convention.

Notice how the test file (math.test.js) is right next to the code file (math.js) in the same directory. This is another convention, and one that is fairly common. We could have placed these two files anywhere within the directory structure of our project, and it wouldn't make much difference. Another common convention is to have all tests separated from the application code and located under a test or tests subdirectory that is next to or just under the src subdirectory.

You might have noticed that the Jest configuration file is actually a JavaScript file itself. This means you can use JavaScript code in your configuration. It's actually quite common for JavaScript and Node.js tools to have an executable configuration file, and I think it's pretty cool that JavaScript can be used as its own configuration language.

8.5.3   *The math library to test*

Now imagine we have added the first function to our new math library. The following listing shows the `square` function. This is a simple function that takes one number and returns the square of that number.

Listing 8.2   A starting point for our new math library (chapter-8/example-1/src/math.js)

```
function square(n) {
    return n * n;            A simple JavaScript function computes the
}                            square of a number. This is the code we'll test.

    ...            You can add more functions for your
                   math library here as you develop it.

module.exports = {            Exports the "square" function so we can use it in our code
    square,                   modules. This is also how we access it from our test code.

    ...            Other functions are exported here as
};                 you add them to your math library.
```

In the future, we would add many more functions to math.js. But for now, we'll keep it short so it can be a simple demonstration of automated testing.

8.5.4   *Your first Jest test*

The `square` function is a simple function with a simple result, and more complex functions always depend on simpler functions like this. To be sure that the complex functions work, we must first test the simple functions. Yes, even though this function is simple, we still want to test it.

Of course, this is JavaScript. We can easily test this function manually using the Node.js REPL. But it's almost as easy to get this function covered under automated testing, which (combined with many other tests for many other functions) can save us time in the future. Not to mention that I'm demonstrating testing here, so if only for that purpose alone, let's write our first automated test.

Listing 8.3 shows the code that tests our nascent math library. The describe function defines a test suite called square function. The test function defines our first test called can square two.

Listing 8.3   A first test with Jest (chapter-8/example-1/src/math.test.js)

```
const { square } = require("./math");    ⟵──── Imports the code we are testing

describe("square function", () => {

      test("can square two", () => {
                                                      Invokes the "square" function
            const result = square(2);        ⟵──┘    and captures the result
            expect(result).toBe(4);    ⟵──
                                                      Sets an expectation that the result
      });                                             will be 4. If the expectation is not
                                                      satisfied, the test fails.
});
```

Creates a test called "can square two"

Creates a test suite called "square function"

We have named this test suite after the function it is testing. You can imagine in the future that we might have other test suites in this file for other functions in our maths library (you'll see some more examples of this soon).

In listing 8.3, we imported our square function from the file math.js. In our test can square two, we then called it with the number 2 as input. You can see that the name of the test implies what the test is actually doing.

> **NOTE**   A good name for a test allows you to instantly understand what is being tested.

We then use the expect and toBe functions to verify that the result of the square function is the number 4. Various combinations of functions can be chained onto the expect function (see the Jest docs for more examples at https://jestjs.io/docs/en/expect, which gives a rich syntax for describing the expected output of the code being tested).

8.5.5   *Running your first test*

Now that we have looked at the code to test and the tests themselves, we are ready to run Jest and see what a successful test run looks like (trust me, I already know this code works). From the terminal in the example-1 directory, run the tests as follows:

```
npx jest
```

You can see the output of the successful test run in figure 8.5. We have one test and one test suite, both have completed successfully.

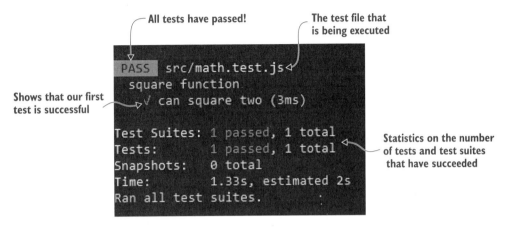

Figure 8.5   The output of our successful test run with Jest

8.5.6   *Live reload with Jest*

Live reloading is important for developer productivity, especially while testing. While coding and writing tests, you can run Jest in live reload mode as follows:

```
npx jest --watchAll
```

That command works for all projects and runs all tests when any code changes. If you are using Git, you can also use this command:

```
npx jest --watch
```

The second version has better performance because it uses Git to know which files have changed (rather than just blindly running all the tests). This is a great way to work. Change some code and the tests automatically run and show you if anything has been broken!

8.5.7   *Interpreting test failures*

All is good and well when our tests are passing, but what about when we have a problem in our code and our tests are failing? Don't wait until you accidentally break your code to find out!

Let's try it now. It's as simple as changing the behavior of our code. For instance, try changing the `square` function to return the wrong result:

```
function square(n) {
    return n & n;
}
```

Notice how I replaced the multiplication operator with the binary AND operator. Let's see what our tests have to say about this.

You can see the output of the now failing test in figure 8.6. When a test fails, Jest finishes with a nonzero exit code. This indicates that a failure happened. We'll make use of this later in our CD pipeline to prevent deployment in circumstances when our tests have failed.

This test failed because we changed the expected behavior of our code. We broke our own code on purpose to see the result, but you can also imagine how a simple typo in our regular development process could have caused this problem in production code. If you didn't have the automated test in place, this problem could easily fall through the cracks of manual testing and later be discovered by a customer. That's embarrassing, to say the least, but it can cause real problems for our business, depending on the nature of the actual bug.

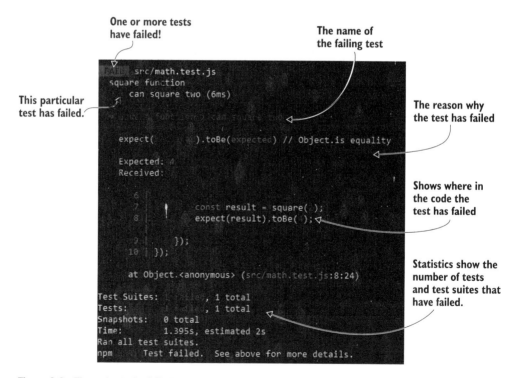

Figure 8.6   The output of a failed test in Jest

Of course, the intention here is not just to test the `square` function. That by itself won't be effective. What we need is to have a large proportion of our code covered by such tests.

A large body of tests gives us an automatic verification system that we run to prove, without a doubt, that our code works as intended. More importantly, it proves to us that our code continues to work in the future as we evolve it. It's handy to note that you can simulate failing code anywhere you like by throwing an exception like this:

```
throw new Error("This shouldn't happen.");
```

The best way to be fearless in the face of errors is to ruthlessly try and cause those in your own code. Once you have seen all the errors, it takes away the fear, and you can focus on understanding and fixing the problem. Simulating or causing problems in code to make sure that our application handles it gracefully is known as *chaos engineering* (check the end of chapter 10 for a reference to learn more about this).

8.5.8 *Invoking Jest with npm*

In chapter 2, we introduced the idea of adding npm scripts to our package.json file so that we can use the conventional npm commands like `npm start`. In chapter 2, we also configured the start script. We'll do the same for the test script here. Once we have configured package.json for this, we can run our test suite by typing:

```
npm test
```

This convention means that we can easily run tests for any Node.js project. We don't have to know if the project is using Jest or some other testing tool! Indeed, you'll see later in this chapter how we'll also run Cypress tests with the same command. The following listing shows our package.json with a test script to run our Jest tests.

Listing 8.4   Package.json with npm scripts for running Jest (chapter-8/example-1/package.json)

```
{
  "name": "example-1",
  "version": "1.0.0",
  "scripts": {                         Setup for running Jest
    "test": "jest",          ◁         by invoking "npm test"    Setup for running
    "test:watch": "jest --watchAll"    ◁                         Jest in live reload
  },                                                             mode
  "devDependencies": {
    "jest": "^25.4.0"    ◁—— Installs Jest as a dev dependency
  },
  "dependencies": {
                                ◁
  }            This project doesn't have any
}              production dependencies yet.
}
```

Note also in listing 8.4, there's an npm script called test:watch. This is configured so that we can run our tests in live reload mode like this:

```
npm run test:watch
```

The test:watch script is my own personal convention—it isn't an npm standard. I use it so that no matter which testing tool I use, I can easily remember how to run my tests with live reload enabled.

8.5.9 *Populating your test suite*

So far, we have only seen a single test, but I'd also like to give you a taste of what it looks like as we grow this test suite. Listing 8.5 shows what math.test.js looks like after adding a second test. (Example-1 doesn't actually contain this new test, but feel free to add it yourself and experiment with it.)

Listing 8.5 Adding the next test (additions to chapter-8/example-1/src/math.test.js)

```
const { square } = require("./math");

describe("square function", () => {

    test("can square two", () => {          Omits the previous
        ...                                  test for brevity
    });

    test("can square zero", () => {
                                             Creates the test
        const result = square(0);            "can square zero"
        expect(result).toBe(0);
    });

    ...             Add more tests to your "square"
                    function test suite here
});

...    Add more tests suites for the math library here
```

As listing 8.5 shows, we can add more tests to our square function test suite by adding more instances of the test function nested inside the test suite's describe function.

The new test, can square zero, is an example of an edge case. We don't need to add any more tests for squaring positive numbers; can square two is enough to cover all positive cases, so we could rename it can square positive number. Then to complete this small test suite for the square function, you should probably also add a test called can square negative number. I'll leave that to you if you'd like to continue working on this.

As we develop our math library, we'll add more math functions and more test suites. For example, we'll add functions like squareRoot and average and their test suites square root function and average function. Remember, we named our test file math.test.js, and that name is general enough that we can add new test suites to it using the `describe` function.

We could also have separate JavaScript code files for each test suite, for instance, square.test.js, square-root.test.js and average.test.js. Note that these are all appended with *.test.js* so that Jest can automatically find them. As we add new libraries in the future, we'll add new test files, as many as we need, to contain all the tests that we create.

You can structure your tests in any way you want. That means you can name those how you like and structure these across files to suit your own needs. When working for a company, however, you'll be expected to follow their existing style and conventions. Whatever convention you follow, I would only ask (on behalf of developers everywhere) that you use *meaningful names* for your tests. Names that make it easy to understand the purpose of the test. Thank you very much.

8.5.10 *Mocking with Jest*

JavaScript is a great language for creating mocks! The dynamic nature of JavaScript makes it particularly easy to create automated tests as well. But what is mocking?

> **DEFINITION** *Mocking* is where we replace real dependencies in our code with fake or simulated versions of those.

The dependencies that we replace can be functions, objects, or even entire code modules. In JavaScript, it's easy to create functions and piece together new objects and data structures that we can use as mocks.

Why do we do this? The purpose of mocking is to isolate the code we are testing. Isolating particular sections of code allows us to focus on just testing only that code and nothing else. Isolation is important for unit testing and test-driven development.

Not only does mocking help isolate the code we are testing, but it can also entirely eliminate the code and processes that would make testing slow. For example, we can eliminate database queries, network transactions, and filesystem operations. These are the kinds of things that can take a huge amount of time *compared* to the code we are testing.

In section 8.6, we'll learn about unit testing and see a real example of mocking, but let's first understand mocking by examining a simple example. Let's say that instead of using the multiply operator in our `square` function, we'll use the `multiply` function as follows:

```
function square(n) {
    return multiply(n, n);
}
```

You might well ask, why are we using a function to do multiplication when there's already a perfectly good operator? That's a good point. Well, I introduced the `multiply` function here primarily because I need a simple example by which to explain mocking. But if you'd like, I can also concoct a great reason why we need this!

Let's just say that we want our math library to work with abstract data types. Instead of working with ordinary numbers, we want it to be able to work with vectors (arrays of numbers), and in this case, the `multiply` function could very well be an extremely complex function that does the computation in parallel on a graphics processing unit (GPU).

Now to isolate our code in the `square` function (which arguably isn't much), we need to mock the `multiply` function. That means we must replace it with another function—one that we can control. We can do this using a primitive form of *dependency injection* (DI). DI is a technique where we inject dependencies into our code rather than hard-coding them. We control what the dependencies are, and that's useful for isolating code for unit testing. In this case, we inject the `multiply` function into the `square` function like this:

```
function square(n, multiply) {
    return multiply(n, n);
}
```

This works because functions are first-class citizens in JavaScript, and these can be passed around like any other value or object. Now let's make use of this from our test. When we call the `square` function, we'll pass in our mock version of `multiply`:

```
test("can square two", () => {
    const mockMultiply = (n1, n2) => {
        expect(n1).toBe(2);
        expect(n2).toBe(2);
        return 4;
    };

    const result = square(2, mockMultiply);

    expect(result).toBe(4);
});
```

Creates a mock version of the "multiply" function

Expects the "square" function to pass the right inputs to the "multiply" function

Hard-codes the mock function to return 4

Passes the mock function into the "square" function instead of the real "multiply" function

Expects to get back the hard-coded value of 4

You are now probably wondering, what's the point of all this? Given that our mock function returns a hard-coded value of 4, what are we actually testing here? You can read it like this: "we are testing that the `square` function invokes the `multiply` function with inputs 2 and 2, and the result received from `multiply` is the value returned from the `square` function."

You might note at this point that we have just implemented the `square` function, tested it, and proved that it works—and the real version of the `multiply` function doesn't even exist yet! This is one of the superpowers of test-driven development (TDD). TDD allows us to reliably test incomplete versions of our code. If that doesn't impress you, I don't know what will!

To make this code work for real, we still need to implement the `multiply` function. This can, in turn, have automated tests applied to it.

OK, so this is a crazy made-up example, but we needed a way to introduce the concept of mocking. It's pretty rare to see DI implemented at such a granular level as I have demonstrated just now. Coming up soon, though, you'll see a more realistic example that replaces entire code modules with mocks.

8.5.11 *What have we achieved?*

We have seen a simple example of testing with Jest and how mocking is used to isolate the code we are testing. Let's wrap up this section with a general recipe for testing with Jest.

CREATING TESTS WITH JEST

1 Create a file for the code you are testing (e.g., math.js).
2 Create a file for your test that matches Jest's naming convention (e.g., math.test.js).
3 Import functions and code modules into your test file.
4 Wrap your entire test suite in a call to the `describe` function and give it a descriptive name.
5 Add each test using a call to the `test` function and give each a descriptive name.
6 Run your tests using `npx jest` or `npm test` (if configured in package.json).

TEMPLATE FOR TEST SUITES

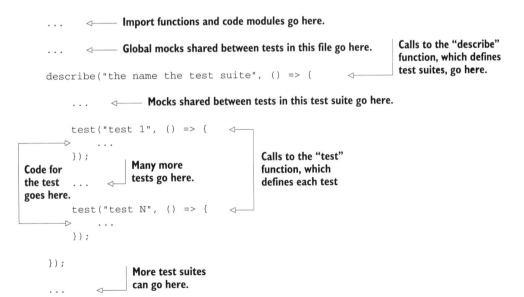

```
test("the name of the test", () => {
```
⟵ Calls to the "test" function, which defines each test. Use a meaningful name for each test!

```
    ...
```
⟵ Mocks used only in this test go here.

```
    ...
```
⟵ Calls the function(s) to be tested and records any result

```
    ...
```
⟵ Inspect results and mocks and states the expectations of the test
```
});
```

8.6   Unit testing

Unit testing for microservices works the same as any other kind of unit testing. We aim to test a single *unit* of code by itself and in isolation from other code. What is a unit? Typically, each test exercises a single function or one aspect of a single function.

What's important with unit testing is the isolation. When we test isolated code, we focus our testing efforts on just that small piece of code. For example, we'd like to test the code for our metadata microservice, but we don't care to test the code for say the Express library or the MongoDB library. Those are dependencies that we assume have already been tested. Instead, we want to test only the code that we have created. To focus on our own code, we must eliminate all other code.

Isolation of code is achieved by *mocking* its dependencies. What this means in terms of our metadata microservice is that we'll substitute the real Express and MongoDB libraries for fake instances that we can control and bend to our will.

Isolation is what makes unit tests run fast. Integration and end-to-end tests don't isolate code. In those types of testing, we exercise the integration of code modules rather than isolated pieces of code.

When running unit tests, we won't start a real HTTP server or connect to a real database. This is the kind of thing that makes unit tests run quickly, and it's why these are at the foundation of the testing pyramid (figure 8.1). We can afford to have 100s or even 1000s of unit tests for our code, and we won't have to wait a long time for our suite of unit tests to complete.

We'll be using Jest to execute our unit tests. Figure 8.7 shows what we'll do with it. Our test code from index.test.js (on the left) is loaded by Jest. Our code to be tested, the code for our metadata microservice from index.js (on the right) is loaded by our test code.

We'll mock Express and MongoDB instead of using the real thing. The test code "starts" our microservice. I say *starts* in quotes because we won't be starting it in the usual way. Unlike in normal execution, Express is mocked so we aren't starting a real HTTP server. Likewise, MongoDB is mocked so we aren't connecting to a real database.

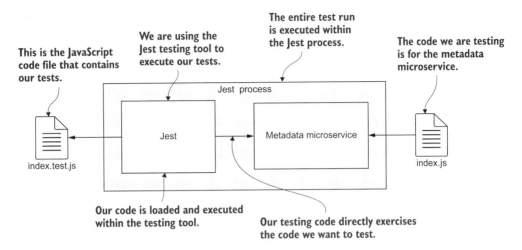

Figure 8.7   Unit testing the metadata microservice with Jest

8.6.1   *The metadata microservice*

We now move on to example-2 in the chapter 8 code repository. To follow along, you'll need to install dependencies:

```
cd chapter-8/example2
npm install
```

Listing 8.6 shows the code we will test. This is a fledgling microservice that will become FlixTube's metadata microservice. This is a REST API whose purpose is to collect, store, search, and manage the metadata associated with each video. The basic setup in the listing is not too different from our first microservice back in chapter 2.

Listing 8.6   The metadata microservice for unit testing (chapter-8/example-2/src/index.js)

```
const express = require("express");
const mongodb = require("mongodb");

function connectDb(dbhost, dbname) {
    return mongodb.MongoClient.connect(dbhost, {
            useUnifiedTopology: true
        })
        .then(client => {
            const db = client.db(dbname);
            return {
                db: db,
                close: () => {
                    return client.close();
                },
            };
        });
```

```
    }

    function setupHandlers(microservice) {

        const videosCollection = microservice.db.collection("videos");

        microservice.app.get("/videos", (req, res) => {          ◁──── Handles requests to
            return videosCollection.find()                              the /videos route
                .toArray()
                .then(videos => {
                    res.json({                        ◁──── Retrieves the records
                        videos: videos                        from the database
                    });
                })
                .catch(err => {
                    ... error reporting omitted ...
                    res.sendStatus(500);
                });
        });

        ...     ◁──── Other handlers can
                       go here later.
    }

    function startHttpServer(dbConn) {          ◁──── Starts the Express
                                                       HTTP server
        return new Promise(resolve => {          ◁──── Wraps in a promise so we can be
            const app = express();                      notified when the server starts
            const microservice = {
                app: app,
                db: dbConn.db,
            }
            setupHandlers(microservice);

            const port = process.env
        ⇒   .PORT && parseInt(process.env.PORT) || 3000;
            const server = app.listen(port, () => {
                microservice.close = () => {
                    return new Promise(resolve => {
                        server.close(() => {          ◁──── Closes the Express server
                    resolve();
                });
                    })
                    .then(() => {
                        return dbConn.close();          ◁──── Closes the database
                    });
                };
                resolve(microservice);
            });
        });
    }

    function startMicroservice(dbhost, dbname) {          ◁──── A new helper function to
        return connectDb(dbhost, dbname)                         collect code to execute when
            .then(dbConn => {                                    the microservice starts
                return startHttpServer(dbConn);
```

```
        });
}
                                                    The main entry point
                                                    for the microservice
function main() {
    ... error checking for environment variables omitted ...

    const DBNAME = process.env.DBNAME;

    return startMicroservice(DBHOST, DBNAME);
}                                                        Starts the microservice
                                                         normally, if this script is
                                                         the main module
if (require.main === module) {
    main()
        .then(() => console.log("Microservice online."))
        .catch(err => {
            console.error("Microservice failed to start.");
            console.error(err && err.stack || err);
        });
}
                              Otherwise, runs the
                              microservice under test
else {
    module.exports = {
        startMicroservice,              Exports the function to start
    };                                  the microservice so we can
}                                       call it from the test
```

Starts the
microservice

Listing 8.6 starts a HTTP server using the Express library and connects to a MongoDB database using the MongoDB library. We added a single handler function for the HTTP GET /videos route. This route retrieves an array of video metadata from the database.

The code we test here will be exercised by calling the function startMicroservice. This is a new function we added to our microservice to help make it more testable. Calling startMicroservice returns a JavaScript object that represents the microservice. We aren't storing the returned object yet. We don't need that for unit testing, but we will need it later when we come to integration testing.

We've made this change to the structure of our microservice in an effort to *design for testing*, and we'll often find ourselves doing this, adapting our code to make it more amenable to testing. Note that we aren't limited to calling startMicroservice. We could, in fact, call any exported function from any of our code modules. Keep that in mind because it's what unit testing is really all about: testing each and every function individually. Now, let's create some tests to confirm that our microservice started and that the /videos route retrieves the expected data.

8.6.2 *Creating unit tests with Jest*

Before we can unit test our code, we need to be able to create mocks for the dependencies. For this example, the dependencies we have are Express and MongoDB. In other situations, you will have different dependencies, like the amqp library for interacting with RabbitMQ.

Listing 8.7 shows the code for our tests. This file defines a single test suite called `metadata microservice` that contains three tests. We have called the file index.test.js to indicate that it tests code contained in the main source file index.js. As you continue to develop your microservice, you'll end up having many more files like this, with tests to cover all the code in your microservice.

The first part of the test suite is devoted to setting up mocks for the Express and MongoDB libraries. Note the use of `jest.fn` to create mock functions that we can use to detect if the function was called, and if so, then what arguments were passed to it. Next, note the use of `jest.doMock`, which allows us to mock entire Node.js modules. These tools are powerful and allow us to replace Express and MongoDB without having to adjust the code we are testing.

The first test in listing 8.7 checks that the HTTP server has been started on port 3000. The second test checks that a handler for the /videos route has been registered. The third test directly invokes the /videos route handler function and checks that it retrieves the required data from the database.

This example is actually quite advanced, but I wanted to get straight to the point and show you some unit testing that is relevant to microservices. If you struggle to understand this code, don't be too concerned. Just try to read it, get the gist of it, and understand which parts of it are for mocking and which parts are for testing.

Listing 8.7   Testing the metadata microservice with Jest (chapter-8/example-2/src/index.test.js)

Defines the test suite for the "metadata microservice"

```
describe("metadata microservice", () => {

    const mockListenFn = jest.fn(                    Creates a mock "listen" function
        (port, callback) => callback());             Creates a mock "get" function
    const mockGetFn = jest.fn();

    jest.doMock("express", () => {                   The Express library is a
        return () => {                               factory function that creates
                                                     the Express app object.
            return {                                 Returns a mock for the
                listen: mockListenFn,                Express app object
                get: mockGetFn,
            };
        };
    });
                                                     A mock for the MongoDB
    const mockVideosCollection = {};                 videos collection

    const mockDb = {
        collection: () => {                          A mock for the
            return mockVideosCollection;             MongoDB database
        }
    };
```

Creates a mock for the Express library

```
const mockMongoClient = {
    db: () => {
        return mockDb;
    }
};

jest.doMock("mongodb", () => {
    return {
        MongoClient: {
            connect: async () => {
                return mockMongoClient;
            }
        }
    };
});

const { startMicroservice } =
    require("./index");

test("microservice starts web server
    on startup", async () => {

    await startMicroservice();

    expect(mockListenFn.mock
        .calls.length).toEqual(1);
    expect(mockListenFn.mock
        .calls[0][0]).toEqual(3000);
});

test("/videos route is handled", async () => {

    await startMicroservice();

    expect(mockGetFn).toHaveBeenCalled();

    const videosRoute = mockGetFn.mock.calls[0][0];
    expect(videosRoute).toEqual("/videos");
});

test("/videos route retrieves data via
    videos collection", async () => {

    await startMicroservice();

    const mockRequest = {};
    const mockJsonFn = jest.fn();
    const mockResponse = {
        json: mockJsonFn
    };

    const mockRecord1 = {};
    const mockRecord2 = {};
```

A mock for the
MongoDB client object

Creates a mock for
the MongoDB module

A mock for
MongoClient

A mock for the
connect function

Imports the code
we are testing

Tests that the microservice
starts the HTTP server correctly

Invokes the code under test

Expects
only I call to
the "listen"
function

Expects that port 3000
was passed to "listen"

Tests that the /videos route is
handled by the HTTP server

Expects the Express "get"
function has been called

Expects that the parameter
to "get" was /videos

Tests that the /videos route retrieves
data from the videos collection in the
database

Invokes the code under test

Mock Express "request" and
"response" objects passed to
our Express route handler

Mocks
the "find"
function to
return
some mock
database
records

Mocks the "find" function to return some mock database records

```
mockVideosCollection.find = () => {
    return {
        toArray: async () => {
            return [ mockRecord1, mockRecord2 ];
        }
    };
};
```

Mocks the structure of the MongoDB library

Expects that the "json" function is called

```
const videosRouteHandler =
    mockGetFn.mock.calls[0][1];
await videosRouteHandler(mockRequest,
    mockResponse);

expect(mockJsonFn.mock
    .calls.length).toEqual(1);
expect(mockJsonFn.mock.calls[0][0]).toEqual({
    videos: [ mockRecord1, mockRecord2 ],
});
});
```

Extracts the /videos route "handler" function

Invokes the "handler" function

Expects that the mock records were retrieved from the database

```
    ...     ◁──── More tests go here!

});
```

You may have noticed in listing 8.7 that I'm using `async` and `await` keywords. I use these a lot in my day-to-day coding, but I haven't used these yet in this book. The reason I've introduced these here is that they fit nicely into Jest tests and make asynchronous code significantly easier to read.

You might be wondering where the `jest` variable actually comes from because there is no `require` statement in listing 8.7 that imports it! This is standard JavaScript, and normally, it would be a problem, but this code is running under Jest. Jest automatically imports the `jest` variable for us. How nice of it to save us a line of code like that.

A large section at the start of listing 8.7 is dedicated to creating the mocks that replace Express and MongoDB. We used `jest.fn` and `jest.doMock` to create mocks. Jest has many other useful functions for mocking and specifying the expectations of the test. See the reference at the end of this chapter to read more about that.

We replaced Express and MongoDB with new JavaScript objects, thus providing our own implementations for the dependencies of the code we are testing. When the code calls these functions, it calls the replacement versions and not the usual ones from the real Express and MongoDB libraries.

If we didn't replace Express and MongoDB, then calling `startMicroservice` would start the real HTTP server and connect to the real database. That normal operation is exactly what we want to avoid when unit testing! It's the kind of thing that makes automated tests run slowly. It won't seem like much of a difference right now because, for the moment, we are only talking about a tiny number of tests. But when you get to running 100s or even 1000s of tests, you will definitely see a big difference.

8.6.3 *Running the tests*

After writing the code and the tests, we are ready to run Jest. From the terminal in the example-1 directory, run the tests as follows:

```
npx jest
```

Or run

```
npm test
```

The output should show one passing test suite with three passing tests.

8.6.4 *What have we achieved?*

We've learned the basics of unit testing with Jest. We mocked the Express and MongoDB libraries, and we tested that our microservice can start and that its /videos route can retrieve records from the database.

This might not seem like much, but you can continue to create tests like this to cover code across all of your microservices. You might even want to try test-driven development (TDD), also known as *test-first development*, where you write code for tests before writing the actual code being tested.

This is a powerful technique that can help you achieve 100% test coverage, a feat that can prove difficult without TDD. At the end of this chapter, you'll find references to learn more about this test-focused method of development if you so desire.

8.7 *Integration testing*

The next step up the testing pyramid (figure 8.1) is integration testing. It's called *integration testing* because, instead of testing code modules in isolation (as we did with unit testing), the emphasis is now on testing code modules functioning together in an integrated fashion. When it comes to microservices, integration testing usually means that we are testing an entire microservice, including all the code modules and code libraries that it depends upon.

It would be nice if unit testing was enough to solve all our problems. Unit testing is effective because unit tests are extremely fast to run. The speed of unit tests means that we'll be more likely to run these frequently and thus catch problems quickly. Unfortunately though, many problems can still be hidden in the integration between code modules where they can't be detected by unit tests.

In a way, integration testing is actually easier than unit testing because we don't have to be concerned with mocking. In fact, if mocking seems too hard, you might find it much easier to start with integration testing. Earlier, when unit testing, we mocked dependencies for Express and MongoDB. We won't be doing that with integration testing. Instead, we'll allow the microservice we are testing to start a real HTTP server and connect to a real database.

Despite the fact that it is easier to write integration tests than unit tests, the setup for integration testing is more difficult. Using a real HTTP server limits the parallelization of our testing because we can only run a single HTTP server at a time on port 3000 (or indeed any other port). Using a real MongoDB database means that we'll need to have a database available for use by the code we are testing.

On top of that, starting the HTTP server and connecting to the database is time-consuming. This is what makes integration tests particularly slow compared to unit tests. All things considered, I won't be surprised if you are now convinced that it's actually unit testing that's easier than integration testing!

> **NOTE** Using the right combination of tests is a balancing act, and we do need integration tests because that's the only way to find problems in the integrated code.

Typically, when we run integration tests against a microservice, we'll interact with it through its official HTTP interface instead of directly, calling its functions as we did for unit testing. There are other ways we could interact with it, depending on how the microservice is implemented. For example, if the microservice uses RabbitMQ, then we can also interact with it by sending it messages.

Figure 8.8 shows what we'll do with integration testing in this section. Again, we are using Jest to test our metadata microservice, but this time, we won't be making use of Jest's mocking facilities. Instead of directly calling code in our microservice to test it, we'll send it HTTP requests and check the responses that come back.

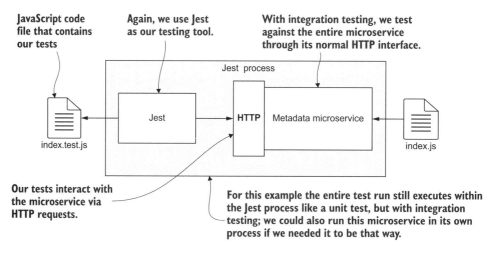

Figure 8.8 Integration testing a microservice with Jest

8.7.1 The code to test

Now we can move to example-3 in the chapter-8 code repository. You can continue to follow along and run these tests. The code we'll test is the same code as in example-2; nothing has changed, so look back to listing 8.6 if you'd like to revise that code.

8.7.2 *Running a MongoDB database*

When doing integration testing, we won't replace our database with a mock version. Instead, we need a real database, and we need to be able to load realistic test data.

To run the integration tests for example-3, you'll need a real MongoDB database up and running. It's not too difficult to download and install MongoDB. You can install it on your development workstation if you haven't already done so. Follow the instructions for your platform here:

https://docs.mongodb.com/manual/installation/

As an alternative, I've included a Docker Compose file in example-3 that starts MongoDB in a Docker container. You can start it like this:

```
cd example-2
docker-compose up
```

8.7.3 *Loading database fixtures*

With a database up and running, now we need a way to load database fixtures on demand. A *database fixture* is a fixed set of test data that we can load into our database for testing. It's called a fixture because we use it to seed our database with a well-known or specific set of data.

Doing this is particularly easy with Jest as we can simply create a JavaScript helper function to load data directly into our database through the regular MongoDB Node.js library. MongoDB is already included in the example-3 package.json, and you can install all dependencies for example-2 like this:

```
npm install
```

MongoDB can be installed in a new project as follows:

```
npm install --save mongodb
```

Note that we'll use the `--save` argument instead of `--save-dev` because MongoDB is actually used in our production microservice, not just in the test code. Even though we use it for testing, we also need it installed as a production dependency rather than a dev dependency.

Listing 8.8 shows a simple function that we can use for loading test data. We can call this function from our test code, and you'll see an example of that soon. We simply need to specify the name of the collection and the data records to load.

In listing 8.8, note how we are accessing the microservice's database through the db field of our `microservice` object (which is saved in a variable as you can see in listing 8.6). This saves having to make multiple connections to the database. We don't need to do that because the microservice has already made the connection, and we can reuse it.

Listing 8.8   A helper function to load a database fixture (extract from chapter-8/example-3/src/index.test.js)

```
// ...

async function
  loadDatabaseFixture(collectionName, records) {        A helper function to
                                                        load a database fixture

    await microservice.db.dropDatabase();               Resets the database (don't
                                                        try this in production!)

    const collection = microservice.db.collection(collectionName);
    await collection.insertMany(records);
}                                           Inserts the test data (our database
                                            fixture) into the database
// ...
```

One of the reasons we use MongoDB in the first place is because it makes it so easy to load test data. You can, of course, do this kind of thing with any database. It's just that some databases, like traditional SQL databases, tend to be more difficult to deal with.

The helper function in listing 8.8 allows us to store test data inline with our test code and to load it on demand into our database. This is quite convenient, but it's also possible to store our test data in distinct data files. That can make it a bit easier to organize. In the section coming up on end-to-end testing, you'll see a different way to load database fixtures.

8.7.4   *Creating an integration test with Jest*

Creating an integration test with Jest is much the same as creating a unit test with Jest. Because we aren't doing any mocking, it actually simplifies our test code quite a bit.

Instead of invoking code directly in our microservice, we'll use HTTP requests to trigger the code we'd like to test. To make HTTP requests, we can use either the Node.js low-level http library that we used in chapter 5 or a library installed through npm. In this case, we'll use the Axios library, which is a more modern library that directly supports `async`/`await`, so it fits nicely with Jest's support for asynchronous coding.

Example-3 already has Axios added to the package.json file. If you installed all dependencies for example-3, then you already have it. Otherwise, you can install Axios in a new project like this:

```
npm install --save-dev axios
```

We are using the `--save-dev` argument here because, in this case, we'll only use Axios in our tests. For that reason, it can be a dev dependency. If you plan to use Axios in your production code though, be sure to install it as a regular dependency using `--save` instead of `--save-dev`.

Listing 8.9 shows the code for our integration tests. This is similar to the code for our unit tests, but instead of mocking dependencies and directly calling into the code to be tested, we are starting our metadata microservice as a real HTTP server. We then use Axios to send HTTP requests to it.

Be careful that you don't run listing 8.9 against a production database! The function that loads the database fixture first drops the entire database. Make sure you only ever run this against a test database! And always backup your production database, just to be on the safe side!

Listing 8.9 Code for integration testing the metadata microservice with Jest (chapter-8/example-3/src/index.test.js)

```
const axios = require("axios");
const mongodb = require("mongodb");

describe("metadata microservice", () => {

    const BASE_URL = "http://localhost:3000";          Sets the base URL for
    const DBHOST = "mongodb://localhost:27017";    ◄── our database server
    const DBNAME = "testdb";

    const { startMicroservice } = require("./index");

    let microservice;
                                                        Starts the microservice,
    beforeAll(async () => {                             including the HTTP
        microservice =                                  server and the database
        ➡ await startMicroservice(DBHOST, DBNAME);  ◄── connection

    });

    afterAll(async () => {
        await microservice.close();    ◄──── Shuts down the microservice
    });

    function httpGet(route) {
        const url = `${BASE_URL}${route}`;
        return axios.get(url);
    }

    async function
    ➡ loadDatabaseFixture(collectionName, records) { ◄─┐
                                                          The helper function
        await microservice.db.dropDatabase();           that loads test data (a
                                                          database fixture) into our
        const collection = microservice.db              database. We defined this
        ➡ .collection(collectionName);                  function in listing 8.8.
        await collection.insertMany(records);
    }                                                  ◄─┘

    test("/videos route retrieves data via
    ➡ videos collection", async () => {    ◄─┐ Tests that a list of videos can be
                                               retrieved via a HTTP request to
                                               the /videos route
```

```
const id1 = new mongodb.ObjectId();
const id2 = new mongodb.ObjectId();
const videoPath1 = "my-video-1.mp4";
const videoPath2 = "my-video-2.mp4";

const testVideos = [
    {
        _id: id1,
        videoPath: videoPath1
    },
    {
        _id: id2,
        videoPath: videoPath2
    },
];

await
    loadDatabaseFixture("videos", testVideos);

const response = await httpGet("/videos");
expect(response.status).toEqual(200);

const videos = response.data.videos;
expect(videos.length).toEqual(2);
expect(videos[0]._id).toEqual(id1.toString());
expect(videos[0].videoPath).toEqual(videoPath1);
expect(videos[1]._id).toEqual(id2.toString());
expect(videos[1].videoPath).toEqual(videoPath2);
});

...

});
```

Creates test data to load into the database (annotation pointing to the test data block)

Loads the database fixture into the videos collection of the database (annotation pointing to loadDatabaseFixture)

Makes a HTTP request to the route we are testing (annotation)

Expects that the received data matches our test data (annotation)

More tests go here! (annotation)

In listing 8.9, there is only one test, but we can easily add more as we develop the microservice. Here again, we test the /videos route. This time, though, we do it through its normal HTTP interface, and the microservice is using a real database instead of a mock.

We aren't testing that the HTTP server starts as we did in the unit tests. That was easy to test then because we had mocked the Express library. Now, though, we aren't mocking anything so it's difficult to explicitly confirm if the HTTP server was started correctly. Although, we can see that we are making a HTTP request to the microservice, which implicitly tests that our HTTP server is functioning.

Note in listing 8.9 how we use Jest's beforeAll function to start our microservice before testing, and then the afterAll function to shutdown the microservice. See how we are saving a reference to the microservice object. This means we can access its database connection and shutdown the microservice when done. Shutting down our microservice is something we never considered before, but it's important here because this might not be the only test suite, and we don't want to leave this microservice running longer than necessary.

You might have realized that as we add more tests to this test suite, we'll run multiple tests against the same microservice. It's not ideal to share the microservice across multiple tests in this way because it makes it difficult to know if each test is independent of the others. But it is significantly faster to do it this way than to separately start and stop the microservice for each test in turn. We could do that to make the test suite more reliable, but you'll be waiting a lot longer for it to finish!

8.7.5   *Running the test*

Running integration tests with Jest is the same as running unit tests. Type

```
npx jest
```

Or, because we configured it in package.json, type

```
npm test
```

Try running this integration test for yourself. Also, try changing code to break the test as we did earlier when unit testing.

8.7.6   *What have we achieved?*

In this section, we learned the basics of running integration tests with Jest. It's pretty much like unit testing, but we left out the mocking. As a result, we ran our code integrated with its dependencies.

When doing integration testing, we are not trying to isolate the code under test (that was the point of unit testing), and we aren't trying to mock any dependencies (which is what helps achieve that isolation). We are, instead, aiming to test the code in its integrated state! That is to say, we are testing it in combination with other code: code in other modules and code in external libraries.

In a sense, integration testing is easier than unit testing because we don't have the concerns of isolation and mocking. Creating integration testing can also be a more efficient use of our time than writing unit tests. That's because integration tests tend to cover more code, and as such, you need to spend less time writing tests.

The big problem with integration tests is that these are slower than unit tests. That is why they have a higher position in the testing pyramid. Consider the unit and integration tests that we have already seen in this chapter. These have tested basically the same thing. But in the case of integration testing, we started a real live HTTP server that connects to a real database. That makes integration tests much slower to execute than unit tests.

8.8   *End-to-end testing*

Now we take the final step up the testing pyramid (figure 8.1). We come to end-to-end testing. This is similar to integration testing except now we aim to test against our whole application, or at least, some cut-down version of it. Here we hope to test our application in its entirety and as close as we can to how it appears in its production environment.

End-to-end testing is possibly the easiest form of testing yet. We don't have to do any mocking, as we did with unit tests. However, we do need database fixtures so that we can load realistic test data.

Traditionally, it would have been difficult to do end-to-end testing against a distributed application. That's because it takes a lot of effort to start all the services. Fortunately, we are now empowered by Docker Compose, which we learned in chapters 4 and 5 and have used since to develop our application. We will now use Docker Compose as a convenient way to boot our microservices application for automated end-to-end testing.

At this point, we are leaving Jest behind and moving onto Cypress, a testing tool for loading and testing web pages. Cypress is powerful and has many features. Here you'll only learn the basics, but that's enough to get started and give you a taste of what it can do. We'll use Cypress to run tests against our application through its front end as served by the gateway microservice. You can see what this looks like in figure 8.9.

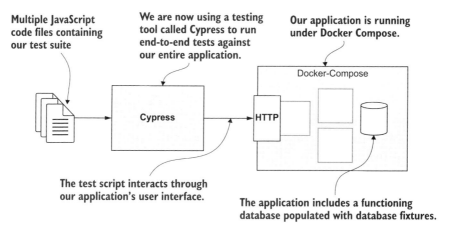

Figure 8.9   End-to-end testing our entire application with Cypress and Docker Compose

Running end-to-end tests requires that we start our whole application and do the testing in a web browser. This makes end-to-end tests the slowest of all the types of testing and is what earns these their place at the top of the testing pyramid.

That said, having a handful of end-to-end tests should be an important part of your testing strategy. End-to-end testing covers a lot of ground, so even though these can take significant time to run, they deliver a lot of bang for buck. Also, this type of testing exercises your application through the front end, which happens to be the point of view of your customer. Needless to say, this *is* the most important perspective from which we can test our application, and it is the primary reason we place such a high value on end-to-end tests.

We now move on to example-4, the final example for chapter 8. Example-4 contains a docker-compose.yaml that boots a cut-down version of FlixTube.

8.8.1 Why Cypress?

Cypress is simply a fantastic all-in-one-tool for testing web pages. It's a visual solution and has a great user interface; we can actually watch it going through the motions of testing our application's front end. You can get a feel for what this looks like in figure 8.10, but to truly understand how powerful it is, you must try it for yourself.

Cypress uses Chrome by default for running tests, but it also automatically detects other browsers on our workstations. We can easily switch between these for cross-browser testing.

Cypress has a great user interface, but it can also run from the terminal in *headless* mode, which means the UI is hidden. During development, we'll spend a lot of time using the Cypress UI to visually test our front end. Ultimately, we'll run it in headless mode so that it fits into our CD pipeline.

When running in headless mode, we can't directly see Cypress interacting with our front end, but Cypress has a super cool feature: it records videos of its test runs. This feature really comes into its own for automated testing. When a Cypress test fails, you can extract the video of the failing test from your CD server so that you can see what happened!

When running the Cypress UI, it automatically supports live reload. All you need to do is to update your code and tests, and Cypress automatically reloads and runs your tests again. Like all the great modern tools, Cypress is open source. You can find the code for it on GitHub here:

https://github.com/cypress-io/cypress

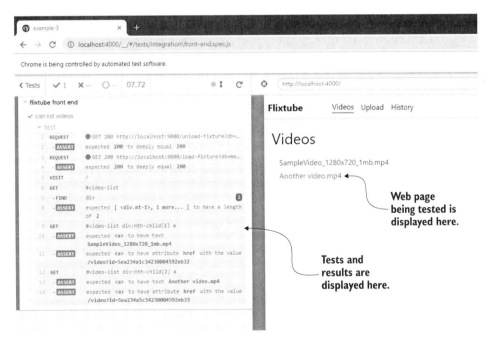

Figure 8.10   The Cypress UI (user interface)

Cypress has other great features that will no doubt impress you. There are references at the end of the chapter so you can continue to learn more about Cypress.

It's not all roses with Cypress, however, and I'd be remiss if I didn't point out a major problem with it. Cypress is based on the Electron framework. This means that it's large and can be quite slow to download/install. This also means it can be difficult, though still possible, to make it work efficiently in your CD pipeline.

For this book and FlixTube, we integrate Cypress and our end-to-end tests into a single code repository. For real projects in the future, though, you might want to split your Cypress tests out to a separate testing repository. Although, normally, it's nice to keep our tests collocated with the code being tested, with Cypress (because it's so big), it can make sense to have these in separate repositories.

8.8.2   *Installing Cypress*

Example-4 already has Cypress added to its package.json. You can install dependencies like this:

```
cd chapter-8/example-4
npm install
```

You can install Cypress to a new project like this:

```
npm install --save-dev cypress
```

Because Cypress, like Jest, is a tool only required for testing, we'll use `--save-dev` to save it as a dev dependency. As mentioned, Cypress is large and installation can take some time. Now might be a good time for a coffee break!

You can see in figure 8.11 the structure of the example-4 project with Cypress installed. This is similar to other project structures we have worked with in earlier chapters. We have a docker-compose.yaml file to build and run our application, and we have code for our microservices in subdirectories.

Some of the structure that you see in figure 8.11 is automatically created for you the first time you start Cypress in a new project. Particularly, Cypress creates many example test files under the subdirectory cypress/integration/examples. I haven't included those examples in the chapter-8 code repository, but you can easily generate these yourself by installing Cypress in a new project and running it. You should try doing that because browsing through those example tests is a great way to learn more about the capabilities of Cypress.

Listing 8.10 shows the Cypress configuration file. This is a JSON file where we can set configuration options for Cypress. For this example, we only need two options. The first is the `baseUrl`, where we set the base URL for the web page we are testing. We'll run it locally (by booting our application with Docker Composer), so the hostname is `localhost`.

The container that runs our gateway is configured to serve the front end on port 4000, which makes the base URL http://localhost:4000. Setting the base URL in the

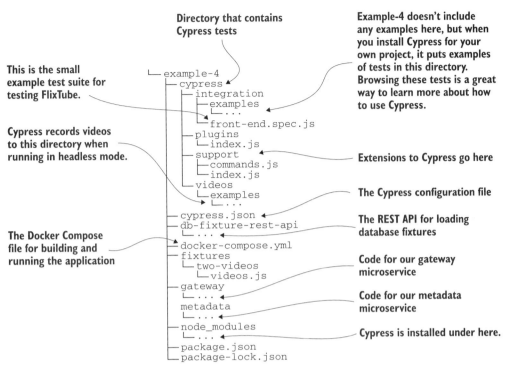

Figure 8.11 Example-4 project structure with Cypress installed

Cypress configuration file is optional. But it's useful in that we can easily redirect our entire Cypress test suite to a new location just by changing that line in the configuration file.

Listing 8.10 Configuration file for Cypress (chapter-8/example-4/cypress.json)

```
{

    "baseUrl": "http://localhost:4000",          ◁──  Sets the base URL that we
                                                        will use to run tests against
    "dbFixturesUrl": "http://localhost:9000"     ◁──  Sets the URL for the
                                                        database fixtures REST API
}
```

The other field we set in listing 8.10 is not a standard Cypress configuration option. We need a way to load database fixtures into our database. For reasons that I'll explain soon, we'll use a separate REST API to do that. The dbFixturesUrl field in the configuration file sets the base URL for that REST API.

8.8.3 Starting the Cypress UI

Now we are ready to start Cypress and run some tests. In your terminal, run the following command from example-4 in the chapter-8 code repository:

```
npx cypress open
```

This opens the first level of the Cypress UI and shows a list of your Cypress test suites. Example-4 only contains a single test suite. Double click the test suite named front-end.spec.js to open the next level of the Cypress UI.

What you see now is a single test to run against the FlixTube UI. The test runs automatically, but at this point, the test should fail because we haven't started our application yet.

8.8.4   *Setting up database fixtures*

Before we start our application, we must be able to load database fixtures. When using Jest earlier, we were able to load data into our database directly from the test code. We can't do this directly from Cypress because it runs in the browser (Cypress is an Electron application-based on the Chromium rendering engine, the basis for the Chrome web browser), and the regular MongoDB npm library doesn't work there. We need a different solution for loading database fixtures.

To load test data into our database, we'll use a separate REST API to manage our database. That means we can make HTTP requests to load and unload database fixtures. We are already using Docker Compose, so it's not difficult to add an extra container into our application. Figure 8.12 shows the structure of our application including the new database fixtures REST API.

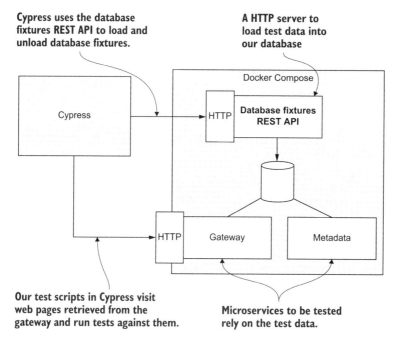

Figure 8.12   Using the database fixtures REST API to seed our database with test data prior to running tests with Cypress

Creating such a REST API is quite a bit of work. However, I already have one that I've used for testing projects in the past. I've included a copy of the code for it under the example-4 project (find it under example-4/db-fixtures-rest-api). You can also find a standalone copy of the code on GitHub:

https://github.com/ashleydavis/db-fixture-rest-api

We won't cover the internals of the database fixtures REST API in this book. We have to draw the line somewhere, but feel free to look over this code on your own. Learning to read the code of others is a valuable experience. Be assured that you won't find anything particularly new here; after all, it's just a Node.js REST API built on Express. That's similar to the microservices you have already seen in this book.

Listing 8.11 is an extract from the example-4 docker-compose.yaml file. It shows that we integrate the database fixtures REST API into our application the same way as any other microservice.

Listing 8.11 Loading the db fixtures REST API with Docker Compose (extract from chapter-8/example-3/docker-compose.yaml)

```
version: '3'
services:

  db:
    image: mongo:4.2.0                    Configures a MongoDB
    container_name: db                    database server
    ports:
      - "27017:27017"
    expose:
      - "27017"
    restart: always

  db-fixture-rest-api:
    image: db-fixture-rest-api
    build:
      context: ./db-fixture-rest-api
      dockerfile: Dockerfile
    container_name: db-fixture-rest-api
    ports:
      - "9000:80"                          Configures the
    environment:                           database fixtures
      - PORT=80                            REST API
      - DBHOST=mongodb://db:27017
      - FIXTURES_DIR=fixtures
    volumes:
      - ./fixtures:/usr/src/app/fixtures:z
    depends_on:
      - db
    restart: always

  ...                  The gateway and metadata
                       microservices are defined here.
```

Listing 8.11 adds the database fixtures REST API to our application, but we still need a way to talk to it from our Cypress tests. For that, we'll make an extension to Cypress that we can use from our tests to load database fixtures.

Listing 8.12 is a snippet of code that shows how we can add a new command to Cypress. This is an example of how we can extend Cypress to do new things. This particular command is called `loadFixture`, and we'll use it in our Cypress tests to load database fixtures.

Listing 8.12 Loading a database fixture under Cypress (extract from chapter-8/example-3/cypress/support/commands.js)

Defines a Cypress command (an extension to Cypress) to load database fixtures via the new REST API

```
Cypress.Commands.add('loadFixture',
    (databaseName, fixtureName) => {

        cy.unloadFixture(databaseName, fixtureName);

        const dbFixturesUrl =
            Cypress.config("dbFixturesUrl");
        const route = "/load-fixture?db=" + databaseName +
            "&fix=" + fixtureName;
        cy.request("GET", dbFixturesUrl + route)
            .then(response => {
                expect(response.status).to.eql(200);
            });
});
```

Unloads test data from the previous test (by calling another helper function)

Reads the URL of the REST API from the Cypress configuration file

Makes a HTTP GET request to the REST API to load the database fixture

Expects that the fixture was successfully loaded (fails the test otherwise)

The `loadFixture` command makes a HTTP GET request to the database fixtures REST API and causes it to load a database fixture from a file (in this case, example-4/fixtures/two-videos/videos.js). In a moment, you'll see how we invoke this command from our test code.

8.8.5   *Booting your application*

We have Cypress installed and ready to go, and we have the ability to load database fixtures. Before we can test our application, we must boot it!

Listing 8.11 was an extract of the Docker Compose file for example-4. The complete file contains the configuration for a cut-down version of FlixTube with gateway and metadata microservices. This is nowhere near the full application, but it's enough that we can write a test to confirm that the list of videos is retrieved from the database and displayed in the front end.

In this case, I've simplified FlixTube just so that I can present it as a simple example for this chapter. Generally, though, it's good to know that we always have the option of cutting back our application to make it easier to test. As our application grows larger, it will eventually become too big to be tested on a single computer using end-to-end tests. At this point, we are forced to chop up our application into smaller testable units. Now, let's start the application using our old friend Docker Compose:

```
docker-compose up --build
```

8.8.6 Creating an end-to-end test with Cypress

Writing end-to-end tests with Cypress is a bit different from writing tests with Jest. In listing 8.13, we use a similar overall structure composed of describe and it functions instead of describe and test (we used those with Jest). describe and it come from the Mocha style of testing.

Mocha is a different testing framework for JavaScript that is still popular, so you might have already heard about it. Cypress happens to be based on Mocha, and that is why these tests look the way they do. Jest actually supports the describe and it format as well, so if you wanted, you could use that same format with both testing tools.

> **Listing 8.13 An end-to-end test of FlixTube with Cypress (extract from chapter-8/example-4/cypress/integration/front-end.spec.js)**

```
describe("flixtube front end", () => {          ⟵── Defines the test suite

    it("can list videos", () => {

        cy.loadFixture("metadata", "two-videos");     ⟵── Loads the fixture named
                                                          two-videos into the videos
                                                          collection of the metadata
        cy.visit("/");            ⟵── Makes Cypress visit the    database
                                       FlixTube home page

        cy.get("#video-list").find("div").
            should("have.length", 2);        ⟵── Checks that two videos (those
                                                 loaded from the database
                                                 fixture) are displayed in the UI

        cy.get("#video-list div:nth-child(1) a")
            .should("have.text", "SampleVideo_1280x720_1mb.mp4")
            .should("have.attr", "href",
              "/video?id=5ea234a1c34230004592eb32");

        cy.get("#video-list div:nth-child(2) a")
            .should("have.text", "Another video.mp4")
            .should("have.attr", "href",
              "/video?id=5ea234a5c34230004592eb33");
    });
});
```

Annotations: "Tests that we can load the list of videos in the FlixTube UI" — "Verifies the details of the first video" — "Verifies the details of the second video"

The first line of code in our test is a call to our loadFixtures command, accessed through the Cypress cy object. The Cypress interface also contains many other functions for loading, interacting with, and testing web pages.

On the next line, we call cy.visit. This is the most important thing you need to know about Cypress. This function is how you make Cypress visit a web page. All other Cypress commands operate relative to the page that is visited.

Here we are visiting the / (root) route on our web page. Note that this is relative to the base URL that we specified earlier in the Cypress configuration file. This navigates the Cypress browser to the FlixTube home page.

Next, we use `cy.get` to get an element from the browser's DOM hierarchy and run tests against it. It checks that we have two videos in the video list and then checks the names and links for each. We know these videos should be displayed in the front end because we have seeded our metadata microservice's database with the two-videos database fixture on the first line of this test. That database fixture loads test data (you can see it in example-4/fixtures/two-videos/videos.js) into the database with all the details of these two videos.

If you already have Cypress open, then you'll have run this test already. The result should look like figure 8.10. You might need to refresh the Cypress UI to run the test after you started the application in the previous section. At this point, you can experiment with breaking this code and seeing the tests fail, just like we did earlier with the unit and integration tests.

Here's an example. Open the file example-4/gateway/src/views/video-list.hbs. This is the HTML that is rendered for the FlixTube home page (in the format of a Handlebars template). Try changing this HTML so that something different is displayed for each video in the list. Once you break the tests, you'll see red for failure instead of the green for success that was shown in figure 8.10.

Just be careful that you never run this test against a production database. Loading a database fixture wipes out the relevant database collections, and you never want to lose production data. You shouldn't be able to do this in production anyway, because you would never run the database fixtures REST API in production! That gives us the capability to load database fixtures, but we only need it for development and testing environments.

> **NOTE** Running the database fixtures REST API in a production environment also gives external access to your database. This is a recipe for disaster, so be careful never to instantiate it in production.

There's so much more you can do with Cypress! This includes clicking buttons

```
cy.get(".some-button").click();
```

and typing values into input fields:

```
cy.get(".some-input").type("Hello world");
```

Cypress even provides facilities to mock your backend REST APIs. You can use this to isolate the user interface for testing! This allows you to do a kind of TDD for user interfaces which, frankly, I find quite amazing. There are references at the end of this chapter so you can continue learning about Cypress.

8.8.7 *Invoking Cypress with npm*

Now we can get set up to invoke our Cypress tests with npm just like we did with Jest. Example-4 is a separate project to the other examples, and we use a different testing tool (Cypress instead of Jest). Nevertheless, we'd like to be able to run Cypress with the conventional npm test script like this:

```
npm test
```

Listing 8.14 shows the setup in package.json to make this work. We have configured the test script to invoke `cypress run`, which executes Cypress in headless mode. This allows us to run Cypress tests from the terminal just like we did earlier with Jest tests.

Listing 8.14   Package.json with npm scripts for running Cypress (chapter-8/example-4/package.json)

```
{
  "name": "example-4",
  "version": "1.0.0",
  "scripts": {
    "test:watch": "cypress open",      ⊲──┐   Invoking the command "npm run
    "test": "cypress run"    ⊲──┐          cypress" opens the Cypress UI
  },                          │
  "dependencies": {},          Invoking "npm test" runs Cypress
  "devDependencies": {         in headless mode to run tests
    "cypress": "^4.4.1",       entirely from the command line
    "mongodb": "^3.5.6"
  }
}
```

The other script we set up is `npm run test:watch` to invoke `cypress open`, which opens the Cypress UI. I like this configuration because I feel that running the Cypress UI (which automatically does live reload) is functionally similar to running Jest in live reload mode (with Jest's `--watch/--watchAll` argument). When I want this functionality, I simply invoke `npm run test:watch`, and I don't have to think about whether I'm in a Jest project or a Cypress project. I just get the result that I'm expecting.

8.8.8 *What have we achieved?*

We've almost come to the end of our journey through the testing landscape. We've seen unit testing, integration testing, and now end-to-end testing.

We've understood the relative performance of tests: integration tests are slower than unit tests and end-to-end tests are slower than integration tests. And we've seen how each unit test covers only a small amount of isolated code. Integration and end-to-end testing can be very effective because these cover much more code with fewer tests.

The question now is how many of each type of test should you have? The answer to this is never set in stone.

But what I can say is that you can, and probably should, have 100s or 1,000s of unit tests. You'll need to have much fewer integration tests and very few end-to-end tests. It's difficult to say how many because it really depends on how long you are willing to wait for a test to run to completion. If you are happy to wait overnight or over a weekend for your test suite to complete, then you can probably afford to have 100s or 1,000s of end-to-end tests as well.

As developers, though, we crave fast and comprehensive feedback. For this, you can't beat unit tests. If you can have a huge amount of code coverage through many extremely fast unit tests, then this is what you should have! That's because this is what will get used by your developers as they are coding throughout every moment of their working day. If your test suite is slow, developers will tend not to use it and not to update it. That's not good for anyone.

At the end of the day, it's not black and white. There isn't even a clear distinction between the different types of tests. Where does unit testing end and integration testing begin? It's not clear. All tests fall on a spectrum, and it's a spectrum with many shades of grey.

8.9   *Automated testing in the CD pipeline*

We have a suite of automated tests. Now we arrive at the real point of automated testing: to put it on automatic!

To truly be automatic, our tests need to operate directly on our hosted code repository. When a developer pushes code changes to the code repository, we'd like to automatically run the test suite to check the health of the code. To achieve this, we must add the tests to our CD pipeline, where they will be an automatic checkpoint in front of production deployment. If the tests pass, our code goes to production. If they fail, our code will not be deployed. It's as simple as that. Figure 8.13 illustrates this scenario.

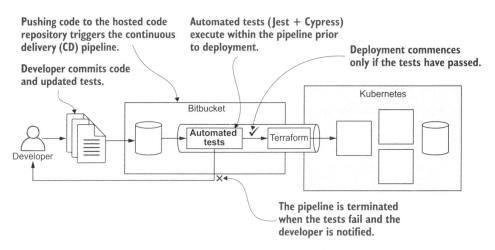

Figure 8.13   Automated testing within the CD pipeline

The reason we spent time earlier discussing the configuration of the npm test script in package.json is because that's how we'll integrate our automated tests into our CD pipeline. As we learned in the previous chapter, a CD pipeline can be as simple as running a shell script (even though some vendors offer fancy GUIs). Adding our automated tests then is easy. Assuming our npm test script is configured, we can simply invoke the following from our deployment shell script:

```
npm test
```

As an example, let's consider adding automated tests to example-4 from chapter 7. Listing 8.15 shows the YAML file for configuring Bitbucket Pipelines. This is the same as the one we used in chapter 7, but now we are invoking npm test prior to invoking the deployment script.

If the automated tests fail, that is to say, that if npm test returns a nonzero exit code, which both Jest and Cypress do if any tests fail, then the pipeline itself fails and is aborted. Failing tests, therefore, prevent deployment to production.

> **Listing 8.15   Running tests in the CD pipeline (an update to chapter-7/example-4/ bitbucket-pipelines.yaml)**

```
image: hashicorp/terraform:0.12.6

pipelines:
    default:
      - step:
          name: Build and deploy
          services:
            - docker
          script:
            - export VERSION=$BITBUCKET_BUILD_NUMBER
            - cd video-streaming && npm install
              && npm test
            - chmod +x ./scripts/deploy.sh
            - ./scripts/deploy.sh
```

Runs tests for the video-streaming microservice from chapter 7 ⟶ (points to `&& npm test`)

Having Jest running in our CD pipeline is fairly easy. The npm install in listing 8.15 installs it.

Running Cypress is more complicated. Because Cypress is so big, you'll need to configure caching in your CD server so that Cypress isn't redownloaded every time the pipeline is invoked. That's getting a bit too involved and is specific to your CD provider, so we don't cover it in this book.

We also need a command in our deployment script that boots our application before running the Cypress tests. This makes things more difficult and is much more advanced. Although beyond the scope of this book, it's definitely worthwhile that you look into this so you can have end-to-end tests running automatically in your deployment pipeline.

8.10 *Review of testing*

Before finishing the chapter, here is a quick review of Jest and Cypress and how we use these to run tests.

Table 8.2 Review of testing commands

Command	Description
`npx jest --init`	Initializes the Jest configuration file.
`npx jest`	Runs tests under Jest.
`npx jest --watch`	Runs tests with live reload enabled to rerun tests when code has changed. It uses Git to know which files have changed.
`npx jest --watchAll`	As above, except it monitors all files for changes and not just those that are reported changed by Git.
`npx cypress open`	Opens the Cypress UI so that you can run tests. Live reload works out of the box; you can update your code and the tests rerun automatically.
`npx cypress run`	Executes Cypress tests with Cypress running in headless mode. This allows you to do Cypress testing from the command line (or CD pipeline) without having to display the user interface.
`npm test`	The npm script convention for running tests. Runs Jest or Cypress (or even both), depending on how you configured your package.json file. This is the command you should run in your CD pipeline to execute your test suite.
`npm run test:watch`	This is my personal convention for running tests in live reload mode. You need to configure this script in your package.json file to use it.

8.11 *Continue your learning*

In this chapter, we learned the basics of automated testing. There's enough here to kick start your own testing regime, but testing is such a huge subject and is a specialization in its own right. To explore the subject further, refer to the following books:

- *Unit Testing Principles, Practices, and Patterns* by Vladimir Khorikov (Manning, 2020)
- *The Art of Unit Testing*, 2nd ed., by Roy Osherove (Manning, 2013)
- *Testing Java Microservices* by Alex Soto Bueno, Andy Gumbrecht, and Jason Porter (Manning, 2018)
- *Testing Microservices with Mountebank* by Brandon Byars (Manning, 2018)

Also see *Exploring JavaScript Testing* by Elyse Kolker Gordon (Manning, 2019), which is a free collection of chapters about testing from other books available from Manning:

- https://www.manning.com/books/exploring-javascript-testing

To learn more about Jest, see the Jest web page and *Getting Started* guide here:

- https://jestjs.io/
- https://jestjs.io/docs/en/getting-started

To learn more about Cypress, see the Cypress web page and documentation here:

- https://www.cypress.io/
- https://docs.cypress.io/guides/getting-started/installing-cypress.html
- https://docs.cypress.io/guides/core-concepts/introduction-to-cypress.html

Summary

- Automated testing is essential for scaling up to large numbers of microservices.
- You learned how unit testing, integration testing, and end-to-end testing fit together in the testing pyramid.
- We created and executed unit tests and integration tests using Jest.
- We created end-to-end tests using Docker Compose and Cypress.
- You learned how to use database fixtures to populate your database with test data for integration and end-to-end testing.
- You learned how to fit automated testing into your continuous delivery (CD) pipeline.

Exploring FlixTube

9

Getting to chapter 9 has been a long road to travel. Along the way, we used numerous tools to build microservices, test those, and deploy them to production. In this chapter, we'll see the fruits of our labor come together in the completed version of the FlixTube example application.

Through this chapter, we'll learn how FlixTube works as a whole and meet some new microservices. We'll revise and consolidate our skills and demonstrate those skills in the context of a complete, although still relatively simple, microservices application.

278

We will start by building and running FlixTube in development. Next, we'll run our tests from chapter 8 against it. Ultimately, we'll deploy FlixTube to our production Kubernetes cluster and create a continuous delivery (CD) pipeline for it.

9.1   *No new tools!*

Congratulations! You have already learned all the main tools you need to start building microservices applications. There is, of course, a deeper level of knowledge to be acquired. There are also many other useful tools that you could learn, and new tools will arrive on the scene in the future.

But, for the purposes of this book, we have learned the minimum amount of tooling to build products based on microservices. As you dive deeper into ongoing development, you'll find problems that are specific to your project, and you'll need to dive deeper into these tools. You'll need to learn a deeper level of Docker, Kubernetes, and Terraform. For now, though, we have enough tools in our toolbox to complete our first version of FlixTube. So let's get to it.

9.2   *Getting the code*

To follow along with this chapter, you need to download the code or clone the repository.

- Download a zip file of the code from here:
  https://github.com/bootstrapping-microservices/chapter-9
- You can clone the code using Git like this:
  ```
  git clone https://github.com/bootstrapping-microservices/chapter-9.git
  ```

For help on installing and using Git, see chapter 2. If you have problems with the code, log an issue against the repository in GitHub.

9.3   *Revisiting essential skills*

As we work through the complete FlixTube example, we will exercise the essential skills we have learned to build, run, test, and deploy microservices. When you see it in a list like this, you realize just how much ground we have covered!

- Running microservices with Node.js (from chapter 2)
- Packaging and publishing our microservices with Docker (from chapters 3 and 6)
- Building and running our application in development with Docker Compose (from chapters 4 and 5)
- Storing and retrieving data using a database (from chapter 4)
- Storing and retrieving files using external file storage (from chapter 4)

- Communication between microservices with HTTP requests and RabbitMQ messages (from chapter 5)
- Testing individual microservices with Jest (from chapter 8)
- Testing the whole application with Cypress (from chapter 8)
- Deploying the application to a Kubernetes cluster using Terraform (from chapters 6 and 7)
- Creating a CD pipeline with Bitbucket Pipelines (chapter 7)

Figure 9.1 illustrates the skills we will revisit and shows their context in the scheme of things. To make the most of this chapter, follow along with the examples. You should get FlixTube running for yourself so you can study it and understand how it works. To test and improve your understanding, you should try making your own changes. Practice is the best way to cement these skills in your mind.

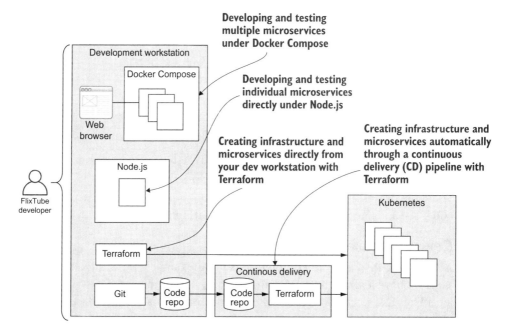

Figure 9.1   Essential skills we revisit in this chapter

9.4   *Overview of FlixTube*

The code for this chapter only includes a single example: the complete FlixTube project. You can find it in the example-1 subdirectory of the chapter 9 code repository. Let's start with a bird's eye view of its structure. Figure 9.2 shows the latest incarnation of FlixTube.

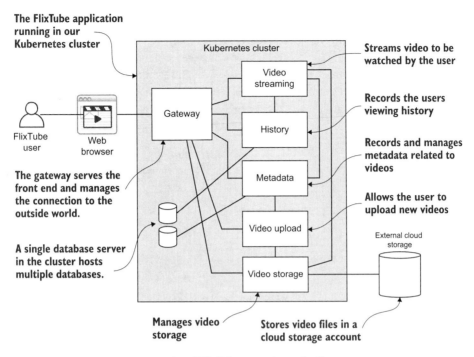

Figure 9.2   Overview of the completed FlixTube example application

9.4.1   *FlixTube microservices*

You already know some of the microservices shown in figure 9.2. For example

- Video streaming (first encountered in chapter 2)
- Video storage (from chapter 4)
- History (from chapter 5)
- Metadata (from chapter 8)

There are also some new microservices that you haven't seen yet: gateway and video upload. Table 9.1 lists the purpose for each of these microservices.

Table 9.1   FlixTube microservices

Microservice	Purpose
Gateway	The entry point to the application. Serves the front end and provides a REST API.
Video streaming	Streams videos from storage to be watched by the user.
History	Records the user's viewing history.
Metadata	Records details and metadata about each video.
Video upload	Orchestrates upload of videos to storage.
Video storage	Responsible for storing and retrieving videos from external cloud storage.

9.4.2 *Microservice project structure*

Before we look at the project structure for the entire application, let's first revisit the structure of an individual Node.js microservice. Open the metadata directory under example-1 in the chapter 9 code repository to follow along.

Using the metadata microservice as an example, figure 9.3 describes the layout of its project. This is a typical Node.js project, and all of FlixTube's microservices have virtually this same structure.

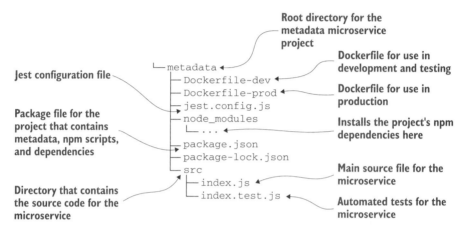

Figure 9.3   The structure of a Node.js microservice project (the metadata microservice)

9.4.3 *FlixTube project structure*

Now, let's look at the structure of the whole FlixTube project. Figure 9.4 shows its layout, including subdirectories for each microservice. Open the example-1 directory from the chapter 9 code repository to take a look for yourself.

For simplicity, FlixTube was built in a single code repository. Using a single repo is a great way to learn development with microservices (it makes it simpler for you), and in general, even after you are an expert in microservices, using a single repo is a simple and convenient way to bootstrap a new microservices application. Of course, using a single repo is also a convenient way for me to share the example code with you.

Having said all that, microservices in production are usually never contained in a single code repository. Using a single repository removes the biggest advantages of using microservices: that they can be independently deployed. Having all the microservices in the single repo means that these will be deployed together (unless you have an unusually smart CD pipeline).

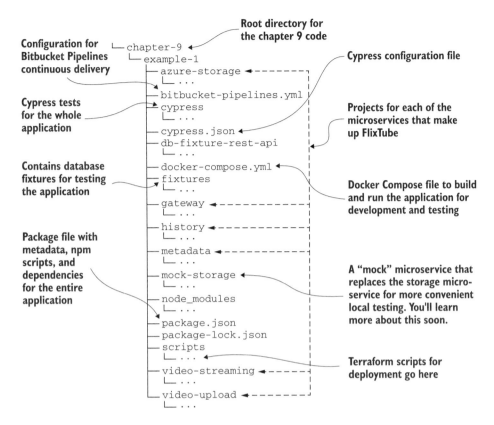

Figure 9.4 The structure of the entire FlixTube project

In real-life situations, microservices are almost always split into separate repositories, and usually, there is a separate repository for each microservice. For the moment, for simplicity and convenience, we'll continue with FlixTube in a single repository. In chapter 11, we'll talk about mono- vs. multi-repos and how we can take FlixTube forward by splitting it out to separate code repositories.

9.5 *Running FlixTube in development*

Our first step is to have FlixTube running on our development workstation (or personal computer). Figure 9.5 shows how it looks in development. Note that we have replaced the video-storage microservice with a mock version of it. We'll discuss the why and how of this soon.

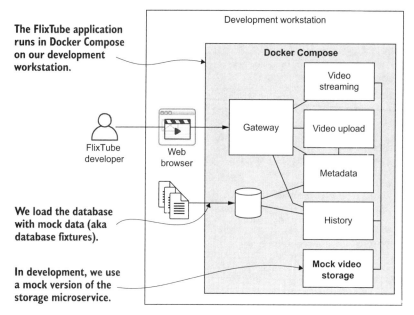

The FlixTube application runs in Docker Compose on our development workstation.

FlixTube developer

Web browser

We load the database with mock data (aka database fixtures).

In development, we use a mock version of the storage microservice.

Development workstation

Docker Compose

Video streaming

Gateway

Video upload

Metadata

History

Mock video storage

Figure 9.5   FlixTube as it now looks in development

9.5.1 *Booting a microservice*

Before booting the whole application, it's worth revising how we start an individual microservice. When developing a new microservice or focusing our current work on an existing microservice, we'll frequently need to run that microservice on its own outside the context of the application.

We are using Node.js for our microservices, so that means running our microservices directly under Node.js on our development workstations. If you followed along in chapter 2 and chapter 8, you'll already have Node.js installed. If not, return to section 2.5.4 in chapter 2 for instructions. Before running a Node.js project, you must first install dependencies like this:

```
npm install
```

To run a Node.js project, use the npm start script convention:

```
npm start
```

This invokes a command line that is specified in the project's package.json file. All microservices in FlixTube follow this common Node.js convention. That means you know how to start any microservice in FlixTube to run it standalone in *production mode*.

What's more appropriate during ongoing development is to run the microservice in *development mode*. This enables *live reload* (first covered in section 2.6.8), so we can edit our code and have the microservice restart itself automatically to include the changes. We use the start:dev script (my personal convention) to run any of the Flix-Tube microservices in development mode:

```
npm run start:dev
```

(You can revise further on production mode, development mode, and live reload. To learn more, return to sections 2.6.7 and 2.6.8 in chapter 2.)

You may have noticed that most of the FlixTube microservices now have dependencies that make them more difficult to start on their own. Most of these either need a database or a RabbitMQ server. Some of them require both. We can deal with this in any of the following ways:

- *Install MongoDB and RabbitMQ on your development workstation.* This is annoying in the short term, but quite useful in the long term.
- *Instantiate MongoDB and RabbitMQ servers containers using Docker or Docker Compose.* This is a convenient, effective, and simple way to do this.
- *Mock the libraries for MongoDB, RabbitMQ and other dependencies.* This is similar to what we did in chapter 8. You'll probably want to do this for your automated testing.

9.5.2 *Booting the application*

Now let's boot the entire FlixTube application using Docker Compose, the useful tool we first encountered in chapter 4 and have used since. Frequently, during day-to-day product development, we'll build and restart our application, and Docker Compose makes this much simpler. Often, we'll take time out to focus on an individual microservice, but we'll still frequently want to test our larger application while we evolve its constituent microservices.

If you followed along in chapters 4, 5, and 8, you will already have Docker Compose installed. If not, refer back to section 4.3.2 and install it so you can follow along. You should now open the example-1 subdirectory from chapter 9 in VS Code to see the code for yourself.

Listing 9.1 reminds us of what a Docker Compose file (docker-compose.yaml) looks like. FlixTube's version of this file is the biggest in this book, so listing 9.1 has been abbreviated for brevity. Most entries in this file are similar, so these can be safely omitted. If you've seen one, you've basically seen them all.

> **Listing 9.1 The Docker Compose file for booting FlixTube in development (abbreviated from chapter-9/example-1/docker-compose.yaml)**

```
version: '3'
services:
                              Starts the container for
  db:           ⟵─────────── the MongoDB database
    image: mongo:4.2.0
    container_name: db
    # ... code omitted for brevity ...
```

```
  rabbit:                                          Starts the container for
    image: rabbitmq:3.8.1-management               the RabbitMQ server
    container_name: rabbit
    # ... code omitted ...
                                          Starts the REST API for
  db-fixture-rest-api:                    loading database fixtures
    image: db-fixture-rest-api
    build:
      context: ./db-fixture-rest-api
      dockerfile: Dockerfile
    container_name: db-fixture-rest-api
    # ... code omitted ...
                                          Builds and starts the video-
  video-streaming:                        streaming microservice
    image: video-streaming
    build:
      context: ./video-streaming
      dockerfile: Dockerfile-dev
    container_name: video-streaming
    # ... code omitted ...
                                          All the other FlixTube
  # ... other microservices omitted       microservices go here.
```

Most FlixTube microservices have been omitted from listing 9.1, but one you can see is our old friend, the video-streaming microservice. There is also the setup for our database (covered in chapter 4), RabbitMQ (covered in chapter 5), and the database fixtures REST API we will use in our automated testing (covered in chapter 8). Now use Docker Compose to build and start FlixTube:

```
cd example-1
docker-compose up --build
```

It takes some time to build and start, especially if you haven't done this before. Docker needs to download and cache the base images.

Now, with the FlixTube application running, open your browser and navigate to http://localhost:4000 to see FlixTube's main page. You'll notice FlixTube has a shiny new user interface (UI)! We'll talk more about that soon. For now, take some time to explore FlixTube's UI:

1 Navigate to the upload page.
2 Upload a video.
3 Navigate back to the main page to see the uploaded video in the list.
4 Click the video to play it.

When you have finished development, don't forget to shutdown FlixTube so that it's not continuing to consume resources on your development workstation. You can do that by pressing Ctrl-C in the terminal where Docker Compose is running and by then invoking

```
docker-compose down
```

9.6 *Testing FlixTube in development*

Testing is essential to the practice of development. We can and should do manual testing, but nothing beats automated testing for efficiency, reliability, and repeatability.

In chapter 8, we looked at multiple ways of testing using Jest and Cypress. We'll revisit those again here. The various tests that we looked at in that chapter are repeated here in the chapter 9 code repo. We'll run those now against the completed FlixTube example.

Of course, any real application will have many more tests than the few we are running here. This is just a demonstration, and I haven't aimed for anything near complete test coverage. Follow along in the coming sections, and try running these tests for yourself.

9.6.1 *Testing a microservice with Jest*

The metadata microservice in FlixTube includes the Jest unit tests from chapter 8. Before running the tests, you'll need to install dependencies:

```
cd chapter-9/example-1/metadata
npm install
```

Now run the tests using the standard npm `test` script convention as follows:

```
npm test
```

This executes the associated command line in the metadata microservice's package .json file that we configured in chapter 8. Figure 9.6 shows the results of a successful test run.

You can also run the tests in *live reload* mode, which means you can edit your code, and the tests will restart automatically. We do this using another npm script called `test:watch` (my own personal convention):

```
npm run test:watch
```

To revise Jest in more detail, return to section 8.5. To revisit the Jest setup for npm and live reload, see section 8.5.8.

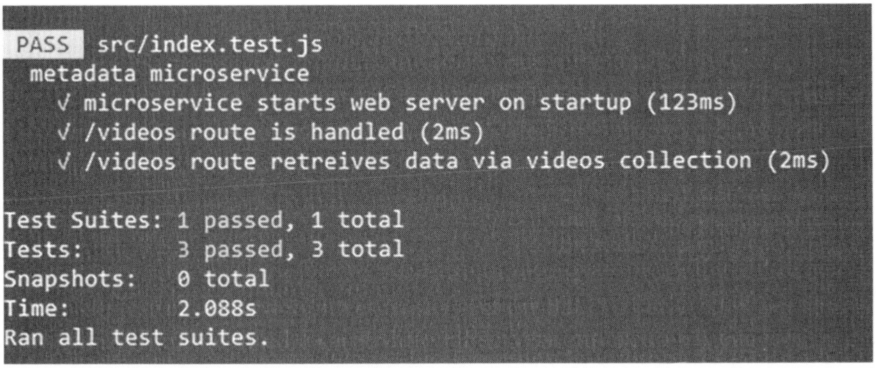

```
PASS  src/index.test.js
  metadata microservice
    √ microservice starts web server on startup (123ms)
    √ /videos route is handled (2ms)
    √ /videos route retreives data via videos collection (2ms)

Test Suites: 1 passed, 1 total
Tests:       3 passed, 3 total
Snapshots:   0 total
Time:        2.088s
Ran all test suites.
```

Figure 9.6 **A successful run of the automated tests for the metadata microservice using Jest**

9.6.2   *Testing the application with Cypress*

We can also run the Cypress end-to-end test from chapter 8 against the FlixTube application. In chapter 8, we ran this test against a cutdown version of FlixTube. Here though, we run it against the full application. To run this test, you'll need to install dependencies for the FlixTube project:

```
cd chapter-9/example-1
npm install
```

Be sure to actually start the application if you haven't done so already:

```
docker-compose up --build
```

Now, run the regular npm test script, which in this case is configured to invoke Cypress:

```
npm test
```

That runs Cypress from the terminal in headless mode. During development, we'll want to bring up the Cypress UI, as shown in figure 9.7. In this case, we'll use the `test:watch` script that we configured to start the Cypress UI:

```
npm run test:watch
```

With the Cypress UI running, we can make code changes that affect our front end and see the results in a very visual way. To revise Cypress in more detail, return to section 8.8. To revisit Cypress setup for npm, go to section 8.8.7.

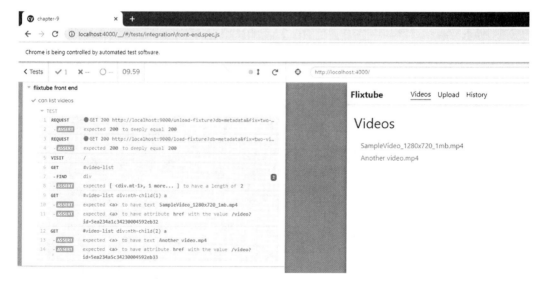

Figure 9.7   A successful test run of the automated tests for the FlixTube UI using Cypress

9.7   *FlixTube deep dive*

By now, you should understand FlixTube from a high level. You know the microservices and the purposes of each. You know how to build, run, and test the application on your development workstation. Before we deploy FlixTube to production, let's first understand some of its deeper details. Throughout this section, we'll look at various aspects of FlixTube:

- Database fixtures
- Mocking the storage microservice
- The gateway
- The FlixTube UI
- Video streaming
- Video upload

9.7.1   *Database fixtures*

We first talked about database fixtures in chapter 8, where we used these to load our database with realistic sets of data prior to running automated tests. We saw database fixtures used for automated testing, but these are also useful for manual testing and even for product demonstrations. Being able to boot your application and have it ready to show, complete with realistic data, is extremely useful!

When unit testing with Jest, we didn't need any data because we mocked the MongoDB database library and were able to replace real data with fake data provided through the mock version of the database library. When integration testing with Jest, we were able to interact with our MongoDB database within our test code by directly using the MongoDB library. This meant we could have test data inline in our test code, but it was convenient not to have to create separate data files for it.

When doing end-to-end testing with Cypress, we had to find a different solution. Because Cypress tests run in the browser (Cypress is built on Electron, which is based on Chrome), we don't have access to the MongoDB library (which only runs under Node.js). In this case, we don't have direct access to manipulate our MongoDB database.

To solve this problem, I created the *database fixtures REST API*. This is a REST API that looks similar to any of the other microservices you have seen in this book. We won't look at its code directly, but if you'd like to look at it yourself, you'll find that it's already quite familiar. The code for the REST API is included in the chapter 8 code repository and copied to the chapter 9 code repository so that we can use it when running our tests against FlixTube. Additionally, you can find the original source code for it on GitHub at https://github.com/ashleydavis/db-fixture-rest-api. You can see the setup for the REST API's container in the Docker Compose file earlier in listing 9.1.

For an understanding of what a database fixture looks like, see listing 9.2. In general, our database fixtures are stored under the fixtures subdirectory of chapter-9/ example-1.

FlixTube only has one database fixture in the file videos.js (shown in listing 9.2). The name of the file denotes the database collection that the data will be stored in. The data from this fixture will be loaded into the videos collection.

The directory that contains the file denotes the name of the fixture. In this case, the name of the directory is two-videos, so the name of the database fixture is two-videos. I've given the fixture this name because its purpose is to load metadata for two videos into our database. In general, we should give meaningful names to our database fixtures so that we can easily remember their purpose.

Each database fixture can consist of many files. Even though here we only have one file for our two-videos fixture, it could have more such files to set the contents of other collections in our database.

Listing 9.2   An example database fixture for FlixTube (chapter-9/example-1/fixtures/two-videos/videos.js)

```
const mongodb = require("mongodb");          ⊲──┐ Imports the MongoDB library
                                                  │ so we can create database IDs
module.exports = [   ⊲──┐ Exports the data that's inserted into the
    {                    │ videos collection of the metadata database
        _id:
➥       mongodb.ObjectId("5ea234a1c34230004592eb32"), ⊲──┐
        name: "SampleVideo_1280x720_1mb.mp4"              │
    },                                                     │ Creates database IDs
    {                                                      │ for new records
        _id:                                               │
➥       mongodb.ObjectId("5ea234a5c34230004592eb33"), ⊲──┘
        name: "Another video.mp4"
    }
];
```

Sets the filenames for the videos

If you ran the Cypress test earlier in section 9.6.2, then you have already used this database fixture! Note that the fixture shown in listing 9.2 is actually a JavaScript file. We can use either JSON format or JavaScript for these database fixtures. JSON is appropriate for static data, but JavaScript is a great option for generating dynamic data. That gives us a lot of flexibility for producing test data. In listing 9.2, see how we use the MongoDB library to produce database IDs for our test data.

9.7.2   *Mocking storage*

For convenience during development, we replaced the Azure version of the video-storage microservice with a mock version. This is similar to the mocking we used in section 8.5.10. Except, rather than replacing functions, objects, and libraries with mock versions, we now replace an entire microservice with a fake version. Figure 9.8 shows what FlixTube looks like when Azure storage has been replaced by the mock storage microservice.

Our mock storage microservice is not a complete fake though! It still does the job of storage, but instead of using cloud storage, it stores videos in the local filesystem. The main reason we do this is not just for testing; it's for the convenience and performance of being able to limit our entire application to our development workstation.

In development we replace the external file storage microservice with a "mock" microservice that uses the local filesystem for storage.

This means we remove the "external" dependency and can now restrict the entire application to a single developer's PC. This makes development much easier and prevents different developers from accidentally interfering with each other.

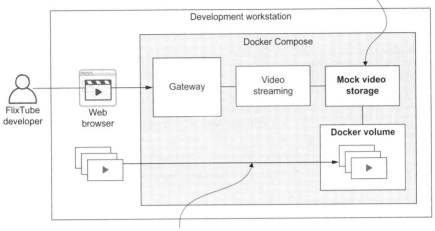

Video files are shared from the developer's workstation into the mock video storage container using a shared Docker volume.

Figure 9.8   Replacing cloud storage with a mock microservice for more convenient and efficient use during development

When running in development, we'd prefer to eliminate external dependencies like connections to cloud storage. In this case, limiting our storage to the local filesystem makes the setup for development easier. Performance is improved because videos are stored locally and not sent out to the cloud. Besides this change, FlixTube works as normal, and the other microservices have no idea that the Azure storage microservice has been kicked out and replaced with a mock version.

Being able to replace complex microservices with simpler mock versions is not just convenient, it might also be necessary at some point in the future. Right now, FlixTube is a small application, but you can imagine as it grows into the world-dominating streaming service it is destined to be that it will become too big to run on a single computer.

At that point, we need to use every trick in the book to make it fit. This includes cutting out microservices that we don't need; for example, you could remove the history microservice from the Docker Compose file if you don't need to test it.

NOTE   Removing or replacing big complex microservices—possibly even whole groups of microservices—is an important technique for reducing the size of our application so that it can fit on a single computer and be able to run during development.

Listing 9.3 shows the setup of our mock storage microservice in FlixTube's Docker Compose file. It looks similar to the configuration of the Azure storage microservice. One thing that's different is the storage subdirectory that is shared between the host operating system and the container. This is the directory where uploaded videos are stored. Sharing it like this means that we can inspect uploaded videos ourselves on the host OS to test that the microservice is functioning correctly.

Listing 9.3 Mock storage microservice setup in the Docker Compose file (extract from chapter-9/example-1/docker-compose.yaml)

```
video-storage:           Sets the DNS name as video-storage. (The other
  image: mock-storage    microservices don't know that the Azure storage
  build:                 microservice has been replaced with a mock version.)
    context: ./mock-storage
    dockerfile: Dockerfile-dev     Instead of building the container from the azure-
  container_name: video-storage    storage subdirectory, we build the mock version
  volumes:                         from the mock-storage subdirectory.
    - /tmp/mock-storage/npm-cache:/root/.npm:z
    - ./mock-storage/src:/usr/src/app/src:z
    - ./mock-storage/storage:
      /usr/src/app/storage:z      Shares the storage directory between the host OS and
  ports:                          the container and stores the videos in this directory.
    - "4005:80"                   You can inspect them from the host to ensure the
  environment:                    mock storage microservice works correctly.
    - PORT=80
  restart: "no"
```

It's a great option for development to be able to replace microservices with mocks. It can help make development easier, but there are times when we need to focus on the real version of the microservice; we need to test it rather than the mock version. At those times, we can simply swap the mock version for the real version in the Docker Compose file. If you like, you can try this for yourself.

Listing 9.4 shows the commented out configuration for the real storage microservice. Simply uncomment this and then comment out the configuration for the mock version. Now rebuild and restart your application. You can now test the real storage microservice in development!

Listing 9.4 The real storage microservice commented out (extract from chapter-9/example-1/docker-compose.yaml)

```
# video-storage:            Uncomment this to include the Azure
#   image: azure-storage     storage microservice in the application
#   build:                   during development. To make this work,
#     context: ./azure-storage    you must then comment out the mock
#     dockerfile: Dockerfile-dev   storage microservice (shown in listing 9.3),
#   container_name: video-storage  effectively replacing it with the real one.
#   ... code omitted for brevity ...
```

Listing 9.5 shows the code for the mock storage microservice. The mock version replaces the /video and /upload routes from the real storage microservice with versions that use the local filesystem. The mock microservice is a drop-in replacement because its REST API conforms to the interface of the real microservice.

Listing 9.5 The mock storage microservice (extract from chapter-9/example-1/ mock-storage/src/index.js)

```
const express = require("express");
const fs = require("fs");
const path = require("path");

const app = express();

const storagePath =                              Sets the path for storing
    path.join(__dirname, "../storage");   ◁────┘  videos in the local filesystem

app.get("/video", (req, res) => {      ◁──┐  HTTP GET route handler that
                                           │  streams a video from storage
    const videoId = req.query.id;
    const localFilePath = path.join(storagePath, videoId);
    res.sendFile(localFilePath);       ◁──┐
});                                        │  Sends the local file directly as a
                                           │  response to the HTTP request

app.post("/upload", (req, res) => {    ◁──┐  HTTP POST route handler that
                                           │  uploads a video to storage
    const videoId = req.headers.id;
    const localFilePath = path.join(storagePath, videoId);
    const fileWriteStream =
        fs.createWriteStream(localFilePath);
    req.pipe(fileWriteStream)                         ◁─────┐
        .on("error", err => {
            console.error("Upload failed.");
            console.error(err && err.stack || err);          Streams the body of the
        })                                                    incoming HTTP request (the
        .on("finish", () => {                                 uploaded file) into a local file
            res.sendStatus(200);
        });                                           ◁─────┘
});

const port = process.env.PORT && parseInt(process.env.PORT) || 3000;
app.listen(port, () => {
    console.log(`Microservice online`);
});
```

9.7.3   *The gateway*

FlixTube has a single gateway microservice. It's called a *gateway* because it acts as a gateway into the application for our users. For the current version of FlixTube, this is the single entry point to the whole application. The gateway provides the front-end UI that allows our users to interact with FlixTube in their web browser. It also provides a REST API so the front end can interact with the backend.

FlixTube doesn't support any kind of authentication yet, but in the future, we'd probably like to upgrade the gateway to authenticate our users. A FlixTube user would have to sign in before the gateway allows them to interact with the backend.

Figure 9.9 shows a potential future for FlixTube with more than one gateway. This illustrates a well-known pattern called *backends for front ends*. Each front end has its own gateway. There is one gateway for access by a web browser; another gateway for access by a mobile app; and another gateway for the FlixTube admin portal.

If possible, we'd want to keep things simple and to support only a single gateway. It's completely OK to share a gateway across multiple types of front ends. But if we find our front ends having different requirements (for instance, different forms of authentication between web and mobile or different security considerations between the web and admin portals), then *backends for front ends* is a pattern that can help.

If we do expand to have multiple gateways, we'd then want to use separate hostnames or subdomains to access them. For example, the main gateway for the browser could use flixtube.com, the mobile gateway using mobile.flixtube.com, and the admin portal using admin.flixtube.com. To assign domain names to your application, you'll need to use a DNS provider to buy domain names and configure each one to point to the IP address of a particular gateway microservice.

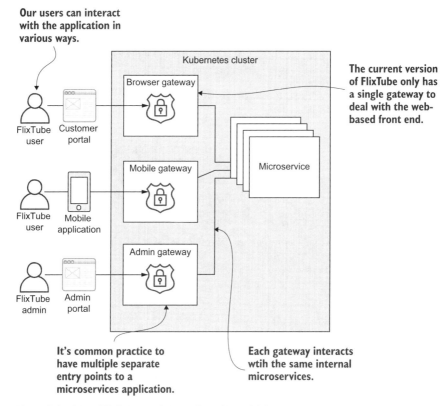

Figure 9.9   What FlixTube would look like with multiple gateways

Forwarding HTTP requests into the cluster is one of the main jobs of a gateway micro-service. We'll see code examples of this in upcoming sections. A more advanced gate-way (FlixTube isn't this advanced yet) will have REST API routes that issue requests to multiple internal microservices. Then it will integrate multiple responses into a single response that is returned to the front end.

For example, imagine a REST API that retrieves an individual user's history. This might require HTTP requests to a user account microservice (FlixTube doesn't have this yet) and the history microservice before integrating a response and sending it to the front end. In this theoretical example, the gateway has merged the responses of both HTTP requests.

9.7.4 *The user interface (UI)*

If you haven't had a chance to explore FlixTube's UI, do so now. Build and start the application as discussed in section 9.5.2, then navigate your web browser to http://localhost:4000.

Figure 9.10 shows the main page of FlixTube (the video list) *after* some videos have been uploaded to it. We can click any video in the list to watch it. We can click between Videos, Upload, and History, in the navigation bar at the top to switch among the main pages.

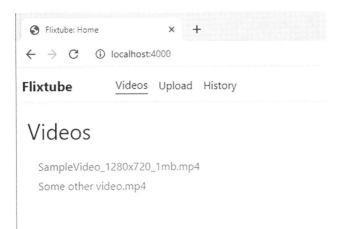

Figure 9.10   The main page of the FlixTube UI shows the list of videos that have been uploaded.

FlixTube is implemented as a traditional server-rendered web page, rather than as a modern single-page application (an SPA) rendered in the browser. If FlixTube were a real commercial application, it would most likely be coded as an SPA using React, Angular, or Vue.

FlixTube uses server-side rendering via Express and the Handlebars template engine with vanilla JavaScript in the front end. The FlixTube front end is plain old HTML, CSS, and JavaScript with no fancy modern frameworks.

Why not use one of the popular modern SPA frameworks? Well, the simple reason is that it's outside the scope of this book. This book isn't about UIs and that's why the front end is as simple as it can be. (Besides that, I didn't want to choose sides and stoke the war between the SPA framework disciples, but all the cool kids use React, right?).

Listing 9.6 is an extract from the gateway microservice's main code file. It shows the HTTP GET route that renders the main page. The main page shows the list of uploaded videos. This route handler starts by requesting data from the metadata microservice. We then render the web page using the video-list template and input the list of videos as the template's data.

> **Listing 9.6   The gateway code that renders the video list web page (extract from chapter-9/example-1/gateway/src/index.js)**

```
app.get("/", (req, res) => {          ⟵  Declares a HTTP GET route handler
    http.request(                         that retrieves the main web page and
        {                                 shows the list of uploaded videos
            host: `metadata`,
            path: `/videos`,
            method: `GET`,
        },
        (response) => {
            let data = "";
            response.on("data", chunk => {                Renders a web page
                data += chunk;                            using the video-list
            });                                           template (listing 9.8
                                                          shows the template).
            response.on("end", () => {                    We pass the array of
                res.render("video-list", {                videos in as the data for
                  videos: JSON.parse(data).videos });  ⟵ rendering the template.
            });

            response.on("error", err => {
                console.error("Failed to get video list.");
                console.error(err || `Status code:
                  {response.statusCode}`);
                res.sendStatus(500);
            });
        }
    ).end();
});
```

Makes a HTTP request to the metadata service to get the list of videos

The code to make the HTTP request in listing 9.6 is using the built-in Node.js `http.request` function, so it's quite verbose. After seeing Axios in chapter 8, you might wonder why I haven't used it instead.

Axios is a fantastic modern library and I highly recommend it! It is simple to use, quite flexible, and it works well with the new `async` and `await` keywords in Java-Script. The reason it's not used in this chapter is that it's easier to control the built-in libraries as a Node.js stream, which we aren't using just yet, but you will see examples of that soon.

I didn't use a JavaScript framework for FlixTube, but I did use a CSS framework (Tailwind CSS). That's so that I could make a nice UI without having to mess about with the nuts and bolts of CSS.

Listing 9.7 shows the main page of FlixTube. This is a HTML document contained within a Handlebars template. Handlebars is a simple and powerful template library that we can use to generate web pages based on data. If you look back to listing 9.6, you'll see that the list of videos is passed as the template data. Now in listing 9.7, you can see that we are generating a sequence of HTML `div` elements from this template data.

When the web browser requests the main page, the gateway microservice requests the data from the metadata microservice. From that data, it renders the HTML to display to the user in their web browser.

Listing 9.7 The Handlebars template for the video list web page (chapter-9/example-1/gateway/src/views/video-list.hbs)

```
<!doctype html>          ◁──── A HTML5 web page
<html lang="en">
    <head>
        <meta charset="utf-8">

        <title>FlixTube: Home</title>
                                              Includes Tailwind CSS. Using a CSS
                                              framework makes CSS much easier
        <link rel="stylesheet"                to deal with!
        ➥ href="css/tailwind.min.css">  ◁──┘
        <link rel="stylesheet" href="css/app.css">  ◁──┐
    </head>                                            Includes FlixTube-
    <body>                                             specific CSS
        <div class="flex flex-col">
  ┌─▷      <div class="border-b-2 bg-gray-100">
  │           <div class="nav flex flex-row items-center mt-1 p-2">
  │               <div class="text-xl font-bold">
  │                   FlixTube
  │               </div>
  │               <div class="ml-16 border-b-2 border-blue-600">
  │                   <a href="/">Videos</a>
  │               </div>
  │               <div class="ml-4">
  │                   <a href="/upload">Upload</a>
  │               </div>
  │               <div class="ml-4">
  │                   <a href="/history">History</a>
  │               </div>
  │           </div>
  └─▷      </div>
                                        The main content
                                        for the web page
            <div class="m-4">   ◁──┘
                <h1>Videos</h1>
     ┌─▷      <div id="video-list" class="m-4">
     │            {{#if videos}}                      Handlebars syntax for rendering
     │                {{#each videos}}                the template from data
```

Renders a navigation bar at the top of the web page

Container for the list of videos

```
                              <div class="mt-1">
This element is repeatedly        <a href="/video?id={{this._id}}">
rendered for each video.            {{this.name}}</a>
                              </div>
                          {{/each}}
                      {{else}}
                          No videos uploaded yet.
                      {{/if}}
                  </div>
              </div>
          </div>
      </body>
</html>
```

This element is repeatedly rendered for each video.

Renders a link to the video from the template data

Displays a message before uploading videos

9.7.5   *Video streaming*

At the heart of FlixTube is video streaming. We first looked at this back in chapter 2, and it's been a theme throughout the book. Now, it's time to see how video streaming works in the completed FlixTube example application. Some of this will be revision, but it's important to see how it works in the bigger context now that we have the gateway microservice and the UI.

Figure 9.11 illustrates the path of a streaming video, starting with external cloud storage on the left and ending with display to the user in the web browser on the right. The streaming video passes through three microservices on its journey to the user. Let's now follow that journey through the code.

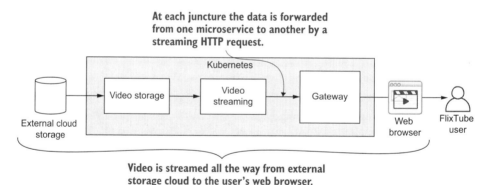

At each juncture the data is forwarded from one microservice to another by a streaming HTTP request.

Video is streamed all the way from external storage cloud to the user's web browser.

Figure 9.11   The path of streaming video through FlixTube

Listing 9.8 is an extract that shows where the streaming video journey starts in the Azure version of the video-storage microservice. The HTTP GET /video route retrieves a video from Azure storage and streams it to the HTTP response. The details of how this works aren't important at the moment, but if you'd like to know, see section 4.4.1.

```
app.get("/video", (req, res) => {
```
The HTTP GET route handler retrieves streaming video from the video-storage microservice.

```
    const videoId = req.query.id;
```
Inputs the ID of the video to be retrieved as a HTTP query parameter

```
    const blobService = createBlobService();
    streamVideoFromAzure(blobService, videoId, res)
        .catch(err => {
            // ... error reporting omitted ...
            res.sendStatus(500);
        });
});
```

Streams the video from Azure storage to the HTTP response

Handles any errors that might occur

Continuing our journey to the video-streaming microservice, listing 9.9 is an extract showing how the HTTP GET /video route *pipes* the streaming video from video storage to its own HTTP response using Node.js streams.

The video-streaming microservice also has another job. It broadcasts the "video viewed" message to other microservices in the application. This kind of *event-driven* programming means that we can later decide to have other microservices respond to the event without us having to update the code for the video-streaming microservice.

As it stands, you might remember from section 5.8 in chapter 5, it is the history microservice that picks up this message and uses it to record the user's viewing history. This use of indirect messaging keeps the video-streaming and history microservices nicely decoupled from each other. It also highlights one of the reasons why microservices applications are so flexible and extensible.

```
app.get("/video", (req, res) => {
    const videoId = req.query.id;
```
Defines a HTTP GET route handler that retrieves streaming video from the video-streaming microservice

```
    const forwardRequest = http.request(
        {
            host: `video-storage`,
            path: `/video?id=${videoId}`,
            method: 'GET',
            headers: req.headers,
        },
        forwardResponse => {
            res.writeHeader(forwardResponse.statusCode,
                forwardResponse.headers);
            forwardResponse.pipe(res);
        }
    );

    req.pipe(forwardRequest);

    broadcastViewedMessage(messageChannel, videoId);
});
```

Forwards the HTTP GET request to the video-storage microservice

Pipes the response (using Node.js streams) from the video-storage microservice to the response for this request

Broadcasts the video viewed message for other microservices to know that the user is watching a video

Our video streaming journey continues to the gateway microservice, the last stop before the UI. The HTTP GET /video route in listing 9.10 pipes the streaming video from the video-streaming microservice to its own HTTP response. This is where the video leaves the cluster, thus delivering the video to the front end.

> **Listing 9.10 Forwarding streaming video through the gateway microservice (extract from chapter-9/example-1/gateway/src/index.js)**

```
app.get("/api/video", (req, res) => {        ◁──── Defines a HTTP GET route handler
    const forwardRequest = http.request(            that retrieves streaming video
        {                                           from the gateway microservice
            host: `video-streaming`,
            path: `/video?id=${req.query.id}`,
            method: 'GET',
        },
        forwardResponse => {
            res.writeHeader(forwardResponse.statusCode,
                ➥ forwardResponse.headers);
            forwardResponse.pipe(res);        ◁──── Pipes the response (using Node.js streams)
        }                                           from the video-streaming microservice to
    );                                              the response for this request
    req.pipe(forwardRequest);
});
```

Forwards the HTTP GET request to the video-streaming microservice

Our video-streaming journey concludes in the UI. You can see the HTML video element in listing 9.11. The source element and its src field triggers the HTTP GET request to the gateway, which triggers the request to video streaming, which triggers the request to video storage. The streaming video is then piped all the way back through video storage, through video streaming, through the gateway, and finally, displayed to the user through the video element in their web browser.

> **Listing 9.11 Playing the video in the front end with the HTML video element (extract from chapter-9/example-1/gateway/src/views/play-video.hbs)**

Uses the HTML video element to display streaming video in the front end

```
<video controls autoplay muted>
    <source src={{video.url}} type="video/mp4">      ◁──── Links to the /api/video route
    Your browser does not support the video tag.            in the gateway microservice to
</video>                                                     retrieve streaming video for
                                                             display in the video element
```

9.7.6   *Video upload*

Video streaming is just one side of the FlixTube equation. The other is video upload, which is how we add videos to FlixTube in the first place. Video upload isn't something we have yet seen in the book, although, it's similar to how video streaming works, so you won't have any trouble with it.

Figure 9.12 illustrates the path of video upload through the application. A video file is selected by the user and uploaded from the FlixTube front end. The uploaded video arrives in the cluster at the gateway microservice before being forwarded through the video upload microservice to the video-storage microservice. There it is safely secured in the external cloud storage. Again we'll follow this journey through the code.

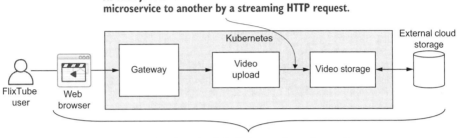

Figure 9.12   The path of a video upload through FlixTube.

Figure 9.13 is a screenshot of FlixTube's Upload web page. If you followed along in section 9.5.2, you will have already seen this and tried uploading a video. The user clicks Choose File and selects a file to upload. Once the upload completes, the UI is updated (as seen in figure 9.13) to give some feedback that the upload completed without error. If an error occurs, the error is displayed instead.

Listing 9.12 is a snippet of the front-end code that uploads the video to the backend. This is using the `fetch` function to upload the video via a HTTP POST request. At this point, you might rightly be thinking why are we using yet another HTTP request library?

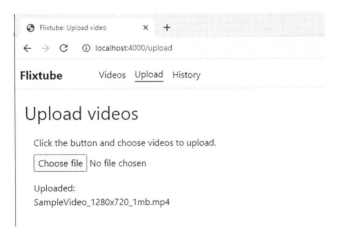

**Figure 9.13   The FlixTube
UI for uploading videos**

Well, normally, we would use something like the Axios library in the front end. However, this is a vanilla JavaScript web page with no build process. That makes it rather difficult to install an npm package like Axios and use it in our front-end JavaScript code; we don't have a way to bundle it into our front end.

The simplest approach that remains is to use something that comes with the browser to make the HTTP request. We could do this using the good old XMLHttpRequest, but that's kind of complicated. Instead, we'll use the more modern `fetch` function, which is also significantly simpler to use. Unfortunately, `fetch` isn't implemented in older versions of web browsers, and that may impact our user base. Fortunately, we only use it here in place of not being able to use Axios.

Listing 9.12   Using `fetch` to upload videos in the front-end code (extract from chapter-9/example-1/gateway/public/js/upload.js)

Uses the browser's "fetch" function to make a HTTP request to the /api/video route

Sets the file to upload as the body of the HTTP request

Sets the HTTP method to POST

Stores the filename and mime type in the request headers

```
fetch("/api/upload", {
        body: file,
        method: "POST",
        headers: {
            "File-Name": file.name,
            "Content-Type": file.type,
        },
    })
    .then(() => {
        // ... Update the UI after the upload ...
    })
    .catch((err) => {
        // ... Handle the upload error ...
    });
```

Executes after the request is successful

Executes if the request fails

After the upload from the web browser, the HTTP POST request lands in the gateway where it is handled by the /api/upload route shown in the following listing. Here we see the request forwarded to the video-upload microservice.

Listing 9.13   The gateway microservice forwards the HTTP POST to the video-upload microservice (extract from chapter-9/example-1/gateway/src/index.js)

Defines a HTTP POST route handler that uploads a video to the gateway microservice

Forwards the request to the video-upload microservice

```
app.post("/api/upload", (req, res) => {
    const forwardRequest = http.request(
        {
            host: `video-upload`,
            path: `/upload`,
            method: 'POST',
            headers: req.headers,
        },
        forwardResponse => {
```

```
            res.writeHeader(forwardResponse.statusCode,
        ➥   forwardResponse.headers);
            forwardResponse.pipe(res);       ⟵  Pipes the response (using Node.js streams)
        }                                        from the video-upload microservice to the
    );                                           response for this request

    req.pipe(forwardRequest);     ⟵   Pipes the request itself (the body of the
});                                    request is the video) to another request
```

Listing 9.14 shows how the video-upload microservice handles the incoming video. At this point, we create a unique ID for the video by creating an instance of MongoDB's `ObjectId` class. The request is then forwarded to the video-storage microservice.

After the upload is successful, the message "video uploaded" is broadcast to let the other microservice services know that a new video is available within the system. The metadata microservice handles this message and records the new video in its database.

Listing 9.14 Handling video upload via HTTP POST (extract from chapter-9/example-1/video-upload/src/index.js)

Defines a HTTP POST route handler that uploads a video to the video-upload microservice

```
➙ app.post("/upload", (req, res) => {                     Extracts the original
                                                          filename from the
    const fileName = req.headers["file-name"];   ⟵       request header
    const videoId = new mongodb.ObjectId();      ⟵   Creates a unique ID for the new video

    const newHeaders = Object.assign({}, req.headers,
    ➥  { id: videoId });                          ⟵
    streamToHttpPost(req, `video-storage`,            Adds the video ID to the headers
    ➥  `/upload`, newHeaders)
        .then(() => {                       Successfully captures the video for the video-
            res.sendStatus(200);    ⟵       storage microservice. This is the most
        })                                  important thing; we can't lose our user's data!
        .then(() => {
            // Broadcast message to the world.
            broadcastVideoUploadedMessage(    ⟵   Broadcasts the video uploaded
                /* params omitted */                  message so that other microservices
            );                                        know a new video has uploaded.
        })
        .catch(err => {
            console.error(`Failed to capture uploaded file ${fileName}.`);
            console.error(err);
            console.error(err.stack);
        });
});
```

Forwards the HTTP request to the video-storage microservice

Finally, the uploaded video arrives in the video-storage microservice, which you can see in listing 9.15. From here the video is saved into Azure storage. Once this whole chain has completed, we have successfully saved a copy of the video the user has uploaded. If you'd like to dive deeper into how a file is added to Azure storage, load the full index.js for the video-storage microservice into VS Code.

> **Listing 9.15   Streaming the video from HTTP POST to Azure Storage (extract from chapter-9/example-1/azure-storage/src/index.js)**

HTTP POST route handler that uploads a video to Azure Storage

```
app.post("/upload", (req, res) => {

    const videoId = req.headers.id;                      Extracts video details
    const mimeType = req.headers["content-type"];        from the request headers

    const blobService = createBlobService();
    uploadStreamToAzure(req, mimeType,
        videoId, blobService)
        .then(() => {                      Streams the video from the
            res.sendStatus(200);           HTTP request to Azure Storage
        })
        .catch(err => {
            // ... error reporting omitted ...       Indicates that
            res.sendStatus(500);                     the upload failed
        });
});
```

Indicates a successful upload

9.8 *Manually deploying FlixTube to production with Terraform*

If you already have FlixTube up and running in development, that's a huge step! In order to make FlixTube available for use by the general public, we now must deploy it to production using the same tools and techniques that we used previously in chapters 6 and 7.

These next two sections are the most challenging in this chapter, but if you can follow along and get through these, it's going to be a great experience for you. If at any time it seems too difficult, feel free to go back and revisit chapters 6 and 7, which have more detailed instructions.

Ultimately, we aim to have a CD pipeline for FlixTube that automatically deploys to production whenever we push updated code to our hosted code repository. Before we get to that though, we must first manually deploy FlixTube. Here's why:

- *When first developing your deployment scripts, you'll do so incrementally.* As you evolve your deployment scripts, you'll need a way to test these, get feedback, and fix issues.
- *In the future, if you discover issues in your CD pipeline, you'll need to have the skills to run deployment scripts in development.* This is necessary so that you can figure out and fix problems.

Figure 9.14 highlights what we'll do. We'll use Terraform to create our infrastructure in the cloud. We'll then use Docker to package and publish our images, and we'll use Terraform to deploy containers to our Kubernetes cluster.

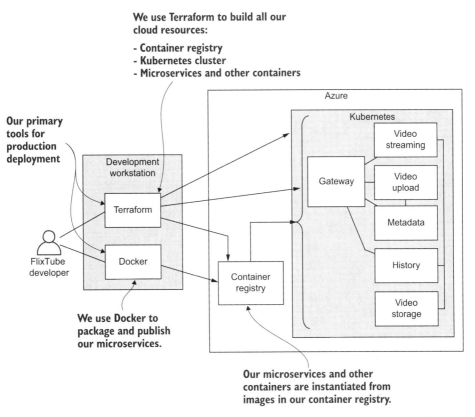

Figure 9.14   Using Terraform to manually deploy FlixTube from the development workstation to production

9.8.1   *The Terraform scripts structure*

Figure 9.15 shows the layout of the scripts directory for FlixTube. You'll recognize some of the code files here from chapters 6 and 7, but there are also some that are new.

Notably, we now see our first use of a Terraform module. The file main.tf in the modules/microservice directory is a reusable Terraform code module. We can use it to deploy all of our microservice without having to repeat this code. We'll look at the code for this module in a moment.

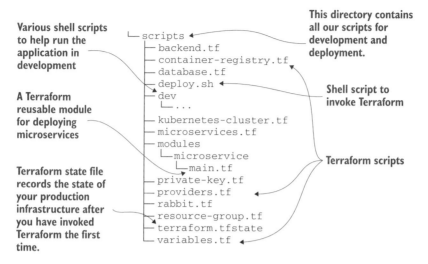

Various shell scripts to help run the application in development

A Terraform reusable module for deploying microservices

Terraform state file records the state of your production infrastructure after you have invoked Terraform the first time.

This directory contains all our scripts for development and deployment.

Shell script to invoke Terraform

Terraform scripts

Figure 9.15   The scripts subdirectory contains the Terraform scripts to deploy FlixTube to production

9.8.2   *Prerequisites*

To deploy FlixTube, you'll need a few tools installed. You'll already have these if you followed along in chapters 6 and 7; if not, you can install these now. First, you need the Azure CLI tool. Check if it's installed like this:

```
az --version
```

If you don't already have the Azure CLI tool, follow the installation instructions here:

https://docs.microsoft.com/en-us/cli/azure/install-azure-cli

You also need Terraform installed. Check if you have it like this:

```
terraform --version
```

Otherwise, install the latest version from here:

https://www.terraform.io/downloads.html

9.8.3   *Azure authentication*

Before deploying infrastructure to Azure, you'll first need to authenticate with your account. If you followed along in chapters 6 and 7, you have already done this. If not, then refer back to section 6.6.2 for detailed instructions. Use the Azure CLI tool to check which account you are currently using by typing

```
az account show
```

Copy the output because you'll soon need values from the id field (your Azure subscription ID) and the tenantID field.

NOTE   Make sure you are using the right account! It might be embarrassing if you accidentally deploy infrastructure to your work account.

You also need to create a service principal that your Kubernetes cluster uses to interact with your Azure account (for example, when it creates an Azure load balancer for you). If you already have a service principal from chapter 6, you can reuse that now; otherwise, create a new one like this:

```
az ad sp create-for-rbac --role="Contributor"
➥ --scopes="/subscriptions/<subscription-id>"
```

Be sure to replace `<subscription-id>` with your actual subscription ID that you noted a moment ago. Then copy the output, which you'll need soon. The values you'll need are from `appId` (which we call `client_id` in our Terraform script) and `password` (which we call `client_secret`) fields. For a more detailed description of creating a service principal, see section 6.11.2.

9.8.4   *Configuring storage*

To deploy FlixTube to production, you also need an Azure storage account. The Azure storage microservice uses this account to store and retrieve videos. If you followed along in chapter 4, you already have an account, and you can reuse that if you like. Otherwise, follow the instructions in section 4.4.1 to create a storage account.

You'll need to create a videos container in your storage account. Note that this isn't a Docker *container*; it's the container concept from Azure storage, a container in which we can store arbitrary files. Make a note of your storage account name and access key. You'll need these soon.

9.8.5   *Deploying the application*

Now it's time to invoke Terraform to evaluate our scripts and deploy FlixTube to production. First, we must initialize Terraform. To do this, initialize Terraform and install the various providers that we need:

```
cd chapter-9/example-1/scripts
terraform init
```

Now invoke Terraform to deploy our infrastructure:

```
terraform apply
```

Before it begins, you must provide values for the following input variables:

- *app_version*—You can just type 1 the first time. For subsequent times that you invoke `terraform apply`, you should increment this number.
- *client_id*—The ID of your Azure service principal that you jotted down in section 9.8.3.
- *client_secret*—The password for your service principal.

- `storage_account_name`—The name of your Azure storage account for storing videos that you jotted down in section 9.8.4.
- `storage_access_key`—The access key for your storage account.

Deploying FlixTube will take some time. Feel free to make a cup of tea (or several).

9.8.6   *Checking that it works*

To check that FlixTube is deployed and functioning, we can load its front end into our web browser. For that, though, we must know its IP address. Just like we did in various sections from chapter 7, we can use the Kubernetes CLI tool to do this:

```
kubectl get services
```

To remember how to install and use Kubectl, revisit section 6.12. You can see the tabular output from Kubectl that is shown in figure 9.16. Find the IP address in the EXTERNAL-IP column for the gateway container. Copy the IP address into your web browser.

You don't need to use any particular port number. We used port 4000 to access the dev version of FlixTube, but FlixTube in production is configured to use port 80. This is the default port for HTTP (because it's the default, we don't need to specify it).

Figure 9.16   Using the Kubernetes command-line tool to get the IP address of the gateway so we can test FlixTube in the browser

You might have noticed that we are using the HTTP protocol here. That's why the browser says "Not secure" next to Fixtube's IP address. For security purposes, we should actually be using (like all modern web servers) the secure version of HTTP, called HTTPS. This stands for Hypertext Transfer Protocol Secure, and we'll mention it again in chapter 11. If all has gone according to plan, you should now be able to navigate the FlixTube UI to upload and play videos.

At this point, feel free to experiment with FlixTube and Terraform however you like. You can make changes to the FlixTube or Terraform code and then apply your changes using `terraform apply`. Do this as many times as you like.

9.8.7 Teardown

When you are done with FlixTube, make sure you clean it all up. Running this infrastructure in the cloud will cost you money. If you only just created your Azure account, you'll be using the free credit that it gives you to try it out, but let's not waste it. Destroy your infrastructure when you are finished with it:

```
terraform destroy
```

9.8.8 Terraform modules

Much of Terraform code in the chapter 9 code repository is the same as that already seen in chapters 6 and 7. However, there's one new thing that needs further explanation.

Remember the Terraform code to deploy a microservice? If you need a refresher, skim over section 7.6. We could get by with simply repeating that same code over and over for each microservice in FlixTube. But most of the code is the same, so it's not an efficient way of working. To cope with this, we'll bring in a more advanced feature of Terraform: Terraform modules.

Terraform modules allow us to write reusable code modules that we can use in different circumstances by supplying different input variables. Listing 9.16 shows the Terraform module that is used to deploy each of FlixTube's six microservices. This looks, more or less, just like any other Terraform code file.

The listing starts with a Kubernetes deployment that instantiates a microservice into our Kubernetes cluster. It ends with a Kubernetes service that makes the microservice accessible within the cluster via DNS. Note that the `type` field of the Kubernetes service is parameterized so that we can enable or disable an Azure load balancer for the microservice. You'll learn more about what a load balancer can do in the next chapter. For now, this is so we can allocate an IP address to the gateway microservices and make it accessible to the outside world. (This is how our customers will interact with our application.)

There's nothing else particularly special about the Terraform code in listing 9.16, other than it being located in the modules/microservice subdirectory. Note the numerous input variables defined at the start of the listing. These are normal Terraform variables, but in this instance, these are the inputs that allow us to customize the module's behavior. For example, we can set the name of the microservice through the service_name variable. We must also pass in details of the container registry that hosts the images for the microservices. Another significant variable is env. This allows us to configure the set of environment variables individually for each microservice.

Listing 9.16 A reusable Terraform module deploys a microservice to Kubernetes (abbreviated from chapter-9/example-1/scripts/modules/microservice/main.tf)

```
variable "app_version" {}          ⟵
variable "service_name" {}

variable "dns_name" {
    default = ""
}

variable "login_server" {}
variable "username" {}
variable "password" {}
                                        Defines variables that are inputs
variable "service_type" {               to this Terraform module
    default = "ClusterIP"
}

variable "session_affinity" {
    default = ""
}

variable "env" {
    default = {}
    type = map(string)
}                                  ⟵
                                                        Defines local variables
locals {                                                to use in this module
    image_tag = "${var.login_server}/${var.service_name}:${var.app_version}"
}

# ... much code omitted for brevity ...

resource "kubernetes_deployment"        Deploys a container to
⟹  "service_deployment" {      ⟵       our Kubernetes cluster

    depends_on = [ null_resource.docker_push ]

    metadata {                          Uses variables to customize the configuration
        name = var.service_name    ⟵   of this module for each microservice

    labels = {
            pod = var.service_name
        }
    }

    spec {
        replicas = 1
```

```
        selector {
            match_labels = {
                pod = var.service_name
            }
        }

        template {
            metadata {
                labels = {
                    pod = var.service_name
                }
            }

            spec {
                container {
                    image = local.image_tag
                    name  = var.service_name

                    env {
                        name = "PORT"
                        value = "80"
                    }

                    dynamic "env" {
                        for_each = var.env
                        content {
                          name = env.key
                          value = env.value
                        }
                    }
                }

                image_pull_secrets {
                    name =
                    ➥ kubernetes_secret.docker_credentials.metadata[0].name
                }
            }
        }
    }

resource "kubernetes_service" "service" {
    metadata {
        name = var.dns_name != ""
        ➥ ? var.dns_name : var.service_name
    }

    spec {
        selector = {
            pod =
    kubernetes_deployment.service_deployment.metadata[0].labels.pod
        }

        session_affinity = var.session_affinity
```

Uses variables to customize the configuration of this module for each microservice

Uses variables to setup environment variables that are specific for each microservice

Deploys a service that makes the container accessible from other containers via DNS

Uses variables to customize the configuration of this module for each microservice

```
    port {
        port       = 80
        target_port = 80
    }

    type               = var.service_type
```

Uses variables to customize the configuration of this module for each microservice

Listing 9.17 shows how we use the Terraform module to deploy our microservices. Only the gateway microservice is shown. The others are omitted because they all look much the same, although, some have different configurations for their environment variables. In the following listing, note how the module is imported, how its source file is specified, and how environment variables are configured.

Listing 9.17   The Terraform microservice module deploys the gateway microservice to Kubernetes (abbreviated from chapter-9/example-1/scripts/microservices.tf)

Imports the microservice Terraform module (the one from listing 9.16) to deploy our gateway microservice

```
locals {
    login_server = azurerm_container_registry.container_registry.login_server
    username = azurerm_container_registry.container_registry.admin_username
    password = azurerm_container_registry.container_registry.admin_password
    rabbit = "amqp://guest:guest@rabbit:5672"
    database = "mongodb://db:27017"
}

module "gateway-microservice" {

    source ="./modules/microservice"

    service_name = "gateway"
    service_type = "LoadBalancer"
    session_affinity = "ClientIP"
    login_server = local.login_server
    username = local.username
    password = local.password
    app_version = var.app_version

    env = {
        RABBIT: local.rabbit
    }
}
```

Sets local variables for use across this script

Specifies the source of the module loaded from the subdirectory ./modules/microservice, which contains the file main.tf (the one from listing 9.16)

Sets input variables to configure the microservice module for the gateway microservice

Configures environment variables that are specific to the individual microservice

```
# ... all other microservices omitted for brevity ...
```

Terraform modules are a more advanced feature of Terraform, and there's still plenty more in Terraform for you to explore. See the end of this chapter for a reference to go deeper into Terraform.

9.9   *Continuous delivery to production*

After manually deploying FlixTube to production, we are now ready to bring the continuous delivery (CD) pipeline online.

You can follow along, but this can be even more challenging than the previous section, especially if something goes wrong! You might have to go back to manual deployment (what we just did in section 9.7) to figure out the problem.

As we did in chapter 7, we'll create our CD pipeline with Bitbucket Pipelines. It should be fairly easy for you to transfer this over to any other CD platform. Like I said in chapter 7, a CD pipeline is really just a glorified shell script, even when some providers also give you a fancy UI.

Porting your deployment shell script from one provider to another isn't difficult. However, Bitbucket is good value because it provides a free tier. It's worthwhile following the instructions here to practice getting this working before you try taking it to a different CD provider. Figure 9.17 illustrates the structure of FlixTube's CD pipeline.

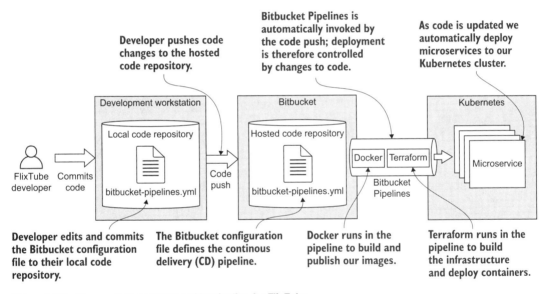

Figure 9.17   The continuous delivery (CD) pipeline for FlixTube

9.9.1   *Prerequisites*

You'll need an account with Bitbucket. You'll already have this if you followed along in chapter 7. Otherwise, signup for a free account at https://bitbucket.org.

9.9.2   *Setting up your code repository*

The next step is to import FlixTube's code into a Bitbucket code repository. Copy the entire contents of the example-1 subdirectory from the chapter 9 code repository to a new location. Create a fresh Git repo here and then push the code to your hosted

Bitbucket repository. Next, enable Bitbucket Pipelines for the repository. Revisit section 7.7.2 for detailed instructions on the Bitbucket repository setup.

Now, configure your environment variables for the repository. You need to add variables for Azure authentication just like you did in section 7.7.6. For security reasons, we'll store sensitive configuration details as repository variables instead of storing these in the code. Like we did in chapter 7, add variables for ARM_CLIENT_ID, ARM_CLIENT_SECRET, ARM_TENANT_ID, and ARM_SUBSCRIPTION_ID. You noted down the values for these variables earlier in section 9.8.3.

In addition, we need to add some new variables to authenticate the video-storage microservice's access to the Azure storage account where we store the videos. For that, also add variables for STORAGE_ACCOUNT_NAME and STORAGE_ACCESS_KEY and set these to the values you noted in section 9.8.4.

9.9.3 *Preparing the backend*

Before the first invocation of your CD pipeline, you need to configure the backend so that Terraform's state file persists between subsequent invocations. For a refresher on Terraform state, revisit section 6.8.7 and section 7.7.4.

Create a different Azure storage container for use by Terraform. You can use the one you created in chapter 7 for this purpose or create a new one. Don't reuse the videos container for this! That would be using the one container for different purposes, and that's the kind of thing that ultimately makes it more difficult to understand and reason about your application.

The Terraform script backend.tf is already configured to store the Terraform state in our Azure storage account. You just need to uncomment the code in that file (you commented it while you were manually deploying FlixTube). Make sure you set the details to your own storage account and container.

Listing 9.18 shows backend.tf after we have uncommented the code. Make sure you rename the resource group and storage account to those that exist in your own Azure account. You'll also need to create an Azure storage container called `terraform`. Terraform will persist its state into this container under the name terraform.tfstate.

Listing 9.18 Terraform backend configuration (chapter-9/example-1/scripts/backend.tf)

Sets the name of the resource group that contains the storage account. Rename this to a resource group that exists in your Azure account.

Sets the name of the storage account in which we store the Terraform state. Rename this to a storage account that exists in your Azure account.

```
terraform {
    backend "azurerm" {
        resource_group_name  =
            "<your-resource-group>"

        storage_account_name =
            "<your-storage-account>"

        container_name = "terraform"
```

The name of the container in which we store the Terraform state. No need to rename this, but make sure the container exists in your Azure account.

```
        key = "terraform.tfstate"                          ◁─────────────┐
    }                                                                     │
                        The name of the file in which we store the Terraform state. This can be set
    }                   to anything, but we are using the default name of the Terraform state file
                        because that makes sense and we can easily remember what it means.
```

9.9.4   *The deployment shell script*

As mentioned earlier, a shell script is usually what's at the heart of any CD pipeline. Listing 9.19 is the deployment shell script for FlixTube. Note that it's barely different from the deployment script from chapter 7. In listing 9.19, some of the code is omitted for brevity, and there's a couple of extra environment variables being passed through to Terraform.

Most of our deployment code is in Terraform code, that's why this shell script remains so small. There is plenty more we could do directly in this shell script if we wanted, for example, building and publishing Docker images. But for FlixTube, at least, we have managed to contain our entire deployment within the Terraform code. To revise the deployment shell script in more detail, revisit section 7.7.3.

> **Listing 9.19   A shell script for deployment using Terraform (extract from chapter-9/ example-1/scripts/deploy.sh)**

Changes to the directory that contains our Terraform scripts

Invokes Terraform apply with auto approve enabled, then runs our Terraform scripts and deploys our infrastructure and microservices

Invokes Terraform initialization

Passing environment variables through for our Terraform scripts

```
        cd ./scripts

        terraform init
        terraform apply -auto-approve \
            -var "app_version=$VERSION" \
            -var "client_id=$ARM_CLIENT_ID" \
            -var "client_secret=$ARM_CLIENT_SECRET" \
            -var "storage_account_name=$STORAGE_ACCOUNT_NAME" \
            -var "storage_access_key=$STORAGE_ACCESS_KEY"
```

9.9.5   *FlixTube's CD configuration*

The final piece of the CD pipeline puzzle is the configuration file. For Bitbucket Pipelines, this is a YAML file that is placed in the root of your code repository. It's called bitbucket-pipelines.yaml. Some other CD providers use similar YAML formats.

Listing 9.20 shows the simple CD pipeline configuration for FlixTube. This is simple because all we are really doing here is invoking the deployment shell script that we saw in listing 9.19. For more details on Bitbucket Pipelines configuration, revisit section 7.7.5.

> **Listing 9.20   CD configuration for Bitbucket Pipelines (chapter-9/example-1/bitbucket-pipelines.yaml)**

```
image: hashicorp/terraform:0.12.6

pipelines:
    default:
      - step:
          name: Build and deploy
          services:
            - docker
          script:
            - export VERSION=$BITBUCKET_BUILD_NUMBER
            - chmod +x ./scripts/deploy.sh
            - ./scripts/deploy.sh
```

Invokes our deployment shell script → points to `- ./scripts/deploy.sh`

9.9.6   *Testing the continuous delivery (CD) pipeline*

Now we are ready to test our CD pipeline. Assuming your repository is configured and you have enabled Bitbucket Pipelines (see section 9.9.2), we need to push an update to the code. We can also trigger a CD pipeline manually in the Bitbucket Pipelines dashboard, but the usual way to trigger deployment is to change some code and push the change to our hosted repository. Let's test that it works.

Try pushing a code change—only a small change is necessary. Maybe change some text in the UI? Then save the file, commit the change, and push it to Bitbucket. You can then watch in the Bitbucket Pipelines dashboard as the pipeline is triggered.

> **NOTE**   The first time the pipeline is invoked, it will take some time as it deploys the first instance of your infrastructure and microservices.

Once it's ready, you can again use `kubectl get services` (like in section 9.8.6) to get the IP address of the gateway to load in your web browser and do some testing. Now you are all set up for continuous deployment! Any code changes you push to Bitbucket will automatically be deployed to production.

9.9.7   *Adding automated testing*

A final step that you can take with your CD pipeline is to add automated testing. The example code for chapter 9 includes some automated tests that you might have tried out earlier in section 9.6. Adding automated testing to your application is as simple as putting the right commands in the right places.

This is simplified because we are following conventions. This means we only need to know one command and that is `npm test`. We don't have to remember whether we are using Jest, Cypress, or some other JavaScript testing framework. Whatever we use, we only need to make sure that the script for `npm test` is configured to invoke it.

As for the right place to invoke this command, that's more difficult because we have our entire application in a single repository and configured with a single CD pipeline. We could invoke `npm test` from our deployment shell script (listing 9.21) or directly from our Bitbucket Pipelines configuration file (listing 9.22). Listings 9.21 and 9.22 show both ways this might work for the metadata microservice.

As you might imagine, this is just the tip of the iceberg. As we build more automated tests for our other microservices, we'll have to invoke `npm test` repeatedly for each microservice. That doesn't seem elegant, but it will be resolved when we transition to a multi-repo scalable deployment architecture. Just hold on until chapter 11 for more on that.

Listing 9.21 Adding automated tests to the deployment shell script

Causes subsequent failing commands in the shell script to fail the entire script

```
set -e
cd ./metadata          Changes directory to the
                       metadata microservice

npm install            Installs dependencies (this installs Jest)
npm test
cd ..                  Runs the tests. If this fails, the shell aborts
                       with an error code. This in turn aborts the CD
                       pipelinewith an error.

cd ./scripts
terraform init
terraform apply -auto-approve \
    -var "app_version=$VERSION" \
    -var "client_id=$ARM_CLIENT_ID" \
    -var "client_secret=$ARM_CLIENT_SECRET"
```
Changes directory back to the main project

Listing 9.22 Adding automated tests directly to the CD configuration file

```
image: hashicorp/terraform:0.12.6

pipelines:
    default:
      - step:
          name: Build and deploy
          services:
            - docker
          script:
            - cd metadata && npm install && npm test
            - export VERSION=$BITBUCKET_BUILD_NUMBER
            -  chmod +x ./scripts/deploy.sh
            - ./scripts/deploy.sh
```

Invokes our automated tests directly from the Bitbucket Pipelines configuration file. If the tests fail, the CD pipeline aborts with an error.

We might even invoke our automated tests directly from our Terraform code. But, arguably, with building and publishing Docker images, we are already doing too much in Terraform. We have taken it beyond its original purpose of provisioning our cloud infrastructure, even though this is a convenient way to bootstrap our microservices application. In chapter 11, we talk about how to refactor our development and deployment processes as we scale up FlixTube.

As noted in chapter 8, running Cypress in the CD pipeline is essentially the same, although, with some additional difficulties. Again we'll invoke `npm test`, but with it configured to invoke Cypress instead of Jest.

The problem with Cypress is that it is big! Installing it into our CD pipeline each time the pipeline is invoked is slow and inefficient (especially if you are paying by the minute for the amount of time your pipeline is executing). If you want to use Cypress in your CD pipeline, then you are going to have to learn how to use the caching facilities from your CD provider. But I'm afraid this book is already too long, so you'll have to tackle that on your own. You can learn more about caching in Bitbucket Pipelines here:

https://support.atlassian.com/bitbucket-cloud/docs/cache-dependencies/

9.10 *Review*

Congratulations! If you followed along in the chapter, you now have FlixTube running in production, and you are all set to continue evolving FlixTube. You can make code changes, test them in development, and then deploy updates to production using CD. Use table 9.2 to review the commands used in this chapter.

Table 9.2   Review of commands in chapter 9

Command	Description
`npm start`	The conventional npm script for starting a Node.js application regardless of what name the main script file has or what command-line parameters it expects.
	Typically, this translates into `node index.js` in the package.json file, but it all depends on the author of the project and how they have set it up. The nice thing is that no matter how a particular project is structured, you only have to remember `npm start`.
`npm run start:dev`	My personal convention for starting a Node.js project in development. I add this to the scripts in package.json, and typically, it runs something like Nodemon to enable live reload of your code as you work on it.
`docker-compose up` ⮕ `--build`	Builds and instantiates an application composed of multiple containers as defined by the Docker Compose file (docker-compose.yaml) in the current working directory
`docker-compose` ⮕ `down`	Stops and *destroys* the application, leaving the development workstation in a clean state
`npm test`	The npm script convention for running tests. This can run Jest or Cypress (or even both) depending on how you configured your package.json file.
	This is the command you should run in your CD pipeline to execute your test suite.
`npm run test:watch`	This is my personal convention for running tests in live reload mode. You need to configure this script in your package.json file to use it.
`terraform init`	Initializes a Terraform project and downloads the provider plugins

Table 9.2 Review of commands in chapter 9 *(continued)*

Command	Description
`terraform apply`	Executes Terraform scripts in the working directory to incrementally apply changes to our infrastructure
`terraform destroy`	Destroys all infrastructure that's created by the Terraform project

9.11 *FlixTube in the future*

Where to now for FlixTube? That's for you to imagine! In chapter 11, we'll discuss the technical aspects of FlixTube's future:

- How do we scale up to cater for our growing user base?
- How do we scale up our development and deployment processes as the application grows and the size of the development team increases?

For now, just imagine the types of microservices you'd like to add to FlixTube in the future. Figure 9.18 gives you some inspiration as to what it might look like as it grows.

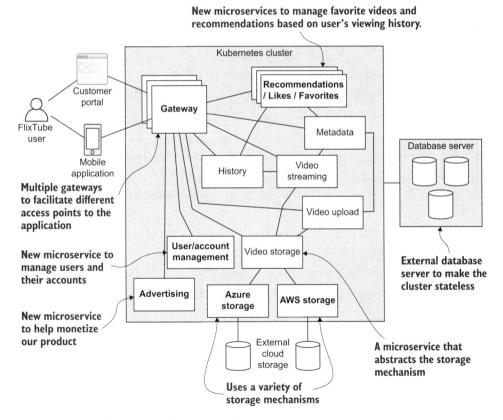

Figure 9.18 What FlixTube could look like in the future

9.12 *Continue your learning*

In this chapter, we studied the structure and layout of the FlixTube example application. We built, ran, and tested it in development. Then we deployed it to production through its CD pipeline.

You have FlixTube running, so what now? Reading any book will only take you so far. The key to you retaining these skills is to practice, practice, and then practice some more. Experiment with the code. Try to add features. Try to add new microservices. Try to break FlixTube just to see what happens. Practicing the art of development is what takes you to the next level.

Development is not without challenges. In fact, it is a never-ending rollercoaster of problems and solutions. When you hit problems with any tool or technology, go back and review the appropriate chapter in this book. You might find the answer you need. Otherwise, you'll need to go deeper and explore other resources.

The final chapters in this book contain guidance that will help you navigate your future development path with microservices. The references at the end of each chapter (including this one) will help you continue your learning journey. But just remember that your key to success and your key to retaining these skills is consistent practice.

To learn about UI development, see the following books:

- *Angular in Action* by Jeremy Wilken (Manning, 2018)
- *Getting MEAN with Mongo, Express, Angular, and Node*, 2nd ed., by Simon D. Holmes and Clive Harber (Manning, 2019)
- *Micro Frontends in Action* by Michael Geers (Manning, 2020)

To learn more about development with microservices, see these books:

- *Microservices in Action* by Morgan Bruce, Paulo A. Pereira (Manning, 2018)
- *Microservices Patterns* by Chris Richardson (Manning, 2018)
- *The Tao of Microservices* by Richard Rodger (Manning, 2017)
- *Microservices in .NET Core*, 2nd ed., by Christian Horsdal Gammelgaard (Manning, 2020)
- *Developing Microservice APIs with Python* by José Haro Peralta (Manning, est, Spring 2021)

To dive deeper into Terraform, see this book:

- *Terraform in Action* by Scott Winkler (Manning, est Spring, 2021)

Summary

- We learned how FlixTube works as a whole and met some new microservices along the way.
- We revisited some of the essential tools needed to build, run, test, and deploy microservices.

- We ran an individual microservice from our FlixTube application in production mode and in development mode, which enables live reload, before booting the entire application.
- We used Jest and Cypress to test FlixTube.
- To make FlixTube available for use by the general public, we deployed it to production and brought the continuous delivery (CD) pipeline online.

Healthy microservices

Errors happen. Code has bugs. Hardware, software, and networks are unreliable. Failures happen for all types of applications, not just for microservices. But microservices applications are more complex, and so problems can become considerably worse as we grow our application. The more microservices we maintain, the greater the chance at any given time that some of those microservices will be misbehaving!

We can't avoid problems entirely. It doesn't matter if these are caused by human error or unreliable infrastructure. It's a certainty—problems happen. But just because problems can't always be avoided, doesn't mean we shouldn't try to mitigate against these. A well-engineered application anticipates and accounts for problems, even when the specific nature of some problems can't be anticipated.

As our application evolves to be more complex, we'll need techniques to combat problems and keep our microservices healthy. Our industry has developed many "best" practices and patterns for dealing with problems. We'll cover some of the most useful ones in this chapter. Following this guidance will make your application run more smoothly and be more reliable, resulting in less stress and easier recovery from problems when they do happen.

This chapter isn't immediately practical; there's no example code in GitHub and you can't directly follow along. Think of it as a *toolbox of techniques* for you to try out in the future as you move forward and continue to develop your own microservices application.

10.1 *Maintaining healthy microservices*

A healthy microservices application is composed of healthy microservices. A healthy microservice is one that is not experiencing problems such as bugs, CPU overload, or memory exhaustion. To understand the health of our application, we need to

- Monitor our microservices to understand their current state
- Take action when problems occur to protect our customers
- Debug and apply fixes as issues arise

Using FlixTube's metadata microservice as an example, figure 10.1 gives you an idea of the infrastructure for a healthy microservice in production. Notice that there are multiple replicas of the microservice, and that requests are evenly balanced between instances of the microservice using a *load balancer*. Should any single microservice go out of commission, the replicas can stand in while the failing instance is restarted.

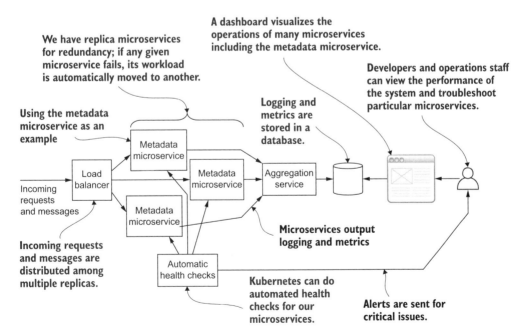

Figure 10.1   Infrastructure for a healthy microservice in production

This redundancy ensures the ongoing reliability of the microservice and the application. In this chapter, we'll learn about replicating microservices on Kubernetes and other techniques to facilitate fault tolerance and recovery from errors.

A microservice can suffer problems even without the dramatic effect of going out of commission. How do we know what's going on in a microservice? It doesn't have to be a black box. We need some kind of logging *aggregation* service (shown in figure 10.1) to combine the logging from all microservices presented in a way that we can understand.

What can we do to ensure that our microservices remain healthy? First, similar to a real medical professional, we must know how to *take the temperature* of our patients. We have numerous techniques at our disposal to help us diagnose the state and behavior of our microservices. Table 10.1 lists the main techniques we'll learn in this chapter to take the temperature of our microservices.

Table 10.1   Techniques for monitoring the state of microservices

Technique	Description
Logging	Outputting information about the behavior of our microservices to show what is happening and when it happened.
Error handling	Having a strategy for managing errors to have a record of what failed and when it failed.
Aggregation	Combining the information from all microservices into a single stream so that we don't have to go searching microservice-to-microservice for the information we need.
Automatic health checks	Configuring Kubernetes to automatically find problems in our microservices.

What happens when something has gone wrong? How do we fix it? Coping with problems that have occurred requires debugging. In this chapter, we'll learn the techniques that we can use to find the cause of a problem so that we can fix it.

10.2   *Monitoring your microservices*

Getting our application into production is just the first step. After that, we need to continually know if our application is functioning or not, especially as new updates to the code are rolled out.

We must have transparency over what our application is doing, otherwise, we have no idea what's going on in there, and we can't fix problems unless we know about them. In this section, we'll look at some techniques for monitoring the behavior of our microservices:

- Logging
- Error handling
- Log aggregation
- Automatic health checks

10.2.1 *Logging in development*

Logging to the console is our most basic tool for understanding the ongoing behavior of our microservices. Through logging, we output a text stream showing the important events, activities, and actions that have taken place within our application.

The stream of logs coming from an application can be thought of as *the history of the application*, showing everything pertinent that has happened over its lifetime. We can use console logging in both development and production. Figure 10.2 illustrates how it works in development.

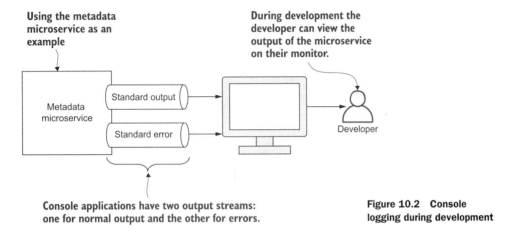

Figure 10.2 Console logging during development

Every microservice, like every process, has two output streams for logging:

1 Standard output
2 Standard error

In JavaScript, we output logging to the standard output channel like this:

```
console.log("Useful information goes here");
```

We output errors to the standard error channel like this:

```
console.error("Useful information goes here");
```

> **NOTE** If you are using a language other than JavaScript, then it will have its own functions for outputting to standard output and standard error.

That's all we need to output to the console. We don't really need a complex logging system. Modern logging aggregation systems usually automatically pick up the standard output and standard errors that are flowing out of a container. We'll see how this works soon.

What should be logged?

Given that logging has to be added explicitly by the developer and it's always optional, how do we choose what to log? Here are a few examples:

- What to log:
  - Pertinent events in your application and details about those
  - Success/failure of important operations
- What not to log:
  - Things that can easily be ascertained from other sources
  - Anything that's secret or sensitive
  - Any personal details about your users

If you find yourself drowning in details from too much logging, feel free to go in and remove logging that isn't useful. For every console log, you just have to ask the question, can I live without this detail? If you don't need it, delete it.

Generally speaking, though, more logs are better than fewer logs. When it comes to debugging in production, you need all the help you can get to understand why a problem occurred. Tracing back through the log is an important step in understanding the sequence of events that resulted in the problem.

You won't be able to add more logging after the problem has occurred! Well, you can if you isolate and reproduce the problem, but that in itself can be difficult. More logging is better because when you do hit a problem, you want to have as much information as possible to help you solve it.

10.2.2 Error handling

Errors happen. Our users suffer. It's a fundamental law of computer programming! Here are some examples of errors:

- Runtime errors (an exception is thrown that crashes our microservice)
- Bad data being input (from faulty sensors or human error in data entry)
- Code being used in unexpected combinations or ways
- Third-party dependencies failing (RabbitMQ, for example)
- External dependencies failing (Azure Storage, for example)

How we deal with errors matters. We must plan to handle and recover from errors gracefully to minimize the harm caused to our users and our business. What happens when errors occur? How will our application deal with these? We must think through these questions and develop an error-handling strategy for our application.

Often in our JavaScript code, we'll anticipate errors and handle these in our code using exceptions, callbacks, or promises. In those cases, we usually know what to do. We can retry the failed operation, or if possible, we might correct the issue and restart the operation if there isn't any automatic corrective action that's obvious. We even might have to report the error to the user or notify our operations staff.

Sometimes we can anticipate errors, other times not. We can miss errors because we didn't know the error could occur or because certain types of errors (e.g., a hard-drive failure) occur so infrequently that it's not worth specifically handling these. To be safe, we must account for errors that we can't even imagine!

What we need is a general strategy for how we handle unexpected errors. For any process, including individual microservices, this boils down to two main options: *abort and restart* or *resume operation.* You can see these error-handling strategies illustrated in figure 10.3.

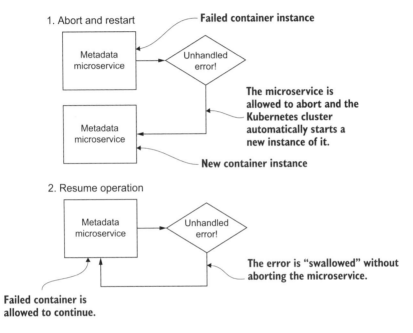

Figure 10.3   Strategies for handling unexpected errors

ABORT AND RESTART

The abort and restart strategy intercepts unexpected errors and responds by restarting the process. The simplest way to use this strategy is to just ignore any errors we don't care about. Any exception that we don't explicitly handle with a try/catch statement in our code results in the process being aborted.

This is the simplest error-handling strategy because it literally means *doing nothing.* Just allow unexpected errors to occur and let Node.js abort our program in response. When a production microservice is aborted, we'll rely on Kubernetes to automatically restart it for us, which it does by default. (This behavior in Kubernetes is configurable as well.)

RESUME OPERATION

The resume operation strategy intercepts unexpected errors and responds by allowing the process to continue. We can implement this in Node.js by handling the uncaught-Exception event on the process object like this:

```
process.on("uncaughtException", err => {
    console.error("Uncaught exception:");
    console.error(err && err.stack || err);
});
```

If we handled the event like this, we take explicit control over unexpected errors. In that case, Node.js will not take its default action of aborting the process. It is simply left to continue as best it can, and we have to hope that the error has not left the process in a bad state.

Printing the error to the standard error channel means that it can be picked up by our production logging system, which we'll discuss soon. This error can then be reported to our operations team, and it doesn't have to go unnoticed.

ABORT AND RESTART: VERSION 2

Now that we understand how to handle uncaught exceptions in Node.js, we can implement a better version of the abort and restart strategy:

```
process.on("uncaughtException", err => {
    console.error("Uncaught exception:");
    console.error(err && err.stack || err);
    process.exit(1);
});
```

In this code, we take explicit control of the handler for unexpected errors. As before, we print the error so that it can be noticed by our operations team. Next, we explicitly terminate the program with a call to process.exit.

We pass a nonzero exit code to the exit function. This is a standard convention that indicates the process was terminated by an error. We can use different nonzero error codes here (any positive number) to indicate different types of errors.

WHICH ERROR HANDLING STRATEGY SHOULD I USE?

To restart or not to restart, that is the question. Many developers swear by abort and restart, and in most situations, it's a good idea to simply let our processes crash. Because trying to recover a microservice after a crash can leave it limping along in a damaged state.

With *abort and restart*, we can monitor for crashes to know which microservices have had problems that need to be resolved. If you couple this with good error reporting, it's a good general strategy that you can apply by default.

Sometimes, though, we might need to use the *resume operation* strategy. For some microservices (for example, microservices that deal with customer data), we must think through the implications of aborting the process.

As an example, let's consider FlixTube's video upload microservice. Is it OK for this microservice to be aborted at any time? At any given moment it might be accepting multiple video uploads from multiple users. Is it acceptable to abort this microservice, potentially losing user uploads? I would say no, but if this is your microservice, you might have a different opinion and that's OK. There is no right way to do this.

> **NOTE** When deciding which strategy to use, it's probably best to default to *abort and restart*, but occasionally *resume operation* will be more appropriate.

10.2.3 Logging with Docker Compose

When using Docker Compose in development, we can see the logging from all our microservices in a single stream in our terminal window. Docker automatically collects the logging and aggregates it into a single stream as indicated in figure 10.4. Obviously, this is useful to get a broad overview of what our application is doing at any given time.

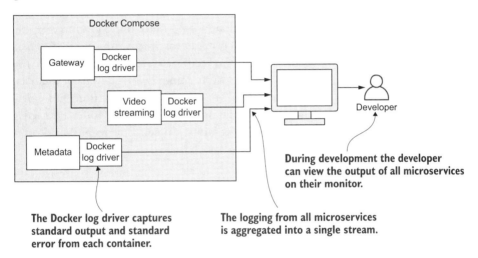

Figure 10.4   When using Docker Compose, Docker aggregates the logging from all our microservices into a single stream.

> ## Redirecting logging to a file
>
> Here's a trick that I find very useful. When we run Docker Compose, we can redirect its output and capture it to a log file. The `tee` command means we can display output both in the terminal as well as saving it to a file.
>
> **This wierd syntax redirects both standard output and standard error.**   **The `tee` command copies its input to the terminal and to the specified file.**
>
> ```
> docker-compose up --build 2>&1 | tee debug.log
> ```
>
> **The normal Docker Compose command we've used since chapter 4!**   **Pipes the redirected output to the `tee` command**

(continued)

Now we can load the log file (in this example, debug.log) in VS code and browse it at our leisure. We can search for particular strings of text. For example, if we are trying to find a problem with the database, we might search for logs that contain the word "database."

I even like to put special codes (character sequences) in my logging to distinguish the logs for particular subsystems of a microservice. This makes it easier to search or filter for the types of logs you are interested in.

10.2.4   *Basic logging with Kubernetes*

When running microservices in development under Docker Compose, we run the application locally on our development workstation. That makes it easy to see the logging from our application and understand what's happening in our code.

Retrieving logging from our production microservices running remotely on Kubernetes is much more difficult, however. To see the logging, we must be able to extract it from the cluster and pull it back to our development workstation for analysis.

Assuming we can authenticate with our Kubernetes cluster, it's fairly easy to retrieve logging separately for individual microservices using Kubectl or the Kubernetes dashboard. Revisit section 6.12 to remind yourself how to authenticate and start using these tools.

KUBECTL

We first met Kubectl in chapter 6, but we'll use it again now to get logs from a particular container running on Kubernetes. Let's say we are running FlixTube as it was at the end of chapter 9 (you can do this and follow along if you like). Imagine that we'd like to get logging from an instance of our metadata microservice.

Given that we could have multiple instances of the metadata microservice (we don't yet, but we'll talk about creating replicas later in this chapter), we need to determine the unique name that Kubernetes has assigned to the particular microservice that we are interested in.

What we are actually looking for here is the name of the *pod*. You might remember from chapter 6 that a Kubernetes pod is the thing that contains our containers. A pod can actually run multiple containers, even though for FlixTube, as yet, we are only running a single container in each pod. After authenticating Kubectl as described in section 6.12.1, now use the `get pods` command to see the full list of pods in our cluster as shown here:

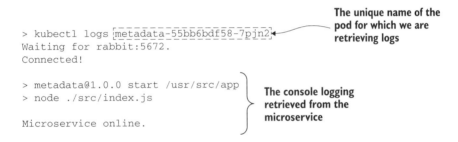

```
> kubectl get pods
NAME                                 READY   STATUS    RESTARTS   AGE
azure-storage-57bd889b85-sf985       1/1     Running   0          33m
database-7d565d7488-2v7ks            1/1     Running   0          33m
gateway-585cc67b67-9cxvh             1/1     Running   0          33m
history-dbf77b7d5-qw529              1/1     Running   0          33m
metadata-55bb6bdf58-7pjn2   ◄───     1/1     Running   0          33m
rabbit-f4854787f-nt2ht               1/1     Running   0          33m
video-streaming-68bfcd94bc-wvp2v     1/1     Running   0          33m
video-upload-86957d9c47-vs9lz        1/1     Running   0          33m
```

The unique name for the pod that contains the single instance of our metadata microservice.

Scan down the list to pick out the name of the pod for our metadata microservice and find its unique name. In this case, the name is metadata-55bb6bdf58-7pjn2. Now we can use the logs command to retrieve the logging for the metadata microservice. In this instance, there isn't much to see, but it's helpful that we know how to do this.

The unique name of the pod for which we are retrieving logs

```
> kubectl logs metadata-55bb6bdf58-7pjn2 ◄───
Waiting for rabbit:5672.
Connected!

> metadata@1.0.0 start /usr/src/app
> node ./src/index.js

Microservice online.
```

The console logging retrieved from the microservice

Just remember to replace the name of the pod with the name of an actual microservice from your cluster. The unique name is generated by Kubernetes, so the name for your metadata microservice won't be the same as the name that is generated for my version of it. Here's the general template for the command:

```
kubectl logs <pod-name>
```

Just insert the particular name of the pod from which you'd like to retrieve the logs.

KUBERNETES DASHBOARD

The other way to view logging for individual containers in your cluster is to use the Kubernetes dashboard. This is a visual way to inspect and explore your cluster, and you can even make modifications to it (although, I don't recommend manually tweaking a production cluster!).

We first met the Kubernetes dashboard in chapter 6. If you've not already done so, you can follow the instructions in section 6.12 to install, authenticate, and connect to your own dashboard. Once connected, you can quickly drill down to any pod to see its log. Figures 10.5, 10.6, and 10.7 show this process. Note in figures 10.5 and 10.6 that there's other useful information that can help us understand the state of our microservices.

Overall status of our cluster

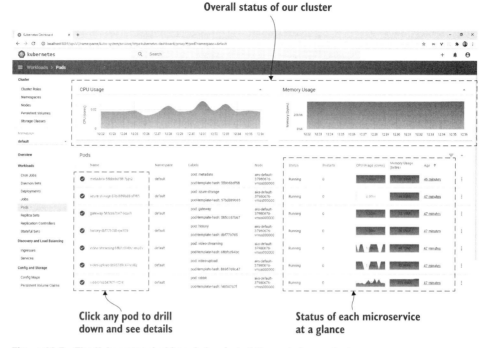

Click any pod to drill down and see details

Status of each microservice at a glance

Figure 10.5   The Kubernetes dashboard showing all the pods in our cluster.

The name of the pod we are viewing

Click here to open logging for the pod.

Click here to open a shell for the pod.

Figure 10.6   Viewing the details of the pod that contains our metadata microservice

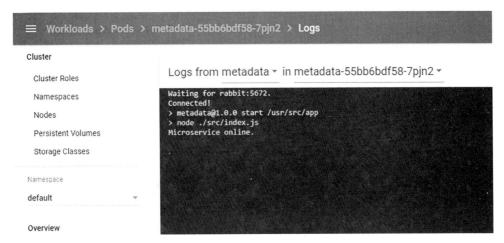

Figure 10.7   Viewing the log for the metadata microservice

10.2.5 *Roll your own log aggregation for Kubernetes*

We can go a long way to finding problems by chasing up logging for each individual microservice as shown in the previous sections. I recommend you do this for as long as feasible because implementing aggregation of logging for Kubernetes is a difficult task.

Eventually, as your application grows, you are going to get tired of chasing down logging separately for each microservice. It's unfortunate that Kubernetes has no built-in way to aggregate logging from containers in the cluster. I do hope the Kubernetes developers provide a simple solution to this in the future; it would be nice if there was a simple way to enable a single stream of logging from the cluster that we can use to monitor the behavior of the whole application.

There are enterprise solutions to this, however, and we'll look at one of those in the next section. The enterprise solutions can be heavyweight and expensive, and these don't necessarily make things any easier. These can also be quite difficult and time-consuming to set up and configure. If you are looking for a lighter-weight solution, you can build your own Kubernetes aggregation system as illustrated in figure 10.8.

The aggregation service shown in figure 10.8 is a lightweight microservice that runs within each Kubernetes node. The difficulty in implementing this is that you must deploy it as a *DaemonSet*. This is a type of Kubernetes deployment that runs a container on each and every node in the cluster. Why do we need this? It's because we need access to the filesystem of each node, where the log files are stored. Kubernetes automatically records standard output and standard error for each container in log files, but those files are available only within the node.

The aggregation service forwards all logging from containers running on the node to an external *collection service*. The collection service is another lightweight microservice. Its only job is to receive incoming logs through HTTP requests and to store those in its database. The database of logs is then displayed to our developers and operations staff through a web-based dashboard.

The logging from all containers on a node is
aggregated into single stream for the node.

An "aggregation service" is deployed to
each node using a Kubernetes DaemonSet.

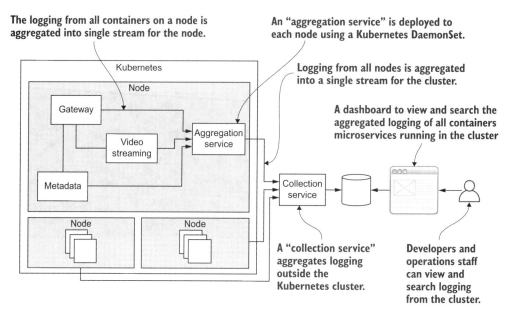

Logging from all nodes is aggregated
into a single stream for the cluster.

A dashboard to view and search the
aggregated logging of all containers
microservices running in the cluster

A "collection service"
aggregates logging
outside the
Kubernetes cluster.

Developers and
operations staff
can view and
search logging
from the cluster.

Figure 10.8   Rolling your log aggregation for Kubernetes

Note that the collection service itself is outside the cluster. We could have put it inside
the cluster, but then problems with the cluster (the exact thing we are trying to detect)
can hinder our ability to collect logging. It can be difficult to debug problems in your
cluster when your log collector is hosted within the cluster that is having the problems.

This kind of hand-rolled logging system actually works pretty well in the early days
of your application. It's a good learning experience to implement this, but only if you
want to drill down deeper into the inner workings of Kubernetes. To learn more and
to try building this for yourself, read my blog post on Kubernetes log aggregation:

http://www.the-data-wrangler.com/kubernetes-log-aggregation/

10.2.6   *Enterprise logging, monitoring and alerts*

A common solution for large scale enterprise monitoring of microservices is the combination of Fluentd, Elasticsearch, and Kibana. Other options specifically for monitoring metrics are Prometheus and Grafana. These are professional enterprise-scalable
solutions for monitoring and alerting. But these can be heavyweight and resource-
intensive, so don't rush into implementing these for your application.

We won't dive into any details on these technologies here because it would be
beyond the scope of this book. It's enough for now to have a brief overview of each of
these technologies.

FLUENTD

Fluentd is an open-source logging and data collection service written in Ruby. You can
instantiate a Fluentd container within your cluster to forward your logs to external log
collectors.

Fluentd is flexible and can be extended by its many plugins. One such plugin is what allows us to forward our logging to Elasticsearch. Learn more about Fluentd by visiting the following web sites:

https://www.fluentd.org/

https://docs.fluentd.org/

ELASTICSEARCH

Elasticsearch is an open-source search engine written in Java. Elasticsearch is what you can use to store and retrieve logging, metrics, and other useful data. Learn more about Elastic search at their website:

https://www.elastic.co/elasticsearch/

KIBANA

Kibana is the most interesting option of all this. It's an open-source visualization dashboard built on top of Elasticsearch.

Kibana allows us to view, search, and visualize our logs and other metrics. You can create fantastic custom dashboards with Kibana. Figure 10.9 shows an example of a dashboard with metrics from a Kubernetes cluster.

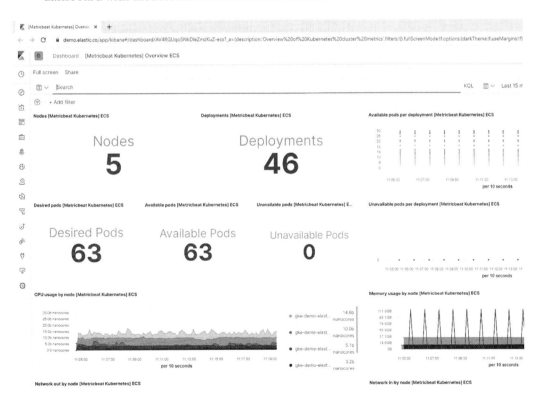

Figure 10.9 Screenshot of a demo Kibana dashboard with metrics from a Kubernetes cluster

The great thing about Kibana, and it can be a real lifesaver, is that you can configure it to automatically alert you when there are problems in your cluster. You specify the conditions under which the alert is raised and the action that is taken.

The paid version of Kibana also has support for email notifications and some other options including triggering of webhooks to invoke whatever custom response you need. Learn more about Kibana from the following websites:

https://www.elastic.co/what-is/kibana

https://www.elastic.co/kibana

You can find Kibana demo dashboards here:

https://www.elastic.co/demos

You can browse the supported notifications here:

https://www.elastic.co/guide/en/kibana/master/action-types.html

PROMETHEUS

Prometheus is an open-source monitoring system and time series database. Alongside Kubernetes, Prometheus is a graduated project of the Cloud Native Computing Foundation (CNCF), which puts it with some very esteemed company.

We can configure Prometheus to scrape metrics from our microservices at regular intervals and automatically alert us when things are going wrong. Learn more about Prometheus here:

https://prometheus.io/

GRAFANA

Whilst Prometheus is great for data collection, queries, and alerts, it's not so good at visualization. We can create simple graphs with Prometheus, but it's quite limited.

It's fortunate then that Grafana, which allows us to create visual and interactive dashboards, is so easy to connect to Prometheus. Learn more about Grafana here:

https://grafana.com/

10.2.7   *Automatic restarts with Kubernetes health checks*

Kubernetes has a great feature for automated health checks that allows us to automatically detect and restart unhealthy microservices. You may not need this particular feature because Kubernetes already defines an unhealthy microservice as one that has crashed or exited. By default, Kubernetes automatically restarts misbehaving containers.

If we aren't happy with the default, Kubernetes lets us create our own definition of "unhealthy" on a case-by-case basis. We can define a readiness probe and a liveness probe for each microservice for Kubernetes to query the health of the microservice. The *readiness probe* shows if the microservice has started and is ready to start accepting requests. The *liveness probe* then shows whether the microservice is still alive and is still accepting requests. Both are illustrated in figure 10.10.

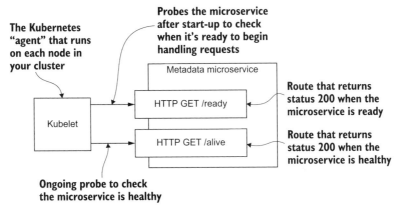

Figure 10.10 Applying automated Kubernetes health checks to the metadata microservice

We can use these two Kubernetes features to elegantly solve the problem we discovered in chapter 5 when we first connected the history microservice to our RabbitMQ server (section 5.8.5). The problem was that the history microservice (or any other microservice that connects to an upstream dependency) must wait for its dependency (in this case, RabbitMQ) to boot up before it can connect and make use of it.

If the microservice tries to connect too early, it's simply going to throw an exception that could abort the process. It would be better if we could simply make the history microservice wait quietly until RabbitMQ becomes available. That is why we used the `wait-port` npm module in chapter 5, but that was an awkward workaround. However, using Kubernetes, we now have the tools for an elegant fix.

The problem as just described only really happens when a microservices application is first booted up. Once your production application is running and your RabbitMQ server is already started, you can easily and safely introduce new microservices that depend on RabbitMQ without them having to wait. But don't start to think that it's not an issue because there is another side to this problem:

- What happens when RabbitMQ crashes and is then automatically restarted by Kubernetes?
- What happens if we'd like to take RabbitMQ down temporarily to upgrade or maintain it?

In both circumstances, RabbitMQ will go offline, and this breaks the connection for all the microservices that depend on it. The default for those microservices (unless we specifically handle it) is to throw an unhandled exception that most likely aborts the microservice. Now any microservices that depend on RabbitMQ will constantly crash and restart while RabbitMQ is down.

This is also true of any system dependencies besides RabbitMQ. Generally speaking, we'd like to be able to take any service offline and have the downstream services wait quietly for that service to become available again. When the service comes back online, the downstream services can resume normal operation.

We can now use the readiness and liveness probes to solve these problems. The following listing shows an update to the Terraform code from chapter 9 that defines readiness and liveness probes for our microservices.

```
container {
    image = local.image_tag
    name  = var.service_name

    env {
        name = "PORT"
        value = "80"
    }

    dynamic "env" {
        for_each = var.env
        content {
          name = env.key
          value = env.value
        }
    }

    readiness_probe {
        http_get {
            path = "/ready"
            port = 80
        }
    }

    liveness_probe {
        http_get {
            path = "/alive"
            port = 80
        }
    }
}
```

Defines a readiness probe for the microservice

Kubernetes makes a HTTP request to the /ready route to determine if the microservice is ready to accept requests.

Defines a liveness probe for the microservice

Kubernetes makes a HTTP request to the /alive route to determine if the microservice is still accepting requests.

If you'd like to try out the code in listing 10.1 for yourself, you can type the updates into the code in the file chapter-9/example-1/scripts/modules/microservice/main.tf. You'll then need to run `terraform apply` to apply the changes to the existing version of FlixTube that you deployed in chapter 9. If you didn't do that or if you have since taken down your production version of FlixTube, running `terraform apply` will deploy a fresh instance of FlixTube.

To make this change, we also have to add HTTP GET route handlers for /ready and /alive to all of our microservices. But what should these routes do?

In the simplest cases, we just have to return a HTTP status code of 200 to indicate success. That's enough to pass both probes, and it lets Kubernetes know that a microservice is both *ready* and *live*. In certain situations (for example, with the history microservice), we can then add additional code to customize the definition of what it means to be ready and live. In any microservice that depends on RabbitMQ, we would add code for

- *A /ready route that returns status 200 only once RabbitMQ becomes available.* This tells Kubernetes that the microservice has entered its ready state.
- *An /alive route that returns an error code when RabbitMQ becomes unavailable.* This causes the microservice to be restarted, but the new microservice (due to the /ready route) won't be placed in a ready state until RabbitMQ comes back online.

A strategy like this solves two problems. First, if we didn't use readiness and liveness probes, our history microservice will constantly start up, crash, and restart while RabbitMQ is down. This constant restarting isn't an efficient use of our resources, and it's going to generate a ton of error logging that we'd have to analyze (in case there's a real problem buried in there!).

Second, we could handle this explicitly in the microservice by detecting when RabbitMQ disconnects and then polling constantly to see if we can reconnect. This would save the microservice from constantly crashing and restarting, but it requires significantly more sophisticated code in our microservice to handle the disconnection and reconnection to RabbitMQ. We don't need to write such sophisticated code because that's what the probes are doing for us. To learn more about pod lifecycle and the different kinds of probes, see the Kubernetes documentation:

https://kubernetes.io/docs/concepts/workloads/pods/pod-lifecycle/

10.2.8 *Tracing across microservices*

I have one last thing to tell you about logging and microservices. It's extremely useful to be able to correlate strings of requests through your cluster. We do this by generating a unique correlation ID (CID) that we can attach to our requests to relate them to each other.

You can see how this works in figure 10.11. When a HTTP request first arrives in our gateway microservice, a unique CID is generated and attached to the request. As the request is forwarded through the system (either by HTTP request or RabbitMQ message), the ID remains attached, and we can use that to trace the path of related requests through our application.

The CID relates all logging, errors, metrics, and other information for the complete chain of requests. This is useful information to have when monitoring or exploring the behavior of our application. If you don't have this, it really isn't obvious where and how a request has penetrated deep into our application.

We can create unique IDs using the uuid library on npm. With that installed, we can create unique IDs like this:

```
const { v4: uuid } = require("uuid");
const cid = uuid();
```

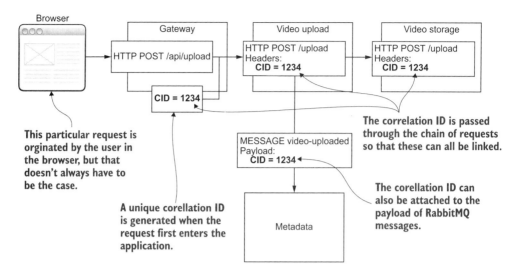

Figure 10.11   Using a correlation ID (CID) to correlate strings of requests through your cluster

We can then attach the unique ID to the headers of forwarded HTTP requests (easy to do with either `http.request` or Axios), or we can add the ID to the payload of Rab-bitMQ messages. To get serious about tracing your requests, you'll need to get Zipkin. This is a tool that allows you to visually trace requests across your application. You can learn more about Zipkin online:

https://zipkin.io/

The code for Zipkin can be found on GitHub:

https://github.com/openzipkin/zipkin

10.3 *Debugging microservices*

With some form of monitoring in place, we can see logging and metrics for our application. We use this to understand its current state and historical behavior. It is useful to have this kind of information in hand when problems occur.

Once a problem has become apparent, we must now put on our detective hats. We need to analyze the information we have to understand *what* went wrong. We then track the clues back to the root cause to find out *why* it happened. Along the way, we'll run experiments to further hone in on the culprit.

Usually, we can't fix a problem until we have identified the cause. Of course, sometimes we can randomly stumble on a solution without knowing the cause. But it's always sensible to be able to ascertain the root cause anyway. That way, we can be sure that the supposed *fix* has actually fixed the problem and not just hidden it.

Debugging is the name of this process of tracking down the source of a problem and subsequently applying an appropriate fix. Debugging microservices is similar to debugging any other kind of application; it's a form of troubleshooting that is part art and part science.

Debugging microservices, though, is more difficult due to the distributed nature of the application. Locating a problem in a single process can be difficult on its own, but finding a problem in an application composed of many interacting processes— that's a whole lot more trouble.

As you might already suspect, searching for the source of a problem is actually the most difficult part of debugging. It's like searching for the proverbial needle in the haystack. If you have any inkling of where to look for the problem, you stand a much greater chance of finding it quickly. That's why developers who are experienced with a particular codebase can find bugs in it much more quickly than those who are less familiar.

After finding the source of the problem, we must now fix it. Fortunately, it is often (but not always) much quicker to fix a bug than it was to find it in the first place.

10.3.1 *The debugging process*

In an ideal world, we'd find and fix all problems during development and testing. Indeed, if you have a thorough testing practice and/or comprehensive automated test suite, you will find many of your bugs before production. If possible, that's the best way because debugging is much easier in development (on your development workstation) instead of in production (where it's likely distributed over multiple servers in a data center). To debug any code, we can follow this process:

1 Gather evidence
2 Mitigate customer impact
3 Isolate the problem
4 Reproduce the problem
5 Fix the problem
6 Reflection

As with anything that's part art and part science, this isn't actually a strictly defined process. Sometimes, we must trace an iterative path through these steps in an unpredictable way. For the purposes of explanation though, let's pretend that we can solve our problem by going through these steps in a straightforward linear manner.

GATHER EVIDENCE

The start of the debugging process is always gathering as much evidence about the problem as possible. This is anything that can help direct us more quickly to the real location of the bug. If we start debugging close to where the problem actually is, we can narrow in on it much more quickly. We need to learn as much as we can about the problem as quickly as possible. That's things like

- Logging and error reports
- Traces for relevant request paths through the system (as described in section 10.2.8)

- Bug reports from users
- Information from the Kubernetes CLI tool or dashboard
- Call stacks for any crash that might have occurred
- The implicated versions or branches of the code
- Recently deployed code or microservices

The reason we must compile this information immediately is that, often, the next thing we must do for the benefit of our customers is to make the problem just disappear as quickly as possible.

MITIGATE CUSTOMER IMPACT

Before attempting to solve or find the cause of the problem, we must ensure that it is not adversely affecting our customers. If our customers are negatively affected, then we must take immediate action to rectify the situation.

At this point, we don't care what caused the problem or what the real long-term fix for it might be. We simply need the fastest possible way to restore the functionality that our customers depend upon. They'll appreciate our immediate action to find a workaround that allows them to continue using our application. There are multiple ways we can do this:

- If the problem comes from a recent code update, revert that update and redeploy the code to production. This is often easier with microservices because if we know the microservice that was updated caused the problem, we can easily revert that single microservice and restore it to the previously working version, say, an earlier image in the container registry.
- If the problem comes from a new or updated feature that isn't urgently needed by the customer, we can disable that single feature to restore the application to a working state.
- If the problem comes from a microservice that isn't urgently needed, we can temporarily take that microservice out of commission.

I can't overstate the importance of this step! It could take hours or days (maybe even weeks at worst) to solve a problem. We can't know ahead of time how long it will take, and we can't expect our customers to standby and wait for that to happen. It's more likely that they'll head over to one of our competitors instead.

What's worse is that solving a problem under pressure (because our customers are waiting on us) is extremely stressful and results in poor decision making. Any fix we apply under stress is likely to add more bugs, which only compounds the problem.

For the sake of our customers and ourselves, we must temporarily ignore the problem and find the fastest way to restore our application to a working state (as depicted in figure 10.12). This takes away the pressure, allows our customers to continue without interruption, and buys us the time we need to solve this problem.

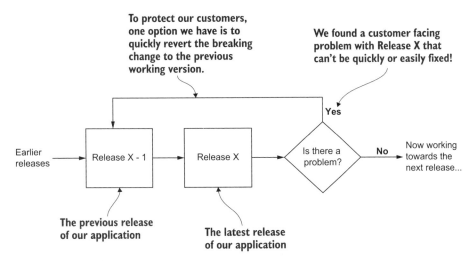

Figure 10.12 Mitigating the risk to our customer after a problem is found by immediately rolling back to a previous working version

REPRODUCE THE PROBLEM

After making sure that the application is working again for our customers, we can now move on to locating the cause of the problem and solving it. To do this, we must be able to reproduce the problem. Unless we can definitely and consistently repeat the problem, we can never be certain that we've fixed it. What we are aiming to do is create a *test case* that demonstrates the bug. That is a documented sequence of steps that we can follow to reliably cause the bug to show itself.

Ideally, we'd like to reproduce the bug on our development workstation. That makes it easier to run experiments to track down the bug. Some problems, though, are so complex that we can't easily reproduce those in development, especially when your application has grown so big (e.g., it has many microservices) that it no longer fits in its entirety on a single computer.

In this situation, we must reproduce the problem in a *test environment*. This is a production-like environment that is purely for testing (it's not customer-facing). Debugging in the test environment (which is similar to debugging in production) can still be difficult, though, and ultimately, we'd still like to reproduce the problem in development.

In the test environment, we can run experiments to further understand which components of the application are involved in the problem, and then safely remove any that aren't contributing to it. Through a process of elimination, we can cut back our application to a point where it is small enough to run in development. At this point, we can transfer from the test environment to our development workstation. We'll talk more about creating test environments in chapter 11.

If we are doing automated testing, this is the point where we should write an automated test that checks that the bug is fixed. Of course, this test fails initially—that's the point of it. We'll use it later as a reliable way to know that the problem has been fixed.

Writing an automated test also ensures that we can repeatedly reproduce the issue. Each and every time we run this test, it should fail, confirming that we have indeed found a reliable way to reproduce the bug.

ISOLATE THE PROBLEM

Once we have reproduced the problem in development, we now start the process of isolating it. We repeatedly run experiments and chip away at the application until we have narrowed down the scope and pinpointed the exact source of the bug.

We are effectively cutting away the space in which the problem can hide, progressively reducing the problem domain until the cause becomes obvious. We are using a *divide and conquer*-style of process as illustrated in figure 10.13.

By the way, microservices are great for this. Our application is already nicely factored into easily separable components. This makes it much easier to pull our application into pieces. In general, it's pretty easy to just drop an individual microservice out of the application (just comment it out of your Docker Compose file!). As you drop each microservice, ask the question: can you still reproduce the problem?

- Yes. That's great. You've just reduced the problem domain by one microservice.
- No. That's great. You've possibly just implicated that microservice in the problem.

Either way, you are iterating your way towards the cause of the problem.

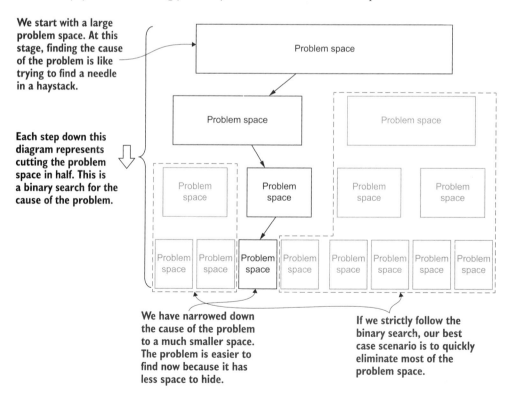

Figure 10.13 Cutting away the problem space until we isolate the exact source of the bug

Sometimes we will quickly identify the source of a problem. At other times, debugging can be a painfully slow, time-consuming, and frustrating process. It depends a lot on our general level of experience, our familiarity with the code base, whether we have seen this *kind* of problem before, and the complexity of the particular problem itself.

> **NOTE** Debugging at its worst requires persistence, patience, and commitment. Don't be afraid to reach out for help. There's nothing worse than being stuck on a problem that you can't solve.

If you know where to start looking for a problem, then you already have a massive head start. You might also be able to take an educated guess at what is causing it. If that works out, you are quite right to skip much of this process and immediately focus your attention on the cause of the bug. However, if you don't know where to look or if your guess turns out to be wrong, you will have to be more scientific about debugging and apply this full process.

FIX THE PROBLEM

You've identified the root cause of the problem. Now you just have to fix it!

Fortunately, fixing problems is much easier than finding them in the first place. Usually, identifying the broken code is enough to make you imagine what the solution would be. Sometimes, it's more difficult, and you'll have to invest some creative thinking to come up with a solution. The hardest part is definitely over though. You have found the needle in the haystack, and now you can work out the best way to remove it.

If you are doing automated testing, and you have already written the failing test that reproduces the issue, then you have a convenient and reliable yardstick to show you when the bug has been fixed. Even if the fix turns out to be difficult, at least you have a way to know for sure that the problem is fixed. That's a useful thing to have as you iterate and experiment your way towards a fix.

REFLECTION

Every time we solve a problem, we should pause for a moment to reflect on what can be done to prevent the problem from happening again in the future, or what could have been done to find and fix the problem more quickly. Reflection is important for us as individuals and as teams to continuously refine and improve our development process.

We might have written an automated test that will prevent this specific problem again in the future. But still, we need something more than that. We should seek practices and habits to help us eliminate, not just this specific problem, but all of this class or kind of problem.

The amount of time that we spend reflecting and then the amount of time we invest in upgrading our development process depends a lot on the problem itself and the severity of it. We should ask questions like

- Is this kind of problem likely to happen in the future such that we should proactively mitigate against it?
- Are the effects of this problem severe enough that we should proactively mitigate against it?

Answering these questions helps us understand how much effort to expend combating this type of problem in the future.

10.3.2 Debugging production microservices

Sometimes we can't get away from it; we literally have to debug our microservices in production. If we can't reproduce the issue in test or development, then our only option is to further understand the problem as it is occurring in production.

If we need to make a deeper inspection than logging can give us, we can use the Kubernetes CLI tool (Kubectl) to open a terminal in any container (at least any that has a shell installed). Once you know the name of the pod (refer back to section 10.2.4), such as the pod that contains the metadata microservice, we can open a shell to it like this:

```
kubectl exec --stdin --tty metadata-55bb6bdf58-7pjn2 -- sh
```

You may have noticed back in figure 10.6 that you can also open a terminal to a pod using the Kubernetes dashboard. Now we can invoke shell commands inside a production microservice.

As you might be able to sense, we are in extremely dangerous territory here. When you are inside a microservice like this, there is the potential for much damage, and any mistakes could easily make the problem much worse! Don't shell into a production microservice on a whim, and if you do, don't change anything. There are better and safer ways to diagnose problems!

This only matters if it affects our customers. If you are instead debugging microservices in your own private cluster or in a test environment, then you aren't affecting any customers; so feel free to push, prod, and poke your microservices however you like—it's a great learning experience to do this! Just don't do it to a production microservice.

10.4   Reliability and recovery

We can't avoid problems, but there are many ways that we can deal with these in our application to maintain service in the face of failures. With our application in production, we have an expectation that it will perform with a certain level of reliability, and there are many tactics we can employ to architect robust and reliable systems. This section overviews a small selection of practices and techniques that can help us build fault-tolerant systems that can quickly bounce back from failure.

10.4.1 Practice defensive programming

A first step is to code with the mindset of *defensive programming*. When working this way, we have the expectation that errors will occur, even if we can't anticipate what those might be. We should always expect the following:

- We'll get bad inputs to our code.
- Our code contains bugs that haven't manifested yet.
- Things we depend on (e.g., RabbitMQ) are not 100% reliable and, occasionally, have their own problems.

When we adopt the defensive mindset, we'll automatically start looking for ways to make our code behave more gracefully in the presence of unexpected situations. Fault tolerance starts at the coding level. It starts within each microservice.

10.4.2 Practice defensive testing

As you are probably aware, testing plays a huge role in building resilient and reliable systems. We covered testing in chapter 8, so all I'd like to say here is simply that testing the "normal" code paths is not enough. We should also be testing that the software we create can handle errors. This is the next step up from defensive programming.

We should be writing tests that actively attack our code. This helps us identify fragile code that could do with some more attention. We need to make sure our code can recover gracefully, reporting errors, and handling unusual situations.

10.4.3 Protect your data

All applications deal with user data, and we must take necessary steps to protect our data in the event of failures. When unexpected failures occur, we need to be confident that our most important data is not damaged or lost. Bugs happen; losing our data should not.

Not all data is equal. Data that is generated within our system (and can hence be regenerated) is less important than data that is captured from our customer. Although all data is important, it's the source data that we must invest the most in protecting.

The first step to protecting data, obviously, is to have a backup. The backup should be automated. Most cloud vendors provide facilities for this that you can enable.

NOTE Don't forget to practice restoring your backup! Backups are completely useless if we are unable to restore those.

At least now, should the worst happen, we can restore lost or damaged data from the backup. In the industry, we have a saying: our data *doesn't* exist *unless* it exists in at least three places. Here are some other guidelines we can follow to protect our data:

- Safely record data as soon as it's captured
- Never have code that overwrites source data
- Never have code that deletes source data

The code that captures our data is some of the most important code in our application, and we should treat it with an appropriate level of respect. It should be extremely well tested. It should also be minimal and as simple as possible, because simple code leaves less space where bugs and security issues can hide.

The reason we should never overwrite or delete our source data is that a bug in that code can easily damage or destroy the data. We know bugs happen right? We are in the defensive mindset, so we are expecting unforeseen problems to happen. To learn more about working with and protecting your data, see my book, *Data Wrangling with JavaScript* (Manning, 2018).

10.4.4   *Replication and redundancy*

The best way to tackle the failure of a microservice is by having *redundancy*. We do that by having multiple (usually at least three) instances of each microservice sitting behind a load balancer, which you can see in figure 10.14. The load balancer is a service that shares incoming requests across multiple microservices so that the "load" is distributed evenly among them.

If any microservice happens to fail, the load balancer immediately redirects incoming requests to the other instances. In the meantime, the failed instance is restarted by Kubernetes. This redundancy means that we can maintain a continuous level of service even in the face of intermittent failures.

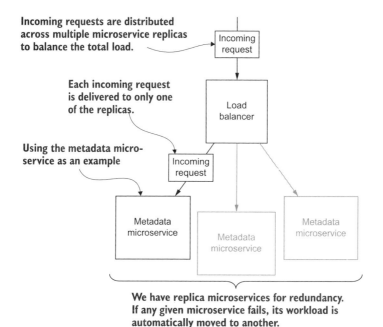

Figure 10.14   A load balancer distributes incoming requests across multiple redundant instances of a microservice.

Redundancy is implemented by *replication*. We also use replication for increased performance, but we'll save that until chapter 11.

Just because our system can handle failures doesn't mean we should tolerate these. All failures should be logged and later investigated. We can use the debugging process from section 10.3 to find and fix the cause of the failure.

IMPLEMENTING REPLICATION IN KUBERNETES

Each of the microservices that we have deployed for FlixTube so far (in chapters 7 and 9) only had a single instance. This is perfectly OK when creating an application for learning (like we did with FlixTube) or when you are in the starting phase of developing your own microservices application. It's just not going to be as fault-tolerant as it could be.

This is easily fixed though, because Kubernetes makes it easy for us to create replicas. The amazing thing is that it is just as simple as changing the value of a field in the Terraform code that we have already written—that's the power of infrastructure as code.

We can easily change the number of replicas by setting the value of the `replicas` property in our Kubernetes deployment. You can see an example of this in listing 10.2, which is an update to the Terraform code from chapter 9.

The number of replicas has been updated from one to three. We can apply this change by running `terraform apply`. Once completed, our microservices all have three redundant instances. With this small change, we have massively improved the reliability and fault tolerance of our application!

The load balancer for our replicas is created by the Kubernetes service defined at the end of listing 10.2. Working through chapters 7 and 9, we always had a load balancer for our microservices, but it distributed the load to only a single microservice! With the change we make in the listing, the load is now being distributed between three instances for each microservice.

Listing 10.2 Creating load balanced replicas of a microservice on Kubernetes (an update to chapter-9/example-1/scripts/modules/microservice/main.tf)

```
resource "kubernetes_deployment"          Configures the Kubernetes
 "service_deployment" {           ◁─────── deployment for each microservice

    depends_on = [ null_resource.docker_push ]

    metadata {
        name = var.service_name

        labels = {
            pod = var.service_name
        }
    }
                                   Sets the replica count to 3. Running
    spec {                         "terraform apply" again creates
        replicas = 3      ◁─────── three replicas of each microservice.

        selector {
            match_labels = {
                pod = var.service_name
            }
        }

        template {
            metadata {
                labels = {
                    pod = var.service_name
                }
            }

            spec {
                container {
```

```
                        image = local.image_tag
                        name  = var.service_name

                        env {
                            name = "PORT"
                            value = "80"
                        }
                    }
                }
            }
        }
    }
}


resource "kubernetes_service" "service" {
    metadata {
        name = var.dns_name
    }

    spec {
        selector = {
            pod = kubernetes_deployment.service_deployment
            ➥ .metadata[0].labels.pod
        }

        session_affinity = var.session_affinity

        port {
            port        = 80
            target_port = 80
        }

        type = var.service_type
    }
}
```

10.4.5 *Fault isolation and graceful degradation*

One thing that microservices are really good at is fault isolation. We do have to take some care, however, to be able to make use of this. What we are aiming for is that problems within our cluster are isolated so that they have minimal effect on the user.

With appropriate mechanisms in place, our application can gracefully handle faults and prevent these from manifesting as problems in the front end. The tools we need for this are timeouts, retries, circuit breakers, and bulkheads, which are described in the following sections.

As an example, let's consider the video-upload microservice. Just imagine that something has gone wrong with it, and it is no longer functional. At this moment, we are working hard to rectify the situation and quickly restore it to a working state. In the meantime, our customers would like to continue using our product. If we didn't have mechanisms to prevent it, errors might go all the way to the front end, bringing our service down, and badly disrupting our customers.

Instead, we should implement safeguards that stop this wholesale disruption of our user base. This is illustrated in figure 10.15. The top part of the figure shows the error propagating all the way to the user and causing problems for them. The bottom part of figure 10.15 shows how this should work: the gateway stopping the error in its tracks, thus containing the fault within the cluster.

We can then handle the situation by showing the user an error message saying that the video-upload feature is currently not available. Video upload might be broken, but our users can continue using the rest of the application.

This is a huge benefit that microservices brings to the table. If we were using a monolith and one of its components (e.g., the video-upload component) was broken, that usually takes down the entire monolith, leaving our customers with nothing. With microservices, however, the fault can be isolated, and the application as a whole can continue to function, albeit in a degraded state.

This idea of fault isolation is often called *the bulkhead pattern,* so named because it is conceptually similar to the actual bulkheads that are used in large ships. When a leak occurs in a ship, it is the bulkheads that prevent the leak from escaping to other compartments and eventually sinking the ship. This is fault isolation in the real world, and you can see how it is similar to a microservices application.

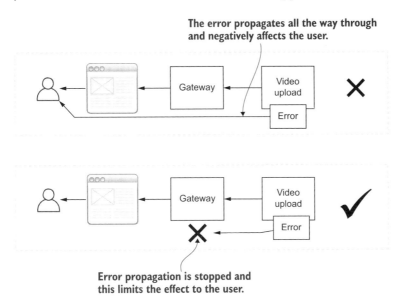

Figure 10.15   Isolating faults within the cluster from the user

10.4.6 *Simple techniques for fault tolerance*

Here are some simple techniques you can start using immediately to implement fault tolerance and fault isolation in your own microservices application.

TIMEOUTS

In this book, we used the built-in Node.js `http.request` function and the Axios code library to make HTTP requests internally between microservices. We control our own microservices, and most of the time, we know those will respond quickly to requests that are internal to the cluster. There are times, however, when a problem manifests itself and an internal microservice stops responding.

In the future, we'd also like to make requests to external services. Just imagine that we have integrated FlixTube with Dropbox as a means to import new videos. When making requests to an external service like Dropbox, we don't have any control over how quickly these respond to our requests. Such external services will go down for maintenance occasionally, so it's entirely likely that an external service like Dropbox will intermittently stop responding to our requests.

We must consider how to handle requests to a service that doesn't respond. If a request isn't going to complete anytime soon, we'd like to have it aborted after some maximum amount of time. If we didn't do that, it could take a long time (if ever) for the request to complete. We can't very well have our customer waiting so long! We'd prefer to abort the request quickly and tell the customer something has gone wrong, rather than have them waiting indefinitely on it.

We can deal with this using *timeouts*. A timeout is the maximum amount of time that can elapse before a request is automatically aborted with an error code. Setting timeouts for our requests allows us to control how quickly our application responds to failure. Failing quickly is what we want here because the alternative is to fail slowly, and if something is going to fail, we'd like to deal with it as quickly as possible so as not to waste our customer's time.

SETTING A TIMEOUT WITH AXIOS

Reading the Axios documentation tells me that the default timeout is infinity! That means by default, an Axios request can literally go forever without being aborted. We definitely need to set the timeout for any requests we make with Axios.

You can set the timeout for each request, but that requires repeated effort. Fortunately, with Axios, we can set a default timeout for *all* requests as shown in the following listing.

Listing 10.3   Setting a default timeout for HTTP requests with Axios

```
const axios = require("axios");
axios.defaults.timeout = 2500;          Sets the default timeout for requests
                                        to 2500 milliseconds or 2.5 seconds
```

RETRIES

We know that HTTP requests sometimes fail. We don't control external services, and we can't see the code for those. It's difficult for us to determine how reliable these are and even the most reliable services can have intermittent failures.

One simple way to deal with this is to simply retry the operation a number of times and hope that it succeeds on one of the subsequent attempts. This is illustrated in

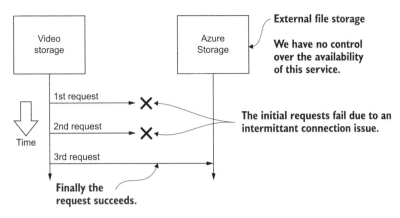

Figure 10.16   Retrying a HTTP request until it succeeds

figure 10.16. In this example, you can imagine FlixTube's video storage microservice requesting a video to be retrieved from Azure storage. Occasionally such requests fail for indeterminable reasons. In figure 10.16, two successive requests have failed due to an intermittent connection error, but the third request succeeds.

Assuming that the network is reliable is one of the fallacies of distributed computing, we must take steps to mitigate against request failures. Implementation in JavaScript isn't particularly difficult. In listing 10.4, you can see an implementation of a `retry` function that I've used across a number of projects. The `retry` function wraps other asynchronous operations such as HTTP requests so these can be attempted multiple times.

Listing 10.4 also includes a helpful `sleep` function used to make pauses between attempts. There's no point immediately trying to make a request again. If we do it too quickly, it's probably just going to fail again. In this case, we give it some time before making another attempt.

Listing 10.5 is an example of how to call the `retry` function, showing how it can wrap a HTTP GET request. In this example, we allow the request to be retried three times with a pause of 5 milliseconds between each request.

Listing 10.4   Implementation of a retry function in JavaScript

Defines a "sleep" function that can
be used to pause between retries

```
async function sleep(timeMS) {
    return new Promise((resolve, reject) => {
        setTimeout(
            () => { resolve(); },
            timeMS
        );
    });
}
```

Wraps a call to
"setTimeout" in a
Promise so that we
await the completion
of the pause

Invokes a callback after the
elapsed amount of time

The callback resolves the Promise.

Sets the duration of the pause

```
async function retry(operation, maxAttempts,
   waitTimeMS) {
      while (maxAttempts-- > 0) {
         try {
            const result = await operation();
            return result;
         }
         catch (err) {
            lastError = err;
            if (maxAttempts >= 1) {
               await sleep(waitTimeMS);
            }
         }
      }
      throw lastError;
}
```

Defines a "retry" function that we can use to make multiple attempts for any asynchronous operation

Makes an attempt at the actual asynchronous operation

Loops for each attempt up until to the maximum number of retries

The operation was a success! This breaks out of the loop and returns the result of the asynchronous operation.

Records the error from the most recent attempt

Handles any error thrown by the asynchronous operation

Pauses for a brief moment before the next attempt (so long as we are not on the last attempt)

Throws the error from the last attempt. We ran out of retries, so we must let the error bubble up to the caller.

Listing 10.5 Using the retry function (an example)

```
await retry(
    () => axios.get("https://something/something"),
    3,
    5
);
```

Calls our "retry" function

The operation to be retried; in this example, it's an HTTP GET request using Axios.

Sets the maximum number of attempts to three

Sets the time between retries to be five milliseconds

10.4.7 Advanced techniques for fault tolerance

We have seen some simple techniques for improving the reliability and resilience of our application. Of course, there are many other more advanced techniques we could deploy for improved fault tolerance and recovery from failures.

We are almost beyond the scope of the book, but I'd still like to share with you a brief overview of some more advanced techniques. These will be useful in the future as you evolve a more robust architecture for your application.

JOB QUEUE

The *job queue* is a type of microservice found in many application architectures. This is a different kind of thing to the message queue we saw in RabbitMQ. It's similar, but it's a level of sophistication above that.

We use a job queue to manage heavy-weight processing tasks. Let's imagine how this could work for a future version of FlixTube. We can say that each video requires a lot of processing after it is uploaded. For example, we'd like to extract a thumbnail from videos. Or maybe, we'd like to convert videos to a lower resolution for better performance playback on mobile devices. These are the kinds of tasks that should happen after a video is uploaded.

Now imagine that 1,000 users have each uploaded a video, all roughly at the same time. We don't have any kind of elastic scaling yet (we'll talk about that in chapter 11). So how can we manage the huge processing workload resulting from so many videos landing in FlixTube at the same time? This is what the job queue does. You can see an illustration of how it works in figure 10.17.

The job queue records the sequence of jobs that need to be performed to the database. This makes it resilient against failure. The entire application could crash and restart, but so long as the database survives, we can reload the job queue and continue processing where it left off. Individual jobs can also fail; for example, the microservice doing the processing crashes, but because failed jobs aren't marked as complete, they'll naturally be attempted again later.

The job queue also allows for control over the performance of this processing. Instead of maxing out our application to process the 1,000 uploaded videos all at once, we can spread out the load so that processing is scheduled over a longer time period. It can also be scheduled across off-peak hours. This means we won't have to pay for the extra compute that might otherwise be required if we wanted to do the processing all at once in a massive burst.

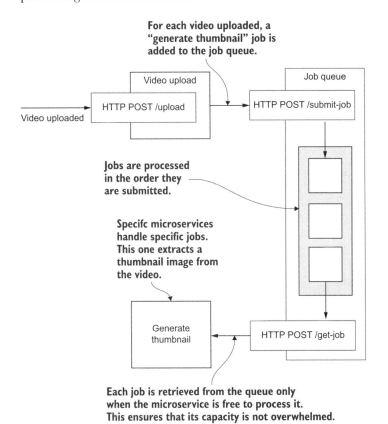

Figure 10.17   A job queue microservice manages a queue of video thumbnail generation jobs.

CIRCUIT BREAKER

The *circuit breaker* is like a more advanced version of a timeout. It has some built-in smarts to understand when problems are occurring, so that it can deal with these more intelligently. Figure 10.18 illustrates how a circuit breaker works.

In normal situations, the status of the circuit breaker is set to On, and it allows HTTP requests to go through as usual (1). If at some point a request to a particular resource fails (2), the circuit breaker flips to the Off state (3). While in the Off state, the circuit breaker always fails new requests immediately.

Think of this as a "super" timeout. The circuit breaker knows the upstream system is failing at the moment, so it doesn't even bother checking. It immediately fails the incoming request!

This failing quickly is why we used timeouts. It's better to fail quickly than to fail slowly. The circuit breaker works by already knowing that we are failing, and so, instead of just failing more quickly, it can fail *immediately*.

Periodically, on its own time (with a delay that you can configure), the circuit breaker checks the upstream service to see if it has resumed normal operation. When that happens, the circuit breaker flips back to the On state (4). Future incoming requests are now allowed through as normal. Implementing a circuit breaker is much more difficult than implementing a timeout or a retry, but it's worth keeping in mind for future use, especially if you find yourself needing a more sophisticated technique.

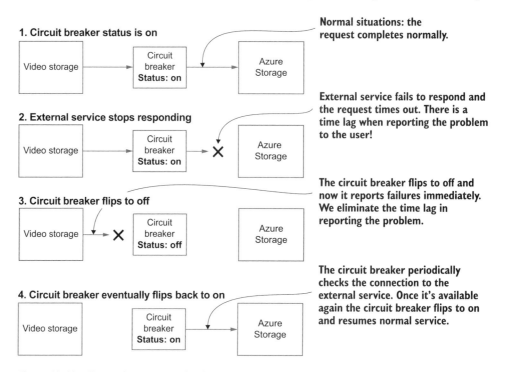

Figure 10.18   Illustrating how the circuit breaker works

10.5   Continue your learning

You now have many techniques in your toolkit for keeping your microservices healthy and reliable! To learn more about building reliable microservices, Manning has released some free chapters relating to microservice stability from the books *Microservices in Action* by Morgan Bruce and Paulo A. Pereira (2018) and *The Tao of Microservices* by Richard Rodger (2017). You'll find these available here:

- https://www.manning.com/books/microservices-stability

There's also a great book about *crash testing* your application:

- *Chaos Engineering* by Mikolaj Pawlikowski (Manning, 2020)

To learn more about logging and monitoring in production, read these books:

- *Unified Logging with Fluentd* by Phil Wilkins (Manning, est Summer 2020)
- *Elasticsearch in Action* by Radu Gheorghe, Matthew Lee Hinman, and Roy Russo (Manning, 2015)

Summary

- Logging and error handling outputs key information used to understand the behavior and state of our microservices.
- Monitoring is key to determining the health of our microservices and detecting problems.
- Aggregation combines the output of all our microservices into a single easily accessible stream of information.
- Kubernetes health checks can be used to automatically detect problems in our microservices.
- When a problem is detected, we must go through a process of debugging to find the cause of the problem and to determine an appropriate fix for it.
- There are many techniques for ensuring reliability and fault tolerance of our microservices, including replicas and load balancing, automatic restarts, timeouts, retries, job queues, and circuit breakers.

Pathways to scalability

This chapter covers

- Scaling microservices to bigger development teams
- Scaling microservices to meet growing demand
- Understanding basic security concerns
- Strategies for converting a monolith to microservices
- Tips for building with microservices on a budget

We've spent the whole book working towards a production microservices application, so where to now? It's time to see what microservices can offer us in the future.

Throughout this book, we've taken many shortcuts that helped us get started quickly and cheaply with microservices. These shortcuts make it simpler to learn microservices and to bootstrap our fledgling application. Even though FlixTube is a simple application built with a relatively simple process, we are still using microservices, and this is an architecture that provides us many pathways towards future scalability.

In this chapter, we discuss how to manage a growing microservices application. How do we scale up to a bigger development team? How do we scale up to meet growing customer demand? We also need to talk about basic security concerns and how they relate to microservices. Then, we'll briefly touch on what it takes to convert an existing monolith to microservices.

We'll finish the book by reiterating the techniques that can make bootstrapping a microservices application simpler, easier, and cheaper. This is practical advice that can help a small team, a startup, or a solo developer kickstart their own microservices application while still having a future full of possibilities for scalability!

11.1 Our future is scalable

Microservices offer us numerous pathways to achieve a scalable product. In this chapter, we will look at the kinds of things we must do moving forward to scale our application and workflow so that we can grow our development team around our growing application. We'll follow up by looking at how to scale the performance of our application for greater capacity and throughput.

You probably don't need any of these techniques yet; you only need these when your application has grown big enough to expand your development team. Or when your customer-base has increased and you need to scale up for better performance.

We are moving into very advanced territory here, and this chapter mostly gives you a taste of the ways in which you can scale your application in the future. This is really just the tip of the iceberg; but it's enough to give you an awareness of the path ahead.

The problems we'll address in this chapter are good problems to have. If you come to the point where you must scale up, that's a good thing. It means your business is successful. It means you have a growing customer base. At this point, you can be really happy you chose a microservices architecture because it makes scaling up much more straightforward.

This chapter isn't intended to be hands on. Think of it as some insight as to where your microservices journey might go in the future. That said, many of these techniques are fairly easy to try, but in doing so, you might make a mistake and inadvertently break your application cluster.

Don't try any of this on your production infrastructure that existing staff or customers depend upon. But do feel free to go back to chapter 9 and follow the instructions there to boot a new production instance of FlixTube. You can use that for experimentation. That gives you a risk-free way to try out anything in this chapter that sounds interesting.

11.2 Scaling the development process

First, let's tackle scaling our development process. In this book, so far, we have experienced the development process and production workflow from the point of view of a single developer working on a small microservices application. Let's now raise our focus up to the level of the team. The simple process we have thus far used can actually work to a certain extent for a small team:

- Developers working on a single codebase, writing and testing code on their development workstations
- Developers pushing code changes to the hosted code repository, which triggers the continuous delivery (CD) pipeline to deploy the application to production

This simple process is a great way to get started and move quickly when building a new application. But we can only take it so far. Our fledgling development process suffers from the following problems:

- *We don't want code going directly from developers to customers.* We'd like our developers to be able to test their code in a production-like environment, but we want that "work in progress" to be buffered from customers to ensure that it works well before inflicting it on them.
- *We don't want developers interfering with each other.* As we grow our development team, developers working in a single code base will be treading on each other's toes more frequently (for example, causing merge conflicts and breaking the build).
- *Our single code repository and CD pipeline is not scalable.* To manage the complexity of our growing application, we must break it apart so that even though the application might grow extremely complex, each individual microservice remains small, simple, and manageable.

To build a scalable development process, expand to multiple teams, and make the most of microservices, we must do some restructuring.

11.2.1 *Multiple teams*

As we evolve our application, we'll be adding more microservices to the mix to implement features and expand our application's capabilities. As the workload grows, we'll also have to grow the team to handle it. At some point, when our single team grows too large, we'll need to split it into multiple teams. This keeps our teams small and allows us to benefit from the communication and organizational advantages that come from small teams.

Applications based on microservices provide natural seams that can be used to carve up the application for development by multiple teams. Figure 11.1 shows what our team structure looks like in the early stages of development, when we are using our simple development process.

Figure 11.2 shows what our structure might look like after we have grown and split into separate teams. We have carved

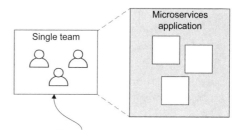

In the early stages of a new microservices application, you'll likely have a single team working across the whole application.

Figure 11.1   When starting a new application, it should be small enough that one team can manage all microservices by themselves.

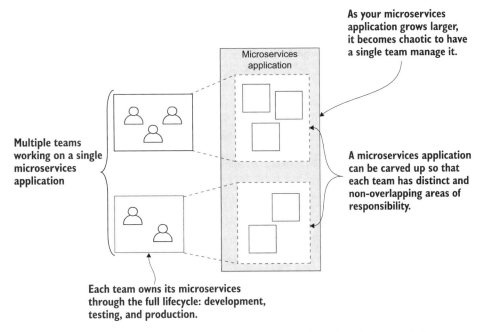

As your microservices application grows larger, it becomes chaotic to have a single team manage it.

Microservices application

Multiple teams working on a single microservices application

A microservices application can be carved up so that each team has distinct and non-overlapping areas of responsibility.

Each team owns its microservices through the full lifecycle: development, testing, and production.

Figure 11.2　As we grow our application, the development can be split so that separate teams are managing independent microservices or groups of microservices.

up the application so that each team is responsible for a different set of microservices with zero overlaps. This helps stop the teams from interfering with each other. Now, we can grow our team of teams to any size we like by dividing our application up along microservices boundaries.

Each team *owns* one or more microservices, and typically, they are responsible for their own microservices—all the way from coding, through testing, and then into production. The team is usually responsible for the operational needs of their microservices, keeping these online, healthy, and performant.

Of course, there are many ways to implement this, and the team structure and development process for any two companies will differ in the details. But, this method of organizing self-reliant teams is *scalable*. This means we can grow a huge company around a huge application and still have an effective development process.

11.2.2 Independent microservices

To this point, the FlixTube application we have developed lives in a single code repository and has a single CD pipeline. You can see in figure 11.3 how this looks.

Using a so-called *mono* (monolithic) *repo* (monorepo) is a great way to get started when working on any new microservices project. It makes the bootstrapping process simpler and easier, and we'll spend much less time creating and maintaining our *development infrastructure* (the infrastructure that supports our development process).

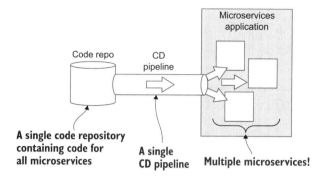

Figure 11.3   When starting a new microservices application, it is simpler to have a single code repository and a single CD pipeline for the entire application.

Having a monorepo and a single CD pipeline makes things easier at the start, but unfortunately, it eliminates a major benefit of using microservices. Having a single repo and CD pipeline means that we have to release all microservices in lockstep. We don't actually have the ability to independently release updates to our microservices! This means that with each deployment, we risk breaking our entire application! This is a situation that's no better than having a monolith! Our deployment process is *monolithic*!

You might recall from way back in chapter 1 that we actually defined a microservice as *a small software process having its own independent deployment schedule* (see section 1.5). We haven't actually achieved that yet, and to gain the most benefit from using microservices, we really have to make those independently deployable. How this should look is indicated in figure 11.4.

Having separate code repositories and multiple CD pipelines allows more granular control over our deployments. If we can independently update our microservices one at a time, then we have a much lower deployment risk. Instead of breaking our entire application with each deployment, we only risk breaking a single microservice.

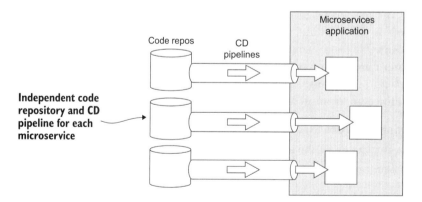

Figure 11.4   As we grow our application, we'll need to split our microservices out to separate code repositories and CD pipelines to gain the benefit that comes with independently deployable microservices.

If changing to multiple repos and CD pipelines seems like a huge amount of work and too much additional complexity, I completely sympathize with you! In fact, I'd argue that this one thing is responsible for much of the perceived complexity normally attributed to microservices.

At this point, I'd like to reiterate that having a monorepo and a single CD pipeline *is* still a good way to start any new microservices application. It keeps things simple in the early days of development. Once you convert to multiple code repositories and multiple CD pipelines, it becomes more complex to manage and maintain, at least at the application level. That just comes with the territory.

Even though our application as a whole will ultimately become incredibly complex (this is inevitable for modern enterprise applications), if we can switch our perspective down to a single microservice, the picture looks very different. Things suddenly seem a lot simpler. Because the complexity gets added slowly, it is more manageable. And by focusing on individual microservices (which are simple) rather than focusing on the whole application (which is bound to be complex), the overall complexity of the application becomes much less impactful.

This is what actually saves the day for complexity in microservices applications. An individual microservice is a tiny and easily understood application with a small codebase. It has a relatively simple deployment process. Each microservice is simple and easy to manage, even though these work together to build powerful and complex applications. This change of perspective from complex application to simple microservice is important for managing complexity.

Splitting our development process into microservice-sized chunks adds some additional complexity, but it pales in comparison to how complex our application may eventually become. By redirecting our focus from whole application complexity to individual microservices, we have essentially freed our application to scale to truly enormous proportions, even when each and every microservice remains just as simple to work with as it ever was.

Don't be too enthusiastic about making this change to independently deployable microservices, however. If you make this change too early, you might find that you are paying for the cost of the transition at a time when it's still too early to gain benefit from it. You don't want to pay the cost before you can make use of the benefit.

Good software development is all about making good trade-offs. Stick with a monorepo and a single CD pipeline for as long as that makes sense for you. But be aware that it's *not* supposed to be this way. As your application grows more complex and as you grow your team, this simple approach eventually breaks down. There comes a point when splitting our deployment pipelines is necessary to scale up, while maintaining a productive development process.

11.2.3 *Splitting the code repository*

Our first task is to split our monorepo into multiple code repositories so that we have a distinct and separate repository for every microservice. Each new repo will contain the code for a single microservice and the code for deploying it to production.

We also need a separate code repository for the Terraform code that creates our infrastructure. This is the code that creates our container registry and Kubernetes cluster. This code doesn't belong to any particular microservice, so it needs its own code repository.

Figure 11.5 illustrates how we can take our FlixTube project from chapter 9 and break it up into multiple code repositories. To build each new repo, we invoke `git init` to create a blank repo, then copy the code into the new repo and commit it. Otherwise, we might want to take the extra steps required to preserve our existing version history (see the following sidebar).

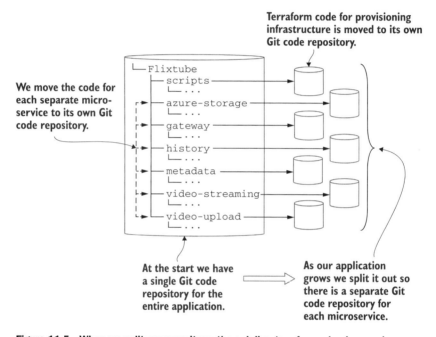

Figure 11.5   When we split our repository, the subdirectory for each microservice becomes its own separate Git repository.

Preserving the version history

When creating new code repositories from old ones, we can use the command `git filter-branch` with the `--subdirectory-filter` argument to save our existing version history. To so this, see the Git documentation for details:

https://git-scm.com/docs/git-filter-branch

You can also search the web for examples of "filter-branch"—there are many!

11.2.4 *Splitting the continuous delivery (CD) pipeline*

Splitting apart our monorepo is fairly easy. At the same time, we must also split our monolithic CD pipeline and this is a more difficult task. We now need to create a separate deployment pipeline for each microservice.

Fortunately, we can create a single microservice deployment pipeline and then reuse it for every microservice (if necessary, making small changes for the custom requirements of each microservice). Our per-microservice CD pipeline will independently deploy a single microservice, triggered automatically when updated code is pushed to the microservice's hosted code repository. Figure 11.6 illustrates this process.

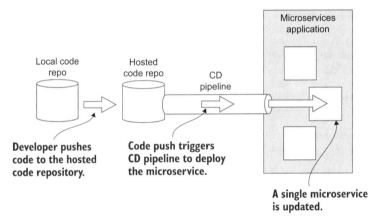

Figure 11.6   Pushing code to the hosted code repository for a microservice triggers the CD pipeline, which deploys a single microservice.

The Terraform code for the deployment of a single microservice is like the code we saw in chapter 9; indeed, it is a cut-down version of that code. We can develop this Terraform code using an iterative process like we did throughout chapters 6 and 7. Once we are happy that the deployment pipeline works for a single microservice, we can copy it into the code repo for every microservice—with the code parameterized by name for each microservice.

Each code repository then needs to have its pipeline enabled and configured. If you are using Bitbucket Pipelines for your CD like we did in chapters 7 and 9, you can enable it for each repository as shown in section 7.7.2. Then you must add a separate configuration file for each repository as illustrated in figure 11.7.

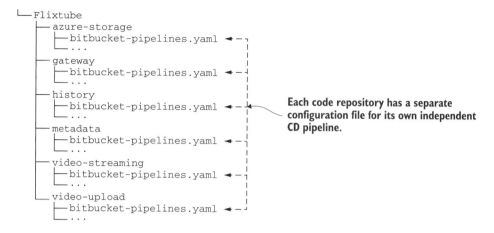

Each code repository has a separate configuration file for its own independent CD pipeline.

Figure 11.7   The code repository for each microservice has its own separate configuration for continuous delivery (CD).

EXTRACTING DOCKER BUILDS FROM TERRAFORM

At this point, we can revisit how we do Docker builds. We are now able to extract these from the Terraform code. If you remember from chapter 7, we kept things simple by having our entire deployment process performed within Terraform.

Actually, that's not 100% true; I didn't mention it at the time, but doing everything within Terraform was a necessary workaround due to how we created all of our infrastructure within Terraform in the first place. This included the creation of our container registry. If we had tried to extract Docker from Terraform, we'd have found that on the first deployment, we couldn't push our images to the container registry because it hadn't yet been created!

This catch-22 situation is not helped by the fact that the Docker provider for Terraform does not support building and publishing Docker images (seriously, it should be upgraded to support this properly). This is why we were forced to use `local-exec` and `null_resource` in Terraform as a kind of ugly hack (see section 7.6.2 for a reminder).

Things are different now though. We've separated our Terraform code into multiple repositories, and our infrastructure code has been separated from our microservices code. In between creating our infrastructure and deploying our microservices, we can build and publish our Docker images simply by invoking Docker directly within the continuous delivery (CD) pipeline (using the `build` and `push` commands that we learned in chapter 3).

We can create a single configuration and then reuse it as a template for each microservice. Our "single microservice" configuration for Bitbucket Pipelines is shown in listing 11.1. We have two steps in this deployment process. The first step directly uses Docker to build and publish the image for the microservice. The second step uses Terraform to deploy the microservice to our Kubernetes cluster.

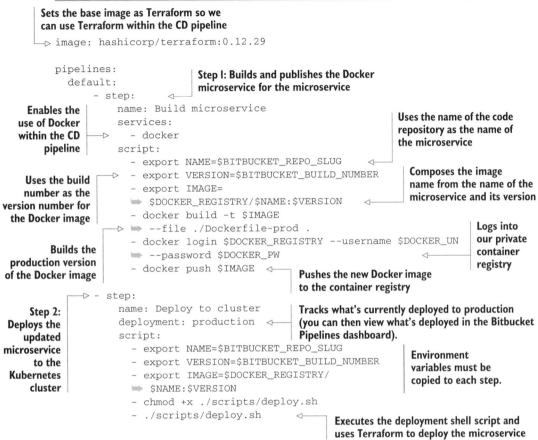

Listing 11.1 Bitbucket Pipelines configuration file for a single microservice (bitbucket-pipelines.yaml)

Sets the base image as Terraform so we can use Terraform within the CD pipeline

```
image: hashicorp/terraform:0.12.29

pipelines:
    default:
        - step:                          ← Step I: Builds and publishes the Docker
            name: Build microservice         microservice for the microservice
            services:
              - docker
            script:
              - export NAME=$BITBUCKET_REPO_SLUG        ←
              - export VERSION=$BITBUCKET_BUILD_NUMBER
              - export IMAGE=
                  $DOCKER_REGISTRY/$NAME:$VERSION       ←
              - docker build -t $IMAGE
                  --file ./Dockerfile-prod .
              - docker login $DOCKER_REGISTRY --username $DOCKER_UN
                  --password $DOCKER_PW
              - docker push $IMAGE        ←
        - step:
            name: Deploy to cluster
            deployment: production        ←
            script:
              - export NAME=$BITBUCKET_REPO_SLUG
              - export VERSION=$BITBUCKET_BUILD_NUMBER
              - export IMAGE=$DOCKER_REGISTRY/
                  $NAME:$VERSION
              - chmod +x ./scripts/deploy.sh
              - ./scripts/deploy.sh        ←
```

Enables the use of Docker within the CD pipeline

Uses the build number as the version number for the Docker image

Builds the production version of the Docker image

Step 2: Deploys the updated microservice to the Kubernetes cluster

Uses the name of the code repository as the name of the microservice

Composes the image name from the name of the microservice and its version

Logs into our private container registry

Pushes the new Docker image to the container registry

Tracks what's currently deployed to production (you can then view what's deployed in the Bitbucket Pipelines dashboard).

Environment variables must be copied to each step.

Executes the deployment shell script and uses Terraform to deploy the microservice

11.2.5 *The meta-repo*

Is using separate code repositories getting you down? Do you find yourself craving the simpler days of managing your application through a single code repository? Well, here's some good news.

We can create a *meta-repo* that ties together all our separate repositories into a single aggregate code repository. You can think of the meta-repo as a kind of virtual code repository. This means we can claw back some of the simplicity and convenience of the monorepo without sacrificing the flexibility and independence of having separate repositories. To create a meta-repo, we need the meta tool, available here:

- https://github.com/mateodelnorte/meta

A meta-repo is configured by creating a .meta configuration file that lists a collection of separate repositories. See figure 11.8 for an example of where a .meta file would live in relation to the FlixTube project. Listing 11.2 shows the structure of this file.

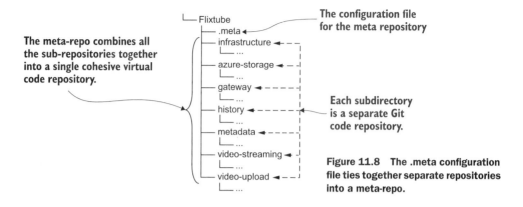

Figure 11.8 The .meta configuration file ties together separate repositories into a meta-repo.

Listing 11.2 Configuring FlixTube's meta code repository (.meta)

```
{
  "projects": {
    "gateway": "git@bitbucket.org:bootstrappingmicroservices/gateway.git",
    "azure-storage": "git@bitbucket.org:bootstrappingmicroservices/
      azure-storage.git",
    "video-streaming": "git@bitbucket.org:bootstrappingmicroservices/
      video-streaming.git",
    "video-upload": "git@bitbucket.org:bootstrappingmicroservices/
      video-upload.git",
    "history": "git@bitbucket.org:bootstrappingmicroservices/history.git"
    "metadata": "git@bitbucket.org:bootstrappingmicroservices/
      metadata.git",
  }

}
```
Lists the separate code repositories that comprise this meta-repo

> **NOTE** In the listing, the code repos link to Bitbucket code repositories, but these could just as easily be GitHub repositories or link to anywhere else where we host our code repositories.

Using meta allows us to run single Git commands that affect the entire collection of repositories. For example, let's say we'd like to pull code changes for all the microservices under the FlixTube project at once. We can use meta to do that with a single command:

```
meta git pull
```

We are still working with separate code repositories, but meta allows us to invoke commands simultaneously against multiple code repositories at once, so that it feels much like we are back to working with a monorepo.

Meta gives us a lot of additional flexibility. We can use it to create our own custom sets of microservices. As a developer on a big team, you can create a meta-repo just for the set of microservices that you normally work on. Other developers can have their own separate meta-repos. You might even like to create multiple meta-repos so that you can easily switch between different sets of microservices, depending on what you are currently working on.

As a team leader, you can create separate meta-repos for different configurations of your application, each with its own Docker Compose file. This makes it easy for your team members to clone the code for a complete set of microservices. Then they can use Docker Compose to boot that application configuration. This is a great way to provide an "instant" and manageable development environment for team members!

11.2.6 *Creating multiple environments*

As we gain customers for our application, it becomes important that we buffer them against problems from ongoing "work in progress" or protect them from new features that are partially completed or only partially tested. The development team needs a production-like environment in which to test their code before putting it in front of customers.

Each developer must test their code on their development workstation, but that's not enough. They must also test their code once it is integrated with changes from other developers. To make it as "real" as possible, this testing should be done in a production-like environment—just not the one that our customer is using!

We need a workflow for our developers to take their changes on a journey from development workstation, through an integration environment, into a test environment, and finally, once all the tests have passed, on to the customer-facing environment. Although no two companies will have exactly the same workflow, you can see what a typical workflow looks like in figure 11.9.

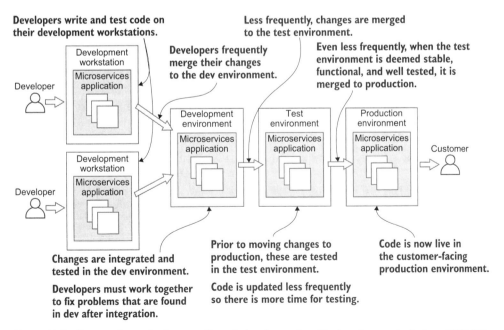

Figure 11.9   Progressing code changes, through development and test environments, before getting to production

Setting up multiple environments is actually simple, and we already have most of what we need in our existing Terraform code that was presented in chapter 9. We had already parameterized our code with an app_name variable that we used to create separate application resources based on the name we assigned to it (revisit section 6.10 where we first added this variable).

We could now use app_name (set from the command line) when invoking Terraform to create different instances of FlixTube for testing and production. We just need to provide different names for each instance. For example, we could set app_name to flixtube-development, flixtube-test, or flixtube-production to create our separate environments.

We can improve on this, though, as in listing 11.3. We can make it simpler to create new environments by introducing a new variable called environment. We then convert app_name to a computed local variable that depends on the value of environment.

Listing 11.3 Setting the app_name local variable to the environment name in Terraform (an update to chapter-9/example-1/scripts/variables.tf)

```
variable "environment" {}
```
Adds a new Terraform variable that specifies the current environment. We need to provide this when running Terraform via the command line, setting it to development, test, or production, for example.

```
locals {

  app_name = "flixtube-${var.environment}"

}
```
Creates a local variable for "app_name" that builds separate versions of the application for each environment (e.g., flixtube-development, flixtube-test, or flixtube-production).

Introducing this new variable (environment) allows us to set the current environment from the command line. Listing 11.4 shows how we input a value from another variable called ENVIRONMENT.

We can reuse the same Terraform project to create as many separate environments as we like, all hosted in the same cloud account but differentiated by name (e.g., flixtube-development, flixtube-test, or flixtube-production). You can use this to create a workflow like that in figure 11.9 or something even more sophisticated, depending on what you need.

Listing 11.4 Updated deployment script to set the environment (an update to chapter-9/example-1/scripts/deploy.sh)

```
cd ./scripts
terraform init
terraform apply -auto-approve \
    -var "app_version=$VERSION" \
    -var "client_id=$ARM_CLIENT_ID" \
    -var "client_secret=$ARM_CLIENT_SECRET" \
    -var "environment=$ENVIRONMENT" \
    -var "storage_account_name=$STORAGE_ACCOUNT_NAME" \
    -var "storage_access_key=$STORAGE_ACCESS_KEY" \
```
Parameterizes our Terraform code by the environment name. We pass in the name of the environment being deployed through an OS environment variable.

11.2.7 *Production workflow*

We can now create multiple environments and use them to stitch together a testing workflow to protect our customers against broken code. The remaining question is, how do we trigger the deployment for any particular environment? This is simpler than you might think.

We can use separate branches in our code repository to target deployments to different environments. Figure 11.10 shows an example setup for this. It's a fairly simple branching strategy, but there are more sophisticated versions in the wild.

Our development team works in the development branch. When they push code to that branch, it triggers a CD pipeline that deploys to the development environment. This allows our whole team to integrate and test their changes frequently, together in a production-like environment.

How frequently should the developers push code changes? As often as possible! Once per day, if not multiple times per day. The less time we have between code merges, the less we'll see errors caused by conflicting changes and bad integrations. This is the idea behind *continuous integration*, an important practice that underpins continuous delivery (CD).

Less frequently (say once per week), we'll merge from the development branch to the test branch. This triggers the deployment to the test environment. Code merges from development to test are less frequent, and this gives us time to test, fix problems, and stabilize the code before we hand it over to our customers.

Finally, when the code in the test branch is good to go (say every 1-2 weeks), we then merge it to the production branch. This deploys updated microservices to

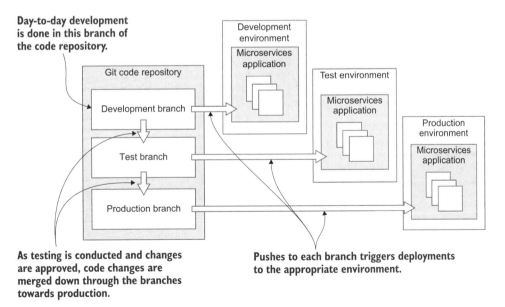

Figure 11.10 Code from development, test, and production branches is automatically deployed to the appropriate environment.

production so that our customers can get their hands on whatever awesome new features and bug fixes we've added.

This workflow can be applied with or without automated testing. It gives plenty of room for testing and allows managers to make a conscious decision to deploy to production. Of course, automated testing makes this so much better and much more scalable! If an automated test fails at any point in the workflow, the deployment is automatically not allowed. When such problems occur, the team must work together to rectify the situation. The addition of good automated testing means we can safely ramp up our deployment frequency, to the point where many modern companies deploy to production on a daily basis.

If we use Bitbucket Pipelines, we can easily configure separate CD pipelines for each branch as listing 11.5 shows. This version of the bitbucket-pipelines.yaml configuration file includes separate sections for each branch. Each section is essentially the same, but we can wire through separate environment variables to configure which production environment is used to deploy each branch.

Listing 11.5   Configuring separate CD pipelines for each branch (bitbucket-pipelines.yaml)

```
image: hashicorp/terraform:0.12.6

pipelines:
  branches:                          ◁────┐ Creates separate CD pipelines for
    development:                           │ each branch in our Git repository
      - step:
          name: Build microservice
          script:
              # ... Commands to build and publish the microservice ...
      - step:                        ◁──┐
          name: Deploy cluster          │ Deploys to the development environment
          script:
              # ... Commands to deploy the microservice to the
                    dev environment ...
    test:
      - step:
          name: Build microservice
          script:
              # ... Commands to build and publish the microservice ...
      - step:                        ◁──┐
          name: Deploy cluster          │ Deploys to the test environment
          script:
              # ... Commands to deploy the microservice to the
                    test environment ...
    production:                       ◁────┐ Configures the pipeline for
      - step:                              │ the production branch
          name: Build microservice
          script:
              # ... Commands to build and publish the microservice ...
      - step:                        ◁──┐
          name: Deploy cluster          │ Deploys to the production environment
```

Configures the pipeline for the development branch

Configures the pipeline for the test branch

```
script:
   # ... Commands to deploy the microservice to the
            prod environment ...
```

One thing to pay attention to when you implement this multi-branch/multi-environment strategy is that each environment needs its own separate Terraform state. We first configured a Terraform backend for CD in section 7.7.4. Back then, we hard coded the connection to Azure storage in the Terraform file backend.tf. We must change this now so that we can set the storage configuration from the command line. We'll then change it for each separate environment.

To start with, we must remove the key field from our backend configuration as shown in the following listing. This is the value that we need to vary, depending on the environment. We'll set it as a command-line argument rather than hard code it.

Listing 11.6 Configuring backend storage for Terraform state with multiple environments (an update to chapter-9/example-1/scripts/backend.tf)

```
terraform {
    backend "azurerm" {

        resource_group_name  = "terraform"
        storage_account_name = "terraform"    ◁
        container_name       = "terraform"


    }
}
```

> You'll have to choose a different name for your storage account. This is a globally unique name so you won't be able to choose terraform.

Configures the backend as in chapter 7, but we remove the "key" field, which we now set separately for each environment.

Now, we can configure the key field for the Terraform backend from the command line as shown in listing 11.7. Essentially, what we do is to tell Terraform to store its state configuration in a file whose name is different, depending on the current environment being deployed. For example, it could be called terraform-development.tfstate for the file that tracks the state of the development environment, and terraform-test .tfstate and terraform-production.tfstate for the other two environments.

Listing 11.7 Updated deployment script to set the backend configuration based on the environment (an update to chapter-9/example-1/scripts/deploy.sh)

```
cd ./scripts
terraform init \
    -backend-config=
   ➥ "key=terraform-${ENVIRONMENT}.tfstate"    ◁
terraform apply -auto-approve \
    -var "app_version=$VERSION" \
    -var "client_id=$ARM_CLIENT_ID" \
    -var "client_secret=$ARM_CLIENT_SECRET" \
    -var "environment=$ENVIRONMENT" \
    -var "storage_account_name=$STORAGE_ACCOUNT_NAME" \
    -var "storage_access_key=$STORAGE_ACCESS_KEY" \
```

> Initializes the "key" field of the backend configuration for the environment we are currently deploying

11.3   Scaling performance

Not only can we scale microservices applications to larger development teams, we can also scale these up for better performance. Our application can then have a higher capacity and can handle a larger workload.

Using microservices gives us granular control over the performance of our application. We can easily measure the performance of our microservices (for an example, see figure 11.11) to find the ones that are performing poorly, overworked, or overloaded at times of peak demand.

If using a monolith, however, we would have limited control over performance. We could vertically scale the monolith, but that's basically it. Horizontally scaling a monolith is much more difficult. And we simply can't independently scale any of the "parts" of a monolith. This is a bad situation because it might only be a small part of the monolith that causes the performance problem. Yet, we would have to vertically scale the entire monolith to fix it! Vertically scaling a large monolith can be an expensive proposition.

Instead, with microservices, we have numerous options for scaling. We can independently fine-tune the performance of small parts of our system to eliminate bottlenecks and to get the right mix of performance outcomes. There are many advanced ways we could tackle performance issues, but in this section, we'll overview the following (relatively) simple techniques for scaling our microservices application:

- Vertically scaling the entire cluster
- Horizontally scaling the entire cluster
- Horizontally scaling individual microservices
- Elastically scaling the entire cluster
- Elastically scaling individual microservices
- Scaling the database

Scaling often requires risky configuration changes to our cluster. Don't try to make any of these changes directly to a production cluster that your customers or staff are depending on. At the end of this section, we'll briefly look at *blue-green deployment*, a technique that helps us manage large infrastructure changes with much less risk.

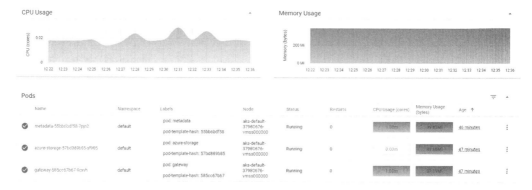

Figure 11.11   Viewing CPU and memory usage for microservices in the Kubernetes dashboard

11.3.1 *Vertically scaling the cluster*

As we grow our application, we might come to a point where our cluster generally doesn't have enough compute, memory, or storage to run our application. As we add new microservices (or replicate existing microservices for redundancy), we will eventually max out the nodes in our cluster. (We can monitor this in the Azure portal or the Kubernetes dashboard.) At this point, we must increase the total amount of resources available to our cluster. When scaling microservices on a Kubernetes cluster, we can just as easily make use of either vertical or horizontal scaling.

Figure 11.12 shows what vertical scaling looks like for Kubernetes. We scale up our cluster by increasing the size of the virtual machines (VMs) in the node pool. We might start with three small-sized VMs and then increase their size so that we now have three large-sized VMs. We haven't changed the number of VMs; we've just increased their size.

In listing 11.8, we change the vm_size field from Standard_B2ms to Standard_B4ms. This upgrades the size of each VM in our Kubernetes node pool. Instead of two CPUs, we now have four (one for each VM). Memory and hard-drive are also increased. You can compare Azure VM sizes for yourself here:

- https://docs.microsoft.com/en-us/azure/virtual-machines/sizes-b-series-burstable

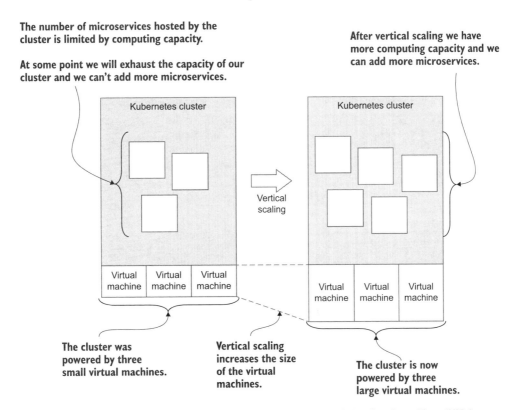

Figure 11.12 Vertically scaling your cluster by increasing the size of the virtual machines (VMs)

We still only have a single VM in our cluster, but we have increased the size of it. Scaling our cluster is as simple as a code change. Again we see power of infrastructure-as-code, the technique where we store our infrastructure configuration as code and make changes to our infrastructure by committing code changes that trigger our CD pipeline.

> **Listing 11.8   Vertically scaling the cluster with Terraform (an update to chapter-9/example-1/scripts/kubernetes-cluster.tf)**

```
default_node_pool {
    name = "default"
    node_count = 1
    vm_size = "Standard_B4ms"        ⟵──┐ Sets a bigger VM for each
}                                         of the nodes in the cluster
```

11.3.2 *Horizontally scaling the cluster*

In addition to vertically scaling our cluster, we can also scale it horizontally. Our VMs can remain the same size, but we simply add more of these. By adding more VMs to our cluster, we spread the load of our application across more computers.

Figure 11.13 illustrates how we can take our cluster from three VMs up to six. The size of each VM remains the same, but we gain more computing power by having more VMs.

Listing 11.9 shows the code change we need to make to add more VMs to our node pool. Back in listing 11.8, we had `node_count` set to 1, but here we have changed it to 6! Note that we have reverted the `vm_size` field to the smaller size of `Standard_B2ms`.

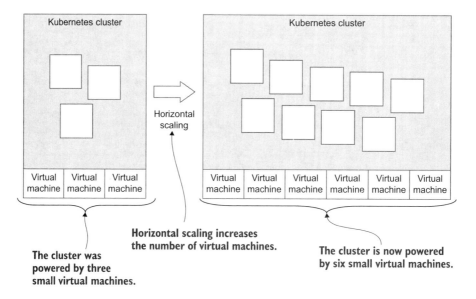

Figure 11.13   Horizontally scaling your cluster by increasing the number of VMs

In this example, we increase the number of VMs, but not their size; although, there is nothing stopping us from increasing both the number and the size of our VMs. Generally, though, we might prefer horizontal scaling because it is less expensive than vertical scaling. That's because using many smaller VMs is cheaper than using fewer but bigger and higher-priced VMs.

> **Listing 11.9 Horizontal scaling the cluster with Terraform (update to chapter-9/ example-1/scripts/kubernetes-cluster.tf)**

```
default_node_pool {
    name = "default"
    node_count = 6              ◁——————  Increases the size of the node pool to 6.
    vm_size = "Standard_B2ms"            The cluster is now powered by six VMs!
}
```

11.3.3 *Horizontally scaling an individual microservice*

Assuming our cluster is scaled to an adequate size to host all the microservices with good performance, what do we do when individual microservices become overloaded? (This can be monitored in the Kubernetes dashboard.)

The answer is that for any microservice that becomes a performance bottleneck, we can horizontally scale it to distribute its load over multiple instances. This is shown in figure 11.14. We are effectively giving more compute, memory, and storage to this particular microservice so that it can handle a bigger workload.

Again, we can make this change using code. In fact, we already did this in listing 10.2 from chapter 10. A snippet of the code is repeated again here in listing 11.10.

We'll set the `replicas` field to 3. In chapter 10, we made this change for redundancy. Having multiple instances means that when any single instance fails the others can temporarily pick up its load while it restarts. Here we make the same change to

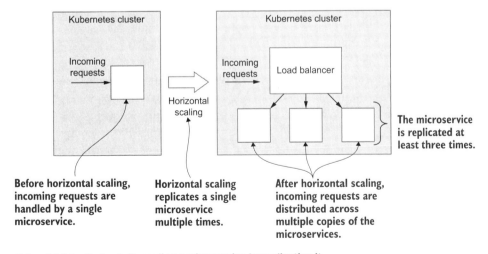

Figure 11.14 Horizontally scaling a microservice by replicating it

the `replicas` field, but this time for performance reasons. Often, we need to make this change for both reasons. We'd like to have redundancy and good performance, and this is solved by creating replicas of our microservices where necessary.

Listing 11.10 Horizontally scaling a microservice with Terraform (an update to chapter-9/example-1/scripts/modules/microservice/main.tf)

```
spec {
    replicas = 3              ◁──────────   Sets the number of replicas for the microservice
                                            to 3. We can now distribute load evenly among
    selector {                              three instances of this microservice.
        match_labels = {
            pod = var.service_name
        }
    }

    template {
        metadata {
            labels = {
                pod = var.service_name
            }
        }

        spec {
            container {
                image = local.image_tag
                name  = var.service_name

                env {
                    name = "PORT"
                    value = "80"
                }
            }
        }
    }
}
```

11.3.4 *Elastic scaling for the cluster*

Moving into even more advanced territory, we can now think about *elastic scaling*, which is a technique where we automatically and dynamically scale our cluster to meet varying levels of demand. At periods of low demand, Kubernetes can automatically deallocate resources that aren't needed. At periods of high demand, it can allocate new resources to meet the increased load. This makes for substantial cost savings because, at any given moment, we only pay for the resources that we need to handle the load on our application at that time.

We can use elastic scaling at the cluster level to automatically grow our cluster when it's nearing its resource limits. Yet again, this is just a code change. Listing 11.11 shows how we can enable the Kubernetes autoscaler and set the minimum and maximum size of our node pool.

You can update the Terraform code in scripts/kubernetes-cluster.tf (from example-1 in chapter 9) from the code in listing 11.11 to enable horizontal scaling for the FlixTube Kubernetes cluster. The scaling works by default, but there are many ways we can customize it. Search for "auto_scaler_profile" in the Terraform documentation to learn more:

https://www.terraform.io/docs/providers/azurerm/r/kubernetes_cluster.html

---

Listing 11.11 Enabling elastic scaling for the cluster with Terraform(an update to chapter-9/example-1/scripts/kubernetes-cluster.tf)

```
default_node_pool {
    name = "default"
    vm_size = "Standard_B2ms"          Enables Kubernetes cluster autoscaling

    enable_auto_scaling = true    ◁─┐   Sets the minimum node count to 3.
                                      This cluster starts with three VMs.
    min_count = 3                 ◁

    max_count = 20                ◁─┐   Sets the maximum node count to 20.
}                                     This cluster can automatically scale
                                      up to 20 VMs to meet demand.
```

11.3.5 *Elastic scaling for an individual microservice*

We can also enable elastic scaling at the individual microservice level. Listing 11.12 is a sample of Terraform code that can give a microservice a "burstable" capability. The number of replicas for the microservice is expanded and contracted dynamically to meet the varying workload for the microservice (bursts of activity).

You can add the code in listing 11.12 to the end of the Terraform code in the scripts/modules/microservice/main.tf file from example-1 in chapter 9. Then, to enable elastic scaling for FlixTube microservices, invoke `terraform apply`. The scaling works by default, but can be customized to use other metrics. See the Terraform documentation to learn more:

www.terraform.io/docs/providers/kubernetes/r/horizontal_pod_autoscaler.html

To learn more about pod auto scaling in Kubernetes, see the Kubernetes docs at:

https://kubernetes.io/docs/tasks/run-application/horizontal-pod-autoscale/

Listing 11.12 Enabling elastic scaling for a microservice with Terraform (an addition to chapter-9/example-1/scripts/modules/microservice/main.tf)

```
resource "kubernetes_horizontal_pod_autoscaler" "service_autoscaler" {
  metadata {
    name = var.service_name
  }
                              Sets the range of instances for this microservice.
  spec {                      It starts at 3 instances and can scale up to 20 to
    min_replicas = 3          meet variable levels of demand.
    max_replicas = 20
```

```
      scale_target_ref {
        kind = "Deployment"
        name = var.service_name
      }
    }
  }
```

11.3.6 *Scaling the database*

The last kind of scaling we'll look at is scaling our database. Back in chapter 4, you might remember we talked about the rule that *each microservice should have its own database* (see section 4.5.4).

There are multiple problems in sharing databases between microservices; one is that it severely limits our scalability. Consider the situation depicted in figure 11.15. We have multiple microservices sharing one database. This is a future scalability nightmare!

These microservices are not independent. The shared database is a fixed integration point among these, and it can become a serious performance bottleneck. If microservices share data, these will be tightly coupled. This severely limits our ability to restructure and refactor in the future. By sharing databases, we are hampering our own future ability to address performance problems.

This scenario can completely destroy the "easy" scaling that we've worked so hard to achieve. If we want to structure our application like this, we might as well not be using microservices at all!

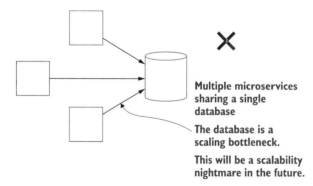

Multiple microservices sharing a single database

The database is a scaling bottleneck.

This will be a scalability nightmare in the future.

Figure 11.15 Why we don't share databases between microservices (except possibly for replicas of the same microservice)

Instead, our application should look like figure 11.16. Every microservice has its own separate database. These microservices are independent, and that means we can easily apply horizontal scaling if necessary.

At this point, I'd like to make it clear that just because we must have separate databases doesn't mean we also require separate database servers. There is a cost to managing database servers, and usually, we'd like to keep that cost down. It's perfectly OK to have a single database server that contains our separate databases as figure 11.17

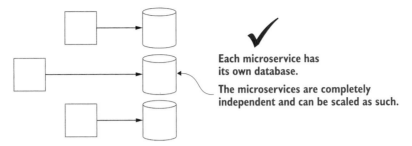

Figure 11.16   Each separate microservice should have its own database.

illustrates. Having just one database server for your whole application makes it simpler and cheaper to get started with microservices.

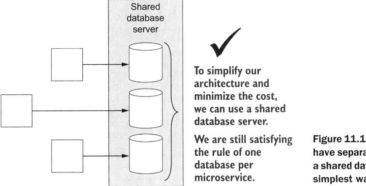

Figure 11.17   It's completely OK to have separate databases running on a shared database server (this is the simplest way to get started).

In the future, if we find that the workload for any particular database has grown too much, we can easily create a new database server and move that database to it as figure 11.18 shows. When needed, we can create dedicated servers for whichever of our databases need the extra compute, memory, or storage.

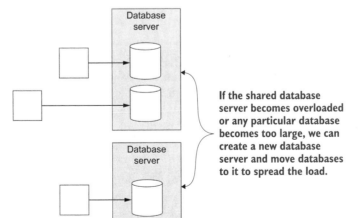

Figure 11.18   As your application grows larger, you can scale it by splitting out large databases into their own independent database servers.

Need an even more scalable database? We used MongoDB in this book, and it offers a database sharding feature (illustrated in figure 11.19). This allows us to distribute a single large database over multiple VMs. You might never need this level of scalability. It's only required for extremely large databases, but it's good to know we have this option if we ever need it.

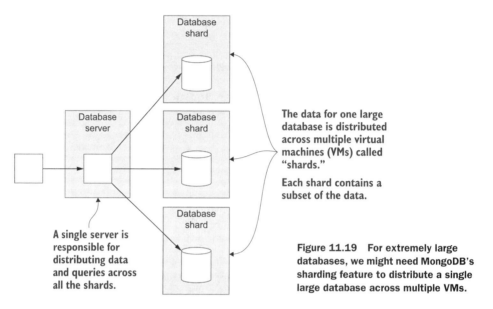

The data for one large database is distributed across multiple virtual machines (VMs) called "shards."

Each shard contains a subset of the data.

A single server is responsible for distributing data and queries across all the shards.

Figure 11.19   For extremely large databases, we might need MongoDB's sharding feature to distribute a single large database across multiple VMs.

11.3.7 Managing changes to infrastructure

Making changes to infrastructure is a risky business, and it needs to be well managed. Make a mistake with any of the scaling techniques you have just read about and you can bring down your entire cluster. It's best that we don't make these kinds of changes to customer-facing infrastructure, so in this section, I present a technique for keeping such risky changes at arm's length from our customers.

The technique is called *blue-green deployment*. We create two production environments and label these as *blue* and *green*. We can easily do this because in section 11.2.6, we parameterized our Terraform code to create different environments distinguished by name.

The first environment we create is labeled as the blue environment. Our customers use our application via our domain name (e.g., www.company.com). We then route them via DNS record to the blue environment. Now, to protect our customers, we'd prefer not to make any risky changes to the blue environment (regular and frequent updates to individual microservices are OK though, because that doesn't risk any impact to the infrastructure).

To make any risky or experimental changes (like experimenting with scaling), we create a whole new production infrastructure that we label as the green environment. Our developers now work in the green environment, so any work they do is separated from the blue environment that our customers use. This is shown in figure 11.20.

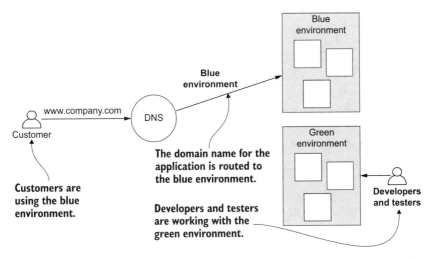

Figure 11.20 Customers use the blue environment, while developers and testers work with the green environment.

Once work on the green environment is completed, is tested, and is known to be working well, we can simply switch the DNS record from blue to green. Our customers can now use the green environment, and our developers and testers can change over to working with the blue environment. This is shown in figure 11.21.

Should any issue be discovered with the new green environment, we can simply flip the DNS switch back to the blue environment and restore working functionality for our customers. In the future, we can continue to flip between blue and green environments, thus keeping our customers protected from potentially risky changes to our infrastructure.

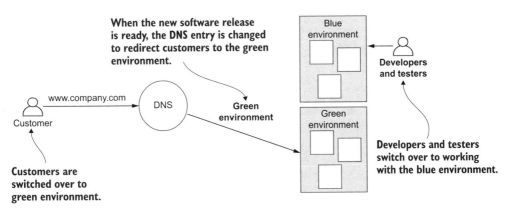

Figure 11.21 When the green environment is ready and tested, customers are switched over to it. Developers and testers then switch to the blue environment and continue working. When the blue environment is ready and tested, customers switch again, and the cycle continues.

11.4   Security

We have briefly talked about security at various points throughout the book. We haven't done it any justice though, because security is very important—even at the early stages of development. So much so that security really deserves its own book.

Well, thankfully, there is a great book on security specifically for microservices: *Microservices Security in Action* by Prabath Siriwardena and Nuwan Dias (Manning, 2020). For now though, let's understand some of the basics.

Every application needs some level of security. Even if your data is not sensitive, you don't want anyone to be able to fraudulently modify it. Even if your systems are not critical, you don't want an attacker to disrupt your system and processes.

We must make effective use of security techniques like authentication, authorization, and encryption to mitigate against malicious use of our application or data. We might also have to structure our data to protect the privacy and anonymity of our customers according to the regulations in our particular region. FlixTube doesn't have any of this yet, although, we have taken some care already with the following:

- *The only microservice exposed to the outside world (and, therefore, exposed to attack) is the gateway microservice.* This is by design! Our internal microservices are not directly accessible from outside our cluster.
- *Although, initially, we exposed our RabbitMQ server and MongoDB database to the world for early experimentation, we quickly closed those off.* We did this to prevent direct external access to these crucial resources. This is important! Don't expose such critical resources to the outside world unless you are 100% sure these are protected against attack.

In the future, we'd like to upgrade FlixTube with at least the following security features:

- An authentication system at the gateway.
- HTTPs for the connection with our customers. This will encrypt their communications, and using an external service like Cloudflare means you can get this online quickly.

Of course, the level of security needed by any given application is only as important as the systems and data we are trying to protect. The amount of security we add to Flix-Tube is going to be much less than the security that's needed by a banking application or government website.

Security has to come from both ends of the organization. Your company should have security policies and a strategy that meets the requirements of the domain and your customers. Then, you and every other developer have a role to play in thinking about and implementing security according to the standards of your company. We should be writing simple, yet secure code. And as with defensive programming (see section 10.4.2), we should adopt a defensive mindset when it comes to security.

First and foremost, when writing code and building microservices, we should ask how would someone attack this system? This primes our mind to proactively address security issues at the time when it can make the most difference: before we are attacked.

11.4.1 *Trust models*

FlixTube's needs are simple enough that we can adopt a security model of *internal trust*, also known as *trust the network* (depicted in figure 11.22). In this model, we do *all* the authentication at the entry point to the system (the *gateway microservice*). The microservices within the cluster all trust each other implicitly and rely on the security of the underlying network to protect them from external attack.

The internal trust model is a simple way to get started with microservices. Simple is often better than complicated when it comes to security because simple offers fewer places for security problems to hide. We must be careful when introducing more complex security, because any kind of added complexity can actually introduce security loopholes.

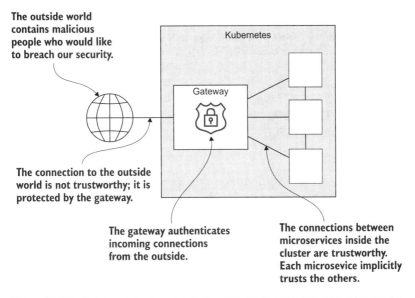

Figure 11.22   An internal trust model. Authentication is applied to external requests at the gateway. Internal microservices trust each other and communicate without authentication.

If your security needs are higher than FlixTube's, then the internal trust model might not be enough. This will also be the case if you have multiple clusters and you have microservices that need to communicate across clusters.

A more secure model that you should consider is called *trust nothing* or *zero trust* (depicted in figure 11.23). In the zero trust model, all connections between microservices—both internal and external—are authenticated. Microservices do *not*

**No connection inside or outside
the cluster is trusted.**

**We view every access point as
a potential violation of security.**

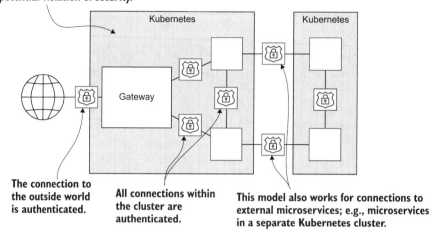

**The connection to
the outside world
is authenticated.**

**All connections within
the cluster are
authenticated.**

**This model also works for connections to
external microservices; e.g., microservices
in a separate Kubernetes cluster.**

**Figure 11.23   A trust nothing model. All connections, both internal and external, are
authenticated. This model supports connections to external microservices.**

automatically trust each other. We are making the assumption that any particular
microservice could be hijacked or compromised, especially if the microservice is hosted
externally in some other cluster.

11.4.2 *Sensitive configuration*

Any application has sensitive configuration data that needs to be protected. You might
remember in chapter 7 that we stored our Azure credentials in Bitbucket repository
variables (section 7.7.6). After splitting out the deployment code for infrastructure
and microservices at the start of this chapter (in section 11.2.3), we also needed a
place to store credentials for our private container registry.

As we build our application, there will be other passwords, tokens, and API keys
that we'll need to store *securely*. We could store any of this sensitive information in our
code, and that would certainly be convenient. But it means that anyone who has or
can get access to our code will also have access to operational information that can
easily be used to subvert or take down our application.

Bitbucket repository or account variables (or similar, depending on your CD provider) are a good way to store this information. You might, however, prefer to have a
solution that's independent of your source control or CD provider. For that scenario,
Kubernetes has its own storage solution for secret configuration. You can read about it
here:

- https://kubernetes.io/docs/concepts/configuration/secret/

If that doesn't suit your needs, there are various other products that can help. As an example, you might like to learn more about Vault, another open source product from Hashicorp (the developers of Terraform). Find out more at

- https://www.vaultproject.io/

11.5 *Refactoring to microservices*

Way back in chapter 1 (section 1.1), I promised that after learning how to build a microservices application from scratch, that we'd eventually come back and discuss more on how to refactor an existing monolith to microservices. How we go about converting a monolith will be different in the details for any given monolith. There are so many ways we could go about this, but in this section, I'll leave you with some basic strategies and tactics for conversion that anyone can use.

The basic idea is the same as any development process. As was introduced in chapter 2 (section 2.4), it's all about iteration, small and simple changes, and keeping the code working as you go (illustrated in figure 11.24).

Conversion of a monolith is a huge job (depending on the size and complexity of the monolith), and a *big bang* conversion is unlikely to be successful. The only safe way to get to the other side is through small and manageable chunks of work, with extremely thorough testing along the way.

We can't just stop working on the product either. We still have a responsibility to add the features and fix the bugs that are requested by the business. It's also essential that we keep the product working; we just can't let problems build up.

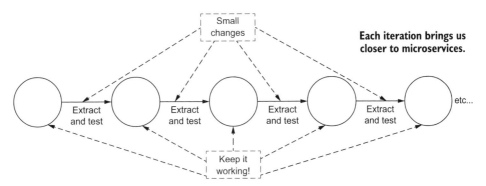

Figure 11.24   **Refactoring a monolith to microservices can only be done in an iterative sequence of small and well-tested steps.**

DO YOU REALLY NEED MICROSERVICES?

Before you start converting your monolith to microservices, you really need to ask: *are microservices really necessary?* The conversion to microservices is likely to be long and difficult. It will introduce significant complexity, and it will test the patience and resolve of your development team.

- Is it really worth the cost of doing the conversion?
- Do you really need to scale?
- Do you really need the flexibility of microservices?

These are important questions. Make sure you have good answers.

PLAN YOUR CONVERSION AND INVOLVE EVERYONE

You can't simply strike out toward microservices in the dark! To stand the best chance of success, you need a documented vision about what your product will look like when you arrive.

Use *domain driven design* (DDD) to model your business as microservices (see the end of this chapter for a book reference). Aim for a simple architecture. Plan for the immediate future and not for the far off uncertain future. Work backward from your architectural vision to what you have now. This is the sequence of changes you must make to convert to microservices. This doesn't have to be planned in detail, but you do need a general idea of where you are going.

We need a vision of what we are building, an idea of how we are going to get there, and an understanding of why this is important. Plans always change. As they say, "a battle plan never survives contact with the enemy" (paraphrased from Helmuth von Moltke, the Elder). But this doesn't mean we shouldn't plan! Instead, we should be planning to allow for change to occur naturally during the process as we learn more about how our application should be structured. And we should revisit and revise our plan, updating it so that it remains relevant for as long as we follow the plan.

The conversion plan should be created together with the team (or a subset of representatives) because implementing this conversion will be a shared and difficult exercise. You need to have everyone invested in it.

It's not enough just to have made a plan. Now you must communicate it to the wider company. Make sure the developers know what's expected of them. Communicate with other business departments, describing it in a language that's meaningful to them, so they know why this is taking place and the value it brings. Everyone, absolutely everyone, must understand the high stakes of this operation!

KNOW YOUR LEGACY CODE

Before and during the conversion, you should invest significant time getting to know your monolith. Create test plans. Conduct experiments. Understand its failure modes. Develop an idea of what parts of it are going to break through each step of the conversion.

IMPROVE YOUR AUTOMATION

Good automation is crucial to any microservice project. Before and during the conversion, you should be constantly investing in and improving your automation. If you aren't already on top of your infrastructure and automation, you need to start working on it right away (even before starting the conversion!). You might find that changing your company's mindset around automation is actually the *most* difficult part of this process.

You need reliable and fast automated deployment (chapters 6 and 7). Any features that you convert should either have automated testing already, or you should implement automated testing with good coverage while you are converting the feature to microservices (chapter 8).

With microservices, you can't get away from automation. *If you can't afford to invest in automation, you probably can't afford to convert to microservices.*

BUILD YOUR MICROSERVICES PLATFORM

Before the conversion starts, you need a platform on which you can host newly created microservices. You need a production environment to host microservices as these are incrementally extracted from your monolith (as shown in figure 11.25).

In this book, you have the recipe to build one such platform. Create a private container registry and create your Kubernetes cluster according to chapters 6 and 7. After creating your first microservice, now create a shared template for your team: a blank microservice that can be the starting point for every other microservice. If you have different types of microservices, create multiple templates, one for each type.

Create your automated testing pipeline and make it easy for developers to use. Create documentation, examples, and tutorials so your developers can quickly understand how to create and deploy new microservices to your platform.

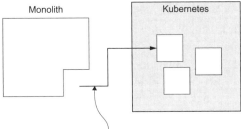

As you extract chunks of functionality from your monolith, instantiate these as microservices in your Kubernetes cluster.

Figure 11.25   Small chunks of your monolith can be incrementally extracted and moved into your Kubernetes cluster.

CARVE ALONG NATURAL SEAMS

Now look for existing components in your monolith that align with microservices in your architectural vision. These present great opportunities for chunk-by-chunk extraction of components from your monolith to microservices as figure 11.26 illustrates.

If you struggle to find natural seams, your job will be much more difficult. If your monolith is a *giant ball of mud* or full of *spaghetti code*, you may have to refactor first or refactor during extraction. Either way, it's going to be tricky. To be safe, your refactoring should be supported by automated testing. It will get messy—be prepared.

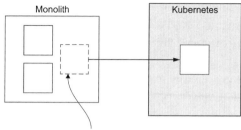

Your monolith will contain components that represent natural seams.

Look for components that are easy to carve out as separate microservices.

Figure 11.26   A monolith will usually have natural seams. Use these to identify individual components that can be incrementally extracted to microservices.

EXTRACT THE PARTS THAT CHANGE MOST FREQUENTLY

When deciding what order to convert components to microservices, prioritize those components that are changing the most. Having those parts of the monolith extracted early to microservices brings immediate and practical benefits, and you'll start to feel the impact straightaway. This early *bang for the buck* should make a measurable improvement to your development pace. It will reduce your deployment risk, and it can help you convince others that the conversion is going well.

AND REPEAT . . .

By repeatedly extracting small chunks to microservices and testing as we go, we'll safely convert our monolith to a microservices-based application (figure 11.27). It's not going to be easy. It will probably take a long time (multiple years, depending on the size and complexity of your monolith). But it is doable! We just have to keep chipping away at it, one small piece by one small piece, until the job is done.

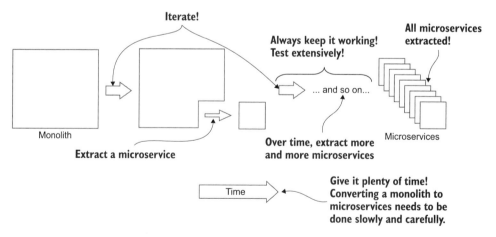

Figure 11.27   Iteratively extract small chunks of your monolith to microservices, always testing and keeping it working. Eventually, your application will be decomposed to microservices.

IT DOESN'T HAVE TO BE PERFECT

When we establish our architectural vision, we are aiming for what I call *the developer's utopia of microservices*. This is the place where we all want to live—*if only we could*. You have to be aware, though, that we aren't really aiming for some perfect instantiation of a microservices application. Sure, that would be nice. But honestly, it's probably not necessary to get all the way there.

Getting to perfection has a diminishing return on investment, and it's rarely going to be worthwhile to try and push all the way through to it. Besides, it's not possible to arrive at perfection because no one will ever agree completely on what that means. But it is still possible to move in that general direction and to make things much better along the way.

Every step on our journey to microservices should be selected to have a positive impact for our customers, our application, our development process, or our business. If at any time we find that continuing along the conversion is not delivering value, we must stop and reassess what we are doing.

Perhaps we are going about it the wrong way? Or, maybe we have now extracted all the value that is possible and pushing further ahead won't continue to improve things. This could leave us with a partially converted monolith, but so what? Whatever works for you is OK. We are all aiming for good outcomes for our business, and we shouldn't feel embarrassed at all about what it actually takes to achieve that, however it might look. If it does the job, it does the job. End of story.

A SPECTRUM OF POSSIBILITIES

As you can see in figure 11.28, there is an infinite spectrum of possibilities between the monolith and the developer's utopia of microservices. Who can say where on this continuum your application belongs? Certainly not me. Only you can decide that.

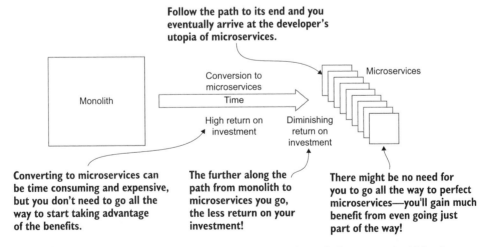

Figure 11.28   A timeline of conversion to microservices. In the early days, you get a high return on your investment (ROI). As you proceed, however, you'll get diminishing ROI, and it might not make sense to go all the way to the developer's utopia of microservices.

11.6   *Microservices on a budget*

Distributed architectures have always been a useful and powerful way to deliver complex applications. Microservices are popular now because of the current confluence and combination of cloud technologies, modern tools, and automation. This has made microservices more achievable and more cost-effective than ever before.

But a microservices application is still a complex thing to build. Even though each individual microservice is simple, you might struggle with the complexities of the application as a whole, especially if you are a small team, solo developer, or a lean startup.

Throughout this book, we have learned various tips and techniques that make it easier to learn microservices and get started with those. These will continue to help you in the future, should you need them. I present these insights here, again, in a more concise form.

- *Educate yourself to use modern tools and make the best use of those!* Rolling your own tools is time-consuming, difficult, and a distraction from what you should be doing: delivering features to your customers.
- *Start with a single code repository and a single continuous delivery (CD) pipeline.* Later, when you have separated out multiple code repositories, create one or more *meta-repos* to bring these back together (as outlined in section 11.2.5).
- *Use a single database server* that hosts one database per microservice.
- *Create a Kubernetes cluster with a single VM.* Create only a single instance for each microservice (no replicas). In the beginning, you probably don't need redundancy or performance. This helps keep costs down.
- *Use external file storage and an external database server, making your cluster effectively stateless.* This lowers the risk for experimenting with your cluster. You might break your clusters, but you won't lose your data. It also supports the blue-green deployment technique presented earlier (section 11.3.7).
- *Use Docker Compose to simulate your application on your workstation for development and testing.* Employ live reload for fast development iterations.
- *In the early days, you might not need automated testing, but it is essential for building a large maintainable microservices application.* When building a minimal viable product (MVP) for a startup, however, you don't need it. It is too early in the product's lifecycle to make such a big commitment to infrastructure. We must prove our product before we can invest in the more advanced infrastructure!
- *You might not have automated testing, but you still need to test!* Set up for efficient and reliable manual testing. You need a script to quickly start your application on a development workstation, from nothing to a testable state, in a short amount of time. You can use Docker Compose and database fixtures to achieve this.
- *Docker makes it easy to deploy third-party images to containers running in your cluster.* That's how we deployed RabbitMQ in chapter 5. You can find many other useful images on DockerHub: https://hub.docker.com/.

- *Invest early in your automation, especially continuous delivery through automated deployment.* You will rely on this every working day, so make sure it works well.

11.7 From simple beginnings . . .

Just look at how far we have come together! We started by creating a single microservice. Then we learned how to package and publish it using Docker. We learned how to develop and test multiple microservices on our development workstation using Docker Compose. Ultimately, we created a production environment in the cloud on Kubernetes and deployed our microservices-based application to it with Terraform.

Complexity management is at the heart of modern development. That's why we invest time learning advanced architectural patterns like microservices.

What a great journey this has been! But I'm sad to say that our time together has come to an end. Your journey will continue, of course, and I wish you all the best in building your own complex applications with microservices.

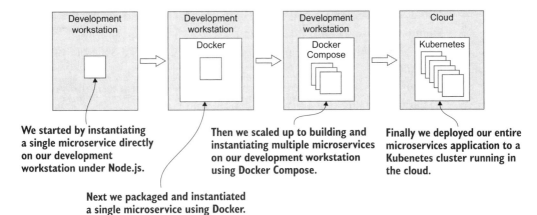

Figure 11.29   Our journey from a single microservice to multiple microservices running in production

11.8 Continue your learning

For one final time, let's finish the chapter with some references to books that will help you learn more and carry your understanding and knowledge forward. To learn more about domain driven design (DDD), read the original book on it:

- *Domain Driven Design* by Eric Evans (Addison-Wesley, 2004)

If you don't have much time, you can find a good summary in the free ebook, *Domain Driven Design Quickly* by Abel Avram and Floyd Marinescu (InfoQ, 2018), available here:

- https://www.infoq.com/minibooks/domain-driven-design-quickly/

To better understand security for microservices, read

- *Microservices Security in Action* by Prabath Siriwardena and Nuwan Dias (Manning, 2020)

To learn more details on theory on development with microservices, pick any of these books:

- *The Tao of Microservices* by Richard Rodger (Manning, 2017)
- *Microservices Patterns* by Chris Richardson (Manning, 2018)
- *Microservices in Action* by Morgan Bruce and Paulo A. Pereira (Manning, 2018)
- *Microservices in .NET Core*, 2nd ed., by Christian Horsdal Gammelgaard (Manning, 2020)
- *Developing Microservice APIs with Python* by José Haro Peralta (Manning, 2020)

Summary

- To gain the most benefit from microservices, we must separate out our code repository and continuous delivery (CD) pipeline. This ensures that each microservice can be deployed independently. It also allows separate teams to take ownership for separate microservices.
- Using a meta-repo, we can regain some of the convenience of the monorepo (mono repository) after we have separated our code repositories.
- Having independent CD pipelines means we'll have a scalable deployment pipeline.
- We can create multiple environments (e.g., development, test, and production) by parameterizing our Terraform deployment code.
- We can configure separate CD pipelines for each branch (e.g., development, test and production) in our code repositories. Pushing code to a branch triggers the pipeline and deploys to the appropriate environment.
- For increased performance, we have numerous options, including
  - We can scale our cluster vertically and horizontally.
  - We can scale our microservices horizontally.
  - We can reserve dedicated compute for particular microservices.
  - We can make use of elastic scaling to automatically scale our cluster and our microservices at times of peak demand.
- We should always have a single database per microservice so that we have options for scaling our data storage.
- Blue-green deployment switches our customers among alternating environments and is a safe way to manage potentially risky infrastructure upgrades.
- Security for microservices is as important as any application, if not more so, given that a microservice application might have many gateways.
- We can employ security techniques such as authentication and authorization to protect access to our system.
- We can employ integrity protection techniques to protect our data and secure privacy and confidentiality for our customers.

- Refactoring from a monolith to microservices can only be accomplished through a series of small and well-tested steps.
- There are many ways we can make microservices more affordable and less complex when we are starting out. This makes microservices an effective and efficient starting point for startups, small teams, and solo developers.

appendix A
Creating a development environment with Vagrant

Vagrant is a tool that allows us to script the creation of a virtual machine (VM). It's typically used for creating a VM to run on our local computer (rather than building a VM to run in the cloud).

Vagrant is a great way to create a Linux-based development environment. It's also great for experimenting with new software (e.g., Docker and Terraform). You can use it so that you don't clutter up your regular development computer with new software.

I used Vagrant extensively on a day-to-day basis for development until just recently. It was really useful as a convenient way to get Docker working on a computer running Windows 10 Home. Now, I use WSL2 (Windows Subsystem for Linux 2). Docker for Windows integrates with that (see chapter 3 for details), so I don't need Vagrant to run Docker anymore.

But Vagrant is still useful for building throwaway environments for development, testing, and experimentation. You can find an example Vagrant setup on GitHub:

- https://github.com/bootstrapping-microservices/example-vagrant-vm

The example Vagrant setup installs Docker, Docker Compose, and Terraform automatically, giving you an "instant" development environment you can use to experiment with the code examples that accompany this book (see section A.6). Note that the example code repositories for the chapters of this book each include a preconfigured Vagrant script that you can use to run the code for that chapter.

A.1   Installing VirtualBox

Before using Vagrant, you must install VirtualBox. This is the software that actually runs the VM within your regular computer (the host). You can download it from the VirtualBox download page:

- https://www.virtualbox.org/wiki/Downloads

Download and install the package that fits your host operating system. Follow the instructions on the VirtualBox web page.

> **NOTE** Vagrant supports other VM providers, like VMWare, but I recommend VirtualBox because it's free and easy to setup.

A.2   Installing Vagrant

Now install Vagrant. This is a scripting layer on top of VirtualBox that allows you to manage the setup of your VM through code (Ruby code actually). You can download it from the Vagrant downloads page:

- https://www.vagrantup.com/downloads.html

Download and install the package that fits your host operating system. Follow the instructions on the Vagrant web page.

A.3   Creating your virtual machine (VM)

With VirtualBox and Vagrant installed, you are now ready to create your VM. First, you must decide which operating system to use. If you already have a production system in place, choose that same operating system. If not, choose a long-term support (LTS) version that will hold up for a long time. You can search for operating systems on this web page:

- https://vagrantcloud.com/search

I'm a big fan of Ubuntu Linux, so for this example, we'll use Ubuntu 20.04 LTS. The Vagrant name for the *box* that we'll install is `ubuntu/xenial64`.

Before creating the Vagrant box, open a command line and create a directory in which to store it. Change to that directory, then invoke the `vagrant init` command as follows:

```
vagrant init ubuntu/xenial64
```

This creates a barebones Vagrantfile in the current directory. Edit this file to change the configuration and setup for your VM. You can learn more about Vagrant configuration here:

- https://docs.vagrantup.com

Now launch your VM:

```
vagrant up
```

Make sure you run this command in the same directory that contains the Vagrantfile. This can take some time, especially if you don't already have the image for the operating system locally cached. Do give it plenty of time to complete. Once it has finished, you will have a fresh Ubuntu VM to work with.

A.4 Connecting to your VM

With the VM booted up, you can now connect to it like this:

```
vagrant ssh
```

Vagrant automatically creates an SSH key and manages the connection for you. You now have a command-line shell into your VM. Any commands you invoke in this shell are executed inside your VM.

A.5 Installing software in the VM

With your VM running and having connected using `vagrant ssh`, you'll now want to install some software. The first thing to do with your new VM is to update the operating system. You can do this in Ubuntu with

```
sudo apt-get update
```

You can now install whatever software you need by following the instructions from the software vendor. To install Docker, see

- https://docs.docker.com/install/linux/docker-ce/ubuntu

To install Docker Compose, see

- https://docs.docker.com/compose/install/

To install Terraform, you simply download it, unpack it, and add the executable to your path. You can download Terraform from here:

- https://www.terraform.io/downloads.html

The example Vagrant setup (next section) installs all these tools automatically. This gives you an "instant" development environment you can use to experiment with the code examples that accompany this book.

A.6 Using the example setup

You can start a VM from the example setup on GitHub available at

- https://github.com/bootstrapping-microservices/example-vagrant-vm

Clone the repository using Git:

```
git clone https://github.com/bootstrapping-microservices/example-vagrant-vm
```

Then change to that repository directory:

```
cd example-vagrant-vm
```

Now boot up the VM:

```
vagrant up
```

Connect a command-line shell to the VM:

```
vagrant ssh
```

This Vagrant script runs a shell script that automatically installs Docker, Docker Compose, and Terraform! Once the VM has started and you have connected you can use all these tools.

A.7   *Turning your VM off*

After you have completely finished with your VM, you can destroy it with the following command:

```
vagrant destroy
```

If you are only temporarily finished with the machine and would like to reuse it again later, suspend it with the following command:

```
vagrant suspend
```

A suspended machine can be resumed at any time by invoking vagrant up. Remember to destroy or suspend your virtual machines when you are not using these, otherwise, they'll unnecessarily consume your valuable system resources.

appendix B
Bootstrapping
Microservices cheat sheet

This appendix summarizes the most useful commands you learned throughout this book.

B.1 *Node.js commands*

See chapter 2 to learn how to install and use Node.js to create microservices.

Table B.1 Node.js commands

Command	Description
`node --version`	Checks that Node.js is installed and prints the version number.
`npm init -y`	Creates a default Node.js project. This creates a stub for our package .json, the file that tracks metadata and dependencies for our Node.js project.
`npm install --save` ➡ `<package-name>`	Installs an npm package. There are many other packages available on npm. You can install any by inserting a specific package name.
`npm install`	Installs all dependencies for a Node.js project. This includes all the packages that were previously recorded in package.json.
`node <script-file>`	Runs a Node.js script file. We just invoke the `node` command and give it the name of our script file as an argument. You can call your script main.js or server.js if you want, but it's probably best to stick to the convention and just call it index.js.

Table B.1   Node.js commands *(continued)*

Command	Description
`npm start`	The conventional npm script for starting a Node.js application, regardless of what name the main script file has or what command-line parameters it expects. Typically this just translates into node index.js in the package.json file, but it all depends on the author of the project and how they have set it up. The nice thing is that no matter how a particular project is structured, you only have to remember `npm start`.
`npm run start:dev`	My personal convention for starting a Node.js project in development. I add this to the scripts in package.json, and typically, it runs something like nodemon to enable live reload of your code as you work with it.

B.2   *Docker commands*

See chapter 3 to learn how to package, publish, and run microservices using Docker.

Table B.2   Docker commands

Command	Description
`docker --version`	Checks that Docker is installed and prints the version number.
`docker container list`	Lists running containers.
`docker ps`	Lists all containers (running and stopped).
`docker image list`	Lists local images.
`docker build -t <tag> --file` ➡ `<docker-file> .`	Builds an image from assets in the current directory according to the instructions in `docker-file`. The `-t` argument tags the image with a name you specify.
`docker run -d -p` ➡ `<host-port>:<container-port>` ➡ `<tag>`	Instantiates a container from an image. If the image isn't available locally, you can pull it from a remote registry (assuming the tag specifies the URL of the registry). The `-d` argument runs the container in detached mode; it won't be bound to the terminal, and you won't see the output. Omit this argument to see output directly, but note that this also locks up your terminal. The `-p` argument allows you to bind a port on the host to a port in the container.
`docker logs <container-id>`	Retrieves output from a particular container. You need to issue this command to see the output when running a container in detached mode.

Table B.2   Docker commands *(continued)*

Command	Description
`docker login <url>` ➥ `--username <username>` ➥ `--password <password>`	Authenticates with your private Docker registry so that you can run other commands against it.
`docker tag <existing-tag>` ➥ `<new-tag>`	Adds a new tag to an existing image. To push an image to your private container registry, you must first tag it with the URL of your registry.
`docker push <tag>`	Pushes an appropriately tagged image to your private Docker registry. The image should be tagged with the URL of your registry.
`docker kill <container-id>`	Stops a particular container locally.
`docker rm <container-id>`	Removes a particular container locally (it must be stopped first).
`docker rmi <image-id>` ➥ `--force`	Removes a particular image locally (any containers must be removed first). The `--force` argument removes images even when these have been tagged multiple times.

B.3   *Docker Compose commands*

See chapters 4 and 5 to learn how to use Docker Compose to simulate a microservices application on your development workstation (or personal computer) for development and testing.

Table B.3   Docker Compose commands

Command	Description
`docker-compose --version`	Checks that Docker Compose is installed and prints the version number.
`docker-compose up --build`	Builds and instantiates an application composed of multiple containers as defined by the Docker Compose file (docker-compose .yaml) in the current working directory.
`docker-compose ps`	Lists running containers that are part of the application specified by the Docker Compose file.
`docker-compose stop`	Stops all containers in the application but persists the stopped containers for inspection.
`docker-compose down`	Stops and *destroys* the application, leaving the development workstation in a clean state.

B.4   *Terraform commands*

See chapters 6 and 7 to learn how to implement infrastructure as code via Terraform to create a Kubernetes cluster and deploy your microservices to it.

Table B.4   Terraform commands

Command	Description
terraform init	Initializes a Terraform project and downloads the provider plugins.
terraform apply ➡ -auto-approve	Executes Terraform code files in the working directory to incrementally apply changes to your infrastructure.
terraform destroy	Destroys all infrastructure that was created by the Terraform project.

B.5   *Testing commands*

See chapter 8 to learn about automated testing for microservices with Jest and Cypress.

Table B.5   Testing commands

Command	Description
npx jest --init	Initializes the Jest configuration file.
npx jest	Runs tests under Jest
npx jest --watch	Runs tests with live reload enabled to rerun tests when code has changed. Jest uses Git to know which files have changed and should be considered.
npx jest --watchAll	As previously, except it monitors all files for changes and not just those that are reported changed by Git.
npx cypress open	Opens the Cypress UI so that you can run tests. Live reload works out of the box. You can update your code, and the tests rerun automatically.
npx cypress run	Executes Cypress tests with Cypress running in headless mode. This lets you test with Cypress from the command line (or CD pipeline) without having to display the UI.
npm test	The npm script convention for running tests. This can run Jest or Cypress (or even both) depending on how you configured your package.json file. This is the command you should run in your CD pipeline to execute your test suite.
npm run test:watch	This is my personal convention for running tests in live reload mode. You need to configure this script in your package.json file to use it.

index